Authentic
Piedmont and Aosta Valley

Touring Club Italiano
President and Chairman: *Roberto Ruozi*
General Manager: *Guido Venturini*

Touring Editore
General Manager: *Alfieri Lorenzon*
Editorial Director: *Michele D'Innella*
Editorial coordination: *Cristiana Baietta*

International Department
Fabio Pittella
fabio.pittella@touringclub.it

Senior Editor: *Paola Pandiani*
Editor: *Monica Maraschi*
Writer and Researcher: *Pietro Ferrario*
with Banca Dati Turistica for Pratical info
Translation and page layout: *Studio Queens, Milan*
Maps: *Touring Club Italiano*
Design: *Studio Queens, Milan*
Cover photo: *The unmistakable silhouette of the Mole Antonelliana towers above the city, surrounded by the Alps. (Realy Easy Star – T. Spagone)*
We would like to thank Pinuccia Cattaneo
for writing the insert about golf and providing the photograph.

Advertising Manager: *Claudio Bettinelli*
Local Advertising: *Progetto*
www.progettosrl.it - info@progettosrl.it

Printing and Binding: *CPM S.p.A., Casarile*

Distribution
USA/CAN – *Publishers Group West*
UK/Ireland – *Portfolio Books*

Touring Club Italiano, Corso Italia 10, 20122 Milano
www.touringclub.it

Code K8Zoo
ISBN-13: 978 – 88365 – 4132 – 4

Printed in March 2007

AUTHENTIC Piedmont and Aosta Valley

SUMMARY

6 What is the Touring Club of Italy?

9 Italy: instructions for use

16 **HERITAGE**

Turin, an elegant city with a character all of its own, and plenty more to explore in the outlying towns, hills and valleys of Piedmont. In the Valle d'Aosta, there are splendid Roman remains at Aosta, and the valleys abound with small towns and villages full of interest, amid magnificent Alpine scenery.

Valle d'Aosta
Aosta
The Western Valle d'Aosta
The Eastern Valle d'Aosta

Piedmont
Turin
Alessandria
Asti
Biella
Cuneo
Novara
Verbano-Cusio-Ossola
Vercelli

94 **SKI**

The mountains of Piedmont and the Valle d'Aosta provide endless scope for skiers. The facilities here were upgraded for the 2006 Winter Olympics. Skiing on the Mt Blanc or Mt Rosa massifs is an experience you are unlikely to forget.

Valle d'Aosta
La Thuile
Courmayeur
Breuil-Cervinia
Valtournenche
Val d'Ayas
Val de Gressoney
Pila

Piedmont
Sestriere
Sansicario
Cesana Torinese
Claviere
Sauze d'Oulx
Bardonecchia
Macugnaga
Artesina-Prato Nevoso
Limone Piemonte

126 **ITINERARIES**

Piedmont and the Valle d'Aosta offer much in the way of scenery and interest, whether you are culture vultures, interested in wine and food, or in search of more energetic pursuits. This guide provides you with expert advice and insight on all aspects of this delightful part of Italy.

Parks
Children
Cinema
Industry museums
Gastronomy route
Walks
Biking routes

156 FOOD

Piedmont is rightly proud of its cuisine, rich with French influences, and its wines include some of Italy's finest DOCG labels. In the Valle d'Aosta, the cuisine is based on simple local ingredients. Wine-production is small but its wines are of very high quality, since traditional farming methods are still used.

Pasta
Hams and Salami
Cheese
Wine
Liqueurs
Cakes
Food Festivals

194 SHOPPING

Shopping in Piedmont is as diverse as you could wish, whether you are searching for haute couture under the porticoes of Turin, or visiting the markets of the region to buy local delicacies, antiques or food.

Arts & crafts
Markets
Fashion

204 EVENTS

The folklore of Piedmont and the Valle d'Aosta includes religious festivals as well as events focusing on local delicacies, while some festivals celebrate local farming traditions.

Music
Folklore

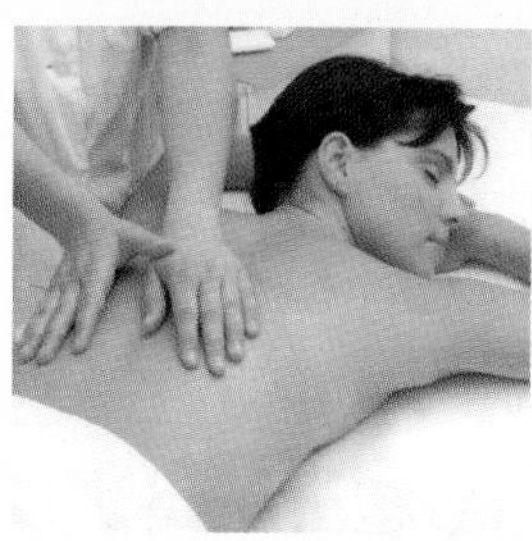

210 WELLNESS

In Piedmont and the Valle d'Aosta there is a wide choice of modern and historic spas in beautiful natural settings, where prestige and traditional treatments goes hand-in-hand with spa technologies on the cutting edge.

Saint Vincent
Acqui Terme
Agliano Terme
Bagni di Vinadio
Bognanco
Garessio
Terme di Lurisia
Terme di Valdieri

216 PRACTICAL INFO

The Practical Information is divided into sections on the hotels, restaurants, farm holidays and places of entertainment we recommend. The category of the hotels is indicated by the number of stars. In the case of restaurants we have awarded forks, taking into account the price of the meal, the level of comfort and service, and the ambience.

WHAT IS THE TOURING CLUB OF ITALY?

Long Tradition, Great Prestige

For over 110 years, the Touring Club of Italy (TCI) has offered travelers the most detailed and comprehensive source of travel information available on Italy.
The Touring Club of Italy was founded in 1894 with the aim of developing the social and cultural values of tourism and promoting the conservation and enjoyment of the country's national heritage, landscape and environment.

Advantages of Membership

Today, TCI offers a wide rage of travel services to assist and support members with the highest level of convenience and quality. Now you can discover the unique charms of Italy with a distinct insider's advantage.

Enjoy exclusive money saving offers with a TCI membership. Use your membership card for discounts in thousands of restaurants, hotels, spas, campgrounds, museums, shops and markets.

These Hotel Chains offer preferred rates and discounts to TCI members!

CHOICE HOTELS EUROPE SM

Mercure
Accor hotels

JOIN THE TOURING CLUB OF ITALY

How to Join

It's quick and easy to join.
Apply for your membership online at **www.touringclub.it**
Your membership card will arrive within three weeks and is valid for discounts across Italy for the entire year.
Get your card before you go and start saving as soon as you arrive.
Euro 25 annual membership fee includes priority mail postage for membership card and materials.
Just one use of the card will more than cover the cost of membership.

Benefits

- Exclusive car rental rates with Hertz
- Discounts at select Esso gas stations
- 20% discount on TCI guidebooks and maps purchased in TCI bookstores or directly online at www.touringclub.com
- Preferred rates and discounts available at thousands of locations in Italy: Hotels - B&B's - Villa Rentals - Campgrounds -TCI Resorts - Spas - Restaurants - Wineries - Museums - Cinemas - Theaters - Music Festivals - Shops - Craft Markets - Ferries - Cruises - Theme Parks - Botanical Gardens

ITALY: INSTRUCTIONS FOR USE

Italy is known throughout the world for the quantity and quality of its art treasures and for its natural beauty, but it is also famous for its inimitable lifestyle and fabulous cuisine and wines. Although it is a relatively small country, Italy boasts an extremely varied culture and multifarious traditions and customs. The information and suggestions in this brief section will help foreign tourists not only to understand certain aspects of Italian life, but also to solve the everyday difficulties and the problems of a practical nature that inevitably crop up during any trip.

This practical information is included in brief descriptions of various topics: public transport and how to purchase tickets; suggestions on how to drive in this country; the different types of rooms and accommodation in hotels; hints on how to use mobile phones and communication in general. This is followed by useful advice on how to meet your everyday needs and on shopping, as well as information concerning the cultural differences in the various regions. Lastly, there is a section describing the vast range of restaurants, bars, wine bars and pizza parlors.

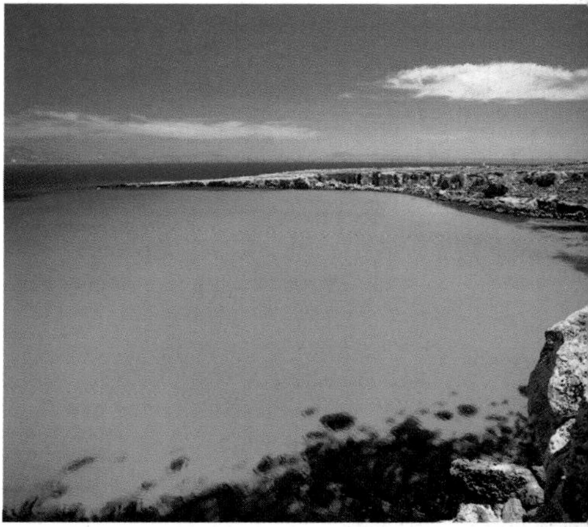

TRANSPORTATION

From the airport to the city

Public transportation in major cities is easily accessible and simple to use. Both Malpensa Airport in Milan and Fiumicino Airport in Rome have trains and buses linking them to the city centers. At Malpensa, you can take a bus to the main train station or a train to Cadorna train station and subway stop.

Subways, buses, and trams

Access to the subways, buses, and trams requires a ticket (tickets are not sold on board but can be purchased at most newsstands and tobacco shops). The ticket is good for one ride and sometimes has a time limit (in the case of buses and trams). When you board a bus or tram, you are required to stamp your previously-acquired ticket in the time-stamping machine. Occasionally, a conductor will board the bus or tram and check everyone's ticket. If you haven't got one, or if it has not been time-stamped, you will have to pay a steep fine.

Trains

The Ferrovie dello Stato (Italian Railways) is among the best and most modern railway systems in Europe. Timetables and routes can be consulted and reservations can be made online at **www.trenitalia.com**. Many travel agents can also dispense tickets and help you plan your journey. Hard-copy schedules can be purchased at all newsstands and most bookstores.

The majestic Basilica di Superga, just outside Turin.

Automated ticket machines, which include easy-to-use instructions in English, are available in nearly all stations. They can be used to check schedules, makes reservations, and purchase tickets.

There are different types of train, according to the requirements:

Eurostar Italia Trains *ES*★ : Fast connections between Italy's most important cities. The ticket includes seat booking charge;

Intercity *IC* and **Espresso** *E* Trains: Local connections among Italy's towns and cities. Sometimes *IC* and *E* trains require seat booking. You can book your seat up to 3 hours before the train departure. The seat booking charge is of 3 Euro.

Interregionale Trains *iR* move beyond regional boundaries. Among the combined local-transport services, the *iR* Trains are the fastest ones with the fewest number of stops. No seat booking available.

Diretto *D* and **Regionale** *R* Trains can circulate both within the regions and their bordering regions. No seat booking available.

DO NOT FORGET: In Italy, you can only board a train if you have a valid ticket that has been time-stamped prior to boarding (each station has numerous time-stamping machines). You cannot buy or stamp tickets on the train.
If you don't have a ticket – or did not stamp before boarding – you will be liable to pay the full ticket price plus a 25 euro fine. If you produce a ticket that is not valid for the train or service you're using (i.e. one issued for a different train category at a different price, etc.) you will be asked to pay the difference with respect to the full ticket price, plus an 8 euro surcharge.

Taxis

Taxis are a convenient but expensive way to travel in Italian cities. There are taxi stands scattered throughout major cities. You cannot hail taxis on the street in Italy, but you can reserve taxis, in advance or immediately, by phone: consult the yellow pages for the number or ask your hotel reception desk or maitre d'hotel to call for you.
Taxi drivers have the right to charge you a supplementary fee for every piece of luggage they transport, as well as evening surcharges.

Driving

Especially when staying in the countryside, driving is a safe and convenient way to travel through Italy and its major cities. It is important to be aware of street signs and speed limits, and many cities have zones where only limited traffic is allowed in order to accommodate pedestrians.
Street parking is organized using road signs and different colored street markings. No line or a white line is for free parking, blue is for paid parking and yellow is for reserved parking (disabled, residents etc). There may be time limits for both free and paid parking. In this case, use your parking disc to indicate your time of arrival.
Although an international driver's license is not required in Italy, it is advisable. ACI and similar associations provide this service to members. The fuel distribution network is reasonably distributed all over the territory. All service stations have unleaded gasoline ("benzina verde") and diesel fuel ("gasolio"). Opening time is 7 to 12:30 and 15 to 19:30; on motorways the service is 24 hours a day.
Type of roads in Italy: The *Autostrada* (for example A14) is the main highway system in Italy and is similar to the Interstate highway system in the US and the motorway system in the UK. Shown on our Touring Club Italiano 1:200,000 road maps as black. The Autostrada are toll highways; you pay to use them. The *Strada Statale* (for example SS54) is a fast moving road that may have one or more lanes in each direction. Shown on our Touring Club Italiano 1:200,000 road maps as red. *Strada Provinciale* (for example SP358) can be narrow, slow and winding roads. They are usually one lane in each direction. Shown on our Touring Club Italiano 1:200,000 road maps as yellow. *Strada Comunale* (for example SC652) is a local road connecting the main town with its sorrounding. Note: In our guide you will sometime find an address of a place in the countryside listed, for example, as

"SS54 Km 25". This means that the you have to drive along the Strada Statale 54 until you reach the 25-km road sign.
Speed limits: 130 kmph on the Autostrada, 110 kmph on main highways, 90 kmph outside of towns, 50 kmph in towns.
The town streets are patrolled by the Polizia Municipale while the roads outside cities and the Autostrada are patrolled by the Carabinieri or the Polizia Stradale.
Do not forget:

- Wear your seat belt at all times;
- Do not use the cellular phone while driving;
- Have your headlights on at all times when driving outside of cities;
- The drunk driving laws are strict – do not drink and drive;
- In case of an accident you are not allowed to get out of your car unless you are wearing a special, high-visibility, reflective jacket.

ACCOMMODATION

Hotels

In Italy it is common practice for the reception desk to register your passport, and only registered guests are allowed to use the rooms. This is mere routine, done for security reasons, and there is no need for concern.
All hotels use the official star classification system, from 5-star luxury hotel to 1 star accommodation.
Room rates are based on whether they are for single ("camera singola") or double ("camera doppia") occupancy. In every room you will find a list of the hotel rates (generally on the back of the door). While 4- and 5-star hotels have double beds, most hotels have only single beds. Should you want a double bed, you have to ask for a "letto matrimoniale". All hotels have rooms with bathrooms; only 1-star establishments usually have only shared bathrooms.
Most hotel rates include breakfast ("prima colazione"), but you can request to do without it, thus reducing the rate.
Breakfast is generally served in a communal room and comprises a buffet with pastries, bread with butter and jam, cold cereals, fruit, yoghurt, coffee, and fruit juice. Some hotels regularly frequented by foreign tourists will also serve other items such as eggs for their American and British guests.
The hotels for families and in tourist localities also offer "mezza pensione", or half board, in which breakfast and dinner are included in the price.
It's always a good idea to check when a hotel's annual closing period is, especially if you are planning a holiday by the sea.

Farm stays

Located only in the countryside, and generally on a farm, "agriturismo" – a network of farm holiday establishments – is part of a growing trend in Italy to honor local gastronomic and wine traditions, as well as countryside traditions. These farms offer meals prepared with ingredients cultivated exclusively on site: garden-grown vegetables, homemade cheese and local recipes. Many of these places also provide lodging, one of the best ways to experience the "genuine" Italian lifestyle.

Bed & Breakfast

This form of accommodation provides bed and breakfast in a private house, and in the last few years has become much more widespread in Italy. There are over 5,000 b&bs, classified in 3 categories, and situated both in historic town centers, as well as in the outskirts and the countryside. Rooms for guests are always well-furnished, but not all of them have en suite bathrooms.
It is well-recommended to check the closing of the open-all-year accommodation services and restaurants, because they could have a short break during the year (usually no longer than a fortnight).

COMMUNICATIONS

Nearly everyone in Italy owns a cellular phone. Although public phones are still available, they seem to be ever fewer and farther between. If you wish to use public phones, you will find them in subway stops, bars, along the street, and phone centers generally located in the city center. Phone cards and pre-paid phone cards can be purchased at most newsstands and tobacco shops, and can also be acquired at automated tellers.
For European travelers, activating personal cellular coverage is relatively simple, as it is in most cases for American and Australian travelers as well. Contact your mobile service provider for details.

Cellular phones can also be rented in Italy from TIM, the Italian national phone company. For information, visit its website at www.tim.it. When traveling by car through the countryside, a cellular phone can really come in handy.

Note that when dialing in Italy, you must always dial the prefix (e.g., 02 for Milan, 06 for Rome) even when making a local call. For cellular phones, however, the initial zero is always dropped.

Freephone numbers always start with "800". For calls abroad from Italy, it's a good idea to buy a special pre-paid international phone card, which is used with a PIN code.

Internet access

Cyber cafés have sprung up all over Italy and you can find one on nearly every city block.

EATING AND DRINKING

The bar

The Italian "bar" is a multi-faceted, all-purpose establishment for drinking, eating and socializing, where you can order an espresso, have breakfast, and enjoy a quick sandwich for lunch or even a hot meal. You can often buy various items here (sometimes even stamps, cigarettes, phone cards, etc.). Bear in mind that table service ("servizio a tavola") includes a surcharge. At most bars, if you choose to sit, a waiter will take your order. Every bar should have a list of prices posted behind or near the counter; if the bar offers table service, the price list should also include the extra fee for this.

Lunch at bars will include, but is not limited to, "panini," sandwiches with crusty bread, usually with cured meats such as "prosciutto" (salt-cured ham), "prosciutto cotto" (cooked ham), and cheeses such as mozzarella topped with tomato and basil. Then there are "tramezzini" (finger sandwiches) with tuna, cheese, or vegetables, etc. Often the "panini" and other savory sandwiches (like stuffed flatbread or "focaccia") are heated before being served. Naturally, the menu at bars varies according to the region: in Bologna you will find "piadine" (flatbread similar to pita) with Swiss chard; in Palermo there are "arancini" (fried rice balls stuffed with

ground meat); in Genoa you will find that even the most unassuming bar serves some of the best "focaccia" in all Italy. Some bars also include a "tavola calda". If you see this sign in a bar window, it means that hot dishes like pasta and even entrées are served.

A brief comment on coffee and cappuccino: Italians never serve coffee with savory dishes or sandwiches, and they seldom drink cappuccino outside of breakfast (although they are happy to serve it at any time).

While English- and Irish-type pubs are frequented by beer lovers and young people in Italy, there are also American bars where long drinks and American cocktails are served.

Breakfast at the bar

Breakfast in Italy generally consists of some type of pastry, most commonly a "brioche" – a croissant either filled with cream or jam, or plain – and a cappuccino or espresso. Although most bars do not offer American coffee, you can ask for a "caffè lungo" or "caffè americano", both of which resemble the American coffee preferred by the British and Americans. Most bars have a juicer to make a "spremuta", freshly squeezed orange or grapefruit juice.

Lunch and Dinner

As with all daily rituals in Italy, food is prepared and meals are served according to local customs (e.g., in the North they prefer rice and butter, in South and Central Italy they favor pasta and olive oil).

Wine is generally served at mealtime, and while finer restaurants have excellent wine lists (some including vintage wines), ordering the house table wine generally brings good results (a house Chianti to accompany your Florentine steak in Tuscany, a sparkling Prosecco paired with your creamed stockfish and polenta in Venice, a dry white wine with pasta dressed with sardines and wild fennel fronds in Sicily).

Mineral water is also commonly served at meals and can be "gassata" (sparkling) or "naturale" (still).

The most sublime culinary experience in Italy is achieved by matching the local foods with the appropriate local wines: wisdom dictates that a friendly waiter will be flattered by your request for his recommendation on what to eat and drink. Whether at an "osteria" (a tavern), a "trattoria" (a home-style restaurant), or a "ristorante" (a proper restaurant), the service of lunch and dinner generally consists of – but is not limited to – the following: "antipasti" or appetizers; "primo piatto" or first course, i.e., pasta, rice, or soup; "secondo piatto" or main course, i.e., meat or seafood; "contorno" or side-dish, served with the main course, i.e., vegetables or salad; "formaggi", "frutta", and "dolci", i.e., cheeses, fruit, and dessert; caffè or espresso coffee, perhaps spiked with a shot of grappa.

The pizzeria

The pizzeria is in general one of the most economical, democratic, and satisfying culinary experiences in Italy. Everyone eats at the pizzeria: young people, families, couples, locals and tourists alike. Generally, each person orders her/his own pizza, and while the styles of crust and toppings will vary from region to region (some of the best pizzas are served in Naples and Rome), the acid test of any pizzeria is the Margherita, topped simply with cheese and tomato sauce.

Beer, sparkling or still water, and Coca Cola are the beverages commonly served with pizza. Some restaurants include a pizza menu, but most establishments do not serve pizza at lunchtime.

The wine bar (enoteca)

More than one English-speaking tourist in Italy has wondered why the wine bar is called an enoteca in other countries and the English term is used in Italy: the answer lies somewhere in the mutual fondness that Italians and English speakers have for one another. Wine bars have become popular in recent years in the major cities (especially in Rome, where you can find some of the best). The wine bar is a great place to sample different local wines and eat a light, tapas-style dinner.

CULTURAL DIVERSITY

Whenever you travel, not only are you a guest of your host country, but you are also a representative of your home country.

As a general rule, courtesy, consideration, and respect are always appreciated by guests and their hosts alike. Italians are famous for their hospitality and experience will verify this felicitous stereotype: perhaps nowhere else in Europe are tourists and visitors received more warmly.

Italy is a relatively "new" country. Its borders, as we know them today, were established only in 1861 when it became a monarchy under the House of Savoy. After WWII, Italy became a Republic and now it is one of the member states of the European Union.

One of the most fascinating aspects of Italian culture is that, even as a unified country, local tradition still prevails over a universally Italian national identity. Some jokingly say that the only time that Venetians, Milanese, Florentines, Neapolitans, and Sicilians feel like Italians is when the national football team plays in international competitions. From their highly localized dialects to the foods they eat, from their religious celebration to their politics, Italians proudly maintain their local heritage.

This is one of the reasons why the Piedmontese continue to prefer their beloved Barolo wine and their white truffles, the Umbrians their rich Sagrantino wine and black truffles, the Milanese their risotto and panettone, the Venetians their stockfish and polenta, the Bolognese their lasagne and pumpkin ravioli, the Florentines their bread soups and steaks cooked rare, the Abruzzese their excellent fish broth and seafood, the Neapolitans their mozzarella, basil, pizza, and pasta.

As a result of its rich cultural diversity, the country's population also varies greatly in its customs from region to region, city to city, town to town. As you visit different cities and regions throughout Italy, you will see how the local personality and character of the Italians change as rapidly as the landscape does. Having lived for millennia with their great diversity and rich, highly heterogeneous culture, the Italians have taught us many things, foremost among them the age-old expression, "When in Rome, do as the Romans do."

NATIONAL HOLIDAYS

New Year's Day (1st January), Epiphany (6th January), Easter Monday (day after Easter Sunday), Liberation Day (25th April), Labour Day (1st May), Italian Republic Day (2nd June), Assumption (15th August), All Saints' Day (1st November), Immaculate Conception (8th December), Christmas Day and Boxing Day (25th-26th December).
In addition to these holidays, each city also has a holiday to celebrate its patron saint's feast day, usually with lively, local celebrations. Shops and services in large cities close on national holidays and for the week of the 15th of August.

EVERYDAY NEEDS

State tobacco shops and pharmacies

Tobacco is available in Italy only at state licensed tobacco shops. These vendors ("tabaccheria"), often incorporated in a bar, also sell stamps.
Since January 2005 smoking is forbidden in all so-called public places – unless a separately ventilated space is constructed – meaning over 90% of the country's restaurants and bars.
Medicines can be purchased only in pharmacies ("farmacia") in Italy. Pharmacists are very knowledgeable about common ailments and can generally prescribe a treatment for you on the spot. Opening time is 8:30-12:30 and 15:30-19:30 but in any case there is always a pharmacy open 24 hours and during holidays.

Shopping

Every locality in Italy offers tourists characteristic shops, markets with good bargains, and even boutiques featuring leading Italian fashion designers. Opening hours vary from region to region and from season to season. In general, shops are open from 9 to 13 and from 15/16 to 19/20, but in large cities they usually have no lunchtime break.

Tax Free

Non-EU citizens can obtain a reimbursement for IVA (goods and services tax) paid on purchases over €155, for goods which are exported within 90 days, in shops which display the relevant sign. IVA is always automatically included in the price of any purchase, and ranges from 20% to 4% depending on the item. The shop issues a reimbursement voucher to present when you leave the country (at a frontier or airport). For purchases in shops affiliated to 'Tax Free Shopping', IVA may be reimbursed directly at international airports.

Banks and post offices

Italian banks are open Monday to Friday, from 8:30 to 13:30 and then from 15 to 16. However, the afternoon business hours may vary.
Post offices are open from Monday to Saturday, from 8:30 to 13:30 (12:30 on Saturday). In the larger towns there are also some offices open in the afternoon.

Currency

As in many other European Union countries, the Euros is the Italian currency. Coins are in denominations of 1, 2, 5, 10, 20 and 50 cents and 1 and 2 euros; banknotes are in denominations of 5, 10, 20, 50, 100, 200 and 500 euros, each with a different color.

Credit cards

All the main credit cards are generally accepted, but some smaller enterprises (arts and crafts shops, small hotels, bed & breakfasts, or farm stays) do not provide this service. Foreign tourists can obtain cash using credit cards at automatic teller machines.

Time

All Italy is in the same time zone, which is six hours ahead of Eastern Standard Time in the USA. Daylight saving time is used from March to October, when watches and clocks are set an hour ahead of standard time.

Passports and vaccinations

Citizens of EU countries can enter Italy without frontier checks. Citizens of Australia, Canada, New Zealand, and the United States can enter Italy with a valid passport and need not have a visa for a stay of less than 90 days.
No vaccinations are necessary.

Payment and tipping

When you sit down at a restaurant you are generally charged a "coperto" or cover charge ranging from 1.5 to 3 euros, for service and the bread. Tipping is not customary in Italy. Beware of unscrupulous restaurateurs who add a space on their clients' credit card receipt for a tip, while it has already been included in the cover charge.

USEFUL ADDRESSES

Foreign Embassies in Italy

Australia
Via A. Bosio, 5 - 00161 Rome
Tel. +39 06 852721
Fax +39 06 85272300
www.italy.embassy.gov.au.
info-rome@dfat.gov.au

Canada
Via Salaria, 243 - 00199 Rome
Tel. +39 06 854441
Fax +39 06 85444 3915
www.canada.it
rome@dfait-maeci.gc.ca

Great Britain
Via XX Settembre, 80 - 00187 Rome
Tel. +39 06 42200001
Fax +39 06 42202334
www.britian.it
consularenquiries@rome.mail.fco.gov.uk

Ireland
Piazza di Campitelli, 3 - 00186 Rome
Tel. +39 06 6979121
Fax +39 06 6792354
irish.embassy@esteri.it

New Zealand
Via Zara, 28 - 00198 Rome
Tel. +39 06 4417171
Fax +39 06 4402984

South Africa
Via Tanaro, 14 - 00198 Rome
Tel. +39 06 852541
Fax +39 06 85254300
www.sudafrica.it

United States of America
Via Vittorio Veneto, 121 - 00187 Rome
Tel. +39 06 46741
Fax +39 06 4882672
www.usis.it

Foreign Consulates in Italy

Australia
Via Borgogna, 2
20122 Milan
Tel. +39 02 77704217
Fax +39 02 77704242

Canada
Via Vittor Pisani, 19
20124 Milan
Tel. +39 02 67581
Fax +39 02 67583900
milan@international.gc.ca

Great Britain
Via S. Paolo, 7
20121 Milan
Tel. +39 02 723001
Fax +39 02 86465081
ConsularMilan@fco.gov.uk

Lungarno Corsini, 2
50123 Florence
Tel. +39 055 284133
Consular.Florence@fco.gov.uk

Via dei Mille, 40
80121 Naples
Tel. +39 081 4238911
Fax +39 081 422434
Info.Naples@fco.gov.uk

Ireland
Piazza San Pietro in Gessate, 2 - 20122 Milan
Tel. +39 02 55187569/02 55187641
Fax +39 02 55187570

New Zealand
Via Guido d'Arezzo, 6
20145 Milan
Tel. +39 02 48012544
Fax +39 02 48012577

South Africa
Vicolo San Giovanni sul Muro, 4
20121 Milan
Tel. +39 02 8858581
Fax +39 02 72011063
saconsulate@iol.it

United States of America
Via Principe Amedeo, 2/10
20121 Milan
Tel. +39 02 290351
Fax +39 02 29001165

Lungarno Vespucci, 38
50123 Florence
Tel. +39 055 266951
Fax +39 055 284088

Piazza della Repubblica
80122 Naples
Tel. +39 081 5838111
Fax +39 081 7611869

Italian Embassies and Consulates Around the World

Australia
12, Grey Street - Deakin, A.C.T. 2600 - Canberra
Tel. 02 62733333, 62733398, 62733198
Fax 02 62734223
www.ambcanberra.esteri.it
Consulates at: Brisbane, Glynde, Melbourne, Perth , Sydney

Canada
275, Slater Street, 21st floor - Ottawa (Ontario) K1P 5H9
Tel. (613) 232 2401/2/3
Fax (613) 233 1484 234 8424
www.ambottawa.esteri.it
ambital@italyincanada.com
Consulates at: Edmonton, Montreal, Toronto, Vancouver,

Great Britain
14, Three Kings Yard, London W1K 4EH
Tel. 020 73122200
Fax 020 73122230
www.amblondra.esteri.it
ambasciata.londra@esteri.it
Consulates at: London, Bedford, Edinburgh, Manchester

Ireland
63/65, Northumberland Road - Dublin 4
Tel. 01 6601744
Fax 01 6682759
www.ambdublino.esteri.it
info@italianembassy.ie

New Zealand
34-38 Grant Road, Thorndon, (PO Box 463, Wellington)
Tel. 04 473 5339
Fax 04 472 7255
www.ambwellington.esteri.it

South Africa
796 George Avenue, 0083 Arcadia
Tel. 012 4305541/2/3
Fax 012 4305547
www.ambpretoria.esteri.it
Consulates at: Johannesburg, Capetown, Durban

United States of America
3000 Whitehaven Street, NW Washington DC 20008
Tel. (202) 612-4400
Fax (202) 518-2154
www.ambwashingtondc.esteri.it
Consulates at: Boston, MA - Chicago, IL - Detroit, MI - Houston, TX - Los Angeles, CA - Miami, FL - Newark, NJ - New York, NY - Philadelphia, PA - San Francisco, CA

ENIT (Italian State Tourism Board)

Australia
Level 4, 46 Market Street
NSW 2000 Sidney
PO Box Q802 - QVB NSW 1230
Tel. 00612 92 621666
Fax 00612 92 621677
italia@italiantourism.com.au

Canada
175 Bloor Street E. Suite 907 – South Tower
M4W3R8 Toronto (Ontario)
Tel. (416) 925 4882
Fax (416) 925 4799
www.italiantourism.com
enit.canada@on.aibn.com

Great Britain
1, Princes Street
W1B 2AY London
Tel. 020 7408 1254
Tel. 800 00482542 FREE from United Kingdom and Ireland
italy@italiantouristboard.co.uk

United States of America
500, North Michigan Avenue Suite 2240
60611 Chicago 1, Illinois
Tel. (312) 644 0996 /644 0990
Fax (312) 644 3019
www.italiantourism.com
enitch@italiantourism.com

12400, Wilshire Blvd. – Suite 550
CA 90025 Los Angeles
Tel. (310) 820 1898 - 820 9807
Fax (310) 820 6357
www.italiantourism.com
enitla@italiantourism.com

630, Fifth Avenue – Suite 1565
NY – 10111 New York
Tel. (212) 245 4822 – 245 5618
Fax (212) 586 9249
www.italiantourism.com
enitny@italiantourism.com

The unique heritage of the Valle d'Aosta, with its spectacular Alpine peaks, offers diverse itineraries for the visitor. Among green valleys carpeted with flowers and majestic cathedrals of rock lie Roman remains and other civic and religious vestiges of Aosta's history. Elsewhere in the valley there are Romanesque and Gothic churches, magnificent medieval castles, fortified houses and lookout towers, for example the beautiful Forte di Bard. In Piedmont, Turin is an elegant, ordered, discreet city with a pleasingly human dimension. Many important vestiges of its past have survived and the quality of its galleries and museums will surprise you.

Heritage

The historic centers of the region's smaller towns, whose history can be 'read' in the stratification of the buildings, are equally delightful.
The architectural legacy left by the Savoys in Turin and the rest of Piedmont deserves a special mention.

Highlights

- The elegant, Savoy pleasure palaces, now a UNESCO World Heritage Site.
- The islands of Lake Orta and Lake Maggiore.
- The Valentino in Turin, a fairy-tale castle set in a park by the Po.
- The Forte di Bard and the picturesque medieval castles of Issogne, Verrès, Fènis and Aymavilles.

Bold, stars and italics are used in the text to emphasize the importance of places and art-works:

bold type ** → **not to be missed**
bold type * → **very important**
bold type → **important**
italic type → **interesting**

Inside

VALLE D'AOSTA

18 Aosta
29 Western Valle d'Aosta
40 Eastern Valle d'Aosta

PIEDMONT

51 Turin
72 Alessandria
75 Asti
78 Biella
80 Cuneo
84 Novara
87 Verbano-Cusio-Ossola
89 Vercelli

AOSTA

Aosta, the regional capital of the Valle d'Aosta, lies in a green valley at the confluence of the Buthier Stream and the Dora Baltea River surrounded by breathtaking Alpine peaks. The steep south-facing lower slopes of the valley, which are called *adret*, are planted with vineyards. On the other side, which is called *envers*, is the mountain resort of Pila. Although there have been settlements here since the 3rd millennium BC, Augusta Praetoria was founded by the Romans in 25 BC to defend the northern frontier of the Empire. Since then, Aosta has maintained its role as a crossing-point on this key route route across the northwestern Alps.

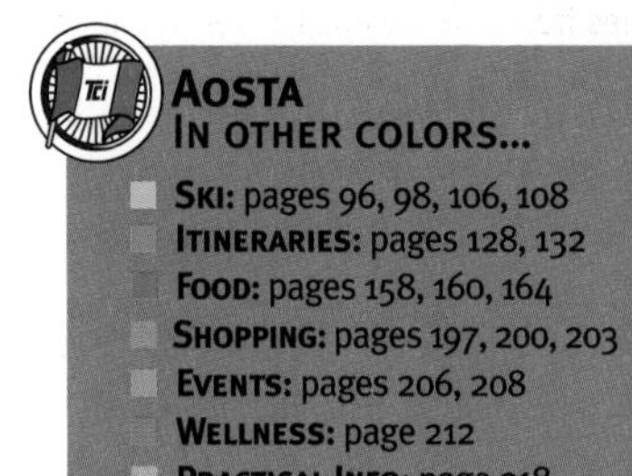

AOSTA
IN OTHER COLORS...
- **SKI:** pages 96, 98, 106, 108
- **ITINERARIES:** pages 128, 132
- **FOOD:** pages 158, 160, 164
- **SHOPPING:** pages 197, 200, 203
- **EVENTS:** pages 206, 208
- **WELLNESS:** page 212
- **PRACTICAL INFO:** page 218

Arco di Augusto/ Arch of Augustus 1

The Arch of Augustus was dedicated to the emperor to celebrate his victory over the indigenous Celtic tribe, the Salassi, in 25 BC. It was put here to formalize the arrival at Aosta of the road from Eporedia (now Ivrea) across the Alps to Gaul and is one of the town's symbols. The single arch with its Corinthian half-columns is striking both for its imposing architectural forms and its somber structure. The roof, which dates from 1912, replaced a similar roof added in the 18th century. In the nearby suburb of Ponte di Pietra, on the far side of the Buthier Stream, you can see a **Roman bridge**, built in the Augustan period on the old riverbed and now in a charming setting.

Complesso Monumentale di S. Orso/Monumental complex of S. Orso 2

This monumental complex is the most important example of medieval buildings in the town and one of the foremost religious complexes in the whole of the Alpine Chain. In front of it is a free-standing Romanesque **bell tower*** with three- and four-light windows (1131), a familiar sight within the urban landscape. The complex comprises the Collegiate church, the cloister and the prior's house. The **Collegiate church*** has a nave with two side-aisles, a crypt and semi-circular apses. The trussed-beam roof dates from 994-1026, when the church was rebuilt above an early-medieval building. In the late 15th century, the facade was added with a high central gable which breaks up

Aosta: Monumental complex of S. Orso

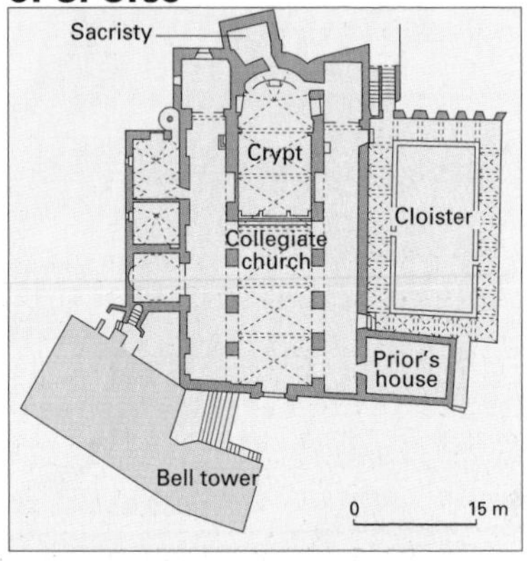

the otherwise blank wall. The interior is decorated in the 15th-century Gothic style. Under the roof (in left aisle) you can still see the remains of the original decoration: fragments of a cycle of **frescoes*** dated to the early 11th century. The fine carved wooden *choirstalls* at each side of the presbytery (where excavations have uncovered a mosaic floor probably dating from the 12th century) date from the late 15th century, whereas the five windows of the central apse date from the early 16th century. The **crypt** below the choir has five small aisles and dates from the Romanesque church (11C). The **Museo del Tesoro**, which, at the time of writing, is not open to the public, contains various *medieval treasures*. The entrance to the **cloister**** (see plan of Sant'Orso for the most interesting capitals), is on the right of the Collegiate church. The cloister has

40 magnificent carved capitals (first half 12C), one of the finest masterpieces of Romanesque sculpture in the Valle d'Aosta. They depict the Salvation of Man through the Incarnation of Christ, with scenes from the Old and new Testaments and the Life of St Ursus. The three parts of the delightful **prior's house*** (1468) to the right of the Collegiate church are supported by five arches. It has elegant windows with flamboyant terracotta decoration and an octagonal tower. It has an interesting little chapel decorated with 15th-century *frescoes* depicting scenes from the Life of St George. Opposite the Sant'Orso complex is the former **church of S. Lorenzo**, of ancient origin but rebuilt several times. Beside it is an ancient lime tree, apparently more than 400 years old. Below the church are the remains of a larger early Christian church built on a Latin-cross plan (5C).

Porta Pretoria ❸

Porta Pretoria was one of the monumental gates built in the eastern wall of the Roman town, in line with the Arch of Augustus. It has lost none of its

The bell tower of S. Orso towers above the old town of Aosta.

Sant'Orso: main capitals to see

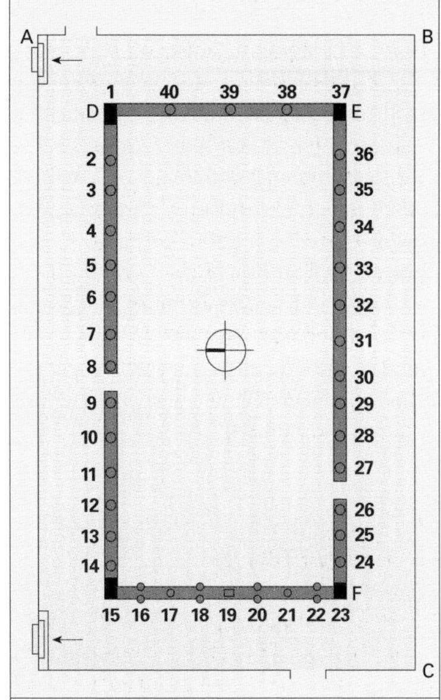

2	Daniel in the Lion's Den
3	The Annunciation
4	The Nativity
5	The Adoration of the Magi
6	The Flight into Egypt
8	The Story of Job
9	Rebecca is asked to marry Isaac
11	The harpies
12	The fox and the stork
16-22	The stories of Esau and Jacob
27-31	The Prophets
32	The stories of St Ursus
33	The Raising of Lazarus; the Apostles
35	The founding of the Collegiate church of S. Orso

grandeur and is still one of the town's most important ancient monuments. It is a double gateway separated by an open central space and dates from the late 1st century BC. Each side of the gateway has three arches built of large blocks. The central arch is higher and broader than the other two. There used to be two defense towers connecting the gate to the walls. The north tower has been incorporated into a medieval fortified house.

Parco Archeologico del Teatro Romano/Archeological park and Roman theater ❹

The archeological park is an excavated area within the town walls, just north of Porta Pretoria. The **theater**** is possibly the most interesting Roman monument to survive from the Roman town of Augusta Praetoria. The back wall of the *cavea* is built of Cyclopean blocks and supported by massive buttresses. Built at the end of the 1st century BC, it could seat more than 3,000 people. It was built large (81.20 m x 64.10 m) to impress anyone arriving from Gaul bound for Rome. Near the theater are the ruins of the 1st-century AD **amphitheater**. This large building (86 m x 76 m) was once connected to the theater by a portico no longer extant. Seven arches of the portico were incorporated

The Roman theater is one of the finest examples to survive from Antiquity in the area of the Alps.

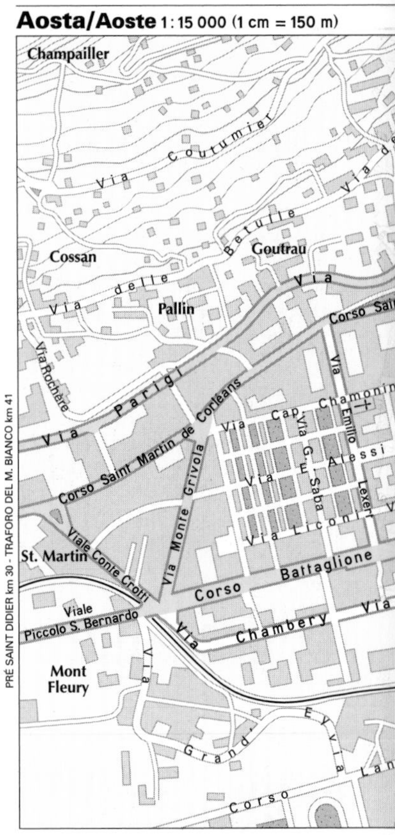

into the *convent of S. Caterina* (founded in the 13C and rebuilt in the 15C). Ruins of the masonry which supported two of the rows of the seating can be seen in the convent orchard.

Le Mura/The walls 5

Many sections of the travertine **walls*** which once surrounded Aosta have survived and are one of the town's cultural attractions. They formed a rectangle measuring 727.5 m x 574 m and included four gates and 20 square two-storey towers placed at regular intervals. Two of the towers have survived intact (Torre del Pailleron and Torre del Lebbroso), while others were transformed or rebuilt in the Middle Ages. They include the *Tour Fromage*, in the eastern section of walls near the Roman theater, now a showcase for contemporary art and, close by, the remains (partially incorporated into medieval buildings) of a Roman tower known as *Casa Tollen*. The high, square **Torre dei Balivi** stands at the north-east corner of the walls. Probably erected in the 12th century, it is now part of a complex of old buildings of various date. The complex, which was subsequently enlarged and altered, used to house the courtroom and was used as a prison until 1984. The **south walls** are particularly interesting because they include two of the towers which have remained intact: the Roman **Torre del Pailleron**, excellently restored in 1891-92 with repairs in brick, and the **tower** known as the **Castello di Bramafam***. This is called a castle rather than a tower because the Challant (who were Viscounts of Aosta in the 13C) built this imposing circular tower with its Guelph merlons above the ruins of a Roman tower. They also built two projecting wings with a west-facing entrance and an arched doorway. Part of the complex stands above the ruins of the *Porta principalis dextera*, one of the Roman gates, discovered in the late

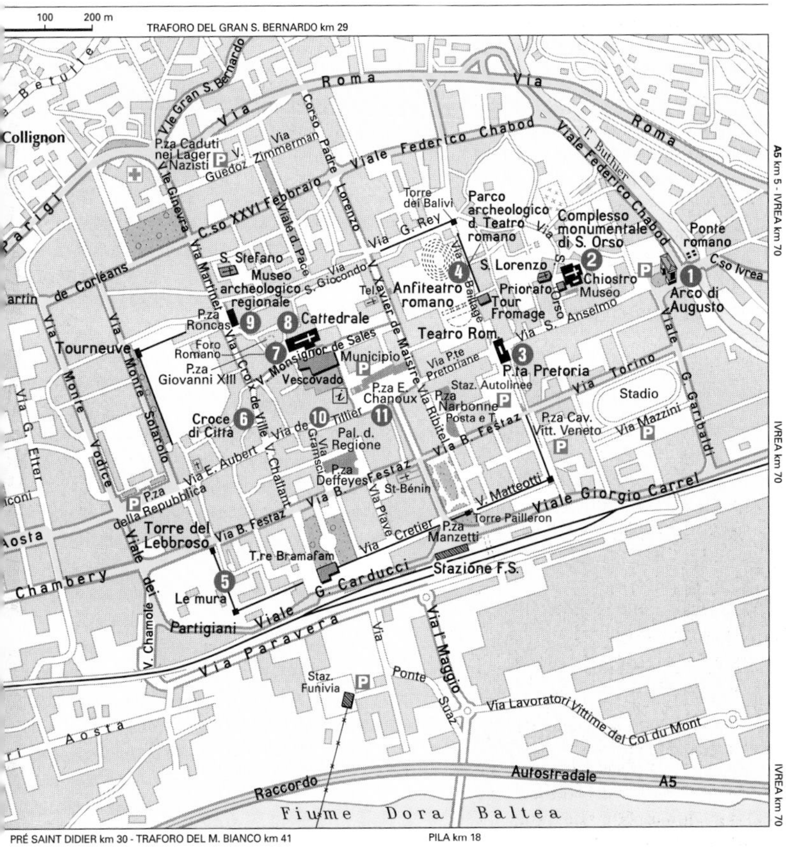

19th century. We recommend making the effort to see the **Torre del Lebbroso**, an important example of an original Roman tower in the Augustan walls. In the 15th century, it was converted into a feudal residence for the De Friour family. In nearby Via Torre del Lebbroso, No. 2 is now the **Biblioteca Regionale e della Città di Aosta**, with a fine collection of about 90,000 books.

The 12C Castello di Bramafam.

Croce di Città 6

Croce di Città was once the crossroads of the Roman town. It began to be associated with the symbol of the Christian religion in 1541, when a *Crucifix* was erected here to commemorate the expulsion of the Calvinists from Aosta. Along with its fountain, in 1841, the Crucifix was moved to **Via Croix de Ville***, an old and very characteristic street which is the center of the social and economic life of the town. On this street is **John Calvin's house**, where the famous reformer stayed (1536) while he was trying to convert the people of Aosta to his religious doctrine. On the right-hand side, notice also the picturesque *Vicolo des Cogneins*.

Piazza Giovanni XXIII 7

This square in front of the cathedral, right in the center of the town, lies above part of the **Roman forum**. Parts of the forum can be seen to the left of the cathedral. From here, beyond the eastern side of a hexastyle temple, you can access a splendid **cryptoporticus****, an impressive rectangular underground gallery (87.10 m x 71.80 m) with barrel vaulting. The double passageway is spanned by a series of mighty arches supported by massive travertine uprights.

Cattedrale/Cathedral 8

Like the church of S. Orso, the cathedral was built in about the year 1000, on the site of an early Christian church (there are guided tours of the excavations). The two bell towers by the apse (with Gothic spires) were part of the Romanesque cathedral dedicated to the Assumption. The neoclassical facade (1848) conceals the beautifully decorated Renaissance facade behind, now part of the atrium. The paintings and sculptural decoration date from 1522. The fine doorway in the right side of the church dates from the 15th century. Inside, decorated in the Gothic style in the second half of the 15th century, is an important **cycle of frescoes*** (dated to between 1030 and 1040, recovered in 1986-91). Note the remarkable *windows* (late 15C-early 16C); in the presbytery, the fragments of *mosaic floor* (12C-13C); the **funerary monument to Tommaso II of Savoy** (first half 15C), and the beautifully carved wooden **choirstalls*** (1469-70). At the end of the right aisle, steps lead down to the **crypt***. The oldest part of it dates from the 9th century. Four of the ten columns have Lombard and Carolingian capitals. The deambulatory now houses the **Museo del Tesoro della Cattedrale***, which contains some particularly fine *artworks*. To the left of the cathedral is the beautiful **cloister***, begun in 1442 and completed in 1460. Built on a square plan, the capitals bear the names of the canons living while it was being built. To the right of the cathedral, a brick arcade (1837) spanning *Via Monsignor de Sales* connects the church to the **Bishop's Palace**. Continuing along this, one of the town's most central streets, you come to a gate on the right which leads into the courtyard. The area was once the site of the *Roman baths*. Like all Roman bath complexes, it had several apsed buildings, a *calidarium* and a *tepidarium*. After visiting the monuments of Roman and medieval Aosta, we suggest you stroll through the **ecclesiastical district**, which can be

Aosta: Cathedral

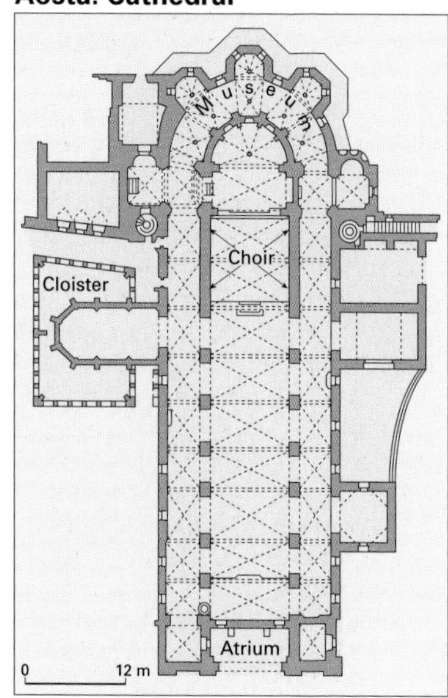

reached by walking between the cathedral and the area where you can view the forum, up Via Conte Tommaso and along Via S. Bernardo di Menthon to *Via S. Giocondo*. This, the old Via dei Preti, is the heart of a district which once enjoyed rights of asylum and special privileges (also known, because of this, as *Rue des Immunités*). Today, this corner of Aosta is still silent and secluded, its long walls concealing the *enclos* (gardens, vegetable patches and orchards) of medieval origin. Nearby is *Via Abate Chanoux*, with its gray medieval houses, built using material from the Roman walls.

Museo Archeologico Regionale 9

A **palazzo** (17C) in **Piazza Roncas***, beautifully **decorated** in 1606, provides access to the town's Archeological Museum, housed in a former 17th-century monastery. On the left, it incorporates the fortified house of the Vaudan family. In 1802, it was transformed by the French into the Challant Barracks. The first museum opened in 1929 following archeological excavations in Aosta and the valley between 1880 and 1925. It acquired considerable prestige as the driving force behind the discovery of other archeological sites which are now also museums. On the ground floor, the exhibits are displayed according to chronology and theme. Here, the *finds* date from the early Mesolithic (7000-6000 BC) to the early Middle Ages. Exhibits particularly worthy of note include the bronze part of a horse's bridle depicting a *battle scene between Romans and Barbarians* (2C) and the **Andrea Pautasso numismatic collection***. The **archeological excavations*** below the museum are well worth seeing. They include the remains of the *Porta principalis sinistra*, one of the four gates of the Roman town, and a series of associated structures. In Antiquity, this was the beginning of the road leading up towards the Great St Bernard Pass. Near Piazza Roncas is the **Torre Tourneuve**, dating from the 12th century, and the **church of S. Stefano**, with 18th-century frescoes on the facade. It contains a huge Baroque gilt wooden high altar, fine carved 18th-century choirstalls and a colossal polychrome *statue of St Cristopher* (second half 15C), carved out of a single block of wood.

Via Jean-Baptiste de Tillier ⑩

In the Middle Ages, this was the street where the merchants lived. It became notorious because of its many stone passageways which enabled people to go from one house to another without going out into the street. The little square where the important chestnut market was once held is the site of the ancient and very interesting **little church of S. Grato**, with its small bell tower on the roof and a Gothic window on the facade. Inside is a *fresco* dating from 1512. Also in Via de Tillier is **Casa Darbelley** and *Palazzo Perrod*, with a neoclassical facade (1820) and a grand courtyard.

Piazza Chanoux ⑪

This large square in front of the Hôtel de Ville (the Town Hall) is the undisputed heart of the modern town, where ceremonies, processions, festivals and markets are held. It is the outward expression of Napoleon's ideas with regard to town planning. These were based on the renewal of architectural and decorative codes in lay terms and the concept of land-use according to the principle of public utility. In 1842, the buildings around the Town Hall were also transformed to provide a suitable background for the town's new center. It was not long before the first hotels were built here, to serve the new phenomenon of tourism. For example, the former *Hotel Couronne*, with a small loggia on the facade, and *Palazzo Frassy*, with majolica decoration in the Art-Nouveau style on its facade (c. 1912), although the building dates from the 19th century. In front of the Town Hall is a *monument to the soldier of the Valle d'Aosta* (1924). The imposing **Hôtel de Ville***, on the north side of the square, with a majestic facade almost 140 m long, was built between 1839 and 1842. The somber monumental neoclassical facade is made up of several symmetrical parts and a portico. The fine statues in front of two of the pillars of the central part of the building symbolize Aosta's two rivers, the *Dora Baltea River* and the *Buthier Stream*.

The splendid facade of the Hôtel de Ville on Piazza Chanoux.

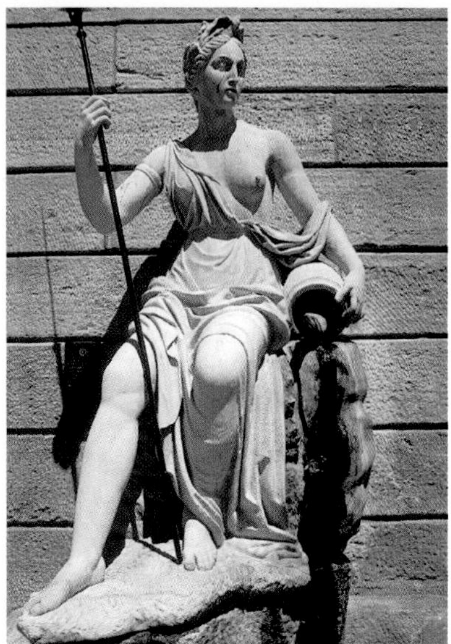

The personification of the Dora Baltea River in front of the Hôtel de Ville.

Mont Fleury and Saint-Martin-de-Corléans (off the map)

Starting at Piazza della Repubblica di Aosta, head west along Corso Battaglione Aosta, until you reach a crossroads. Beyond it, on the left, you can see the *Castello di Mont Fleury*, a charming, late-18th-century building. If you turn right at the crossroads towards the hillside along Viale Crotti, and keep left, Corso Saint-Martin-de-Corléans will bring you into the district of the same name. Behind the *church of Saint-Martin-de-Corléans* (dating from the 17C but with a late-Romanesque bell tower) is the **Parco Archeologico dell'Area Megalitica di Saint-Martin-de-Corléans***, a site used for cult worship and a burial ground dating from the 3rd millennium BC and occupied until the Medieval period. From the church of Saint-Martin, walk uphill to Via delle Betulle, and continue to walk right following this road which runs parallel to the SS 26 road at the bottom of the valley. The locals call this road *la panoramica*. After a while, just below the level of the road, you will see two old villas with farms attached which are worth a visit. The first is **Cascina Martinet**, an old farm restored in the 19th century. The second, slightly further downhill, recognizable by its tower with a wooden balcony on the top, is **Villa Torrione**. This farm was given by the Viscount of Aosta to the canons who ran the Pilgrims' Hospice on the Great St Bernard Pass in 1177.

Villa Romana della Consolata/Roman Villa at Consolata (off the map)

Beyond the point where Via delle Betulle joins Viale Gran San Bernardo, Via Roma and Viale Chabod lead to the district of Consolata. Here, just north of the town walls, you can see the remains of a Roman villa from the late Republican period, with its original walls and mosaic floors with geometric motifs. Built on a rectangular plan, the villa is composed of large residential rooms connected to the service rooms and storage rooms. It was probably inhabited until the 5th century. During the phase of continuous occupation, building work seems to have been undertaken, especially in the large *tablinum*.

The late 18C Castello di Mont Fleury.

DAY TRIPS

CHARVENSOD [4 km]

Many of the villages under this town's administration have marvelous views of Aosta, the valley of the Dora and the beginning of the Valle del Gran San Bernardo. The *chapel of S. Colomba* was built in 1622, in an area called *Duys*, where there has been a church since the 12th century.
The castle of the bishops of Aosta (14C) is now a ruin.

COLLE DEL GRAN SAN BERNARDO [34 km]

Since very early times, this has been a crucial crossing point between the Po Valley and Central and Western Europe. The pass (2,473 m) lies in a valley with very little vegetation and is covered in snow for most of the year. The Celts certainly knew about the pass and used it, and the Romans built a consular road over it. Over the centuries, the pass was crossed by Charlemagne (in 775), probably also by Henry IV on his way to Canossa (in 1077), by Frederick Barbarossa (in 1174 and 1175) and finally by Napoleon's army (15-21 May 1800). The flat valley at the top of the pass is called the **Plan de Jupiter**. There is a hotel there, the *Albergo Italia*, a *statue of St Bernard* (1905), patron saint of mountaineers, and an Italian customs post. At the far end of the valley, beyond the Swiss customs post, is **Lake Gran San Bernardo**. Beside the lake are the ruined steps of a small *temple* dedicated to Jupiter, after whom the valley is named. Nearby they discovered the ruins of a Roman staging post. The **Hospice** is the most impressive building on the pass.
The current one dates from 1821-25 and replaces the original hospice built here in about 1050 to provide shelter for travelers crossing the pass. It was possibly founded by St Bernard himself, then an archdeacon in Aosta. Today it is run by an Augustinian community.
It was here that the famous St Bernard's dogs were bred and trained to help travelers lost in the snow. Inside the hospice is the **Museo del Colle del Gran San Bernardo**, which has finds from excavations conducted on the consular road across the pass. They include coins, votive objects, and a small natural history collection.
Before the oldest part of the complex around the church is the *tomb of General Louis-Charles Desaix*, who died fighting at the battle of Marengo, built by Napoleon in 1806, and the **Treasury***, which houses some valuable *artworks*. The Baroque **church** dates from 1686. It has fine wooden choirstalls, part of which were inlaid when the church was built.
The *altar* on the right contains the remains of St Faustina, formerly in the catacombs in Rome and donated by Leo XII in 1828.

Lake Gran San Bernardo at the top of the pass between Italy and Switzerland.

The 15C bell tower of Gignod Parish church with the Alps in the background.

ÉTROUBLES [16 km]

Tourism and dairy farming are the main resources of this town situated on the left bank of the Artanavaz Stream and surrounded by woods and meadows. The *Parish church* (1815) has a remarkable 15th-century *bell tower* with a spire. The charming medieval center is a sort of open-air museum, with sculptures and frescoes by Italian and foreign contemporary artists.

GIGNOD [8 km]

The town is set in a splendid sunny position on the east bank of the Buthier Stream. The **Parish church of S. Ilario** stands on the site of the castle built by the Gignod family, dominating the town. It has a huge *bell tower* (1481) with two-light windows. The church was built in the 15th century in the Gothic style, and was altered subsequently. (The facade dates from the 19C). It is famous for its fine cycle of **frescoes*** which date from about 1480, one of the most important in the region. Note also the 16th-century *windows*, the Baroque *high altar* and the small **museum**, with *artworks, liturgical and sacred objects* and a couple of worked silver *processional crosses*. Just below the old town center is a short square medieval *tower* which was part of the fortifications that defended the valley. Not far from Gignod, on the opposite side of the valley, at the small town of *Ayez* is a 15th-century **fortified house** with stone walls and carved lintels above the windows.

GRESSAN [4 km]

The merloned tower of **Castello La Tour de Villa** stands at the entrance to this picturesque little town. Today the castle is still a private residence. The central tower dates from the Romanesque period and the surrounding parts of the building from the 15th century, but were altered in the early 20th century. The merlons on the tower and the curtain wall also date from the 15th century. From the embankment in front of the castle you can see the old, free-standing *Tour de la Plantà* with massive perimeter walls 2 m thick. Further downhill, surrounded by orchards, is the pretty little church of **S. Maria Maddalena***, rebuilt in the 15th century. It has 15th-century *frescoes* on the facade and more inside. The 12th-century **bell tower** is all that remains from the Romanesque church.

OYACE [20 km]

A panoramic road which follows the right bank of the Buthier di Valpelline Stream leads up to the town. A tower mentioned in a document of 1197, the **Tournalla**, dominates the town from a high rocky spur. According to tradition, and possibly because there are no other examples of octagonal towers in the region, it is said to have been built by a group of fleeing Saracens in about 1000.

PARCO NATURALE DELLA CÔTE DE GARGANTUA [15 km]

This area of moraines formed by the glacier which once occupied the valley of the Gressan Stream is now a small nature reserve. It has a rare type of vegetation dating from the period when, once the glaciers had retreated, the climate of the Alpine Chain was much warmer and drier than it is now. Preserved by the unusual microclimate of the area, the vegetation consists mainly of low bushes and shrubs.

POROSSAN [4 km]

Near this small town on the left bank of the Buthier Stream is a spectacular 15th-century **canal-bridge**, which can be seen from a small bridge in the fields of *La Chapelle*. It is an impressive feat of hydraulic engineering resting on a single-arch bridge 70 m high, built to guarantee the water supply to the areas of Saint-Christophe and Quart.

QUART [8 km]

The villages of this municipality based in *Villefranche* are scattered around an area of varying height. It includes *Alpeggio Fontin*, thought to be the farm where the Valle d'Aosta's most famous cheese, Fontina was first made.
From the late 12th century, the lords of Quart ruled the feud from their gloomy **castle** here, dominating the valley from a rocky knoll. It acquired its present form between the 14th and 16th centuries under the Savoy rulers who took over power. There are still traces of the Savoy *coats-of-arms* and *stuccoes* above the doorway leading into chapel (17C). The **Necropolis of Vollein*** is situated within the vast municipality of Quart. It dates from the early Aeneolithic (between 3000 and 2500 BC) and is interesting not only from the point of view of archeology, but also in terms of landscape, situated as it is in a rocky area with wonderful views of the mountains. So far, 60 tombs have been found. The grave-goods suggest that it belonged to a tribe of Anatolian origin. Below the burial ground are traces of an adjoining settlement.

The massive castle once ruled by the lords of Quart.

SAINT-CHRISTOPHE [3 km]

The town comprises three villages scattered around the hillside. By walking down to the right of the garden around *Castello Passerin d'Entrèves*, you reach the *Parish church*. Built in the Romanesque style, it has an 19th-century facade and an imposing stone **bell tower***. The height of the tower was raised in the 15th century. The ground floor of the tower is a chapel with a large wooden *statue of St Cristopher* (15C).

SAINT-OYEN [18 km]

Like other towns in the valley, this one is surrounded by meadows used for grazing dairy cattle which provide the milk for the flourishing local dairy industry, especially Fontina cheese. What distinguishes it is the fact that it has a very old fortified monument, **Chateau Verdun**. In 1137, the castle was given to the monks of the Great St Bernard Pass, who turned it into an annex of the Hospice on the pass and used it as a farm. Today, Chateau Verdun still provides accommodation for individuals or small groups in a quiet natural setting. The *Parish church* is very old, but was rebuilt in 1820.
It contains a gilt, silver *reliquary* inlaid with precious stones made by a Swiss goldsmith in the 17th century. Close by, in **Saint-Léonard**, it's worth visiting the medieval **Castello di Bosses**, a striking rectangular building dating from the 15th century (although the original building is older). Various events and exhibitions are held here.

SANTUARIO DI PONT-SUAZ [5 km]

This very old pilgrimage church, with its sloping roof extending forwards protecting the facade and decorated with a fresco of the *Crucifixion*, is traditionally a favorite pilgrimage site of vine-growers. From the 18th century onwards, they would come here to ask the Madonna to free them from the scourge of the disease which afflicts the vine called peronospora. According to local tradition, the crypt was used for practicing exorcism.

THE VALLE DI OLLOMONT [17 km]

This small, quiet valley of the Buthier di Ollomont Stream is really an exception in the scenario of the Valle d'Aosta. None of the paths are difficult, its undulating hills are dotted with tiny villages, and the silence is broken only by the shrill alarm calls of the large marmot population. The valley, once often frequented by smugglers, has always been regarded as one of the most obvious ways to cross into Switzerland. The **Fenêtre Durand Pass** (2,802 m) at the head of the valley,

Scattered villages in the quiet, narrow Valle di Ollomont.

is quite easy to negotiate and is one of the very few passes between the Valle d'Aosta and Switzerland that does not involve crossing a glacier. **Ollomont**, the only town in the valley (although the road goes on to *Glacier*), has a beautiful *Parish church* which is unusually high for a mountain church. It was founded in 1775 and enlarged in 1868. If you are interested in scenery and wildlife, we recommend the walk to the **Tour del Belvedere** (8.5 km, about 3.5 hours). This circular walk starts at *Rey*. At first the path is fairly level, after which there are uphill and downhill sections. It passes through pleasant wooded scenery with wonderful views.

THE VALPELLINE [20 km]

The town is situated near the confluence of the Buthier di Ollomont Stream and the Buthier di Valpelline Stream, in a valley used for farming which is popular with visitors in the summer. The houses of the old town center have long wooden balconies. The **Parish church of St-Pantaléon** and the *bell tower* with two-light windows and a pyramidal pointed spire date from the 18th century. (The *bell* (1736) is famous for its particularly harmonious sound). The church has a fine Baroque greenstone *doorway*. Inside is a beautiful marble *altar* (17C). The **museum** here has a collection of sacred *artworks*: note the painted leather *altar frontal* (17C).
Near the church is *Casa La Tour*, a medieval building rebuilt in the 18th century with a large roofed area used for farm-work, supported by round pillars. The largest town in the **upper reaches of the Valpelline** is **Bionaz**. Here you can see the *Parish church of S. Margherita*.
It incorporates decoration from the late-Romanesque, 13th and 18th centuries, and has a late Romanesque bell tower. Bionaz is surrounded by large meadows, whereas, higher up, the landscape becomes more severe, with rocks and cliffs. This is the setting of **Lake Place Moulin**, a large artificial lake built in 1965 to regulate the flow of water to the hydroelectric power stations further down the valley.
As a result of the building of the dam, 650 m long and 146 m high, the village of *Prarayer*, at the north-east end of the lake, was partially submerged. It is now a hiking and climbing center. One particularly famous route leads to the *Aosta refuge* (2,788 m).

Lake Place Moulin, in the reaches of the Valpelline.

WESTERN VALLE D'AOSTA

The area described in the following pages can be subdivided, in terms of geographical location and landscape, into three separate parts. The first is the short section of La Plaine (that is, the bottom of the valley of the Dora Baltea River) between Aosta and the winding gorge just above Avise, known, significantly, as the Pierre Taillée (meaning 'cut stone'). The second comprises the three valleys of the Mt Gran Paradiso massif (and the Parco Nazionale del Gran Paradiso), the Val di Cogne with the Valnontey, the Valsavarenche, the Val di Rhêmes, and the Valgrisenche to the west. The last is the upper Valle della Dora, which stretches beyond the Pierre Taillée to the foot of Mt Blanc and, along with the area around Courmayeur and the side-valleys of La Thuile (or Piccolo San Bernardo), the Val Veny and the Val Ferret, is called the Valdigne. This is an area of serious mountains, with thrilling views of Mt Gran Paradiso and, in the Valdigne, Europe's highest mountain, Mt Blanc. What's more, the area has plenty of interesting little towns to explore. Historically speaking, as well as medieval castles and a large number of Romanesque bell towers, a complex network of roads, trading and traditions has developed which are still important from the social and cultural point of view today. In other words, with its historical heritage, landscape, and wildlife, the area has enormous potential for the visitor in terms of sport, culture and recreation.

From La Plaine to the Valdigne

The area covered by the SS 26 road stretches from the bottom of the Dora Baltea valley to the lip of the valley of Courmayeur.

Sarre, pleasantly situated on the hillside, is surrounded by vineyards and orchards interspersed with chestnut woods and spruce forest. Although it was founded in the 11th century, the *Parish church*, with its 17th-century lines, is noted for its exquisite Romanesque **bell tower*** with two- and three-light windows. The **Castello di Sarre**, outside the town, is also worth a visit. Built in the 12th and 13th centuries, and transformed in the 18th century, it is now a **museum**. Its collection includes furnishings, portraits, prints and various other precious objects.

Saint-Pierre is situated on a hillside among expanses of apple orchards and vineyards. Here archeologists discovered the remains of a settlement of hut-like buildings dating from the late 4th-early 3rd millennium BC, so far the earliest evidence of settlement in the Aosta valley. The **castle** and the lovely Romanesque **bell tower*** of the church of S. Pietro look rather strange as a result of a 19th-century facelift. The medieval castle was converted into a noble residence in the 17th century. It is also famous because of its museum: the **Museo Regionale di Scienze Naturali*** which illustrates various aspects of the Valle d'Aosta's natural environment. The mineralogical and petrographic collections are followed by a section devoted to the climatic and glacial aspects of the region. Then there are

Saint-Pierre: Castle of Sarriod de la Tour

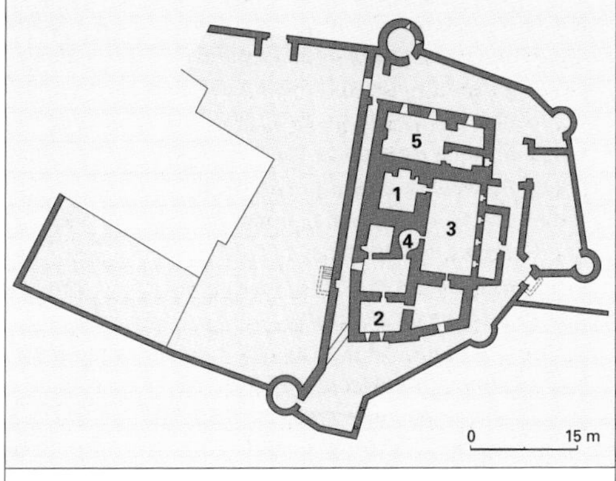

1 Ancient tower
2 Chapel
3 Room below the 16C hall
4 Staircase
5 Room below the 15C hall or "Room of the Heads"

Saint-Pierre: the church of S. Pietro and the castle.

sections about the flora and fauna, their origins and the most important species, and dioramas of the valley's four typical natural environments. Sections devoted to the valley's bird, mammal and insect species complete this interesting collection. Another monument worth seeing in Saint-Pierre is **Castello Sarriod de La Tour***, situated just outside the town and, in terms of architectural interest and state of preservation, more attractive than the previous one. Founded in the late 14th century, the castle has round towers, an imposing square keep and a beautiful **spiral staircase** with hand-carved stone steps. Inside the castle, note the *Sala delle Teste (Room of the Heads)*, with a fine late 15th-century wooden ceiling, and the *chapel*, with fragments of **frescoes** depicting the figure of Christ: one of the few surviving 13th-century cycles of its kind. Near Saint-Pierre is **Bois de la Tour***, a pleasant area for walking with picnic tables and an exceptional viewpoint, and **Comba di Vertosan**, a beautiful valley with lots of scope for hikers and mountain-bike enthusiasts.

Villeneuve, situated on the banks of the Dora (where there are opportunities for white-water rafting) lies on an old trading route. At the entrance to the town is a large medieval *tower-house*. The **church of S. Maria*** with its cemetery is situated on a high terrace above the Dora Baltea. Built in the archaic Romanesque style, it dates from the 11th century. The *bell tower* with its one-, two- and three-light windows dates from the 12th century. The interior is divided into a nave and two side-aisles, each of irregular shape and with an apse. There is a delightful *crypt* below the main apse. Just before the church, a small path leads uphill to **Châtel-Argent** with its very obvious round *keep*. The castle is mentioned in a document of 1175, but its present form dates from the late 13th century. Other features of architectural interest include the stone chemin-de-ronde and the remains of an old chapel with an elegant doorway in its facade.

Arvier lies in a valley cultivated with vineyards which cover the hillside in a series of steps. The wooded area outside the town has plenty of trails for hikers. The town is dominated by two buildings: the Romanesque bell tower of the *Parish church* (17C) with a spire and one-, two- and three-light windows, and the remains of the 13th-century **Castello La Mothe**, which has a square tower with windows with stone cross-members. The town is arranged around Rue Lostan, interesting on account of its 16th-century houses. Similar buildings are also to be found at nearby *Liverogne*. Here, from the bridge spanning the Dora di Valgrisenche there is a good view of a Roman bridge which has been incorporated into later buildings. Not far away lie the impressive ruins of **Castello di Montmayeur**, in a dominant position above the beginning of the Valgrisenche. It was erected in 1271 and rebuilt in 1312. The round merloned keep and the surviving sections of the higher set of walls are very dramatic. Because of its position, in the 19th century it was nicknamed the *Nido di avvoltoi* (Vultures' nest).

Avise*, a small town on the left bank of the Dora Baltea, is surrounded by green meadows, clumps of trees and vineyards. The old town is well preserved. The **Castello d'Avise***, situated on the left as you enter the town, dates from the late 15th century and was obviously built more for residential than defensive purposes.

Throughout the castle there is an unusual emphasis on ornament and decorative features. For example, the tower on the west side, with its corbeled embrasures, and the facade facing the valley, with beautifully decorated large and small windows. Further on is *Castello Blonay*, consisting of a solid 12th-century tower and a building which is possibly earlier, with 15th-century windows. At Avise, too, next to the 19th-century *Parish church of S. Brizio*, stands the ubiquitous late-Romanesque bell tower, decorated with two-light windows.

La Salle, set in a magnificent position on a broad plateau surrounded by woods and cultivated as meadows, orchards and vineyards, has several interesting buildings. The *Parish church of S. Cassiano* which was rebuilt the first time in the 17th century and again in the 19th century in the neoclassical style, has a fine Romanesque bell tower with two-light windows and a spire. Inside, the **museum** has several fine *artworks*. Note also **Maison Gerbollier**, where open-air concerts and other events are held in summer.
From La Salle, a panoramic road follows the hillside north-west towards the remains of the 13th-century **Castello di Châtelard**. It has a high round tower and ruined fortified walls. The next town, **Cheverel**, has an *ethnographical museum 'L'Uomo e il Pendio'*. Before the village of **Derby-Villaret** the SS 26 road passes through the **Pierre Taillée** gorge, where you can see cuts in the rock, arches and buttresses made by the Romans to build the terracing for the Roman road across the Little St Bernard Pass. Beyond a tunnel, (when there is suddenly a splendid *view* of Mt Blanc), the town, situated on both sides of the river and the main road, is composed of old buildings. The *Parish church*, built in the 15th-century and altered several times since, has a Romanesque bell tower.

Morgex, situated on the Dora, is surrounded by a broad circle of mountains. The **Parish church of S. Maria Assunta** was rebuilt in the 17th century but its Romanesque bell tower confirms that it is of earlier date. Recent research has ascertained the existence of an early Christian building dating from the late 5th to mid-6th centuries. On the edge of the town is **Castello di Archet**, an imposing complex of buildings (12C). Next to it is a merloned tower probably dating from the late 10th century. A few kilometers from Morgex, near Ruine Alta, is **Castello Pascal de la Ruine**, a remarkable 15th-century building with several parts, latterly used as a farm. It has some interesting late-Gothic features, such as very small windows and doors. The road from Morgex across to La Thuile via Colle San Carlo is very scenic.

Pré-Saint-Didier is situated at the confluence of Dora di Verney, or Dora di La Thuile Stream, and the Dora Baltea River and is famous for its splendid views of Mt Blanc. From here, the feature called the Dente del Gigante (Giant's Tooth) is quite obvious. Much visited in Roman times because of the health-giving properties of its thermal springs, Pré-Saint-Didier has a spectacular **gorge*** gouged out of the rock by the Dora di Verney Stream. From the cultural point of view, the **Parish church of S. Lorenzo** is very interesting architecturally. Despite subsequent alterations to the church fabric, its Romanesque origins are still obvious. The small 11th-century Romanesque bell tower is decorated with one- and two-light windows.

The Orrido della Dora gorge at Pré-Saint-Didier, a popular rafting location.

Cogne in summer.

The Cogne valley

This is one of the most charming valleys in the area and becomes obvious as you drive towards it. The road climbs gradually higher between the forested slopes on either side. The sharp ridges and the jagged peaks of Mt La Grìvola and Mt Grand Nomenon appear up ahead above a succession of outcrops and expanses of forest. We are in the eastern part of the Graian Alps. After crossing the Grand Eyvia Stream, the road passes the ruins of two disused iron foundries, which formerly played an important role in the valley.

Only a few kilometers from Aosta, **Aymavilles**, in a verdant valley with meadows, orchards and vineyards, is a popular holiday center with various interesting monuments. It is also known for its marble quarries (the marble from here is called *bardiglio*). The **castle****, set in a position dominating the town from above, is unusual, being a wonderful combination of a feudal fortress and a delightful Baroque residence. The main part of the castle is built on a rectangular plan with four high round angle towers. Two of the sides have rectangular merlons and two have indented merlons. The original building dates from at least 1287 and was probably a square keep. In about the mid-14th century, the four corner towers were added, giving the castle its characteristic outline. In 1728 four more blocks with broad loggias connecting the towers were added, decorated in the Baroque style. The **Parish church of St-Léger**, beyond the town, on the Cogne road, has Baroque lines as a result of the rebuilding in 1762 of a building mentioned in 1145. It has a late-Romanesque *bell tower* (and a bell cast in 1372). Inside, the ancient **crypt** is very interesting. It has thick walls with pillars and arches, and two aisles with very low, ribbed cross-vaulting, dating from the last quarter of the 10th century. The **Accademia di S. Anselmo**, conceived with the idea of promoting the study of local archeology and history, has some interesting collections. They include ancient objects, some remarkable works of art, sacred furnishings and a numismatic collection. At the tiny hamlet of *Pondel*, a Roman bridge which is also an **aqueduct*** spans the Grand Eyvia Stream. This daring structure was built across the gorge at a height of 52 m above the water. Pondel (or Pont d'El)

Castle of Aymavilles, with its four distinctive round towers.

was built (as a Latin inscription on the keystone of the arch of the aqueduct records) during the consulship of Augustus (3 BC) by C. Avillius and C. Aimus Patavinus, two mine-owners, who financed the project. The huge single arch (56 m long and 2.4 m wide) had a covered passageway to allow people and animals to cross, with a roofed entrance at each end. The top of the bridge, which has no roof and dates from a later period, was used as an aqueduct.

The Roman bridge-cum-aqueduct at Pondel built in 3 AD from local stone.

On the east side of the Valle del Grand Eyvia is **Ozein**. The village lies in a beautiful area with flat meadows and terracing. In the older part of the village, part of the stone houses was used for storing hay. The structures called *rascards* (wooden buildings resting on mushroom-shaped bases with walls made of overlapping tree-trunks) prevented rodents from stealing the provisions stored inside.

Cogne lies in a broad, sun-kissed hollow surrounded by woods, on the northern edge of the Parco Nazionale del Gran Paradiso. This is one of the places where you can access the park. One of the delightful features of the town is the lovely and unspoiled **field of Sant'Orso**, a triangular piece of land that has been saved from the clutches of the developers. In the oldest part of the **historic center**, slightly higher up than the rest of the town, are some traditional rural houses which have central courtyards with earth floors. Some of them have pointed doors and windows and wrought-iron decoration. Near the *Parish church of S. Orso*, the *statue* of the saint on the facade dates from the early 17th century. The church contains late 17th-century Baroque altars and an aluminum *statue of St Barbara*. In Piazza del Municipio (where there is an incredible *view* of Mt Gran Paradiso), the iron *fountain* was cast in 1809. The **Museo Minerario Alpino**, housed in the former mining village, describes the longstanding relationship between Cogne and the local mines which exploited the vast local deposits of magnetite (possibly the most prized of all the iron-ore minerals). The mines certainly existed in the 15th century and are possibly even older. They were finally closed down in 1979. The museum illustrates how the ore was extracted with the aid of plans, photographs, tools, scale models and audiovisual aids. There is also a large section devoted to the most important (former) mines in the local area.
In the Cogne area, there are still many testimonials to centuries of mining: industrial buildings that were used as houses for the workers and service buildings, north-west of the town, the blocks of houses at *Colonna*, occupied by miners until 1960, and the *Costa del Pino mine-entrance*. Just outside Cogne, *Lillaz* marks the beginning of a footpath leading to the Finestra di Champorcher Pass. On average the **walk** takes about 4.5 hours. The path winds up through coniferous forests, past mountain farms overlooking vast expanses of meadows, home to many different flower species.

The **Valnontey**, all of which lies within the territory of the Parco Nazionale del Gran Paradiso, winds up from Cogne towards the snow and glaciers of the massif. A road leads from Via del Gran Paradiso up to the *fortified house of Villette*, built in the 13th century and restored after a fire in the 16th century. It consists of two stone buildings, one of which has a fine Gothic two-light window. At *Valnontey*, on the other side of the river, is the **Giardino Botanico Alpino Paradisia*** (see page 132), which contains about 1,500 plant species from the Alps and other mountain regions. Not far from the garden, a mule-path leads up to the *Vallone del Loson*, to the **Vittorio Sella refuge**, situated on a plateau which opens out into vast expanses of meadows. The walk takes about 2.5 hours. This is one of the best places in the park for sightings of ibex, chamoix and marmots. At **Épinel**, monuments include a 15th-century *building* with an imposing cut-stone doorway, the *church of Ss. Fabiano e Sebastiano*, dating from 1699, and some characteristic 17th-century stone houses, some of which have *rascards* at the top. It's worth the short walk to see the **fortified house of Tarambel**, in the meadows east of Épinel. Dating from the 13th century, this small building once controlled traffic travelling up and down the valley. It has a doorway with a rounded arch made with small hand-hewn pieces of stone resting on massive jambs, set slightly above ground-level. This small, unusual mountain-style building has great charm.

Meadows and snow-capped peaks above Pont, at the top of the valley.

The Valsavarenche

Even more than Val di Cogne, the almost straight Valsavarenche runs through the National Park towards the Mt Gran Paradiso massif. This is Alpine scenery at its best.

Introd/*Plan-D'Introd* can be reached by crossing the Dora di Rhêmes Stream above a spectacular gorge with rock walls covered in vegetation. It lies in a pleasant position between the Savara Stream and the Dora di Rhêmes Stream. The almost circular **castle** with a square keep looks down over the town. The castle already existed in 1244, when it was described as having battlements. To the right of the road that climbs up to the castle, note also the old **Cascina Ola**, an interesting rural building from the point of view of decoration and ingenious functional features, dating from the 16th century. Not far from here is the 16th-century *Parish church* with a fine Baroque carved wooden high altar with marquetry work.

Valsavarenche/Dégioz, shares the name of the valley in which it lies. It is situated in a fan-shaped area of meadows at the foot of an ancient landslide. It has a **Parish church**, the **Madonna del Carmine**, with late-neoclassical lines, and a bell tower with two-light windows dating from 1483. Inside is the **Museo Parrocchiale della Madonna del Carmelo**, with some valuable exhibits, including a 14th-century polychrome wooden *statue of Our Lady of the Fountain*.

The small village of **Eau-Rousse**, named after a nearby cliff with red striations, lies at the far side of a hollow with terraces, a few houses and the *rascards di Maisonasse*. Eau-Rousse is another starting-point in Valsavarenche for walks in the beautiful Parco del Gran Paradiso.

Below **Pont**, magnificently situated at the head of the upper Valsavarenche, is an open rocky gorge lined with pines and larches. This is the wildest stretch of the Savara Stream. Above the grassy valley are the slopes and waterfalls of Mt Gran Paradiso. Just beyond are the baitas of **Pont**. Above the town is **Mt Gran Paradiso*** (see pp. 128-129), first climbed in 1860. Water from the mountain flows down into the Orco Stream on one side and into the Dora Baltea River on the other. This is the backbone of the homonymous park.

Extensions of Gran Paradiso form three large ridges separating the Valsavarenche from the Val di Cogne, and the Valle di Locana in Piedmont. These ridges are criss-crossed with footpaths for ascents, descents, traverses and fine ridge-walks. The walk to the **Vittorio Emanuele II refuge** takes about 2.5 hours. It constitutes the first part of the easiest route to the summit of Mt Gran Paradiso. With luck you may have sightings of some of the species of fauna which inhabit the park. The refuge, situated in severe glacial landscape, has magnificent views.

The Rhêmes valley

This valley lies on the western edge of the Parco Nazionale del Gran Paradiso. It is famous for its beautiful scenery, its views and its natural setting, where pastoral activities are still practiced much as they have been for centuries.

The road climbs up past meadows with clumps of trees, small villages and cultivated fields to **Rhêmes-Saint-Georges**, set in a green valley, a center for Alpine skiing, rock- and ice-climbing, and horse-riding in the nearby woods. The old village of *Coveyrand-Vieux* has houses several storeys high, with an intricate system of covered passageways and roofs with projecting eaves which allowed people to walk about in the depths of winter in comparative comfort. Adjoining the 15th-century *church* of S. Giorgio with its bell tower with two-light windows is the small **museum**, with interesting exhibits dating from the 15th century.

Looking back from the middle of the valley, there are good views of the villages of the municipality of Rhêmes-Saint-Georges, and the white bell tower of the church. Higher up, in an Alpine setting of meadows and woodland, is the picturesque village of **Melignon**. There is a chapel with a bell tower with a spire and a house frescoed in 1849. From here you can see the glaciers higher up, and the imposing shapes of Mt Granta Parey and *Mt Grande Rousse*.

Rhêmes-Notre-Dame, the last village in the valley, is quiet and isolated. The old center has conserved much of its traditional appearance. It lies in a vast area of meadows surrounded by forests and high mountains which form a particularly dramatic setting. The *Parish church of the Assunta* has a 15th-century bell tower with a spire and a one-light window. Set on the western edge of the Parco Nazionale del Gran Paradiso, the town has a Visitors' Center with a **museum**. It has interesting information about the fauna of the park and, in particular, the project to re-introduce the bearded vulture. For obvious reasons, it also attracts large numbers of walkers and climbers. In fact, it lies on the route of the Alpine path called Alta Via No. 2, between Champorcher and Courmayeur. From here it is also possible to cross the Alps into the upper Val Soana (in Piedmont) and the Val d'Isère (in France).

There are small clusters of traditional houses in the top of the valley, such as *Pont* (which has the same name as the village described in the description of the

The baitas of Pellaud in the upper reaches of the Valle di Rhêmes.

Mt Granta Parei towering above the valley.

Valsavarenche), where one of the houses is particularly striking for its size and complexity, with features dating from the 17th century. The houses of *Pellaud* date from the 17th and 18th centuries. The last village is *Thumel*, a group of *baitas* set in a spectacular expanse of meadows. Just above it, the cowsheds of *Fos* are situated in a very scenic area. Thumel is the starting-point for the footpath which, in about 1.5 hours, winds up to **Benevolo refuge**, set in the middle of the glacial head of the valley, with views across to the majestic rock walls of Mt Granta Parei. It's a lovely walk, partly because of the rich flora resulting from the limestone substrata and the fairly frequent sightings (rare elsewhere) of the Alpine chough.

The Valgrisenche

Much of the valley is still unspoiled. The lower part of the valley is broad and picturesque, while the top ends at the mountain chain on the border with Val d'Isère, and the spectacular glaciers of the Aiguille de la Grande Sassière. The road which winds up the valley is interesting from the point of view of Alpine scenery and views. It begins at Arvier, passes through Planaval and ends at the town of Valgrisenche.

Below the valley, the small **sanctuary of Rochefort** can be seen high up, surrounded by in the chestnut forest. It can be reached by following a footpath marked with Neogothic pillars depicting the *Stories of the Passion*, starting at the tiny village of *Rochefort*. Next to the pilgrimage church, which dates from 1833, is an old *oratory* which has magnificent views. The narrow bottom of the Valgrisenche has steep cliffs dotted with pines and spruces on either side. From here there are views of the Ghiacciaio del Rutor, and the massive face of Mt Montmayeur. Below the ruined castle is a rocky gorge. The water of the Dora di Valgrisenche Stream flows down between fallen boulders and pine-trees forming two beautiful waterfalls.

The small village of **Planaval** overlooks a flat valley which once contained a lake. The old part of it is well-preserved and includes traditional houses dating from the 17th century. A *fortified house* dating from 1312 has been incorporated into a modern building. The houses here have features in common with other parts of the Valle d'Aosta, but some have features from the area of the Canavese further east. The former are large stone houses with three or four floors, long wooden balconies and sloping roofs with strongly projecting eaves. The houses with Piedmontese influences are almost entirely built of stone with large, round pillars supporting the projecting eaves. In both cases, the houses mainly date from the 17th and 18th centuries. Common features to look out for include ramps for the animals and covered passageways where the houses are built closer together.

The little town of **Valgrisenche**, which has the same name as the valley, is situated in a flat area dotted with smooth boulders, with numerous streams and clusters of tiny houses in a valley of meadows and forests. It is a popular holiday center in summer and winter (offering hiking, climbing, trekking, Alpine and Nordic skiing, snowboarding, horse-riding and so on). Most of the houses are clustered around the main street. It has a pretty central square with a fine late-Romanesque *bell tower* and the *church of S. Grato*. The church houses the small but interesting **museum**. Above the Valgrisenche is **Lake Beauregard**. The pleasant walk around the lake takes about 3 hours.

The Valle del Piccolo San Bernardo

Named after the famous Little St Bernard Pass which leads across into Savoie, the valley is also named after the Dora di Verney (or Dora di La Thuile) Stream which flows down this valley, the Valle di Verney and the Valle di La Thuile. The valley is steep, with few signs of habitation until La Thuile, the main town, where it opens out into green rolling meadows.

The oldest part of **La Thuile** (called *La Veulla*), an important summer holiday resort and even more popular in winter, is focused around the charming square of the **Parish church of S. Nicola**. The church is of Romanesque origin but was rebuilt in 1796, and has a 15th-century bell tower. Inside is a polychrome wooden *Crucifix* dating from the 16th century. As you climb up the valley, before reaching the town, the Dora di Verney, or Dora di La Thuile Stream forms the Orrido di Pré-Saint-Didier, a gorge with pine and spruce forests on either side. Above it, the valley broadens out into a grassy valley surrounded by thick forests dominated by the glaciers and mountains higher up.

Cotton grass in flower near the Ghiacciaio del Rutor.

Colle San Carlo

A pleasant panoramic road leads from La Thuile towards *Campo del Principe Tommaso*, set among larches and fir trees, to **Colle San Carlo**. This is the start of the walk to the summit of *Mt Tête d'Arpy* (about 20 mins), where there are extraordinary views across to Courmayeur and the Mt Blanc massif. Beyond the col, the scenery is dominated by thick coniferous forest.

The **Piccolo S. Bernardo/Little St Bernard Pass*** can be reached by the panoramic final section of the SS 26 road, which curves up, past the old village of **Pont Serrand**, in a lovely setting, with the 15th-century *chapel of S. Bernardo*. This important Alpine pass opens out at the top into a sort of plateau spanning the watershed between the valleys of the Dora Baltea and the Isère, which also marks the border between France and Italy. Next to the *Memorial to the victims of Nazi Concentration Camps* (1955) lie the remains of the *Mansio in Alpe Graia*, a Roman building on the consular road to Gaul and, close by, the *fanum*, a Gallic-Roman sanctuary. A little further along the plateau is a **cromlech**, a funerary precinct dating from the Early Iron Age. This unusual prehistoric monument consists of a stone circle with a diameter of 72 m formed by small blocks of stone standing between 2 m and 4 m apart.

Courmayeur and Mt Blanc

Situated in the upper reaches of the Valdigne, where the presence of the gigantic Mt Blanc massif is overwhelming, **Verrand** is an old town with marvelous views and an interesting setting.

Not far away is **Courmayeur****, skiing and mountaineering capital of the area. It is situated below the enormous massif of Mt Blanc in a beautiful valley of fir trees and larches. It has a **historic center** with the **church of Ss. Pantaleone e Valentino** ❶ and a fine Romanesque *bell tower* with a spire with one-, two- and three-light windows. Inside the church is a neoclassical black marble altar, and two fine Baroque wooden altars with twisted columns. The building opposite the church is also interesting and is the *headquarters of the Alpine Guides*. It also houses the **Museo Alpino Duca degli Abruzzi** ❷ where you can find out everything you ever wanted to know about mountaineering, from the display of mountaineering equipment, photographs, diaries and other information about climbing in the Alps and international expeditions. In the town center, **Via Roma** ❸ is a busy shopping street with rastaurants and cafés, while **Via Marconi** ❹ is an old street that has been saved from the developers. In the piazza, **Torre Malluquin** ❺, is all that survives of the 14th-century castle. Suggestions for day-trips from here include *Plan-Gorret*, which has splendid **views*** of Mt Blanc and the Mt Rutor massif, the *Bertone refuge*, another place with **marvelous views***, and **Dolonne**, an old town with houses with late-Gothic features. Further on is *La Saxe*, where the 19th-century buildings are packed close together, and **Entrèves**, where there is an interesting *fortified house* dating from 1391 with stone walls and windows.

Mt Blanc**, the highest mountain in the Alps (4,807 m) and in Europe as a whole, stretches from the Col de la Seigne to the south-west and the Col du Gran Ferret to the north-east. Its white profile is dotted with pinnacles, rocky outcrops and jagged ridges, while its slopes are a series of steep winding valleys filled with glaciers. The most northerly part of the massif includes the great pyramid of *Mt Dolent*, the *Ghiacciaio della Brenva* and the *Ghiacciaio del Miage*. From the point of view of mountaineering, this area provides endless challenges for climbers, with routes of every level of difficulty and some of the longest, most demanding ice and snow routes in the Alpine chain. The **Traversata del Bianco**** is the name of

Courmayeur 1 : 25 000

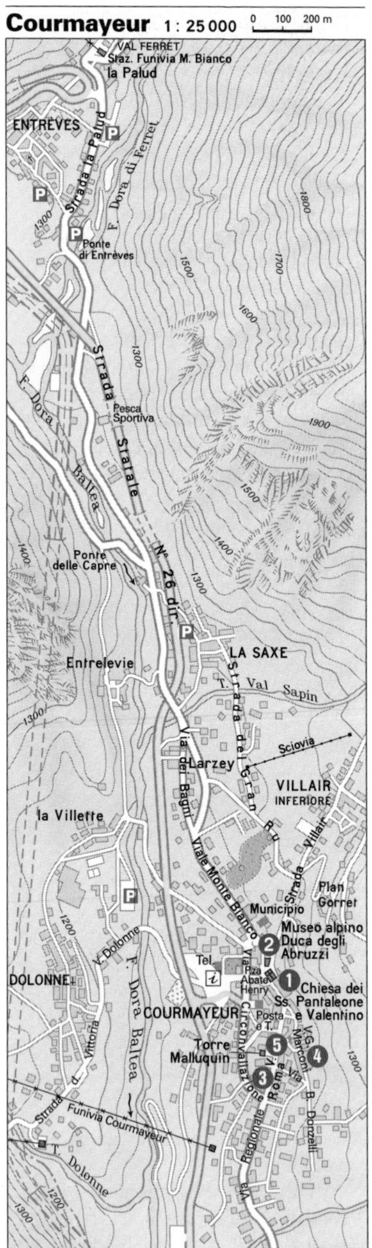

the cable-car system which crosses the Mont Blanc massif, the longest in the world. Needless to say, it offers unparalleled views of the range. *Pavillon du Mont Fréty* is the site of the **Giardino Botanico Alpino Saussurea**, one of Europe's highest botanical gardens, while the *Aiguille du Midi* is the highest point of the crossing with the most spectacular views. (If you do decide to make the

Ghiacciaio del Miage in the Val Veny.

crossing, make sure you are equipped for high altitude and remember to take your passport!)

The **valleys of the Mt Blanc range**, the Val Veny and the Val Ferret run almost parallel to the Aosta side of this magnificent massif. For centuries this area was only used for summer grazing, but the advent of naturalists and mountaineers has led to the development of the area for tourism. Mountaineering, hiking, access to climbing routes, and discovering magnificent natural scenery: that is why people come here. The **Val Veny**, with its river, the Dora di Veny Stream, has lovely views of Entrèves, the Val Ferret and the peaks of the Grandes Jorasses. Looking up towards the Ghiacciaio della Brenva, you will see the **sanctuary of Nôtre-Dame-de-la-Guérison**, and the final seracs of the Ghiacciaio di Brenva, where enormous blocks of ice occasionally plunge towards the valley. The valley broadens out further up to provide wonderful **views*** of the Mt Blanc range above the coniferous forests.
The last inhabited village in the valley is **La Visaille**.

In the **Val Ferret** the *Dora di Ferret Stream* has a broad bed of gravel and conifers on either side. Above it are the imposing mountains of the Grandes Jorasses. This valley has splendid **views*** of the whole chain of Mt Blanc, as well as beautiful Alpine scenery. Higher up, the valley broadens out and so do the views. From here you can see up the Val Veny and the beginning of the valley leading up to the Little St Bernard Pass. Further on, up on your left, is the Ghiacciaio di Frébouge and the little village of **Arnouvaz**. It takes less than 2.5 hours to walk from here along the dirt road that follows the valley floor to *Pré de Bar*, where a footpath leads up to the grassy **Col du Grand Ferret**.

The magnificent Mt Blanc massif has the longest cable-car system in the world.

EASTERN VALLE D'AOSTA

The eastern part of the region is a small area with plenty of character in terms of landscape. However, it is also an interesting tourist destination because of its potential in terms of culture, wildlife, sport and recreation. The monuments in the lower part of 'La Plaine' (as this part of the Valle d'Aosta is called), and the charm of both the valley and the mountains in this part of the Valle d'Aosta (where the tourist infrastructure compares favorably with other more famous and much visited parts of Italy) will delight the visitor. The variety of landscape, its wide-ranging views, its extraordinary castles, and the colors of the vineyards on the hillside terraces are just a few examples of the many interesting things to see. From the historical point of view, the valleys of Mt Rosa (the Gressoney and Val d'Ayas valleys) are particularly interesting because of their specific ethnic groups. People of French Provençal origin settled on the lower slopes of the valley while people of Germanic origin (the Walser, from the Swiss area of Valais) settled higher up.

La Plaine between the Canavese and Aosta

The tour of La Plaine begins at Pont Saint-Martin with its famous Roman bridge. It continues on the SS 26 road, following the line of the Roman road, up the lower valley of the Dora Baltea River, passing splendid castles en route.

Pont Saint-Martin stands at the confluence of the Lys and Dora Baltea rivers and is the gateway to the Valle d'Aosta from the Po Valley. Its important strategic position is emphasized by the *Porta della Valle d'Aosta*, a stone gateway with a cross on the top, built in the 19th century at one end of the spectacular **Roman bridge***. The bridge, built on bedrock across the Lys, is a splendid feat of engineering. It was built in the 1st century BC and consists of a single low round arch, 23 m high and 6 m wide. Another building in the historic part of town is the 15th-century building known as *'l Castel*, while the ruins of the *castle* (13C) lie on a rocky spur overlooking the town. To the left of it is the Neo-Gothic *Castello Baraing*, built between 1883 and 1893.
Near Perloz, an interesting town in the lower Valle del Lys, is an old abandoned *cemetery* and the late 16th-century *Parish church* (the frescoes on the facade are from the same period). The **sanctuary of Nôtre-Dame-de-la-Garde**, also near Perloz, is situated in a panoramic position.
The interior was frescoed in the 19th century. The pilgrimage church contains many votive paintings and a *statue of the Madonna and Child* which possibly dates from the 13th century.

The small town of **Perloz*** is a quiet, picturesque conglomeration of stone houses. Features of interest include the 14th-century *Castello Valleisa* and the *fortified house of the Vallaise de la Côte family*, dating from the 14th-15th centuries (note the two original wooden upper floors).
The 17th-century *Parish church of S. Salvatore* contains a large fresco of the *Last Judgement* (1677). There is an interesting **walk** from Perloz to the tiny village of **Chemp** that takes just over

The Roman bridge at Pont Saint-Martin.

2 hours. The route passes a chestnut wood, small ancient *traditional hamlets*, and semi-deserted villages with interesting traditional architecture. The route starts at *Pont Nantey*, passes the *chapel of Ruine (18C)* and the villages of *Badéry*, *Darbelley* and *Crétaz*, before arriving at Chemp.

Donnas is overlooked by hills with terraced slopes planted with vineyards. The town has several charming features. On the western edge of the town there is a stretch (222 m) of the **Roman consular road*** dating from the 1st century BC. Not only is the road impressive and scenic. It also shows us how the Romans built roads in mountainous terrain, with the foundations of bare rock of the same depth as the layers composing the actual road surface. Notice the *Roman milestone* marking the distance from Aosta, and the ruts left by centuries of passing carts.

The **Gola di Bard**, dominated by the fortress of the same name, is a deep gorge with vertical walls. This is one of the most dramatic testimonials left by the huge glacier which, until about 10,000 years ago, occupied the area which is now the bed of the Dora Baltea River. The gorge contains some examples of an interesting geological phenomenon known as **giants' kettles**, conical cavities (4 m wide and 7 m deep) gouged out of the rock by the water which flowed below the glacier which once occupied the valley. You can see quite a spectacular example of one from the path which leads from the church of Bard up to the fortress. The **Forte di Bard****, a large fortified structure built between the steep walls of the gorge, stands on an inaccessible rocky hill. This ancient fortress, rebuilt in 1830-38, should not be missed. It enables you to admire an impressive feat of military engineering which has survived for more than 150 years. It also houses some interesting museums in various parts of the fortress (called *Opere*) connected by a network of panoramic elevators. The exhibitions are supported by state-of-the-art technological aids (multimedia, sound and light effects), while the approach to the exhibits is strictly scientific. The fort also contains a small hotel, a restaurant, a café, a herbalist's, a shop selling high-quality craft products of the Valle d'Aosta, and another selling books and postcards. Beyond these are the exhibitions. The first elevator takes you to **Opera Ferdinando**. *Opera Superiore* contains the **Museo del Forte e delle Fortificazioni**, which illustrates the transformations which have taken place over the centuries in strategies of attack and siege and the corresponding changes in defensive structures, especially in the mountains. *Opera Inferiore* houses the **Museo delle Frontiere**, which is about the history of the Western Alps and the relations between the various peoples that have occupied its slopes over the centuries. Higher up, *Opera Mortai* is where the cannons used to be positioned and the building next-door, formerly the *powder*-magazine, has been converted into a teaching room for visiting school groups. **Opera Vittorio**, at the top of the second elevator, houses the exhibition **Le Alpi dei Ragazzi** (Alps for Kids). The aim of the exhibition is to enable kids to learn about the mountains around Bard and have fun at the same time. The long, covered chemin-de-ronde connecting the lower parts of the fort to the ones higher up has been organized as a **Time-scale**,

The Fort of Bard controls access to the Valle d'Aosta from the Po Valley.

a succession of pictures and information depicting the history of the Western Alps. **Opera Carlo Alberto**, the highest part of the fortress, has a broad *courtyard* which is used for theatre productions and concerts. It contains the **Spazio Vallée Culture**, which highlights the region's enormous historical and cultural heritage. On the first floor is the **Museo delle Alpi**, Bard's main attraction. The museum takes visitors on a virtual journey of discovery into the Alps. The mountains are presented from the various points of view of the people who live there. In the basement you can visit the **dungeons**. Below the promontory is the old **town***, which has many interesting old buildings. One is the *house* just below the fortress,

Arnad: apse of the church of S. Martino.

Casa Ciuca, a late-medieval noble residence which contains a *wine-shop* (the huge old *wine-cellars* are splendid) and a *hostel*. Just beyond it, on the same side of the street, is **Casa Challant*** (second half 15C). Inside, one of the polychrome coffered ceilings has been preserved. In Piazza del Municipio, the *Town Hall* occupies two old buildings: the former town hall, subsequently converted into a hotel, and the **Parish church of the Assunzione di Maria**, built in the mid-19th century on the site of an earlier building (the *bell tower* dates from the 12C-13C). Near the cemetery there are some **rock carvings** which date from around 3000-2700 BC. On the way out of Bard, there is a bar containing some *arches* of a bridge-viaduct which was part of the Roman road. On the opposite side of the Dora from Bard, **Hône** marks the beginning of the Valle di Champorcher. Its **Parish church**, dating from the 19th century with a stone *bell tower* from 1730, has a wooden *pulpit* and *choirstalls*, both from the 19th century, and three Baroque wooden *altars* dating from the late 18th century. Next-door is the small *Museo di Arte Sacra*.

Arnad is dominated by the 17th-century *Castello Vallaise* and the ruins of the 14th-century *Castello Superiore*. It is very popular with rock-climbing enthusiasts because of its excellent climbing walls. In the nearby *Vallone di Machaby* (just past Castello Superiore), is the **sanctuary of Madonna delle Nevi**. The present lines date from 1687-89. Just outside the town, the **church of S. Martino*** is one of the valley's finest examples of Romanesque architecture. Built between the 11th and 12th centuries, it was altered in the 15th century. The facade has a fine 15th-century **doorway**. *Inside*, there are three low aisles, also the **museum**.

Issogne*, on the orographic right side of the Dora Baltea, is famous for its large, square **castle****. Although it has no external decoration, it contains a luxurious noble residence. It is built around a vast, splendid Renaissance **courtyard** with the *Pomegranate Fountain* in the middle. The sides of the courtyard are frescoed with noble *coats-of-arms*. In the lunettes of the front portico, which has painted ribbed vaulting, are delightful *frescoes* depicting scenes of everyday life. On the ground floor, be sure to see the *dining-room*, furnished with 15th-century furniture, the *kitchen* and the *Hall of Justice*, frescoed with *hunting scenes and the Judgement of Paris*. On the first floor, beyond the *bedrooms of the Countess* and *Count Renato*, is the *chapel*, with Gothic

Castle of Issogne

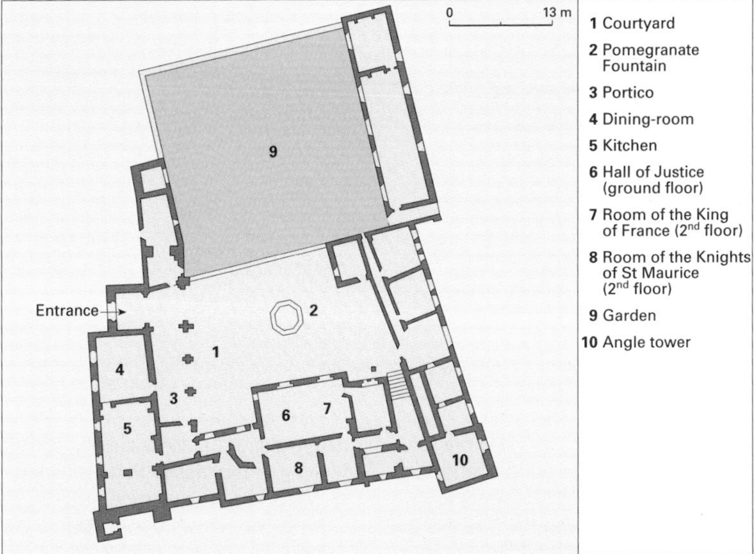

vaulting decorated with *frescoes*.
On the second floor is the *Room of the King of France* (with a 15th-century *four-poster bed*), so called because of the gold *fleurs-de-lis* painted in the coffers of the *ceiling* and the *fireplace*, with the Valois coat-of-arms and the motto *Vive le Roi* (Long live the King), and the *Room of the Knights of St Maurice*, with a fine coffered ceiling painted with the cross of the order.

Verrès* stands at the confluence of the Evançon Stream and the Dora Baltea River. As well as its fine castle, it also has a lovely Collegiate church. This is situated in the highest part of the town, is small but very characteristic, surrounded by narrow streets with steps lined with old stone houses. The **Collegiate church of Ss. Egidio e Agostino** was built in 1775-76 on the site of a Romanesque church. A Gothic *chapel* dating from 1407 has been incorporated into the building. Another feature to survive from the 15th century is the fine *doorway*, in the left wall of the church. Next to the church stands an imposing stone building dating from 1512, the **abbey of S. Egidio** (St Gilles), founded by Augustinian monks in about 1000. The **Challant castle*** stands on a high rocky hill in a strategic position for controlling the mouth of the valley. It is a massive, square building dating from 1390 and was modified in 1536. It had to be enlarged because of the use of fire-arms during a siege. This necessitated the building of a set of defensive walls with embrasures that could withstand an artillery attack. This compact stone structure with walls 2.5 m thick is regarded as one of the finest examples of late-Gothic military architecture in the Valle d'Aosta. Near the castle is the farm-house called **La Murasse**, with a square tower.

Montjovet is situated in the gorge of the same name wedged between steep slopes with terracing covered with vines. The most interesting part of the town is **Borgo**, which is medieval, with the *church of S. Rocco*. From the small meadow to the left of the church, there is a beautiful view of the valley. In the foreground are the medieval remains of **Castello di Montjovet** with a square *tower* dating from the 10th-11th century.

Saint-Vincent*, famed for the beneficial effects of its thermal water since Antiquity is certainly worth visiting for its fine monuments. Some of the lower structures of the **Ponte Romano/Roman bridge*** ❶ have survived, including a *ramp at one end*. The water of the **Stabilimento Termale/spa complex** ❷, set in a fine

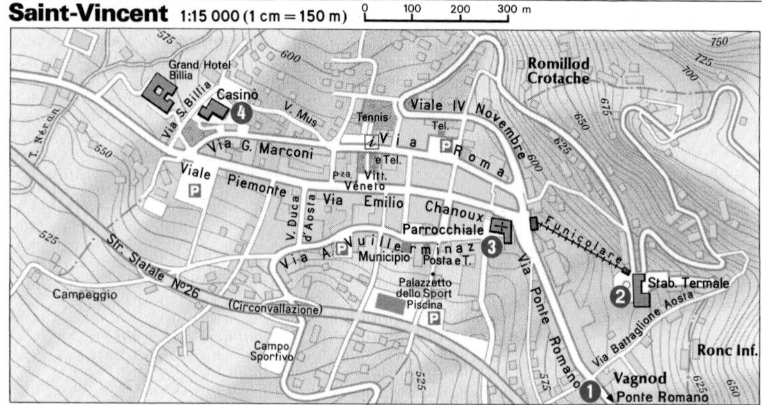

panoramic position, has given the town a reputation as a spa center, attracting many famous people. The water is particularly effective in the treatment of problems of the liver and the digestive tract, gastroenteric ailments and skin problems, but also because of the important fact that it actually tastes good. The complex can be reached by *cable-car* (the ride is free). The **Fons Salutis spa complex** still has a 20th-century facade whereas the interior and the infrastructures are of later date. From the garden terrace in front of the building there is a splendid view over the town of Saint-Vincent and quite far up the Valle della Dora. The **Parrocchiale/Parish church*** ❸ stands on the site of a large Roman building dating from the 4th-5th century (the remains can be seen underground) and is built on a Romanesque plan. The oldest part, dating from the 11th century, is the crypt with three aisles. The central apse and the triumphal arch date from the 15th century, the cross-vaulting dates from the 17th century, while the facade and the first two bays of the church date from the 19th century. On the outside of the church, the most interesting part is the apse. The apse of the left aisle has fine Romanesque decoration and the central apse is Gothic and has some 16th-century *frescoes* on the underside of its Gothic vaulting. The imposing **bell tower** has a Romanesque base, with 16th- and 17th-century additions higher up. Inside the church there are **frescoes** dating from the mid-15th century. At the beginning of the left aisle, the windows belong to the **Museo Parrocchiale di S. Vincenzo**. Its collection includes carved wooden *statues*, a stained-glass *window* of Flemish origin (1561) and various *sacred objects*. Finally, the **Casino** ❹ deserves a mention. It can be reached by walking along the pedestrian Via Chanoux, then along Viale Piemonte, with lovely views. On the left of the building with mirrors which houses the Casino is the **Grand Hotel Billia**, a beautiful Art-Nouveau building dating from 1907.

Châtillon has many of the typical characteristics of towns in La Plaine (the name given to the eastern part of the Valle d'Aosta). The town center is dominated by its medieval *castle*, which was transformed into a noble residence in the 18th century. (The garden is open to the public.) A staircase, which contains Roman funerary *inscriptions* found in the nearby cemetery, leads up from the center to the **Parish church of S. Pietro**. The church has a small *museum* containing antique furnishings, gold- and silver-ware, and wooden statues. **Castello di Ussel** stands on a high promontory south-west of the town. The fortress was built in the mid-14th century and was a prototype for other similar forts in the Valley. Today it is used for exhibitions. One of the best reasons for visiting it is that it has marvelous views from the ramparts.

The medieval **Castello di Fénis****, the most famous castle in the Valle d'Aosta stands in an isolated position outside the **town***. Its double set of fortifications make it look particularly magnificent. Built in about 1340 on the site of an earlier fortress, it was given a double set of walls because it is built on low ground in a position which is little suited to defense. Very soon, however, in addition to being used for defense, it was used as a residence and place of representation. The entrance in the *square tower* leads into the **courtyard*** with loggias above, where there is a beautiful semi-circular staircase and splendid **frescoes*** dating from the first half of the 15th century. On the ground floor you can visit the *armory*, the *dining-room*, the *larder*, the *garrison's kitchen*, the *study* and the *tax-office*. On the floor above is the **chapel**, with some fine *frescoes* painted in about 1420. Other rooms on the first floor include the *baronial hall*, with pieces of 15th-century furniture, and the *bedrooms of the counts*. Just beyond Fénis is the town of **Nus**, with the remains of the *Castello di Pilato*, built between the 14th and 15th century. From Nus a road winds up into the **valley of the Saint-Barthélemy Stream** into lovely, unspoiled mountain scenery. The fact that there are very few towns here makes the valley very popular with hikers.

The Gressoney valley

The valley follows the course of the Lys Stream, with its plentiful supply of water and many waterfalls. Much of the valley is unspoiled and even the old towns are well preserved.

In the lower part of the Valle di Gressoney, with its wonderful views, are the towns of **Tour d'Héréraz**, named after its *tower*, now a bell tower and originally Roman and **Lillianes**, notable for its *Parish church of S. Rocco*. **Fontainemore** has many buildings in the traditional mountain style and is surrounded by picturesque villages scattered among the woods, with houses and chapels (some of which have frescoes) built of stone and wood. Just beyond the last town you can see the gorge known as the *Orrido di Guillemore*, gouged out of the living rock by the Lys, which forms a high and very noisy waterfall at this point.

Issime, situated in the middle of a broad hollow, is the first town in the valley where the people are of Walser origin. The fine 17th-century **Parish church of S. Giacomo Maggiore*** has a nave and two side-aisles, a large *fresco* on the facade dated 1698 and several interesting *altars*. Inside the church is a small *museum* containing liturgical objects and wooden sculptures. Issime is the starting-point for many walks in the area, where hikers can enjoy not only the wildlife but also the local ethnography and architecture. One of them is the walk of about 1.5 hours to the **Vallone di S. Grato** where you can see numerous *rascards*. At the 18th-century *chapel of St-Grat* there is a lovely view over the Issime valley. Just beyond Issime is the **sanctuary of Madonna delle Grazie,**

The medieval castle at Fénis, possibly the most spectacular in the region.

TCI HIGHLIGHTS

The Walser

A wave of migration that lasted 300 years, ending in the 15th century, brought groups of farmers from an area of Switzerland on the far side of the Alps, to the valleys on the south side of the Mt Rosa. Laden with household goods, farm tools and equipment, families of farming folk crossed the Alps by narrow mule-paths in search of land to cultivate and colonize. This was the beginning of the epic of the Walser, as these people were called (they spoke a Germanic dialect) by the people with whom they came into contact, after their land of origin (Valais). In the Valle d'Aosta the Walser settled mainly in the Valle di Gressoney and the Val d'Ayas, in unused land, in areas which were inaccessible and unpopulated. It was precisely the fact that the Walser communities remained isolated that enabled them to preserve their language, traditions and culture for centuries. Even today, exploring the lands of the Walser means taking a step back in time. Their houses are striking in their simplicity. They have broad balconies which were used for drying and storing hay. The ground floor was used as a cowshed, the first floor contained the bedrooms, and the top floor was used for storage. The elegant costumes traditionally worn by women were made of black and red fabric, and were worn with a white blouse decorated with beautiful lace trimmings and hats embroidered with gold filigree. Their language is also very interesting. Philologists have traced it back to an early branch of modern German. At Issime they still speak a dialect known as Töitschu, whereas, at Gressoney, they speak Titsch, which resembles modern German more closely. In order to preserve their sense of identity and in memory of the great migration which spread the Walser people all over the southern edge of Mt Rosa, today, many young people from the Walser villages follow the route known as the Great Walser Footpath. Using very old paths, they make an interesting tour of the mountain massif not only in Italy, but also making forays into Switzerland, Austria and Liechtenstein. As far as the Valle d'Aosta is concerned, the walk starts at Gressoney-Saint-Jean, and passes through Gressoney-La Trinité, the Val d'Ayas, into the upper Valtournenche, and descends from there to Zermatt, in Switzerland.

dating from the 18th-19th century with a fine Baroque carved wooden altar. Nearby is the town of **Gaby**, a surprising 'enclave' in the middle of Walser territory where the French Provençal dialect has survived. Situated in a favorable position, sheltered by the mountains, it has a medieval *bridg*e and the *Parish church of S. Michel*e, with a frescoed presbytery.

Gressoney-Saint-Jean* is one of the most interesting towns in the Western Alps, both because of its history and its lovely position. It nestles in a hollow at the foot of Mt Rosa, and from it you can see the glaciers of Mt Lyskamm glistening in the sun. Before reaching the main part of the town, you encounter a road which leads to **Belvedere** (with lovely views). Here, set in the middle of coniferous forest, is Castel Savoia (early 20C) where Queen Magherita of Savoy spent the summers until 1925. It is a strange building with several towers built in a pseudo period style, faced in local stone. Its internal *decoration* is original and it has a fine oak staircase. Next to the royal residence is an **Alpine garden** which contains about 1,000 species of Alpine plants, mostly of ornamental value. At the entrance to Gressoney-Saint-Jean is the **Alpenfauna Museum Beck-Peccoz**, housed in an early 20th-century building, which contains examples of the most important species of fauna in the region. It also has a historical section with hunting weapons and trophies. The **Villa of Baron Beck-Peccoz**, a luxurious residence with broad balconies and spires, was built in 1888. Inside it is beautifully furnished and each room has a different enameled ceramic Bavarian stove (notice them particularly in the first floor rooms). The villa is surrounded by a large park with larches and fir trees. The **borgo***, as the center of Gressoney-Saint-Jean is called, is the most typical and best-preserved of all the towns in the Valle del Lys. It has interesting examples of traditional buildings and focuses mainly around two lovely squares: *Piazza Umberto I*, surrounded by 17th- and 18th-century buildings, and *Piazza Superiore*, with late 19th-century buildings, dominated by the **Parish church of S. Giovanni Battista**. The church has a fine *bell tower*, a *portico* dating from 1626 with 14 small *frescoed shrines* and a small *museum*.

The Parish church at Gressoney-Saint-Jean.

The little town of **Gressoney-La-Trinité** has an extraordinary setting below the Mt Rosa massif. In the summer, there is plenty of scope for hikers. One suggestion is the thrilling ascent to the refuge known as the **Capanna Regina Margherita**, the highest refuge in Europe. Another is the hiking route known as **Alta Via N. 1**, also called the Via dei Giganti (Giants' Way) because it includes some of the giants of the Alpine Chain: Mt Rosa, Mt Cervino (the Matterhorn) and Mt Blanc. This route, which is only suitable if you are extremely fit, is usually divided into 8 sections, each of which involves 6 or 7 hours of serious hiking.

The Champorcher valley

The unusual morphology of the valley, a true paradise for nature-lovers, has made it possible to promote tourism without spoiling its beauty. In fact, the valley has many lovely features: lakes, streams, waterfalls, springs, peat-bogs, and many species of animals, plants and flowers.

Pontboset, a small town surrounded by chestnut woods, has retained its traditional rural appearance, with a number of stone granary-houses. Even the more typically 'urban' buildings have features associated with farming practices (for example, covered balconies which were used for drying hay and other commodities).
The interesting **chapel of Gom** with Classical-style lines has a fine Baroque *altar*, and there is a characteristic stone hump-backed **bridge** which was erected over the Ayasse Stream in 1676. Beyond the bridge, a footpath leads to the two tiny hamlets of **Crest di Sopra** and **Crest di Sotto**, in a beautiful panoramic setting. After Pontboset is another interesting area, with small groups of houses with traditional architectural features: **Dogier**, which has some *rascards*, an old communal *oven* and a *farm complex* dating from the 18th and 19th centuries; **Salleret** , which has a little 18th-century *chapel* with a frescoed facade; **Mellier**, which is built on both sides of the stream, with many period buildings, including a *granary-house* with a sun-dial and a *chapel* dating from 1727 with *frescoes* on the facade.

The tourist resort of **Champorcher** is the valley's largest town. It is gaining a reputation for its pristine Alpine landscape and also for its farming activities, which limit the amount of building possible. **Château** has an old merloned *tower*, all that remains of a castle destroyed in 1212. Above the tower is a small village which has preserved its

traditional appearance.
Here, built over a vertical drop down to the stream and near a scenic viewpoint, is the *Parish church of S. Nicola* (first half 16C), which has some fine 17th-century wooden *altars* and an interesting *museum*.

Dondenaz, on the edge of the Parco Naturale del Mont Avic, is the starting-point for many hiking trails. There is a famous walk to the **Finestra di Champorcher Pass**, which has fantastic views. On the way back from the Finestra di Champorcher, don't miss **Lake Miserin**, one of the loveliest in the Western Alps. Standing next to the lake is the *sanctuary of Madonna della Neve*, and a mountain refuge.

The Val d'Ayas

The lower valley is called the Valle di Challand, while the upper valley is called the Canton des Allemands (Canton of the Germans), in reference to the medieval colonization of the valley by the Walser. In less than 30 km, the landscape changes from orchards and chestnut woods to beechwoods, coniferous forest, rocks, glaciers and magnificent Alpine scenery.

At **Challand-Saint-Victor**, in the village of *Sizan*, the *Parish church of St-Victor*, has a 17th-century stone *doorway* and some Baroque *altars*. It also has an interesting *museum*.
Higher up, the valley becomes more typically Alpine and, at a certain point, the land levels out. This is the setting of the well-preserved little town of *Arcésaz*. Perched high on a cliff above the town, above broad-leaved deciduous and coniferous forests, are the ruins of a Romanesque fortress, **Castello di Graines***.
Probably dating from the 11th century, it has a set of defensive walls with a massive square *tower* in the middle. Beside the tower are the remains of a small *chapel*. Higher up, you pass the 16th- 17th-century *chapel of S. Valentino*, with a frescoed facade and a strange stone *altar* dating from the 17th century in the shape of a small church. Further on is the old town of **Brusson**. Its picturesque stone and wood houses huddle below the lovely *Parish church of S. Maurizio*, the town's main monument.

At the top of the valley, which opens out into a broad hollow, is **Antagnod***, which must have one of the best views of Mt Rosa. This small historic town has picturesque cobbled alleyways, and houses built of stone and wood, proof of the continuity of the valley's traditional building techniques.
The beautiful **Parish church of S. Martino** towers above the town.
It has an interesting carved wooden **high altar** mostly painted in gold, dating from between 1700 and 1713.
To the right of the church, in the *chapel* of the cemetery, is a small and interesting **Museo di Arte Sacra**.
The **Casa degli Challant** is very interesting from the point of view of local building techniques. The house has an external spiral staircase built inside a round, 15th-century tower, and long wooden balconies. Now the house is a shop selling and exhibiting local craft products.

The Parish church at Sizan (Challand-Saint-Victor).

Situated in the so-called 'Canton des Allemands' (the Walser part of the valley), **Champoluc's** main attraction is its lovely mountain scenery. This is the ideal place for hikers and wildlife enthusiasts. If you are interested not only in natural landscape but also in mountain architecture and ethnography, we suggest you return to Champoluc on foot. Starting at the little village of *Saint-Jacques*, the **footpath** follows the tarmac road along the valley floor but a little higher up. The path passes many interesting examples of mountain architecture: *rascards* in mountain farms, little country churches and houses in tiny villages.

Traditional architecture at Saint-Jacques, in the upper Val d'Ayas.

The Valtournenche

The Valtournenche has wonderful scenery to offer the visitor, both in the hollow of Cervinia, and in the less-frequented side-valleys, where sometimes you have only the icy wind blowing down from the glaciers for company.

Antey-Saint-André has a splendid position, since it is south-facing and sheltered from the wind, and has incredible views of Mt Cervino (which we know better as the Matterhorn). The oldest part of the town, called *Bourg*, lies above the old main road and below the **Parish church of S. Andrea**, which dates from the 12th century. Some features of the earlier stone church are still visible. It has a fine late-Gothic *doorway* and a *bell tower*. The various hamlets which comprise the town of **La Magdeleine** are scattered over a high panoramic terrace above the Marmore Stream. At *Messelod*, it's worth visiting the 17th-century *chapel of S. Rocco*, which has frescoes on the facade. There are other interesting buildings at *Clou*, including some *rascards*, a *house* with a sun-dial (there are several in the village) and some old *mills* by the stream.

Torgnon*, which lies on a broad moraine, surrounded by undulating meadows and thick forest, is one of the best places to admire the summit of the Matterhorn. Other attractions include some fine examples of traditional Alpine architecture, for example, numerous *rascards*, and granaries with solid walls called *greniers*. At **Mongnod**, the **Parish church of S. Martino** is built in the Neo-Gothic style. It has an interesting **museum**. Beyond Mongnod lies **Triatel**, where the **Museo Etnografico del Petit Monde*** is named after the stream which flows through the village. (Water from the stream still drives an old *mill*, which has recently been restored). This fascinating ethnographical museum enables you to see the various types of traditional non-residential building techniques in one place (stone foundations, wooden structures and roofs covered with stone slabs). It occupies three buildings of the community which were once used as workshops and for storage. On the right is a long row of **rascards***, where hay and grain used to be stored. They are supported by mushroom-shaped pillars which aerated the building and kept out the rodents. It contains an exhibition about farming activities and animal husbandry in the mountains.
Next to its stands the little church of S. Rocco (1630). Opposite the *rascard* is the **grandze**, where meat, bread, butter and cheese was stored. Inside it is a reconstruction of how such foods were produced and stored.
On the first floor is a reconstruction of a 19th-century bedroom. Next to the *grandze* is the **grenier** (grainstore), which is also supported by pillars and

was used for storing food. It contains information about the various craft techniques involved in wood-production. The three buildings, built between 1463 and 1503, are perfectly preserved.

The fact that the village of **Chamois*** can only be reached by cable-car or on foot adds to its charm. Situated on a natural shelf surrounded by woodland and mountain farms, it consists of a few traditional wood and stone houses.

Valtournenche, the largest town in the valley, is in fact a conglomeration of several small villages scattered over a vast plateau high above the Marmore Stream. The most important buildings are situated on the main square of **Pâquier**, where the Town Hall is located. In quiet **Piazzetta delle Guide**, plaques testify to the fact that some of the most legendary Alpine guides of the Matterhorn were born here. The plaques are fixed to the facade of the Town Hall. Behind it is a 17th-century **rascard*** which was once used as a storeroom and is now used for temporary exhibitions. On one side of the square is the **Parish church of S. Antonio**, with a *bell tower* dating from between 1760 and 1763. Inside is the small **museum** which contains *sacred artworks*. The artificial **Lake Cignana** is the starting-point for many walks in the area. The footpath to the lake starts at *Barmasse*, where Bronze Age rock carvings depicting work tools have been found. About 3 hours' hike from the artificial lake is an area with magnificent scenery including some natural lakes (Lake Balanselmo, Lake Dragone and the Great Lake). Just beyond Valtournenche, where the valley narrows, the road passes close to the **Orrido di Gouffre de Busseraille,** a gorge 35 m deep and more than 100 m long, gouged out of the bedrock by the Marmore Stream. This is a very spectacular gorge because it contains many caves, giants' kettles and a waterfall 10 m high.

Breuil-Cervinia*, one of Italy's most famous and prestigious tourist resorts, has gained an important reputation in Italy's scenario of worldly living.
The town is situated below the highly spectacular peak of **Mt Cervino (the Matterhorn)****, a mountain which is unique in terms of its shape and beauty. The town nestles in a hollow surrounded by *high mountains*.
Higher up, near the top of the cable-car of the *Little Mt Cervino*, is the highest and largest **ice-cave** in the world (with a diameter of 26 m, and an average height of 5 m).
The cave can be reached by walking along a tunnel 50 m long, dug out of the ice.

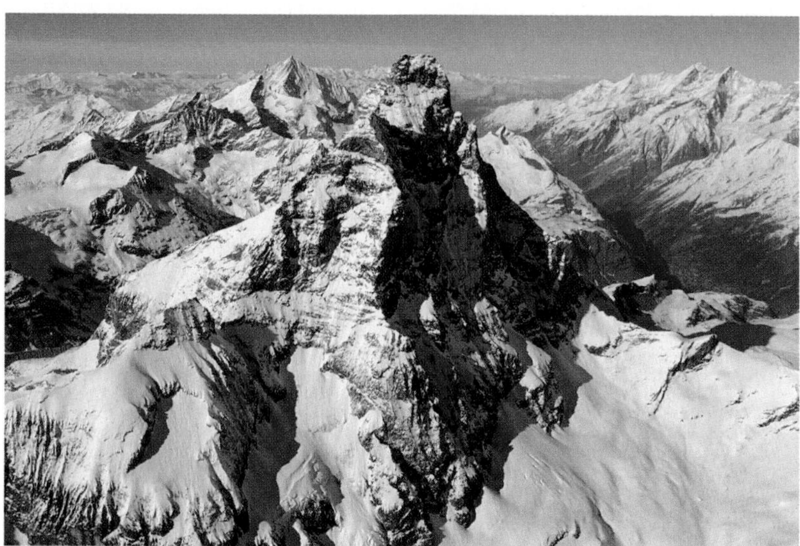

The summit of the Matterhorn, 4,478 m high, one of the most majestic sights in the Alps.

TORINO/TURIN

This city, situated at the narrowest point of the Po Valley, where the western hills of Monferrato slope down towards the Po, embraced by the Alpine Chain, is excellently located at the foot of several Alpine valleys. The earliest settlements found in the area of the present city date from the 3rd century BC, but the city was actually founded in the year 29. During the Gallic Wars, Julius Caesar founded a Roman colony here with the name of Augusta Julia Taurinorum, from which Turin developed. In the 10th century, the city came under the influence of the Savoy dynasty. Later the city became a free commune and was occupied several times by the French, but eventually Turin became the capital of the Duchy of Savoy. In 1720 the Duke of Savoy was offered the title of King of Sicily (later exchanged for Sardinia) and Turin became the capital of the kingdom. The Congress of Vienna (1815) and the Restoration gave Piedmont Genoa and Liguria, thus unwittingly laying the foundations for a process which would eventually lead to the Unification of Italy (1861). The city of Turin and the area around it not only has an Egyptian Museum with the world's second-finest collection of Egyptian artifacts after Cairo, but also offers the pleasure palaces built by the Savoys, designated a UNESCO World Heritage Site.

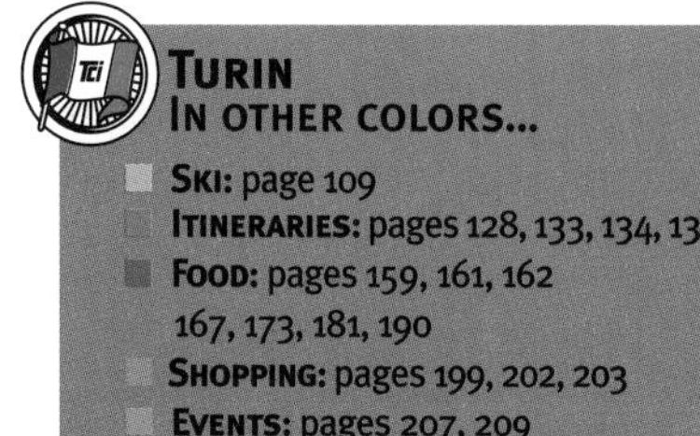

TURIN
IN OTHER COLORS...

- **SKI:** page 109
- **ITINERARIES:** pages 128, 133, 134, 138
- **FOOD:** pages 159, 161, 162 167, 173, 181, 190
- **SHOPPING:** pages 199, 202, 203
- **EVENTS:** pages 207, 209
- **PRACTICAL INFO:** pages 230, 231

Piazza Castello ❶

Piazza Castello is the hub of Turin and encapsulates its identity. The area in front of Palazzo Madama, with its fountains, rows of benches and *statues*, and the small square in front of the Palazzo Reale form a large pedestrian precinct. From here you can admire the uniform rows of porticoes and facades overlooking the streets around the square, their continuity interrupted only by the domes of S. Lorenzo and the Chapel of the Holy Shroud. Apart from the small square in front of the Palazzo Reale (royal palace), the whole of Piazza Castello is surrounded by porticoes: pleasant places where you can walk and enjoy the city's shops and historic cafés.

Palazzo Madama ❷

This palazzo in the center of Piazza Castello embodies centuries of Turin's history. Not only is it the fulcrum of

Palazzo Reale and Palazzo Madama, the strongholds of Savoy power, overlooking Piazza Castello.

Torino 1: 15 000 (1 cm = 150 m)

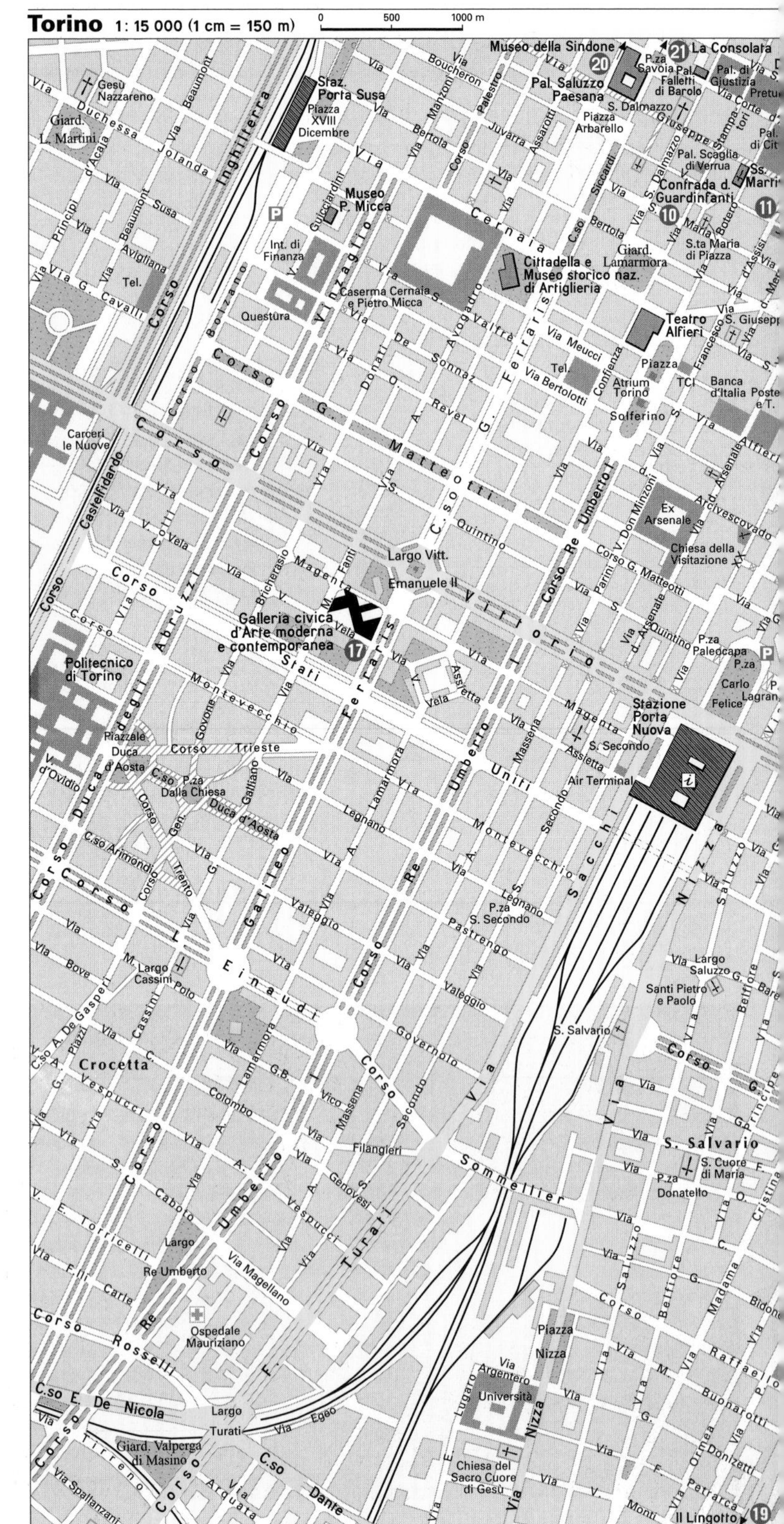

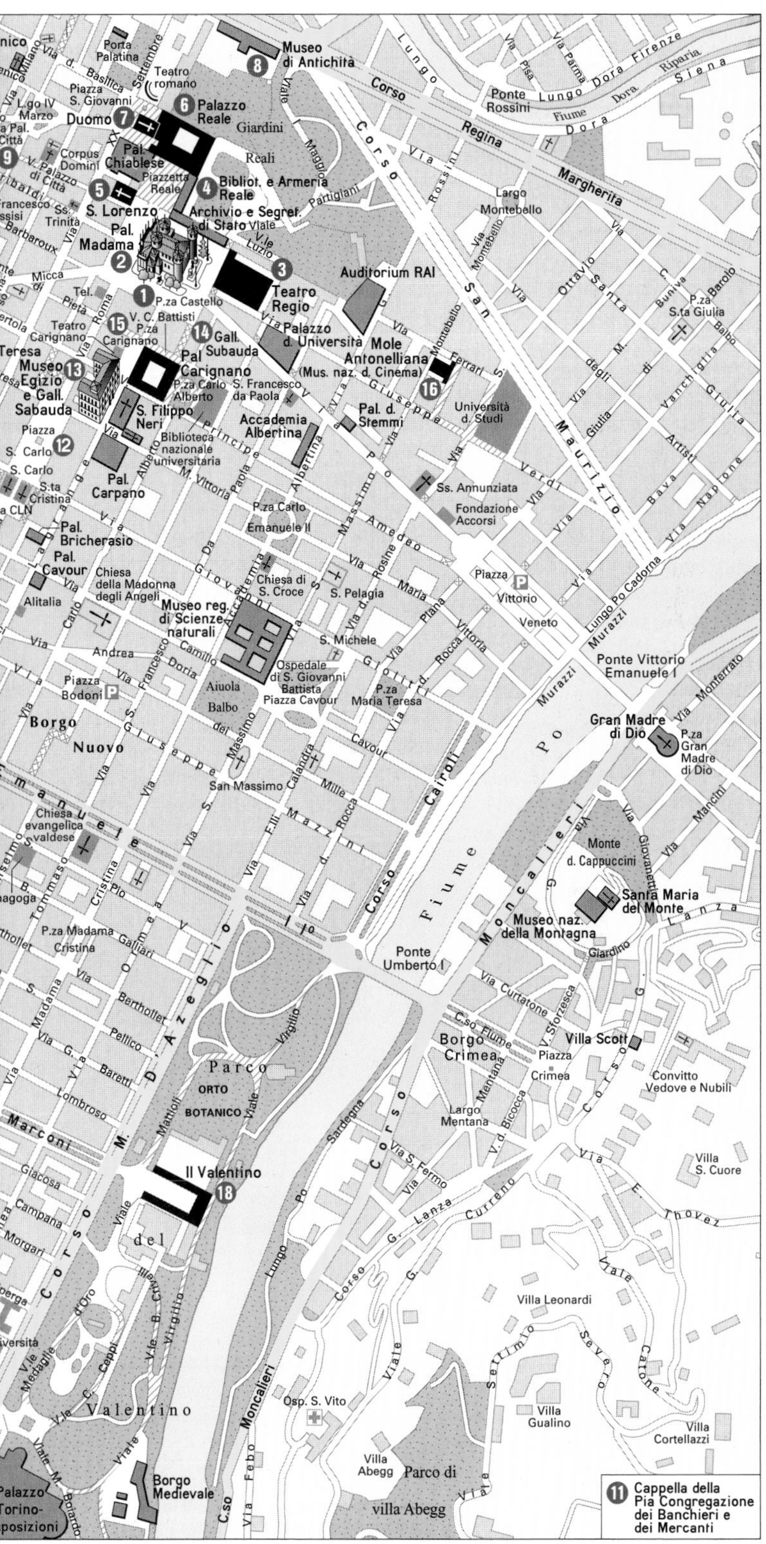

11 Cappella della Pia Congregazione dei Banchieri e dei Mercanti

the immediate surroundings but of Turin's historic center as a whole. The differing facades of the building can be attributed to numerous construction phases. The sides and back with the four towers are built of dark-red medieval bricks. The towers nearest the Baroque facade are actually of Roman date. In complete contrast, the beautiful pale stone facade is a masterpiece of early 18th-century architecture by Filippo Juvarra. The facade of the palace is like a monumental stage-set with nine large windows, through which the light becomes part of the architectural composition. The three central openings with windows behind, spanned by four gigantic grooved columns, form a vast loggia overlooking the square. At the top is a high balustrade with statues and vases. The inside of this Baroque wing is even more extraordinary: from the vaulted entrance-hall, two symmetrical flights of stairs lead majestically up to right and left. The whole setting is lavishly decorated. There are shell motifs and low reliefs in the atrium, urns and cherubs on the walls, and rose motifs and pateras on the high, barrel-vaulted ceiling. On the ground floor, in the *Sala del Voltone*, you can see the excavations of the medieval courtyard, the foundations and fragments of Roman paving beneath the glass floor. The entrance to the **Museo Civico di Arte Antica**** and the Gothic and Renaissance art collections are on the ground floor. Upstairs, next to the splendidly restored royal apartments on the first floor, is the huge *Salone del Senato*, once seat of the Senate. The top floor contains the ceramics, glass, ivory and fabric collections. The three floors of the museum are connected by a state-of-the-art glass lift and a spiral staircase in the southeast tower. From the top, there are splendid views over Turin. The museum was created in the 19th century to preserve Turin and Piedmont's artistic and historical collections. It began with part of the royal collections and has continued to grow over the years as a result of acquisitions, and donations and legacies from private individuals.

In addition to its *art gallery*, with works dating from the 15th to 18th centuries, illuminated manuscripts and sculpture collections, the museum has an important collection of decorative and applied arts, a seemingly endless display of ceramics (more than 4,000 pieces) reflecting different periods and styles (majolica and porcelain produced by Europe's leading manufacturers), and exquisite collections of engraved and painted glass, enamels, gold, silver, ivories, and period furniture and furnishings. Strangely, the museum's two prize exhibits were not part of the original collection: the fascinating and mysterious **Portrait of an Old Man**** by Antonello da Messina (1476) and part of the Duc de Berry's *Book of Hours*, known as **Les Très Riches Heures de Milan****, illuminated between 1380 and 1450 by, amongst others, the Flemish painters Hubert and Jan van Eyck.

Teatro Regio/Royal Theater ❸

By crossing the top of Via Po and continuing under the porticoes, we come to the front of the Teatro Regio. The *bronze gate* decorated with an

Leonardo da Vinci's self-portrait in the Biblioteca Reale.

abstract motif entitled *Musical Odyssey* is by Umberto Mastroianni (1994). In 1936 the theater, built between 1738 and 1740, was completely destroyed by fire. The only part to survive was the facade, which continues the architectural theme of the rest of the piazza. The design for the new theater (opened in 1973) kept the original front of the building but gave it a completely new interior, which is hidden from the square. The new design with its curving shapes is highly original. Seen from above, the theater looks like an enormous saddle. Its curving side-walls are built of brick, with an eight-pointed star motif, contrasting with the extensive use of glass. Inside, the foyer is a wide-open space arranged on three levels with exposed architectural features. The auditorium is shaped like a half-open shell, the aisles forming lines which converge on the stage. Boxes are arranged around the edge in a descending gradient. The stage is the second-largest in Europe, the largest being at the Opéra in Paris. It has a complex structure which allows all kinds of daring stage-effects and is dominated by a large scenery control tower.

Biblioteca Reale and Armeria Reale/Royal Library and Royal Armory ❹

At the far end of the porticoes is the entrance to the Royal Library and the Royal Armory, both of which occupy the building situated east of the Piazzetta Reale. The Royal Library on the ground floor is a beautiful rectangular room with a frescoed barrel-vaulted ceiling. It has a fine collection of books and manuscripts (including illuminated codices on vellum, books of hours (prayer books) and some of the earliest printed books). Its finest exhibits are a collection of drawings by Leonardo da Vinci, including the famous **Self-portrait**** in red ink, a preliminary study for the face of the angel in the *Virgin of the Rocks* in the Louvre, and his ornithological treatise, the *Codice sul Volo degli Uccelli*. (However, these works are only displayed during special exhibitions.) A large *staircase*

The historic setting of the Royal Library, created by King Carlo Alberto of Savoy.

(1738-40) leads up from another door to the Royal Armory.
The elegant staircase is still decorated with the original colors, ranging from pale ochre to gray. The Armory was created in 1837 by King Carlo Alberto of Savoy. This is one of Europe's most important collections and includes exhibits from East and the West, and many items made in the arsenals of Turin and Genoa. The collection is displayed in three rooms: the *Sala della Rotonda* by architect Pelagio Pelagi, the *Galleria del Beaumont* and the *Sala del Medagliere Reale*. It contains *weapons* from the prehistoric, classical and medieval periods, but especially beautifully decorated examples from the 16th century.
There is a fabulous set of German suits of armor and another attributed to a famous late 16th-century armorer from Lombardy, Pompeo della Cesa. There are swords, stilettos, spears and fire-arms of all shapes and sizes, but perhaps the most extraordinary exhibit of all is the 17th-century suit of armor made for the knight Don Diego Felipe de Guzman, who was more than 2m tall. There are many weapons which once belonged to members of the House of Savoy (who reigned from the constitution of the Italian state in 1861 to the creation of the Italian Republic in 1946), such as the *set of hunting*

arms of Carlo Emanuele II (1650). There are also 19th-century weapons, ranging from *Napoleon Bonaparte's sword* to weapons which belonged to the Savoy counts, dukes and kings. The wooden horses covered with horse-hide, mounted by knights in armor, are very striking.

Chiesa di S. Lorenzo ❺

On August 10, 1557, the day dedicated to St Lawrence, Emanuele Filiberto of Savoy (known as *Testa 'd Fer* meaning Iron Head), ruler of the Spanish Netherlands, led the Imperial army in the Battle of San Quintino and inflicted a crushing defeat on the French. It was a fundamental date for the Savoy dynasty. According to the terms of the Treaty of Cateau-Cambrésis (1559), it thus regained the lost Duchy of Savoy, with Turin as its new capital. On the eve of the battle, the brave *condottiero* made a vow that, if he won, he would build a splendid church dedicated to St Lawrence. The vow was honored, but much later. Emanuele Filiberto did not enter his new capital in triumph until February 1563 and, to begin with, he kept his vow by simply restoring the existing church of S. Maria del Presepio. However, in 1666, work started on what was to become the present church of S. Lorenzo. The architect in charge was Guarino Guarini and his design was so highly acclaimed that he was appointed architect and mathematician to the ducal court of Carlo Emanuele II. He remained in Turin until 1681, leaving behind many testimonials to his genius. The dome is very obvious from the piazza, but the church seems to lack a proper facade. In fact, Guarini's church was never completed.
As a result the entrance to the church looks like that of a civic building. Inside, to enter the church, you must first cross the *Oratorium dell'Addolorata*, the former hall of the church of S. Maria del Presepe, which was altered in the 19th century. The interior is very striking indeed. Light pours into the church from the windows in the **dome****. Built on an octagonal plan, the dome has convex sides and opens out at the bottom into chapels glistening with gold and polychrome marble. All of it, including the decoration and the furnishings, are part of Guarini's original master plan. The unusual elliptical presbytery has an *altar* which is another of Guarini's masterpieces. Looking up into the dome, you can admire the harmony of the design but it may make you feel dizzy! Its complex structure is divided by 16 intersecting arches which form a beautiful star pattern. If you look hard, the lines and spaces above the windows look like huge oriental masks with their mouths open.

Church of S. Lorenzo

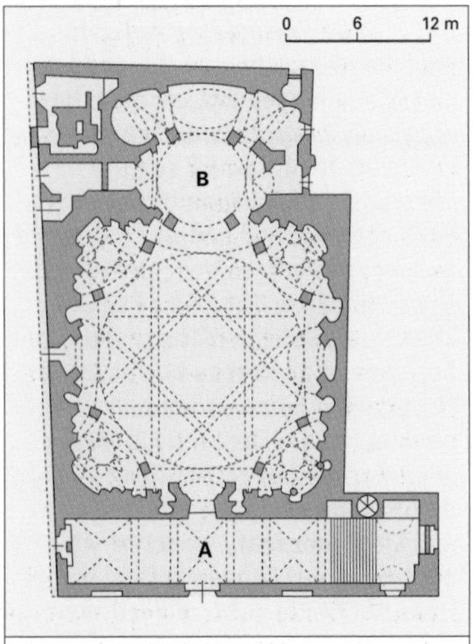

A Oratory of the Addolorata
B Elliptical presbytery, with altar by G. Guarini

Palazzo Reale/Royal Palace ❻

In 1997, the Palazzo Reale, together with the pleasure palaces around Turin built by the Savoys, were designated a UNESCO World Heritage Site. Following Emanuele Filiberto's decision to move the capital of the Duchy of Savoy from Chambéry to Turin, in 1583, he invited all the greatest architects of the time to participate in a competition to design the new ducal residence. Ascanio Vittozzi won, and remained in the service of the duchy until his death in 1615. Vittozzi contributed in a major way to the transformation of Turin into a capital worthy of the name.
The facade of the new Palazzo Ducale was completed in 1586 with a long gallery connecting the right-hand side of the palace to the castle. Vittozzi was

succeeded by Carlo di Castellamonte and Carlo Morello. The latter built the '*padiglione*', a wing of the palace which used to seal off the Piazzetta Reale, connecting the gallery to Palazzo Chiablese on the left-hand side. This was destroyed in the early 19th century. Throughout the 17th century, the palace was a hive of craftsmen and painters. On the first floor, the reception rooms facing the square were decorated with beautiful carved gilt wooden ceilings, complemented by huge allegorical paintings on the theme of the virtues, commissioned by the duke. In the great *Hall of the Swiss* there is a depiction of the legendary origins of the Savoy family. Many of the walls are adorned by valuable tapestries. As the dynasty was gradually establishing its supremacy, new features were added to the palace. Carpenters and stucco craftsmen were summoned to embellish the interior. In about 1690, the Viennese painter Daniel Seyter depicted the pomp of Vittorio Amedeo II in his allegorical frescoes on the ceiling of the gallery named after him, the **Galleria del Daniel**. The Ducal Palace became the Royal Palace when Vittorio Amedeo II was crowned King of Sicily in 1713. (Seven years later he exchanged it for the crown of Sardinia.) The next two decades marked the golden period of architect Filippo Juvarra, who designed the **'Scissors Staircase'** and the **Chinese Room**. The first is ingeniously designed with a double flight of steps connecting the first and second floors. The second reflects the vogue of the Rococo period for the Orient, with pieces of Chinese lacquered furniture, partly acquired by Juvarra himself and partly imitated by local cabinet-makers.

In the 1830s, Benedetto Alfieri succeeded Juvarra and continued the work of decorating the palace. Having been desecrated during the Napoleonic period, the palace again became a symbol of royal power under King Carlo Alberto. The palace regained its lost splendor under the supervision of an architect from Bologna, Pelagio Pelagi. This architect profoundly altered the appearance of the reception rooms (the *Hall of the Swiss*; the *ballroom* decorated with 20 white marble columns and neo-classical motifs) using new stylistic themes, ranging from archeological motifs from Ancient Egypt to Gothic Revival. The Unification of Italy had only been achieved two years before (1861) when he made his last remarkable transformation of the building: the complete restructuring of the *monumental staircase*, which, with its monumental statuary, celebrates the Glory of the House of Savoy. With the subsequent transfer of the capital of Italy from Turin to Florence (1865) and then to Rome (1870), the palace ceased to be a royal

From the early 17C onwards, the Savoy court was based in Palazzo Reale.

residence and became a place haunted by historical and artistic memories. During the 1890s, the facade of the palace was restored to its original architectural lines. Today, the elegant white facade plays a large part in making Piazzetta Reale, and Piazza Castello as a whole, one of Turin's most delightful spots. Behind the palace, and closely related to its historical and architectural ups and downs, are the **Giardini Reali**, the royal gardens, surrounded by 17th-century fortifications, and containing two delightful *casini* or pleasure houses, but at the time of writing, the gardens are being restored.

Duomo/Cathedral ❼

The cathedral, erected between 1491 and 1498, is dedicated to St John the Baptist. The comparitively small size of the building and its beautiful white marble facade provide a stark contrast to the trend for monumentality which was to become fashionable in the Baroque period and later. However, it has a fine symmetrical facade, its curving top reflecting the position of the nave and two side-aisles behind. The jambs and lintels of the three doors are beautifully carved. The *bell tower of S. Andrea* is Romanesque in style despite dating from the second half of the 15th century. The height of the tower was raised according to a design by Juvarra (1720-23).
The church is built on a Latin-cross plan, is full of light and mainly reflects the Gothic style. On the back of the main facade is the **tomb of Giovanna d'Orlier de la Balme**, a lady of the court, by a 16th-century French sculptor. The devotional chapels in the side-aisles, often built into the walls, are enhanced with fine **paintings and sculptures** dating from the 16th to 19th centuries. In the *transept*, overlooked by a monumental Baroque *gallery*, with an organ, note the *sacristy*, the elaborate *royal tribune* and, below, in a special fire-proof glass chamber, the **Sacra Sindone**** (Holy Shroud). To the left of the bell tower of St Andrew is the 1st-century **Roman theater**. From the perimeter fence you can see the external pilasters of the *cavea* (auditorium), the rows of seating and the flat *orchestra*.
The **Porta Palatina***, the most obvious monument dating from the Roman period, also dates from the 1st century and is one of the best-preserved examples of a Roman city gate.
Built of red brick, it has two towers with 16 sides and small windows, connected by a facade of which only the outer wall remains.

Cathedral

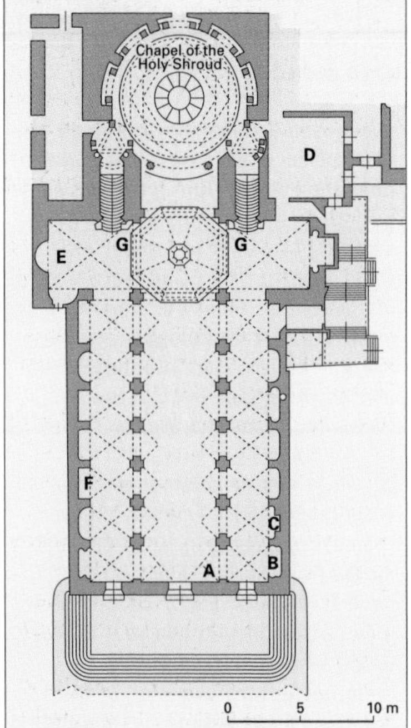

A Tomb of Giovanna d'Orlier de la Balme
B Large statue of the Virgin
C Polyptych, Chapel of the Shoemakers' Guild
D Sacristy
E Royal box and, below, the Holy Shroud
F Tomb of the Blessed Pier Giorgio Frassati
G Steps leading to the Chapel of the Holy Shroud

Museo di Antichità/Museum of Antiquities ❽

Providing continuity with the Roman remains in the archeological park opposite, the Museum of Antiquities is also situated on Via XX Settembre.
The museum is divided into three sectors, each with a different theme. One deals with the archeology of Turin, with artifacts from public and private buildings, testimonials of funerary rites and a 2nd-century inscription where the

name 'Julia Augusta Taurinorum' appears for the first time. Another section contains artifacts from the Piedmont region, from the proto-historic to Roman and Medieval periods. The prize exhibit of this section is the **treasure of Marengo**, a small collection of beautifully crafted artifacts, mainly silverware, dating from the 1st to 3rd centuries.
The royal greenhouses contain other collections: Cypriot finds, prehistoric and protohistoric artifacts from various European cultures, but especially from the Italian peninsula: *Etruscan collections*, *Greek vases*, *Greek* and Italiot sculpture; *Graeco-Roman sculpture*, including a red porphyry **bust with a cuirass**, an original 4th-century work, and finds from excavations conducted in the territory of the Savoys.

Piazza Palazzo di Città ⑨

This was once the market square of Piazza delle Erbe. It was redesigned in its present form in 1756 by Benedetto Alfieri, who surrounded it by a portico with two rows of columns and opened up the view along Via Palazzo di Città to Piazza Castello. It is overlooked by **Palazzo di Città**, the City Hall, a 17th-century building which was considerably altered in the following century. In the middle of the square is the *monument to the Green Count*, Amedeo VI, so called because he liked to wear and dress his retinue in green. The statue is by Pelagio Pelagi (1853) and depicts the count fighting during the crusade of 1366.

Contrada dei Guardinfanti/ Guardinfanti District ⑩

The dense network of streets to the left of Via Garibaldi, between Via S. Tommaso and Via Stampatori, is known as Contrada dei Guardinfanti. It is named after the shops which, until the 19th century, sold the crinolines worn by noble-women (originally to disguise the fact that they were pregnant, but later merely as a fashion accessory). The district has retained its medieval appearance and, coming from the more spacious areas of Baroque expansion, the streets suddenly seem dark and narrow. They are overlooked by many fine buildings and shops. Some of the streets (Via Mercanti and Via Stampatori) are still named after the guilds which had their workshops there. Not far away, on the street of the same name, is the beautiful 14th-century **church of S. Francesco d'Assisi**, which was altered in the 17th century.

The 16C courtyard of Palazzo Scaglia di Verrua.

Cappella della Pia Congregazione dei Banchieri e dei Mercanti ⑪

This chapel can be accessed from Via Garibaldi through the *Casa dei Gesuiti*, with its fine cross-vaults and little domes, and the old cloisters, now an information point and exhibition center. Consecrated in 1692, the building, decoration and furnishing of the chapel was financed by the wealthy congregation of bankers and merchants. It has a remarkable *frescoed ceiling*. Note also the wooden *sculptures of the Doctors of the Church*, painted to look like marble. There is also an unusual *mechanical universal calendar* (1835). In Via Stampatori notice **Palazzo Scaglia di Verrua***, a fine example of Mannerist architecture from the second half of the 16th century.

Piazza S. Carlo ⑫

Piazza S. Carlo is Turin's most famous square. Its monumental enclosed space is the city's '*salotto*' (drawing-room) and has always been the heart of the social and public life of the people of Turin. Based on the royal squares of Paris, it was designed in 1637 by Carlo di Castellamonte. Formerly, the land was occupied by the city walls which once surrounded the 'old town'. In the center of the square is the **equestrian monument to Emanuele Filiberto*** (1838), known by the Torinesi as *il caval d'brons* (the bronze horse). It depicts the victorious duke in the act of sheathing his sword after the Battle of San Quintino. The same tactic used to make Piazza Castello look uniform was applied to Piazza S. Carlo. It owes its perfect symmetry to the duke's plan to give the land around the square to his nobles on the condition that they built their private residences according to Castellamonte's unitary plan. Each house was a large, rectangular building with a central garden, a spacious entrance-hall on the ground floor, and a great hall on the first floor. *Palazzo Solaro del Borgo* is the best example. At road level, the longer sides of the square are lined with broad, airy porticoes. Two of the city's historic cafés are situated below them (**Caffè San Carlo** and **Caffè Torino**) and *Confetteria Stratta*, still with its 1836 decor. Between Piazza S. Carlo and Piazza Castello is **Via Roma**, rebuilt in the 1930s, with porticoes housing some of Turin's most elegant shops.

Museo Egizio/ Egyptian Museum ⓭

Turin's Egyptian Museum, which is accessible to the disabled, is the world's most important collection after Cairo and one of the city's best-known monuments. After the Napoleonic period, the vogue for collecting Egyptian antiquities became very popular. Bernardino Drovetti from Piedmont, who was Consul General of France during the occupation of Egypt, collected more than 8,000 items: statues, sarcophagi, mummies, papyri, amulets and jewels. In 1824. King Carlo Felice acquired Drovetti's collection and, combining it with finds from the collections of classical antiquities of the House of Savoy, created the world's first Egyptian Museum. In the early 20th century, the museum's new director, Ernesto Schiaparelli, began to make new acquisitions as well as personally conducting excavations in Egypt. As a result, by the 1930s, the collection had grown to more than 30,000 exhibits illustrating every aspect of the Ancient Egyptian civilization: splendid art, everyday objects, rites associated with their belief in the after-life and the techniques used by Egyptian craftsmen, from the pre-dynastic period (4,000 BC) to Late Antiquity (5th-6th C AD). The many exhibits include the following highlights: a reconstructed **pre-dynastic oval funerary chamber*** containing the body of a man in the fetal position, one of the earliest-known examples of natural mummification; the **royal papyrus***, a complete list of all the pharaohs from the 1st to the 18th dynasty which (together with the famous Rosetta Stone, kept in the British Museum in London, and the Palermo Stone, copies of which are displayed here) have been

A statue of Amenhotep I.

Harpist, fragment of a mural from Thebes.

Orazio Gentileschi: Annunciation, houses in the Galleria Sabauda.

fundamental in the study and interpretation of the Egyptian language; the **tomb of Ini***, with a sarcophagus and rich grave-goods laid out on a cowhide; a **painted linen cloth*** depicting a funeral ceremony; the reassembled **rock-cut Temple of Ellesiya*** (1430 BC); and the **statue of Ramses II in Majesty***.

Galleria Sabauda/ Savoy Gallery ⓮

As well as being patrons of armorers, the Savoys had a passion for commissioning and collecting works of art. Every duke and king, but also members of the princely branches of the family, contributed to the dynastic collections over the centuries, building them up into one of Italy's most important art collections. The year after his accession to the throne (1832), Carlo Alberto created the Galleria Sabauda (*Sabauda* means 'of the House of Savoy'). It contains works of the Italian School dating from the 15th and 16th centuries; paintings by Piedmontese masters from the 14th to 16th centuries, including a **Virgin Enthroned with Sts Ubaldo and Sebastian***; and, finally, a splendid collection of works by Flemish and Dutch masters, including masterpieces such as Jan van Eyck's **Stigmata of St Francis**** and Rembrandt's **Portrait of an Old Man***, and precious examples of Baroque painting (landscapes, still lifes and battle scenes). The Savoy collection dating from 1550 to 1630 includes works by Flemish, Venetian, Lombard and Mannerist painters. The collections made between 1630 and 1730 include Francesco Cairo's **Herodias with the Head of John the Baptist***. Of the works commissioned between 1730 and 1831, there are two lovely landscapes depicting Turin at that time (**Side-view of the Royal Gardens** and **View of the Old Bridge Spanning the Po**). The collection of early art, displayed in the form of a 'house museum', in addition to furniture, fabrics, jewelry and precious objects, includes Duccio di Buoninsegna's **Madonna Enthroned with the Child and Two Angels**.

Piazza Carignano ⓯

This square may not share the monumental grandeur of other places in the city, yet this quiet corner has more artistic, historical and literary associations than anywhere else in Turin. It is dominated by the undulating red-brick facade of Palazzo Carignano. Opposite is one of the city's institutions: the **Teatro Carignano***, built in 1711 and completely rebuilt after a fire in 1787. The interior is beautifully decorated with marquetry, gilt stucco and red velvet, with frescoed panels in the ceiling. **Palazzo Carignano**** has been recognized by UNESCO as a World Heritage Site. Its unusual curved facade follows the outline of the two symmetrical staircases inside and the great oval hall in the center, the real fulcrum of the building. This was a very innovative feature and proved to be of critical importance in the history of Italian and European Baroque. In addition to its unusual lines, unusual effects were created by using bricks to face the building. Special bricks were made to create particular patterns, rendered even more effective by their pinkish-red color. The entrance-hall with its columns, where the double staircase

Piazza Carignano, a traditional meeting-place for the Torinesi.

leads up to right and left, has a majestic feeling of wide-open space. The **Museo Nazionale del Risorgimento***, housed in Palazzo Carignano, is one of the few museums devoted to the history of the Italian nation. It contains testimonials about the Savoy kingdom from 1706, year of the heroic stand against the siege of Turin by the French army of Louis XIV and, in fact, the beginning of the political independence of the state of Piedmont. It illustrates the most important steps towards the creation of the Italian state. The exhibits include a reconstruction of the *cell at Spielberg* in which Silvio Pellico (writer and patriot, champion of the cause of national independence from Austrian rule) was imprisoned, posters and newspapers from the period of the Risorgimento, and memoirs and relics from the Wars of Independence. You can look down on the **Chamber of the Subalpine Parlament***, the precursor of Italian Unification, see rooms devoted to WWI, and the **Chamber of the Italian Parliament**, a poignant achievement, since it was never used. It was finished in 1871, by which time the capital had been moved to Florence and then Rome.

Mole Antonelliana ⑯

The Mole, named after the visionary architect who designed it (Alessandro Antonelli), towers above the city and is Turin's best-known symbol, partly because it can be seen from many points in the city. Structurally, the Mole is a combination of neo-classical features and daring vertical design. Based largely on Neogothic principles, it seems to herald the huge tower blocks of the 20th century. In fact, the charm of this symbol lies in the fact that it is virtually impossible to link it to any single architectural style. Above the massive square base (a peristyle, a pronaos, and two tiers of Corinthian columns with large glass windows and another layer set slightly further back from the lower layers) is a large four-sided dome which culminates in a small temple with two tiers of columns. Above it, the spire rises vertically, ringed by a series of small round balconies with diminishing circumferences. At the top of the spire, like a spearhead probing skywards, is a star. When completed, the height of the Mole (167.5 m) set a new European record for a brick-built building. You can get up to the 'temple feature' at the top of the dome in the glass lift.
At the top, the **view** over Turin and the surrounding landscape is unbeatable. On a clear day, the chain of the Alps all around seems remarkably close. The Mole now houses the **Museo Nazionale del Cinema****. For further information see p. 135.

Galleria Civica d'Arte Moderna e Contemporanea ⑰

Turin's modern art gallery, referred to as GAM, with its 20,000 exhibits, rivals Rome's national art gallery as Italy's most important collection of modern and contemporary art. The works are displayed according to period and provenance. The exhibition begins with works by 19th-century Italian artists and continues with 20th-century art by both Italian and foreign artists. There are Avant-garde works, modern 'classics', expressions of the neodada, informal and pop art movements, with special emphasis on *arte povera*, which began in Turin. Some works in the collection are worth coming to see in their own right: Modigliani's **La Ragazza Rossa**; a series of **paintings** by Felice Casorati and **sculptures** by Arturo Martini. The section devoted to the 19th century is full of surprises, both in terms of figurative art and sculpture. Partly as a result of the success of this gallery, in 2002, the **Fondazione Sandretto Re Rebaudengo*** was built on the outskirts of Turin to promote exploration of the visual arts: painting, sculpture, photography, video and performance, with particular emphasis on works by young artists embarking on careers in this field.

The Valentino ⑱

The **Parco del Valentino****, Turin's largest park, is situated on the banks of the Po and is a favorite place for walking. It can be divided into three parts: the most northerly part, between the *monumental arch to the Artillery Regiments* (1930) and the *Botanical Garden*; a middle section stretching from the Castello Valentino to the Borgo Medievale; and finally the most southerly section laid out around the *rock garden* and exhibition center of Torino Esposizioni. The paths and avenues of the park provide plenty of scope for hikers, joggers and dog-walkers. There are large grassed areas, open-air cafés and boathouses overlooking the river. You can take a boat trip from the jetty here, or the more energetic can try their hand at canoeing on the Po. In 1729, the **Botanical Gardens** were founded by royal decree. They contain 12,000 plants species from all over the world, some of them perfectly acclimatized in glasshouses. It also has important collections of *historical herbariums*, an *iconographic collection* and a *botanical library*.

The **Castello del Valentino***, designated by UNESCO as a World Heritage Site, a grand pleasure palace overlooking the river, looks like a French *château*. Its steeply-sloping slate roof with dormer windows is very reminiscent of buildings in France. The central part of the facade facing the river is decorated with arches and windows and a symmetrical double staircase. The palace was built in the 17th century for Marie Christine of

Castello del Valentino with its towers reflected in the Po.

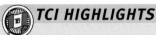

TCI HIGHLIGHTS

THE FLOWERING OF TURIN'S ART-NOUVEAU STYLE

In 1902, the First International Modern Decorative Arts Exhibition introduced the city to the wonders of Art Nouveau. Special pavilions were set up in Parco Valentino to display the new architectural trends (and were only dismantled several years after the event). Sinuous, elegant and refined in every detail, the floral style began to appear in particular areas of the city in the architecture, in the decorative arts and even in fashion. One such area extends from the beginning of Corso Francia (from Piazza Statuto to Piazza Bernini), the district also known as Cit Turin (dialect for 'little Turin'). Here, during the early years of the 20th century, villas and palazzi began to appear decorated with little wrought-iron balconies, polychrome-glass windows and bay windows on the corners. One of them (No. 65 Via Cibrario) belonged to Guido Gozzano, a poet who symbolized that fleeting, carefree moment poised between the old and the new. Starting at Piazza Statuto, No. 8 bis Corso Francia, Villa Raby, has strongly projecting bay windows on the corners and a beautiful wrought-iron gate. On the parallel Via Piffetti, at No. 3, Palazzo Mazzetta (1908), the wrought-iron decoration is inspired by a peacock's tail. No. 5, Palazzo Masino, dates from the same period. Here, note the parapet of the balcony decorated with sphinx-like figures and the G motifs, signature of architect Giovanni Gribodo. He also designed the villas at Nos, 10-12, whose facades have symmetrical proportions, but which differ in terms of the materials and the decorative motifs used. No. 3 Via Beaumont, Casa Tasca (1903), has florid decoration on the facade and between the windows (notice the vertical corner sequence of stone balcony-open bay window-small wrought-iron balcony). Casa Fiorio (designed by Giuseppe Velati Bellini) at No.5 Via Cibrario has elegant, somber floral and abstract decoration. Back in Corso Francia, at the corner of Via Principi d'Acaja (No. 11), Casa Fenoglio-La Fleur, designed by Pietro Fenoglio in 1904, is one of the most photographed examples of Art Nouveau in Turin. (Note the original canopy in colored glass and wrought iron at the top of the corner tower, which resembles the corolla of a flower (see photo). No. 32, Casa Maciotta (again by Fenoglio, 1904) has a characteristic hexagonal corner balcony protected by a slender gazebo. Although the area around Corso Francia has many examples of this architectural style, it is by no means the only area of Art-Nouveau buildings in Turin. There are other good examples around Piazza Crimea, near Parco Valentino, and in the Crocetta district.

France, who used it as a pleasure palace, a venue for tournaments, jousting, parties and river battles. The beautiful decoration of the first floor rooms, with frescoes and gold and white stucco-work, dates from 1633-42. The artists were Isidoro Bianchi and his sons Pompeo and Francesco, who based their work on mythological themes and deeds of the members of the House of Savoy, especially in the *central hall* and the *Moncalieri apartment*. On the opposite side is the *Turin apartment*, decorated between 1646-49 and 1662. Beyond the courtyard of the castle is the **rock garden**, an elaborate series of flower-beds, lawns, small bridges, hedges and paths, crossed by a small stream. The **Borgo Medievale**, a faithful reconstruction of a 15th-century fortified Piedmontese village, was built on the banks of the Po in 1886. The purpose of the Borgo was to recreate a medieval atmosphere. A drawbridge leads into it through the gateway of the *Torre di Ogliànico*. On the left is the *Albergo dei Pellegrini*, preceded by an area with a fountain and an oven. On either side of the street are reconstructions of medieval houses, churches and towers from towns in Piedmont. Below the porticoes on either side are craft workshops including a blacksmith's, a pottery and a paper mill. In the little square below the *castle* is the *Issogne Fountain* (1927). A porticoed ramp, a copy of the entrance to the castle of Fénis in the Valle d'Aosta, leads into the **castle** courtyard. The entrance-hall leads into the courtyard, where the bodyguard of Verrès is usually on duty. The larder, the kitchen, and the dining-room are on the ground floor. The bedroom, the chapel and the great hall are located on the first floor. The rooms have all been reconstructed with great care. The Borgo is still a focus of initiatives to promote medieval culture. Leaving the Borgo Medievale behind and continuing with the river on your left, you soon come to the **Fountain of the Months*** on a slight rise. This beautiful fountain was built in 1898 and is supposed to depict Turin's four rivers (the Po and its three tributaries: the Sangone, the Dora Riparia and the Stura), surrounded by allegorical statues representing the months of the year.

The Lingotto ⓳

The Lingotto, the original Fiat car factory, was very large indeed. It consisted of two blocks 507 m long and 24 m wide linked by 5 horizontal blocks, with 5 floors of engineering workshops, situated south of the city center between the hills on the far side of the Po and the backdrop of the Alps. The cars were tested on the extraordinary **elliptical**, **parabolic test-track** on the roof of the building (1 km long and 24 m wide). It was built in a series of modules. This can be seen on the facade and in the regular spacing of the pillars and open spaces inside. At each end, a **spiral ramp** links the various floors of the building and is its most spectacular feature. The cars were driven from the production line directly up to the test-track. However, the changing needs of production lines eventually rendered the factory obsolete and the building was gradually abandoned, finally closing in 1983. In the mid-1980s, an international competition was held. The winning design was entered by the architect Renzo Piano. During the following decade, the various parts of the factory were used to stage a whole series of cultural events: concerts of classical music, prestigious theatrical productions, important exhibitions and temporary exhibitions focusing on art and town-planning. The actual restructuring of the factory began in 1991, when the body-shop was reorganized as premises for exhibitions and trade fairs.
In 1993, work began on the engineering workshops (about two-thirds of the whole factory), and was completed in 2002. The result is an ingenious new multifunctional center which has preserved the dimensions, spacing and facade of the old factory. Today, in addition to the conference center and the area devoted to trade-fairs, the Lingotto is a multi-functional complex where culture and commerce, work-places and residences, open areas and production areas exist side by side. The new features include the **Auditorium*** (Renzo Piano, 1993-94), a state-of-the-art concert hall with perfect acoustics, and the '*garden of wonders*', the delightful garden occupying the space in the middle of the building. On the top, overlooking the test track, are two of Renzo Piano's brilliant 'inventions': the **Bolla** (1994), a bubble-like conference hall in blue glass suspended 40m above the ground, and the **Scrigno**, the steel box housing the Pinacoteca Agnelli.
The **Pinacoteca Giovanni e Marella Agnelli*** contains works from the vast private collection of the Agnelli family, selected according to the criteria of 'art which inspires simple esthetic pleasure and pure emotions', in accordance with the wishes of its founders. Modern and contemporary masterpieces are housed in an exquisite setting created by architect Renzo Piano. They include views by 18th-century Venetian *vedutisti* (including 6 Canalettos), the *Halberdier*

FIAT: BIRTH AND EVOLUTION OF AN INDUSTRIAL CITY

Four letters, a clever acronym which sounds like a Latin imperative encouraging people to produce (meaning 'let it be made'), a story more than a century old, an ongoing story today. FIAT stands for Fabbrica Italiana Automobili Torino. It was founded in 1899 in the noble Palazzo Bricherasio, near Piazza S. Carlo. The investors included Giovanni Agnelli, an ambitious 33-year old businessman from Villar Perosa. In 1904, FIAT became an unmistakable trade-mark on a blue oval background, tastefully designed in the Art-Nouveau style by Carlo Biscaretti di Ruffia. Giovanni Agnelli had decided to embark on a real challenge. (In the 1920s he was made a Senator.) The Italian car industry was still at the embryo stage and investing everything in it at that time was considered very risky. But Agnelli knew what he was doing. The company reported exponential growth for more than 80 years, hand in hand with the gradual growth and development of Italian industry as a whole. In the mid-1960s, when Avvocato Giovanni Agnelli, named after his grandfather, the founder, took over as Chairman of the company, Fiat employed almost 160,000 people, in a city which the 1961 census recorded as having a population of just over one million. More than anything else, FIAT stands for the Agnelli family. Many maintain that, in the 20th century, the owners of FIAT played a key role, replacing the role played by the Savoys in the 19th century. Although the Savoy dynasty had done its best to steer the tiny state of Piedmont towards the geographical and political Unification of Italy, the Agnelli 'dynasty' was responsible for creating a different dimension of Italy, namely its economy, and the social changes it brought with it. An Italy which, especially after WWII – first with the years of mass immigration from the south and the economic boom, then the struggles of the proletariat – radically changed its face.

in a Landscape by Tiepolo, 2 pure neo-classical sculptures by Antonio Canova, Impressionist paintings by Manet and Renoir, and 7 important **works** by Matisse, executed between 1920 and 1948; two Picassos, examples of Italian Avant-garde art and a **Nu couché** by Amedeo Modigliani.
20 minutes' walk from the Lingotto, overlooking the Po, is the **Museo Nazionale dell'Automobile***, the only museum of its kind in Italy.
It illustrates the development of personal transportation from its very origins to the present day.
It is one of the finest collections in the world and contains all kinds of vehicles, from the first self-propelled artillery tank (1729) to futuristic electric models powered by solar energy, sports cars, racing cars, mass-produced models and prototypes, early motor-driven carriages (more like carriages than cars), and weird-looking dragsters which once broke speed records.

Museo della Sacra Sindone/ Museum of the Holy Shroud 20

Via S. Domenico contains the *church of the Santo Sudario*, a small jewel of Piedmontese Rococo (1734-35).
In the crypt is the Museum of the Holy Shroud, created with the purpose of conserving and promoting the story of the Holy Shroud and the scientific research that has probed into the origins of this famous relic.
The material on display, including a multimedia facility, provides a complete picture of the historical, scientific, religious and artistic background to the Shroud. The objects exhibited include the casket in which it was brought from Chambéry to Turin in 1578, rare and precious documents dating from the 16th to 19th centuries, the plates of the first official photographs of the Shroud (taken in 1893 and 1931), three-dimensional depictions of the relic, and photographs taken through an electronic microscope, making it possible to detect minute traces of

pollen, blood, aloe and myrrh.
From the historical and artistic point of view, one of the most important pieces in the collection is the casket made of silver and precious stones in which the Shroud was kept until 1998. A photograph of the sacred relic is on display.

La Consolata 21

Small, secluded Piazzetta della Consolata is one of the quietest, most charming corners of central Turin. It contains the church of Santa Maria Consolatrice, a Romanesque bell tower, an old herbalist's shop and one of the city's best-known historic *caffetterie* (cafés) and confectioners. The *bell tower* is much older than the church and probably dates from the 10th century. Originally it was a lookout tower. At the base of the tower you can see stones from earlier buildings of Roman date. On the side facing the square is a stone with a relief depicting a fallen tree. The bell tower was added 1406. The *church of S. Andrea* was built in 1678 to a design by Guarini. The hexagonal church was accessed through an elliptical hall. In 1729, Juvarra added an oval presbytery. In 1860, the neo-classical pronaos was added. Inside, to the right, steps lead down into the old *chapel of the Madonna delle Grazie*, decorated with marble and stuccoes. On the walls are delightful votive paintings giving thanks for divine grace. An archway leads into the *sanctuary of the Consolata*, with its high frescoed dome.

La Consolata: the Romanesque bell tower.

TCI HIGHLIGHTS

The Holy Shroud

The Shroud ('Sindone' in Italian) is a yellow piece of woven linen cloth with a herring-bone motif, 4.37m long and 1.11m wide. Impressed on it is the figure of a man who has been tortured and killed by crucifixion. It shows signs of wounds to his face, head and body, and a more obvious knife-wound between the ribs on the right-hand side of the body. There are many obvious coincidences linking the trials of this man to the Passion and death of Jesus Christ, as described in the various versions of the Gospels. Despite scientific objections to the authenticity of the relic, for centuries, this extraordinary and mysterious object has been a subject of great fascination. The first certain news of the Shroud appears in the mid-14th century, in France, although, prior to this, the relic seems to have made a long journey from Jerusalem to Anatolia, and from there to Constantinople, before falling into the hands of Goffredo di Charny. The Savoys bought the relic from him in 1453 and, for more than a century, it was kept in Chambéry. In 1578, Emanuele Filiberto transferred it to his new capital, Turin, and it has been there ever since. In 1694 it was placed in the chapel between the royal palace and the Duomo, designed specially for the relic by Guarino Guarini. During its long history it has escaped a series of disasters. In 1532, when a fire destroyed the chapel of Chambéry Castle, the Holy Shroud was damaged (the repairs were not removed until the summer of 2002). Then, one night in April 1997, Guarini's chapel was all but destroyed, but the relic was saved again.

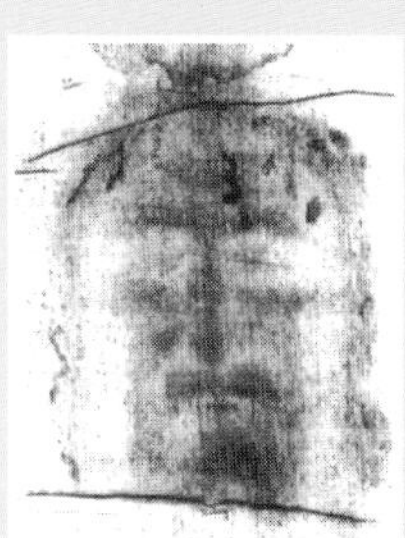

DAY TRIPS

BASILICA OF SUPERGA [9 km]

If you look out from the top of the hill of Superga with your back to the basilica, Turin lies at your feet with the circle of Alpine peaks beyond.
In 1717, King Vittorio Amedeo II commissioned Juvarra to build a church here. It took 14 years to complete and, in 1731, the church was solemnly consecrated. The shape of the church, according to Juvarra's design, seems to continue the shape of the hill on which it stands. Beyond the long pronaos with eight Corinthian columns stands the round church, with a dome supported by a drum. On each side of the church is a symmetrical bell-tower, attached to the wings of the adjoining monastery. Built on a circular plan, the church has two main chapels and four secondary chapels. Left of the altar is the **chapel of the vow**. A doorway in the left side of the basilica leads down below the church to the **tombs of the kings*** and princes of Savoy, who were buried here from 1731 onwards. A tunnel leads to the central chapel (1773-78), decorated with marble, stucco and *statues*.
Off the cloister is the *room of the popes*, which contains portraits of all the popes who have ascended the papal throne.

IVREA [50 km]

Ivrea's famous **castle** (c. 1358-1398) is built on a square plan with four round brick-red angle towers and a large central courtyard. Not far away is the **cathedral**, built in the 10th century in the Romanesque style. The crypt, with its fragments of frescoes, the octagonal tiburium and the two bell towers by the apse date from this period. The cathedral has been radically altered over the centuries. The facade, with a tympanum crowned by statues, is neo-classical (1854). The Baroque interior, which contains many fine *artworks*, is built on a Latin-cross plan. The nave and two side-aisles culminate in a raised medieval deambulatory.
In Via Arborio note the 18th-century **Palazzo del Seminario**, built according to a design by Filippo Juvarra.
On one wall of the portico in the courtyard is a fragment of 12th-century *mosaic* from the floor of the Romanesque cathedral.
Outside the historic center is the **Roman amphitheater**, built around the turn of the 1st century. You can still see part of the *cavea*, a corridor leading to the center of the arena, and the foundations of the podium.
The **church of S. Bernardino** dates from the mid-15th century and contains a remarkable fresco cycle depicting **Stories from the Life of Jesus***, in 20 panels (late 15th C).

TCI HIGHLIGHTS

«...DEFEATED ONLY BY FATE»

Three rooms in the cloister of the basilica are now the Museo del Grande Torino, with documentation and memorials of the great Torino soccer squad which, on May 4, 1949 perished in the Superga plane crash. A plaque behind the church pays tribute to their memory. There is no doubt that 'Grande Torino', as the club was called, possibly the greatest team in the history of Italian soccer, was also the most popular. Captained by soccer champion Valentino Mazzola, it achieved astounding results (winning five championships between 1943 and 1949 and contributing ten of the eleven members of the Italian national team). More importantly, in the eyes of Italy, it represented the new, fresh, successful face of a country that had emerged destroyed and humiliated from WWII. When the plane carrying the whole team crashed into the hill of Superga, the news spread like wildfire through the streets of Turin. In no time, a procession of people dressed in black began to make its way towards the hill. Half a million people attended the funeral service, the streets of Turin and the stands of the Filadelfia football stadium where Toro had played fell silent. It was the beginning of a legend.

Ivrea: the Romanesque 10th-century cathedral and, beyond, the famous castle with the 'Red Tower' (c. 1358-1398), a symbol of Ivrea.

PALAZZINA DI CACCIA DI STUPINIGI [9 km]

The Palace of Stupinigi, designated a UNESCO World Heritage Site, and situated south of the city, is not actually a royal residence, merely a grand hunting lodge to satisfy the hunting whims of the Savoys. It was Filippo Juvarra who, in about 1729, created this monument to the king's passion for hunting by designing a majestic 'villa of delight', surrounded by gardens and an extensive park. The building, with four wings arranged around a large central oval hall, is crowned with a large bronze statue of a stag. The palace now houses the Museo di Arte e Ammobiliamento. The collection includes 18th-century furniture, paintings, wallpaper, fabrics, furnishings of various kinds, statues, ornamental panels and painted doors. Look out for the paintings of stag-hunting scenes (1772-78) in the Groom's Room of the king's apartment, also the fresco on the ceiling of the antechamber of the queen's apartment. The fresco decoration of the central hall is particularly magnificent. Towards the end of the route, in the apartment of the Prince of Carignano, there is a gallery of relics dating from the Napoleonic period. The gardens, laid out after 1740, are surrounded by the Parco Naturale di Stupinigi.

SACRA DI S. MICHELE [37 km]

This impressive monument is one of the most striking symbols of the region. The complex of the 'Sacra' is a cluster of religious buildings and ruins built into the summit of *Mt Pirchiriano* at an altitude of 962 m. The abbey was founded in the year 983, with money donated by a nobleman, Ugo de Montboissier. Situated on the pilgrim route to Rome, the Sacra soon became one of the most important Benedictine monasteries, and its library was famous. It became increasingly influential and, at one point, controlled churches and abbeys in Italy, France and Spain.
Over the centuries, the early Romanesque structures were incorporated into buildings in the French Gothic style. The earliest building, of which traces can be seen in the crypt of the church, dates from 983-87. The following parts of the old abbey complex have survived: the remains of the original chapel, the church dating from the 12th and 13th centuries, the cloister, the pilgrims' hospice, and a few of the fortifications. Walking from the car park by the ruins of the *monks' tombs* (Romanesque in date) up the long sloping path, you see the *guest quarters*, formerly a pilgrims' hospice, on your left. The entrance or *porta di ferro* (iron gate) in a small tower was once part of the fortifications. From here, steps lead up to a terrace with splendid **views** across the plain. You also get a good view of the

whole complex higher up, especially the apses of the church. A steep staircase called the *Scalone dei Morti* (Staircase of the Dead), thus called because monks were occasionally buried in the walls on either side, leads up to the church. At the bottom, on the left, a gigantic pillar supports the ceiling and the floor of the church above. At the top of the staircase is the magnificent **gateway of the Zodiac***. The capitals are carved with the *stories of Samson* and of *Cain and Abel*, and the jambs on either side are carved with *imaginary figures* and the *signs of the Zodiac*. After yet another flight of steps you reach the **church of S. Michele***. The late Romanesque doorway with a pronounced embrasure in the right side of the church is made of green and gray stone. Inside, the nave and two aisles are separated by cruciform pillars. These support the cross-vaults, decorated with fine *frescoes*, *high reliefs* and *sculptures*. The frescoed choir, part of the Romanesque church, is irregularly shaped at the end of the nave. Steps lead down to the *crypt*, where three chapels stand side by side. They were altered in the 19th century. This is part of the early medieval structure. Much of the film "The Name of the Rose" was filmed here.

SUSA [54 km]

The center of this little town has seen centuries of history, and still has many Roman and medieval features. In **Borgo dei Nobili**, the houses have medieval doors and windows. The **church of S. Francesco**, with a facade decorated with small gables, and the monastery attached date from the mid- 13th century. The **amphitheater** discovered as a result of floods in 1961 dates from the 2nd century AD. It is fairly small, with an oval arena measuring 45m x 47m. The **castle** is now the **Museo Civico**. It contains collections of natural history, Egyptian artifacts, archeological finds from excavations around Susa, coins and historical documents. The **cathedral of S. Giusto*** overlooks the square named after it. Founded in about 1020, the early Romanesque building was altered several times. In the 14th century it was rebuilt in the Gothic style, and was altered again in the 16th and 18th centuries. The fine *bell tower* has six storeys separated by hanging arches and the upper part of the tower is illuminated by two-, three- and four-light windows. At the back of the church is a Gothic apse, and the end of the nave is crowned with small arches and a small bell tower. Inside, near the modern side-entrance, the *baptistery* contains a large green marble bowl. In the apse are some beautiful 14th-century carved wooden **choirstalls**. There is also a large wooden *lectern* dating

Sacra di S. Michele

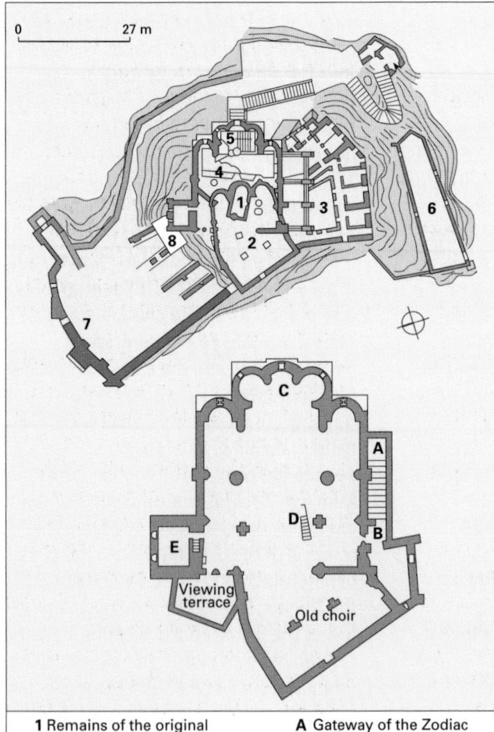

1 Remains of the original chapel (10C-11C)
2-4 Church (12C-13C)
3 Cloister
5 Staircase of the Dead
6 Guest quarters
7 Remains of fortifications
8 Terrace

A Gateway of the Zodiac
B Church doorway
C Presbytery, with large windows
D Stairs to the crypt
E Bell tower

from the same period. The sacristy and the chapter house contain several remarkable *artworks*.
On the far side of the Parco di Augusto (once the Roman Forum) is the **Arch of Augustus***, dating from 9 and 8 BC. Built of white marble from Foresto, it has a single arch almost 9 m high. A frieze in low relief runs across the top.

VENARÌA REALE [9 km]

In 1997, Venarìa Reale was designated a UNESCO World Heritage Site. It may be regarded as the Versailles of the Savoys. It wasn't just a palace for hunting parties, balls and flamboyant receptions, but a whole complex of buildings which constituted a sort of satellite of the city of Turin. As well as the palace, the plan included a whole village and gardens, and the huge park of La Mandria, with another smaller royal palace and village. The most important families of the royal court built palaces in the **village of Altessano Superiore**, redesigned in 1658, with three squares which form a sequence on the road running through the Contrada Grande. The actual **royal palace** complex is the result of various alterations to the original design of 1658. The *courtyard of honor* is on the right, near the lower garden, whereas the left part of the courtyard is sealed off by the Galleria di Diana. Opposite is the earliest part of the complex, the *Palazzo di Diana*, built by Castellamonte between 1660 and 1663. The palace is named after its elaborately decorated great hall, the **Salone di Diana*** (with its allegorical frescoes, stuccoes, busts of satyrs, nymphs and hunting trophies). The *frescoes on the ceiling*, which depict Diana being crowned by Jupiter as the goddess of all forms of hunting, are by Jan Miel (1661-63). Miel was court painter and was active in introducing the new ideas of the Classical movement to Piedmontese painting in the 17th century. Built in the late 17th century to connect the palace to the stables, between 1716 and 1718, the **Galleria di Diana**** was completely transformed by Filippo Juvarra. Not only is the gallery one of his masterpieces, it is the most memorable feature of the whole of the Venarìa. It is 80m long and perfectly proportioned. It is a 'theater of light' because of the way the light enters through windows

Filippo Juvarra's elegant Galleria di Diana at the Savoy pleasure palace of the Venarìa.

arranged to illuminate the elaborate stuccoes. Juvarra was also responsible for the **orangery*** and the magnificent **stables**** (1722-27), buildings of extraordinary grandeur. The **gardens***, which Castellamonte based on 16th-century gardens in Rome, were gradually altered over the years, according to the latest vogue. Try to see Juvarra's extraordinary *'appartamenti verdi'*, long lines of trees planted at the sides and end of the ornamental garden, and shaped as if they were real rooms with walls and ceilings.
La Mandria is the estate that was used as a horse stud and to rear the game required to satisfy the Savoy's passion for hunting. The *castle* La Mandria, regarded as the hunting lodge of the Venarìa, became a royal residence under Vittorio Emanuele II, who converted part of the stables into a private apartment. The buildings parallel to the old stables were also part of the farm and the horse stud.
The 19th-century *farms of Vittoria and Emanuella* are part of the same complex, despite being slightly further away. In 1978, the Piedmont Region decided to protect this area with its deer and wild boar by creating the **Parco Naturale Regionale La Mandria**. This is all that remains of the natural forest which once covered the entire Po Valley.

ALESSANDRIA

The founding of Alessandria (1168) is associated with the long struggle between the papacy and the Holy Roman Empire. The town, initially on the side of the Holy Roman Emperor, subsequently switched sides, and was re-christened Alessandria in honor of Pope Alexander III. Renowned historically as a military stronghold, over the centuries, thanks to its strategic position on the Tànaro River, it attracted the attention of many military men. From Frederick Barbarossa to Napoleon Bonaparte, the town's history is dotted with military events which have influenced the development of the town on the plain between the Tànaro and Bòrmida rivers. A case in point is the Cittadella (fortress), built between 1733 and 1745, a fine example of military architecture. Alessandria was a military target during WWII and was subjected to intense Allied bombing.

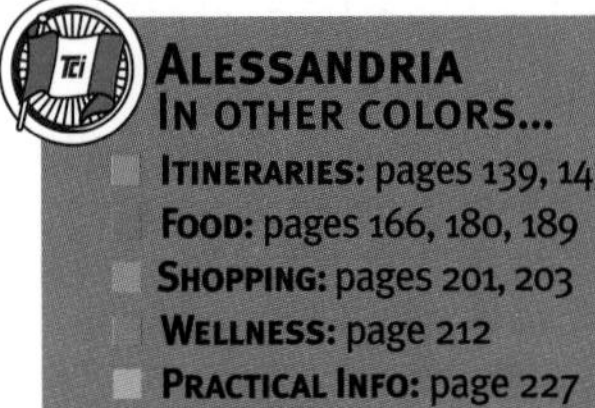

Piazza della Libertà ❶

Piazza della Libertà (1803), a vast rectangular square bordered with trees, is the heart of the town. On the south side of the square is the porticoed **Palazzo Municipale** (1772-1828). To the north is the *post office* (1939-41), decorated with a large Fascist *mosaic*. To the east lies **Palazzo della Prefettura e della Provincia**, one of the town's most important Baroque buildings. It has a majestic octagonal entrance-hall and broad stairs. The reception rooms are still decorated in the 18th-century style with ornamental panels above the doors, mirrors, fireplaces and frescoed ceilings depicting mythological themes.

Cattedrale/Cathedral ❷

The cathedral, built in 1810 on the site of the previous church, overlooks *Piazza Giovanni XXIII*. It has a fine neo-classical

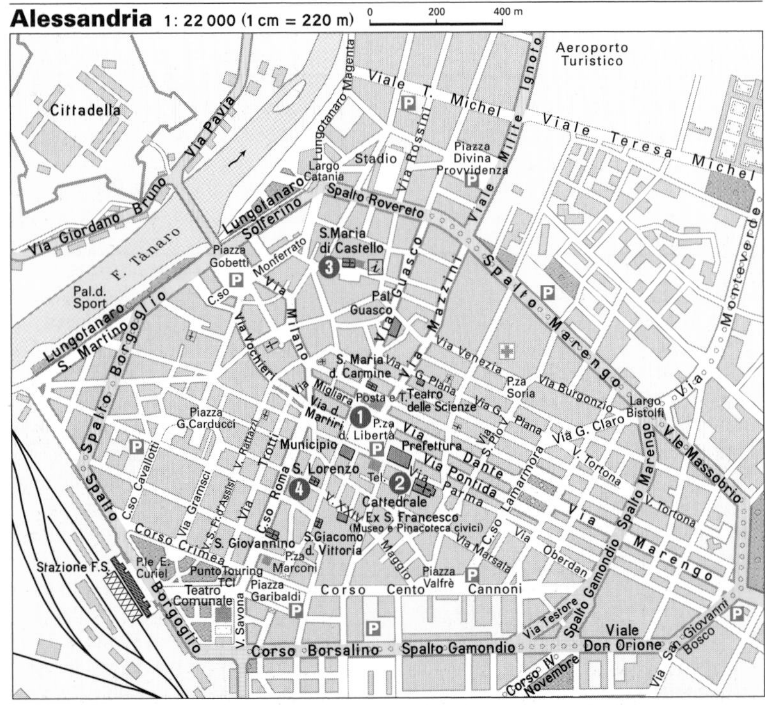

facade (1822-23) and a tall bell tower with a spire which was only completed in 1922. Inside, the nave was frescoed in the 19th century. The drum supporting the dome is decorated with statues of the patron saints of the 24 cities of the Lombard League. (The Lombard League was an alliance formed in 1167 by most of the cities in northern Italy to counter the attempts of Holy Roman Emperor Frederick Barbarossa to bring Italy within his sphere of influence.)

S. Maria di Castello ❸

This church, founded in 1470 (although not completed until 1545), was built on the site of two earlier churches (some ruins can be seen under the floor). Its lines are mainly based on the late Gothic style. It has a fine Renaissance doorway. Inside the church is a wooden *Crucifix* dating from about 1480 and a 16th-century polychrome terracotta *Deposition*. In the presbytery are some late 16th-century carved wooden choirstalls and the high altar (1640). In the left transept is a *Madonna*, a polychrome stone carving in high relief (15C). In the refectory of the adjoining monastery is a *Crucifixion* dating from 1520.

S. Lorenzo ❹

Work on the church dedicated to St Lawrence began in 1770-72. The magnificent interior was decorated by the Lombard mural painters Giovanni Pietro and Pietro Antonio Pozzo, and there are two interesting *paintings* by A. Lanzani.

DAY TRIPS

ACQUI TERME [34 km]

This small town, famous even in Antiquity for its sulfur-rich springs, is also renowned for its cakes and confectionery, truffles and red wines. On the right of Corso Italia, beyond the medieval arch, a staircase leads up Vicolo della Schiavia to the splendid *Piazza del Duomo*. The imposing Romanesque **cathedral** (1067), still has three splendid apses, the transept and the bell tower (completed in the 13th century) from the original church. The broad 17th-century portico on the facade protects a beautiful marble *doorway* dating from 1481. Inside, the nave and four side-aisles are separated by pillars. The pulpit an[...] are carved with fine Ren[...] Below the presbytery is [...] three broad aisles and a [...] columns. In the Sala dei [...] triptych of the **Madonna** [...] (c.1480). The **basilica of** [...] town's oldest church, stands in *Piazza Addolorata*. It dates from the early Christian period and was rebuilt between 989 and 1018. The three polygonal apses probably date from the first church, while the rest of the church was restored in 1927-30. On the other side of the Bòrmida River, near the *Ponte Carlo Alberto*, are the ruins of a **Roman aqueduct** dating from the Augustan period (1C).

SACRO MONTE DI CREA [43 km]

One of Piedmont's most famous and visited sanctuaries, and a UNESCO World Heritage Site, the Sacro Monte consists of a church, 23 chapels and 5 hermitages situated on a wooded hill in a panoramic position. The complex dates from the 12th century and has been altered several times. The Romanesque **basilica of S. Maria Assunta** was enlarged in 1483. In 1608-12, the monks built a majestic facade incorporating a portico. Inside, the nave and two side-aisles are separated by pillars supporting pointed arches and cross-vaults. In the apse is a panel depicting the *Madonna and Child with Saints* dating from 1503. Note the **chapel of St Margaret**, right of the altar, with important 15th-century frescoes by Lombard and Piedmontese painters. In the chapel on the left, above the altar, is the *Madonna di Crea*, a small 14th-century statue of cedar wood. In the *treasury*, note the *portraits of Guglielmo di Monferrato* and *his wife Anna d'Alençon*. The **chapels**, begun in 1590, contain interesting sculptures, whereas the **hermitages** are smaller chapels below the steps leading up to the church. The **Parco Naturale Regionale del Sacro Monte di Crea** was created to protect the wildlife, landscape and monuments of the area. Inside the park, very different plant species manage to live side by side (thermophilic plants, which thrive in temperate climates, and microthermal plants, which grow in cool environments). Mammals in the park include badger, fox, dormouse, and squirrel, whereas bird species include raptors and passerines.

a: Sacro Monte

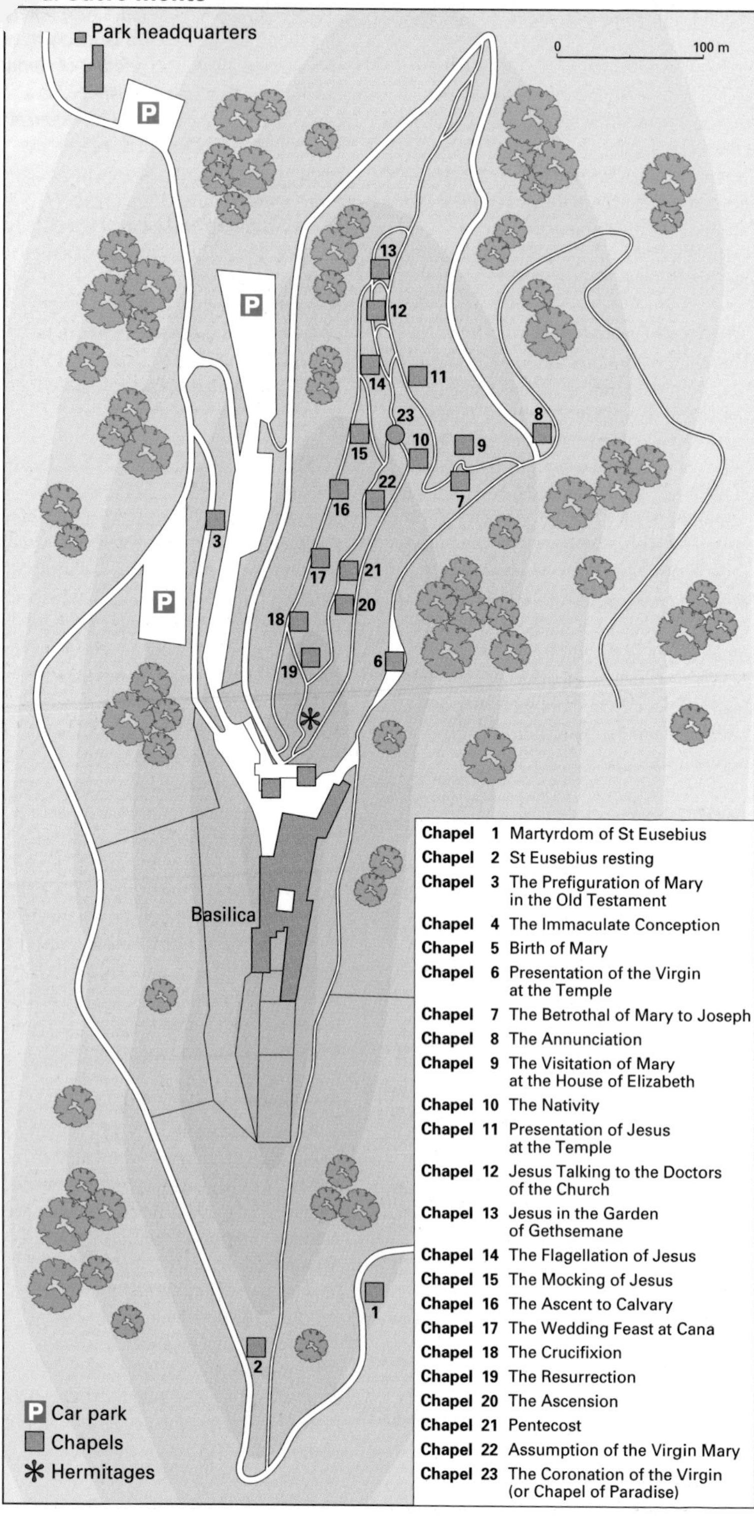

Chapel	1	Martyrdom of St Eusebius
Chapel	2	St Eusebius resting
Chapel	3	The Prefiguration of Mary in the Old Testament
Chapel	4	The Immaculate Conception
Chapel	5	Birth of Mary
Chapel	6	Presentation of the Virgin at the Temple
Chapel	7	The Betrothal of Mary to Joseph
Chapel	8	The Annunciation
Chapel	9	The Visitation of Mary at the House of Elizabeth
Chapel	10	The Nativity
Chapel	11	Presentation of Jesus at the Temple
Chapel	12	Jesus Talking to the Doctors of the Church
Chapel	13	Jesus in the Garden of Gethsemane
Chapel	14	The Flagellation of Jesus
Chapel	15	The Mocking of Jesus
Chapel	16	The Ascent to Calvary
Chapel	17	The Wedding Feast at Cana
Chapel	18	The Crucifixion
Chapel	19	The Resurrection
Chapel	20	The Ascension
Chapel	21	Pentecost
Chapel	22	Assumption of the Virgin Mary
Chapel	23	The Coronation of the Virgin (or Chapel of Paradise)

ASTI

Asti is a fascinating town with a rich artistic heritage, renowned for its excellent wines and delicious food. It lies in the heart of the Monferrato hills, on the right bank of the Tànaro River, at the confluence with the Bòrbore Stream. The old town center, with its narrow, winding medieval streets is very picturesque. The oldest part of the town is called the Recinto dei Nobili (literally, Enclosure of the Nobles). The name refers to the fact that, in the Middle Ages, it was occupied by fortified houses and towers belonging to noble families in the area. You can still discern the original structure of the Recinto today, despite Baroque and 19th-century additions. Some of the towers are still standing and you can see some of the features of the fortified houses (particularly brick and tufa arches).

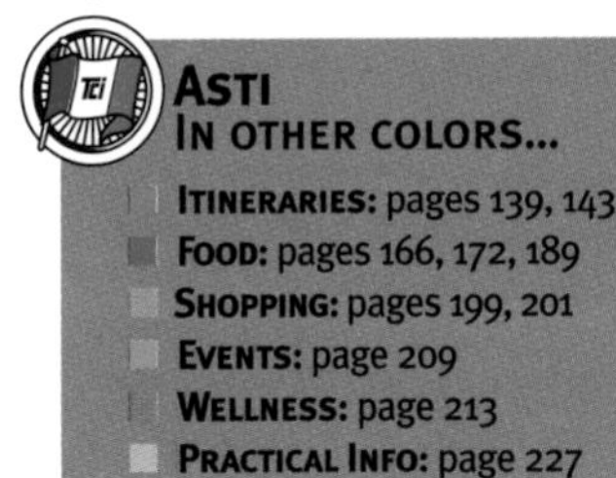

Piazza Vittorio Alfieri ❶

The square was named after one of the town's most famous sons, poet and playwright Vittorio Alfieri. Palazzi with porticoes line three sides of the square, which was laid out between 1860 and 1870 above the old military parade ground. In the center is the *monument to Vittorio Alfieri* (1862) and, opposite, *Palazzo della Provincia* (1958-61).

S. Secondo ❷

According to tradition, the church stands where the saint was martyred in 119. This fine Gothic building was rebuilt between the second half of the 13th century and the mid-14th century on the site of a 7th-10th-century church. The facade, completed in 1462, is divided into three parts. Three doors with embrasures are framed by columns with capitals. Above

Asti 1: 20 000 (1 cm = 200 m)

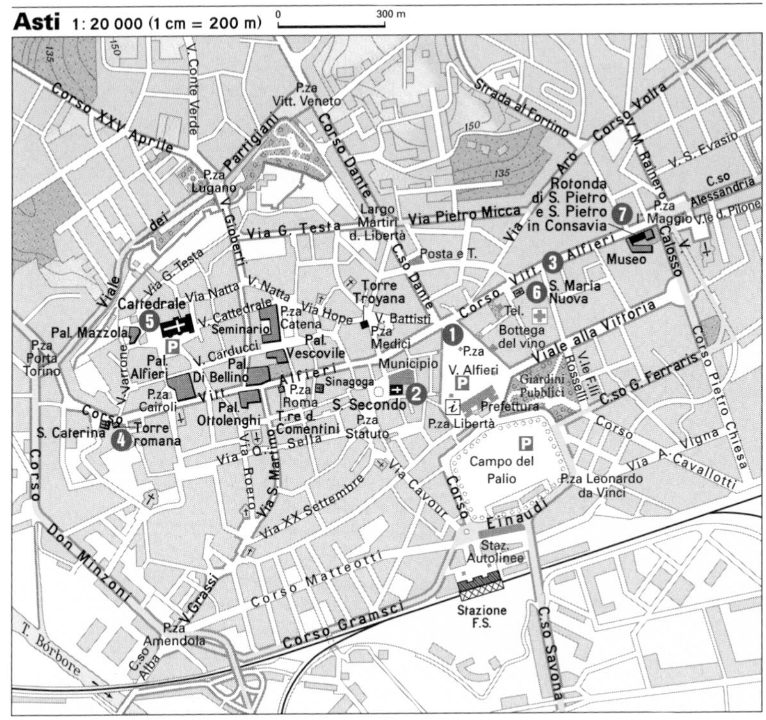

each door is a rose-window. The central window is decorated with intricate stone-carving and a low relief dating from the 15th century. Only the central apse belongs to the earlier church (late 13th century). The splendid 10th-century Romanesque bell tower is visible from the courtyard of *Palazzo di Città*, left of the church. Built on a Latin-cross plan, the nave and side-aisles are separated by pillars, from which ribs spring to form pointed arches. In the 2nd and 3rd chapels of the right aisle, there are fragments of early 15th-century *frescoes*. Flights of steps on either side of the presbytery lead down to the *crypt*, which was part of the original building and possibly dates from the 7th century. The short aisles are divided by six small columns with sandstone capitals, and converge on a small apse, shrine of the 16th-century silver reliquary containing the remains of St Secondus.

Corso Vittorio Alfieri ❸

The elegant, paved, slightly sloping main street is overlooked by some of the town's most elegant 18th-century palazzi. In *Piazza Roma*, just off the Corso, is a late 19th-century Neogothic building and the 13th-century *Torre Comentina*. Buildings of note on the Corso include: **Palazzo di Bellino,** a medieval fortified house restored in 1751; *Palazzo Ottolenghi*, a medieval building restructured in 1740; the **crypt of St Anastasius*** and the **Museo Lapidario**, an archeological park-cum-museum. The crypt has column bases, columns and capitals dating from the late-Roman period. Finally **Palazzo Alfieri**, where Vittorio Alfieri was born, is an 18th-century transformation of a 13th-century palazzo, with a magnificent central courtyard.

Peach-trees in bloom in the Monferrato hills.

Torre Romana/Roman Tower ❹

Continuing along the main street, inside Palazzo del Michelerio, is the former church of Gesù (1549) and, more particularly, the *cloister of Gesù*, a masterpiece of local 16th-century architecture, with perfect lines. Further on, where the road becomes wider, stands the *Torre Romana* or *Torre Rossa*, dating from the Augustan period (1C). It has 16 sides and was possibly once part of an old gate. The top of the tower, decorated with small arches and columns, dates from the late 11th century. Beyond this point, opposite the Baroque *church of S. Caterina* (1766-1773), is a high wall with seven pointed arches, part of the old city walls.

Cattedrale/Cathedral ❺

This majestic brick cathedral is one of Piedmont's most important Gothic buildings. It was built between 1309 and 1354 above the remains of an earlier church and has been altered several times over the centuries. The lower part of the facade is decorated with narrow blind arches and three Gothic doorways (c.1450). The upper facade is divided into three sections by two pilaster strips ending in pinnacles. It has three rose-windows and is crowned by a cornice of small intersecting blind arches. In the right-hand wall of the church, which has tall, narrow, one-light windows separated by buttresses, is a remarkable **porch*** in the flamboyant Gothic style (post-1450), with delicate reliefs and exquisitely carved statues. The Romanesque bell tower was rebuilt in 1266 and the height of the tower was lowered in the 17th century. The well-illuminated nave and slender side-aisles, separated by cruciform pillars, are built on a Latin-cross plan. The walls and ceiling are entirely covered with late-17th-century frescoes, and there are many other interesting *artworks*. The **treasury** is worth visiting and contains some very valuable objects.

On the left side of the cathedral is the courtyard of the oratory and the *priest's house*, an old brick building with a small tower. Opposite the cathedral stands the late 17th-century *church of S. Giovanni*, built on the site of a 9th-century church. The nave with its large curved one-light windows belongs to the original church. Below the church is the interesting **crypt of St John** (8C), with four splendid columns made of Egyptian granite and syenite with anthropomorphic carved capitals. Not far away, in *Piazza Medici*, stands the **Torre Troyana*** (13C), 38 m high, with Romanesque two-light windows and Ghibelline merlons.

S. Maria Nuova ❻

The church was rebuilt in the 14th century on the site of an earlier Romanesque church, and altered again in the 17th and 19th centuries. The lower part of the bell tower dates from the original church (11C). Inside is a remarkable *Madonna Enthroned with the Child and Saints* by Gandolfino d'Asti (1496) in its original frame. The beautiful *Chiostro dei Canonici Agostiniani* adjoining the church dates from 1591.

Rotonda di S. Pietro and S. Pietro in Consavia ❼

In Piazza I Maggio is an unusual museum complex consisting of the Battistero or Rotonda di S. Pietro, the church of S. Pietro in Consavia and the cloister. The Rotonda, one of Asti's most important Romanesque monuments, was built in the 12th century and was based on the Church of the Holy Sepulchre in Jerusalem. Used as a baptistery, it is a low, octagonal building surrounded by mighty buttresses. Above is an octagonal drum crowned with small arches. The interior of the building is round with eight short columns with alternating bands of brick and sandstone and square capitals. These support the octagonal dome, the walls of which were frescoed in the 17th century. You walk through the baptistery to enter the *church of S. Pietro in Consavia*, an example of 15th-century architecture between the Gothic and Renaissance styles. Note the terracotta friezes around the windows and on the cornices. The cross-vaulting of the *cloister of the Pilgrims' Hospice* is supported by columns. A door leads into the **Museo Archeologico e Paleontologico**, which has exhibits dating from the Roman, Barbarian and Medieval periods, an Egyptian collection and a fossil collection.

DAY TRIPS

S. MARIA DI VEZZOLANO [40 km]

The abbey, a magnificent example of late Piedmontese Romanesque, was founded before 1086. Throughout the Middle Ages, it was a center of power which administered extensive domains. The church, the cloister and the chapter-house of the abbey are still standing. The **church**, like some of the adjoining buildings (late 12C). It has a fine facade completed in the early 13th century, with alternating bands of brick and sandstone. It is divided into three by two buttresses and has a doorway with beautiful carved reliefs and a two-light window decorated with *statues*. The decoration uses a typical motif of Po Valley churches of this period: superimposed tiers of blind arcading supported by short columns. Inside, there are two naves with apses (the third was incorporated into the cloister) separated by pillars supporting pointed arches and cross-vaulting. In the first bay of the main nave is a marble **rood-screen** in the French style, extremely rare in Italian churches. It is supported by five pointed arches and decorated with two tiers of fine **low reliefs*** dating from 1230-35. In the main apse, the jambs of the right-hand one-light window are decorated with beautiful **carvings**. In the **cloister** are fragments of painted decoration from the 13th-14th centuries.

Abbey of S. Maria di Vezzolano

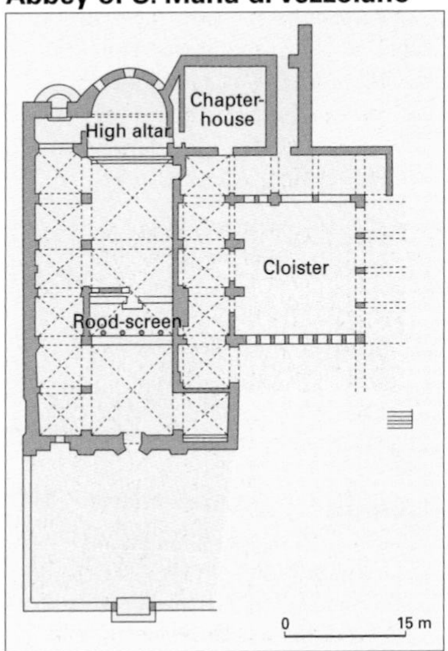

BIELLA

The town, one of the capitals of Italy's textile industry, and the administrative capital of the recently-created Province of Biella, is situated on the lower slopes of the Alps. The Roman town was founded on the site of a Celtic settlement situated on the Cervo Stream. Today there are three parts to Biella. Old-fashioned Piazza up on the hill overlooks Piano, where the town subsequently developed, while the newest part, Chiavazza, is further down, on the left bank of the Cervo. There are many castles in the province (many now private residences), but there are also examples of 17th century architecture. The sanctuaries known as 'Sacri Monti' were built on hills and are linked by panoramic roads. A case in point is the famous sanctuary of Oropa, designated a UNESCO World Heritage Site.

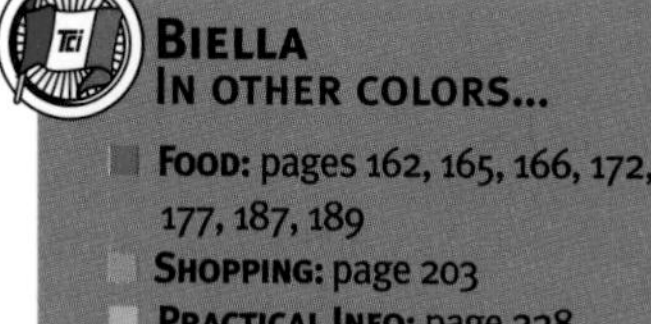

BIELLA IN OTHER COLORS...

FOOD: pages 162, 165, 166, 172, 177, 187, 189

SHOPPING: page 203

PRACTICAL INFO: page 228

SS. Trinità ❶

Begun in 1626 and completed in 1750, the church of SS. Trinità is decorated inside with 17th-century stuccoes and frescoes. It has a fine wooden **shrine** above the high altar by a woodcarver from Biella, Giovanni Vaglio (17C).

Biella 1 : 19 000 (1 cm = 190 m) 0 200 400 m

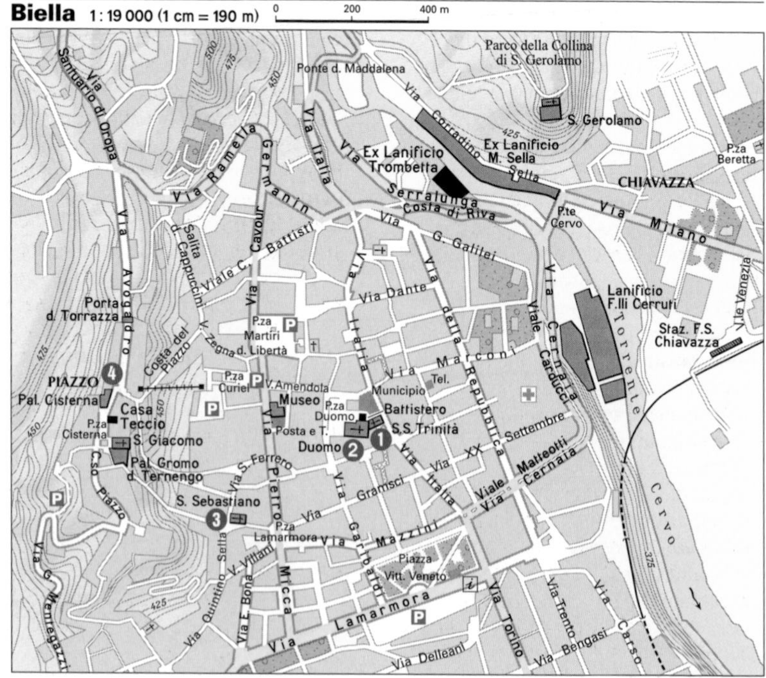

Latin-cross plan. The Gothic vaulting above the nave and two side-aisles is decorated with beautiful *frescoes*. There are also some interesting fragments of *paintings* from the 15th-16th centuries. Near the cathedral is the Romanesque **bell tower of St Stephen**, with one- and two-light windows. To the left of the cathedral is the **Baptistery***, one of Piedmont's most important pre-Romanesque buildings (7C-11C). Built on a square plan, with four semi-circular apses

Duomo ❷

The church was begun in 1402 on the site of an earlier church. In 1772, it became the cathedral and a Neogothic facade was added in 1826. The interior is built on a divided into three parts by pilaster strips, it was constructed with pebbles and bricks using a herring-bone motif. Solid buttresses support the octagonal drum on the top of the baptistery, decorated with blind niches, with a small lantern of later date on the top. Above the door is a fine *low relief* dating from the Roman period (2C). Inside are fragments of frescoes from the 13th-14th centuries.

S. Sebastiano ❸

This remarkable example of Renaissance architecture is one of the town's most prestigious monuments. Work on the church began in 1502 and was completed in 1551, but the present facade replaced the original in 1882. The harmonious, elegant interior consists of a nave and two side-aisles. They are divided by slender columns which have dosserets carved with low reliefs. The barrel vaults of the nave, the apse and the dome are decorated with *frescoes*. Over the altar in the chapel at the end of the right aisle, note the altar-piece depicting the **Assumption*** (1543). The marquetry work in the apse, the **choirstalls** and the *lectern* is by Gerolamo Mellis (1545). Adjoining the church is the lovely **cloister** (1560) of the former monastery of S. Sebastiano, now the interesting **Museo del Territorio**. Near the Cervo Stream is the former woolen mill **Lanificio Trombetta**, a marvelous 19th-century example of industrial archeology.

Biella Piazzo ❹

Biella Piazzo is situated on the hill overlooking Biella Piano. In **Piazza Cisterna** is the noble 16th-century facade of **Palazzo dei Dal Pozzo della Cisterna**. The main part of the building is decorated with floral friezes in the Gothic style. The palazzo is surrounded by medieval buildings. They have porticoes with pointed arches supported by pillars and columns with capitals, and windows with terracotta decoration. One of the best examples is **Casa dei Teccio**, on the left-hand side of the piazza. On the corner of the square is the **church of S. Giacomo** (13C), with a 14th-century facade and bell tower. To the right of the church, **Palazzo Gromo di Ternengo** has a Renaissance courtyard overlooked by two storeys with loggias, a portico and terracotto decoration.

DAY TRIPS

PANORAMICA ZEGNA [41 km]

The Panoramica Zegna, the SS 232 road is 26km long. The most scenic part of the route is between Trivero and Rosazza. First it climbs up the side of Colle S. Bernardo, passing *Caulera*, Bocchetto di Stavello and Bocchetto di Margosio. There are splendid views of Mt Rosa, especially in summer, when the hillside is covered with rhododendrons. Then the road winds up onto Mt Marca to **Bielmonte**. This is the highest point of the park of **Oasi Zegna**, created with the aim of protecting this part of the Alps.

SANCTUARY OF OROPA [13 km]

The Sanctuary of Oropa, is one of Western Europe's oldest sanctuaries dedicated to the Virgin Mary. The founding of the pilgrimage site here is attributed to St Eusebius (4C), first bishop of Vercelli, but it is first documented in 1207. The vast complex comprises the old church, the new church and twelve chapels. The **old church** was rebuilt between 1600 and 1637 on the site of a 13th-century church (note the frescoes from this period). Inside, the *chapel of St Eusebius* contains the revered wooden statue of the **Black Madonna** (13C). Building of the grand **new church** began in 1885, however, problems ensured that it wasn't completed until 1960, when it was finally consecrated. The interior is divided into two large central chambers. In the second is the high altar by Giò Ponti, with statues and low reliefs. The first **chapels** were built in the early 16th century, but construction of the actual Sacro Monte, dedicated to the Virgin Mary, began in 1620. The chapels depicting the following scenes are particularly worthy of note: the *Wedding Feast at Cana* and the *Coronation of the Virgin* (or *Paradise*), where there are 156 statues. In 2005, the area became the Riserva Naturale Speciale del Sacro Monte di Oropa. Together with the nearby Riserva Naturale del Monte Mars in the Aosta Valley, the reserve is a huge protected area spanning the border of two regions. Next to the church is a cable-car which takes visitors up to the glacial **Lake Mucrone**, a starting- point for many walks in the surrounding mountains.

CUNEO

Cuneo (the word means 'wedge' in Italian) was founded in 1198. In medieval times it was strategically important because of its situation on a wedge-shaped plateau formed by the confluence of two rivers: the Gesso and the Stura di Demonte. The town is built on a grid plan around the main thoroughfare formed by the medieval, porticoed Via Roma and Corso Nizza. The oldest part of the town is concentrated on the peninsula between the rivers in Contrada Mondovì, where there are many 17th- and 18th-century buildings. Piazza Duccio Galimberti, which has elegant 19th-century buildings with long porticoes, is the heart of the town and acts as a link between the old town and the new.

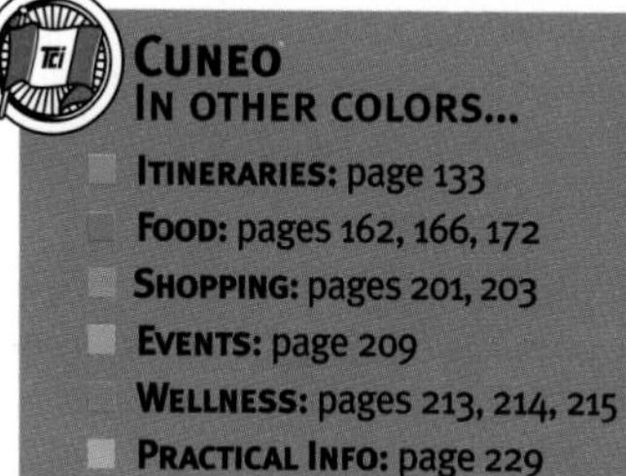
Cuneo in other colors...
- **Itineraries:** page 133
- **Food:** pages 162, 166, 172
- **Shopping:** pages 201, 203
- **Events:** page 209
- **Wellness:** pages 213, 214, 215
- **Practical Info:** page 229

Cattedrale/Cathedral ❶

At the beginning of Via Roma, lined by characteristic porticoes, stands the cathedral of Nostra Signora del Bosco, rebuilt in 1662 on the site of a medieval chapel. The neo-classical facade from 1865. Inside the church, built on a Greek-cross plan, the dome (1835) is decorated with frescoes. In the apse is a remarkable *Purification*. Notice also the fine wooden choirstalls and the *pulpit* (1668). The sacristy contains the *diocesan treasury*, with precious chalices and reliquaries.

S. Chiara ❷

The deconsecrated church of S. Chiara, now used for exhibitions, was begun in 1712 and completed in 1719. Altered in

Cuneo 1 : 20 000 (1 cm = 200 m)

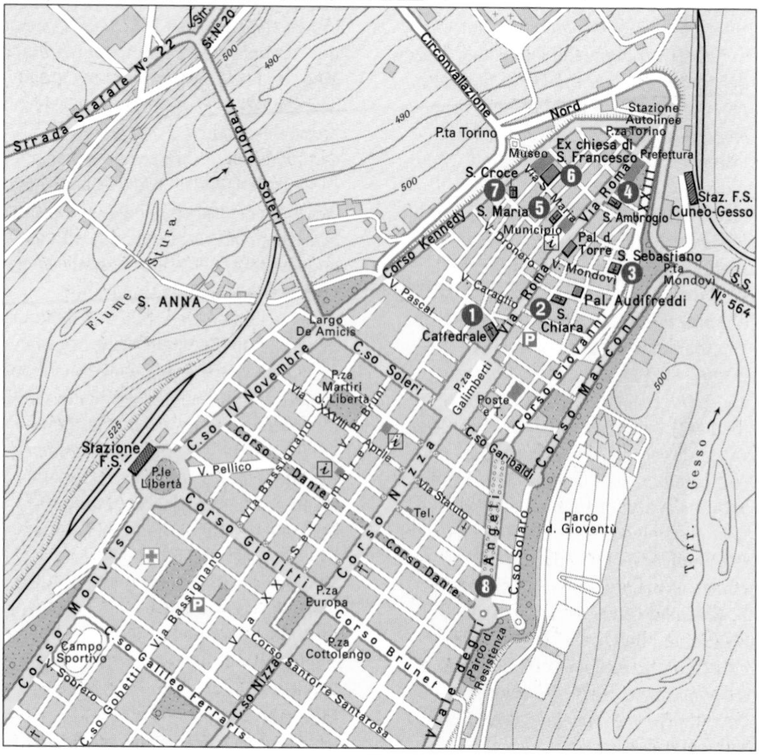

the 19th century, it has a curved facade divided into two tiers. The quiet, striking interior contains interesting *frescoes* and 18th-century decoration.

S. Sebastiano ❸

The church of S. Sebastiano stands on *Via Mondovì*, a medieval street lined with porticoes. On the same street is the 15th-century *synagogue*, which was modernized in 1884 and is decorated in the late-Baroque style. The facade of the church dates from 1880. Inside there are some remarkable *works* by Giovanni Antonio Molineri (in the vaults and the apse), *choirstalls* dating from 1595 and some 16th-century paintings.

S. Ambrogio ❹

The original church dedicated to St Ambrose dates from 1231 but it was rebuilt between 1703 and 1743. Subsequently the facade and the *apse* were added. The apse was frescoed in 1870-80. The striking, elegant interior is built on a Greek-cross plan, with a marvelous interplay of arches, vaulting and ribbing. Above the crossing of the transept is a dome with a lantern.
On Via Roma is **Palazzo Municipale**, dating from 1631, once a Gesuit monastery, and **Palazzo della Torre**, so-called because it incorporates the medieval tower of the town hall.

S. Maria ❺

Hugged by buildings on either side, the church of S. Maria has a facade decorated with statues. It was built in 1665, but in 1726 the rectangular apse was made semi-circular. There are interesting frescoes on the ceiling, and good *paintings* behind the high altar and in the first chapel of the left aisle.

Ex chiesa di S. Francesco/Former church of S. Francesco ❻

The former church of S. Francesco is the town's most important example of medieval architecture. The building, built on Gothic lines, has a 15th-century facade divided into three parts by two pilaster strips and decorated with terracotta friezes and pinnacles. The fine marble doorway dates from 1481. Above it is a tympanum with a rose-window. The mighty bell tower, with its octagonal pyramidal spire, dates from 1399.

The adjoining cloister with frescoed lunettes leads into part of the monastery, now the **Museo Civico**. It has sections devoted to archeology, the Middle Ages, an ethnographic collection and a beautiful collection of rag dolls dressed in local Cuneo costume.

S. Croce ❼

On the same street stands the magnificent church of S. Croce, built between 1709 and 1715. It has an unusual concave facade with two tiers, ending in an elegant curved tympanum with the remains of frescoes. The interior consists of two intersecting elliptical halls. In the apse is a fine carved wooden *bishop's throne* in the French Gothic style and an altar-piece in a marble frame (18C). Don't miss the painting in the first chapel of the left aisle, a splendid **Madonna and Child with Sts Bernardino of Siena and St Augustine**.

Viale degli Angeli ❽

The long tree-lined Viale degli Angeli winds along the eastern bastions of the town, not far from the Gesso Stream, to the **sanctuary of S. Maria degli Angeli**, which has a rich historic and artistic heritage.

DAY TRIPS

ALBA [61 km]

Alba has a fine medieval center contained within an almost circular perimeter which follows the line of the old city walls. It has many picturesque towers and fortified tower-houses which give the town special appeal. The **church of S. Domenico** is particularly interesting and one of the most important Romanesque and Gothic buildings in the Po Valley. It was built between the end of the 13th century and the early 14th century and was subsequently altered several times. The facade, divided into three parts by pilaster strips, has a lovely rose-window and a beautiful doorway with an embrasure. There is a fresco in the lunette above. The fine polygonal apse dates from the late 13th century. The interior is divided by round pillars into a nave and two

The charming medieval towers and fortified houses of Alba.

side-aisles with ribbed cross-vaulting. In the last bay of the left-hand aisle there are interesting *frescoes* dating from the 14th and 15th centuries. In the second bay is a delightful marble sculpture (*The Cross*).
The **Cathedral**, built in the late 15th century in the Gothic style by adapting the earlier Romanesque church, was altered several times between the 16th and 19th centuries. The three doorways on the facade date from the original Romanesque church (11C). The fine 13th-century *bell tower* incorporates the original massive Romanesque belfry. The interior, built on a Latin-cross plan, is divided into a nave and two side-aisles. These rest on cruciform pillars and Gothic arches which support ribbed vaulting.
The polygonal apse contains magnificent carved and inlaid wooden **choirstalls** made in the 16th century.
In Via Cavour stands the *Torre Astesiana*, with one- and two-light windows, the medieval *Loggia dei Mercanti*, with a portico and a terracotta frieze, an old *tower* and a fine *house* with Gothic decoration and traces of Gothic windows.

BOSSEA CAVE [43 km]

The Grotta di Bossea is the final part of a large karst system below the Maudagna-Corsaglia watershed.
The cave, which is about 3 km long, is one of the most interesting in Italy in terms of its magnificent limestone formations and the fossil remains found there. This remarkable karst phenomenon is situated at an altitude of 829 m in the narrow valley of the Corsaglia River, and is full of spectacular features (the height difference to be negotiated is 120 m, while the temperature in the cave is about 10°C/50°F). Beyond the first corridor is an enormous cave, where the various features have been given names: the *Hall of the Landslides*, where the many stalactites have human shapes, the *Canopy*, a fantastic marble-like formation of strange shapes, the *Hall of the Bells* and the huge *Hall of the Temple*. A skeleton of *Ursus spelaeus*, a bear species once native to the region, has been reconstructed here with bones found in the cave.
A steep climb, called the *Calvary*, leads to the *Castle*, a limestone formation resembling a castle. Then, beyond the *Hydrangea Bridge*, is *Lake Ernestina* where the chamber echoes to the sound of a large waterfall. This is the first of a series of underground lakes you encounter as you proceed through other chambers and tunnels, all full of the most spectacular limestone formations.

SAN COSTANZO SUL MONTE [19 km]

Just north of Dronero, on the south side of Mt S. Bernardo, is one of Piedmont's most interesting monuments. This small, very old church (supposedly founded by the Lombards in 712) was rebuilt in the Romanesque style. The back of the church, dating from the 12th century, is a wonderful example of architecture of the period, dominated by an octagonal tiburium decorated with small arches and three semi-circular apses decorated with pilaster strips.
You can see traces of the old bell tower on the right-hand side. The front of the church, rebuilt between the 17th and 18th centuries, is in the Neogothic style. Inside, the nave and

Bossea Cave Plan

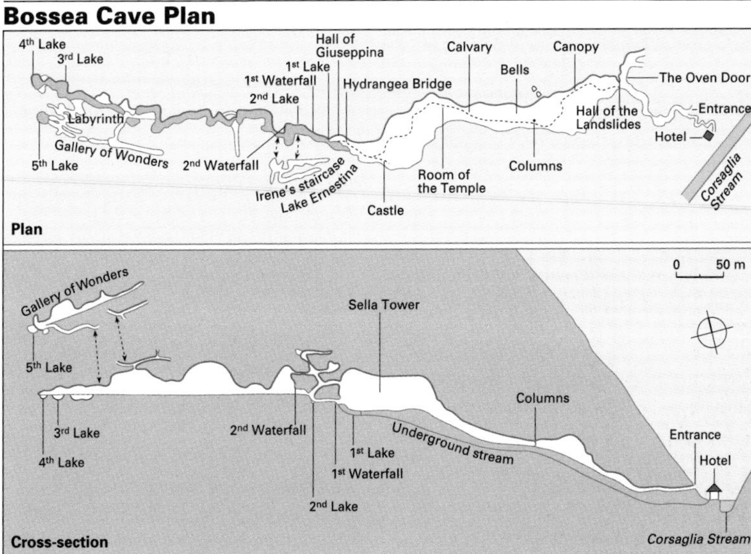

two side-aisles are preceded by a vestibule. The Romanesque part of the church has beautiful carved capitals while the nave is decorated with fragments of Romanesque frescoes. The crypt below the church, also in the Romanesque style, has three aisles.

SANCTUARY OF VICOFORTE [34 km]

The Sannctuary of Vicoforte is one of Piedmont's best-known monuments, with its three facades and bell towers. Next to the pilgrimage church, the Cistercian monastery has a large late-Renaissance cloister and a lovely *frescoed refectory*. The church, built on an elliptical plan, has an ellipsoidal **dome*** supported by eight buttresses, interspersed with elegant rectangular windows. A high atrium leads into the church, which is very striking because of its sheer size. The dome and the drum with its windows rest on eight pilasters and eight arches. Above the dome is a lantern. The frescoes on the ceiling, which cover an area of about 6,000 m^2, depict the *Glory of the Assumption with the Holy Trinity*, and *saints* and *doctors of the Church*. In the center of the building, raised and surrounded by a balustrade, is the **Temple of the Pillar,** decorated with 18th-century statues of *Hope* and *Charity*. In the silver and bronze frame in the center, made in 1751, is a fresco of the *Madonna and Child* (15C). There are interesting *chapels* around the edge of the church, while the frescoed ceiling is decorated with fine *paintings*.

Sanctuary of Vicoforte

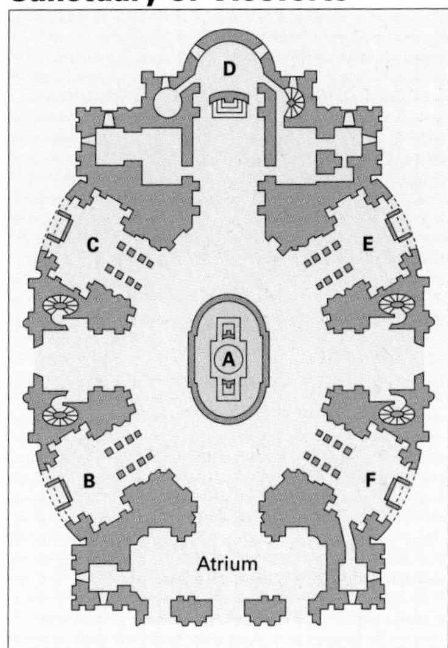

- **A** Temple of the Pillar
- **B** Chapel of St Bernard
- **C** Chapel of St Joseph
- **D** Apse with frescoes by F. Biella and altar-piece by F.A. Meyer
- **E** Chapel of St Francis of Sales
- **F** Chapel of St Benedict

NOVARA

Most of the buildings in Novara's small historic center date from the 19th century. Many have neo-classical facades. The oldest building of all is the Baptistery of the Duomo. Monuments dating from the medieval period include the Duomo, the cloister of the priest's house, the chapel of St Sirus (with fine 12C Romanesque frescoes) and the Broletto. The Basilica of S. Gaudenzio was built during the transition from Mannerism to Baroque. In the 19th century, Antonelli added a daring dome 121m high which has become the symbol of the town. This is a town with a human dimension and a historic center reminiscent of a 19th-century drawing-room. In the distance are the peaks of the Alpine Chain.

NOVARA
IN OTHER COLORS...

ITINERARIES: page 155
FOOD: pages 159, 165, 170, 173, 175, 177, 181, 190, 193
SHOPPING: pages 199, 203
PRACTICAL INFO: pages 229, 230

Duomo/Cathedral ❶

The large neo-classical cathedral stands on Piazza della Repubblica. It was built on the site of a Romanesque church. Features dating from the earlier church include the massive bell tower (the top was added in the 16C), the cloister of the priest's house and the Oratory of St Sirus. The splendid facade is preceded by a pronaos with four granite Corinthian columns and a quadriporticus. The left side continues, connecting the cathedral to the baptistery. Inside, imposing stucco columns separate the nave from the side-aisles, while the spaces are hung with Flemish *tapestries* (1565). In the presbytery are beautiful fragments of the black and white **mosaic floor** of the Romanesque church (11C-12C), depicting the *Temptation of Adam and Eve*. Nearby, in the *oratory of St Sirus* (12C) is a damaged but important cycle of frescoes from the same period (**Stories from the Life of St Sirus***). A doorway in the right aisle leads into the courtyard of the bishop's palace and the **cloister of the priest's house**, surrounded by porticoes with short, octagonal pillars. The north side dates from the 11th century while the other three date from the 12th century. The courtyard houses the **Museo Lapidario della Canonica**, with early altars, sarcophagi, funerary inscriptions and architectural fragments.

Novara 1: 25 000 (1 cm = 250 m)

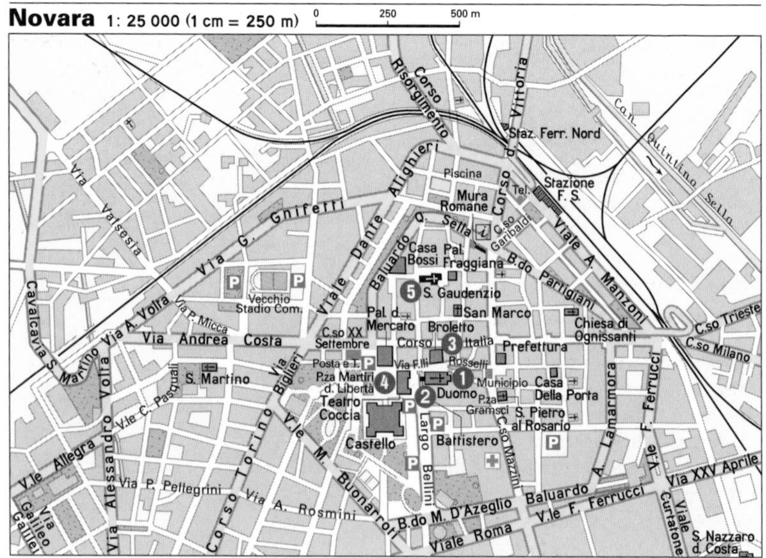

Battistero/Baptistery ❷

Possibly the oldest early-Christian baptistery in the Po Valley, it was built in the 5th century on a multifoiled octagonal plan. The high domed tiburium, decorated outside with small arches and niches, was added in the early 11th century. Inside, the building is decorated with alternating semicircular and rectangular niches. There are also traces of the original floor, some mosaics and, below glass, the full-immersion baptismal font. Up in the loggia, the 8 large panels with splendid **frescoes*** (c.1019) are some of the most important examples of pre-Romanesque painting in the region.

Broletto ❸

The Broletto is a complex of medieval buildings with a wide courtyard, accessed from the north side of Piazza della Repubblica. *Palazzo dell'Arengo* or *Palazzo del Comune* dates from 1206 and has a large porticoed atrium. The top of the building is decorated with a frieze depicting scenes of courtly life. On the east side is *Palazzo dei Paratici* (seat of the town's medieval guilds, 14C and 15C). On the south side is *Palazzo del Podestà*, a magistrate's house. Built in 1346 and rebuilt in the mid-15th century, it has a portico, frescoes on the facade and five one-light windows with terracotta decoration. The Broletto houses the interesting **Museo Lapidario del Broletto**.

Piazza Martiri della Libertà ❹

The broad, rectangular square has porticoes on three sides and, in the middle, the *equestrian monument to Vittorio Emanuele II* (1881). On the south side is the *Castello Visconteo-Sforzesco*. On the north side, the pediment of the neo-classical **Palazzo Orelli** or *Palazzo del Mercato* (1840) is decorated with allegorical and mythological scenes. The main facade faces Largo Costituente. Here is the so-called **Barriera Albertina**, two small identical neo-classical buildings dating from 1837. Occupying the east side of the square is the Classical-style *Teatro Coccia* (1886). Near Piazza Martiri della Libertà, on the corner with Via Pier Lombardo, is **Casa Bossi**, a fine example of a 19th-century noble residence.

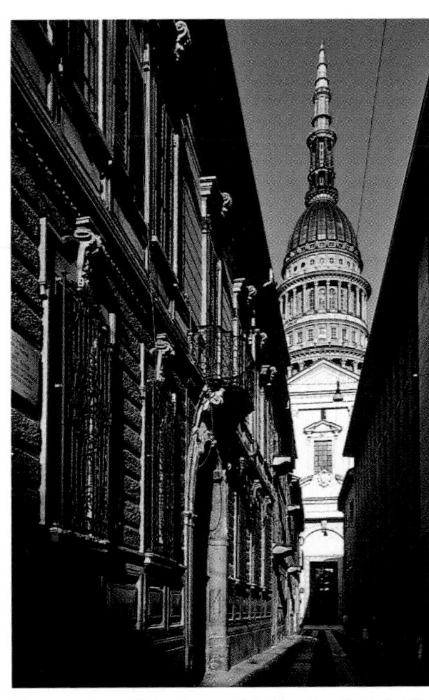

Novara: view of the dome of S. Gaudenzio from Via Pier Lombardo.

S. Gaudenzio ❺

The church of S. Gaudenzio, begun by Pellegrino Tibaldi in 1577 and completed in 1659, has a fine Baroque bell tower (1753-86). The **dome***, built by Alessandro Antonelli between 1844 and 1886 above the crossing of the transept, rests on four pairs of large arches which form a square above the pillars of the transept. The *interior*, built on a Latin-cross plan with three chapels on each side separated by pairs of half-columns, contains many fine *artworks*.

DAY TRIPS

ARONA [38 km]

Arona is situated opposite the Rocca d'Angera on the Lombardy side of Lake Maggiore, between the lake and the hills further inland. It has a pleasant historic center with some interesting works of art. The elegant **Piazza del Popolo**, with its magnificent views of the lake, is the heart of medieval Arona. A road winds up the hill from here to the colossal statue of S. Carlo Borromeo, locally known as **S. Carlone***, more than 20m high. There is a splendid view of the surrounding area.

ORTA SAN GIULIO [45 km]

Orta San Giulio is a charming little town in a splendid position on the eastern shore of Lake d'Orta, opposite the Isola di San Giulio. The town is a maze of narrow, steep, winding streets. The old houses and Baroque palazzi have porticoed courtyards and pretty wrought-iron balconies. This charming, elegant lakeside resort attracts many visitors. On the main square stands **Palazzotto della Comunità** (1582), supported by a broad portico. To the right of it is *Casa Giani* (15C-16C) with a loggia; *Casa Margaroni*, with a small portico; *Palazzo Gemelli*, (late 16C) with a frescoed facade and a 17th-century rusticated doorway. At the top of the broad slope leading up from the square is the **Parish church of S. Maria Assunta**, with a doorway in Oira marble dating from 1485. The **Isola di San Giulio***, interesting historically and in a delightful setting, can be reached by boat from Orta San Giulio in a few minutes. The church on the island, the **Basilica of S. Giulio***, is one of Piedmont's most important Romanesque monuments. On either side of the facade is a small 12th-century tower. The pronaos dates from the 16th century. The massive bell tower with its three-light windows dates from the 12th century. *Inside*, pillars separate the nave from the two side-aisles. It has a raised transept, a crypt containing the relics of the saint, and an octagonal tiburium decorated in the Baroque style. The church abounds in *works of art*, including frescoes (14C and 15C), and, by the 4th pillar of the left transept, a magnificent carved **pulpit*** in black Oira marble resting on 4 columns (1110-1120). The **Sacro Monte di Orta***, a UNESCO World Heritage Site, dominates Orta San Giulio from the top of the promontory, now a Riserva Naturale. There are two parts to the hill: the hillside with its ancient broad-leaved deciduous trees, and the monumental area on the top, where the lovely paths, trees and grassed areas are carefully tended. The *Sacro Monte*, begun in 1591 and completed in 1760, contains 20 chapels (the 21st is unfinished). They contain frescoes (17C and 18C) and 376 painted, life-size, terracotta statues depicting scenes in the Life of St Francis of Assisi. Across the lake, perched on a rocky promontory above vertical cliffs, is the **sanctuary of Madonna del Sasso**. Built in the 18th century in the Baroque style on a Greek-cross plan, it contains interesting cycles of *frescoes* and a fine **Pietà** (16C).

Orta San Giulio: Palazzotto della Comunità with its characteristic portico and sun-dials, dating from 1582, in Piazza Mario Motta.

VERBANO-CUSIO-OSSOLA

Verbania, conceived in 1939 by uniting the towns of Intra and Pallanza, is the capital of the province of Verbano-Cusio-Òssola. (Cusio is the Roman name for the area of Lake Orta.) The town thrives on the tourism generated by the fact that it is attractively positioned on the shores of Lake Maggiore. Pallanza, of Roman foundation, looks out across the lake towards the Borromeo Bay near Stresa. The town's buildings are medieval and Baroque. Some of the villas have magnificent gardens, built in the 18th and 19th centuries. The town is a lakeside garden, the ideal place for anyone wanting to spend a relaxing holiday in beautiful, soothing landscape.

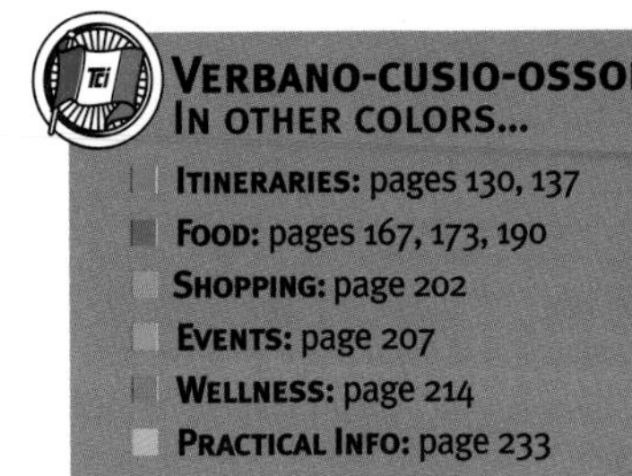

VERBANO-CUSIO-OSSOLA IN OTHER COLORS...

ITINERARIES: pages 130, 137
FOOD: pages 167, 173, 190
SHOPPING: page 202
EVENTS: page 207
WELLNESS: page 214
PRACTICAL INFO: page 233

Lungolago/Esplanade ❶

In Via Cietti, near the *Lido*, is *Casa De Latti* (14C). Continuing along Viale delle Magnolie you come to Piazza Garibaldi, with lovely views over to the islands of Golfo Borromeo. Beyond the old harbor is the Villa del *Kursaal*. Its beautiful garden looks over to the little *Isola di S. Giovanni*, and its 17th-century *Palazzo Borromeo*, set in luxuriant vegetation. The esplanade continues beyond the **Promontorio della Castagnola***, thus named because it was once covered with chestnut trees. These splendid villas surrounded by delightful gardens, are decorated in the Eclectic and Art-Nouveau styles.

Oratorio di S. Remigio ❷

This little church dedicated to St Remigius is a delightful Romanesque building

Verbania 1: 21 000 (1 cm = 210 m) 0 200 400 m

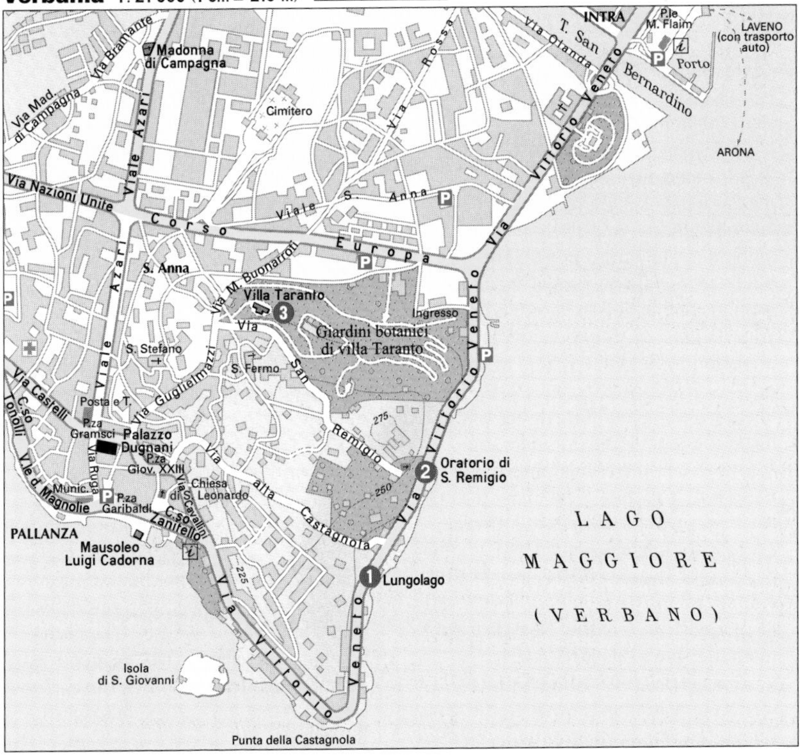

dating from the 11th-12th centuries with a 16th-century portico. Inside are fragments of 12th-century frescoes, two 15th-century frescoes (an Assumption and a Deposition) and another depicting the *Madonna and Child* (1528).

Villa Taranto ❸

The villa, which dates from 1875, was named after the Duke of Taranto, a title given by Napoleon to an ancestor of the last owner of the estate, the Scotsman Captain Neil MacEacharn. This famous English-style landscaped **garden****, with its paths, terraces, lawns, fountains, waterfalls and pools, contains hundreds of plants and trees, brought here between 1931 and 1936. It constitutes one of the finest collections anywhere of European and exotic botanical species. There are eucalyptus, magnolias, water lilies, lotus flowers, and rare tropical plants as well as chestnuts, birches, tulips, dahlias, paulownias, asters, azaleas, narcissus, rhododendrons, hydrangeas and magnificent beeches. In spring, when the flowers are in bloom, the garden with its lakeside setting is a marvelous sight.

DAY TRIPS

ISOLE BORROMEE [3 km]

Isola Bella** lies offshore from Stresa. Until the late 16th century, it was just a small fishing port. In 1632, Count Carlo III Borromeo decided to build a pleasure palace here for his wife, Isabella d'Adda. And so the monumental **Palazzo Borromeo*** was built, surrounded by one of the finest examples of an Italian Baroque *garden*. This compact, 4-story building is preceded by beautiful flights of steps. It houses the **Museo Storico e Artistico**. The decoration and furnishings of the luxurious rooms (the *Ballroom*, the *Alcove Room*, the *Throne Room*, the *Bedroom*) is original. The underground rooms have been made into artificial *caves* with tufa walls inlaid with marble and shells. The *art gallery*, *chapel* (1884) and the *Galleria degli Arazzi* with its splendid 17th-century Flemish tapestries are well worth a visit. The **garden*** is divided into ten terraces which slope gradually down to the lake. Decorated with statues and fountains, it has many rare and exotic plants.
On the last terrace is a magnificent stone *theater*, with a unicorn, the symbol of the Borromeo family, on the top. Most of **Isola dei Pescatori***, north-west of Isola Bella, is a picturesque little fishing-town with narrow, winding streets and charming views. **Isola Madre***, the largest of the islands, has a splendid **botanical garden** with rare and exotic plant species. Various species of birds roam free here, especially white peacocks. The garden is laid out around another of the Borromeo residences, an 18th-century villa with huge rooms. It houses *collections* of furniture, paintings and sculptures, as well as two unusual collections of 18th- and 19th-century marionettes and 19th- and 20th-century dolls. It also has a collection of scripts and scenery from miniature theaters.

STRESA [25 km]

This well-known lakeside resort is set in a lovely position opposite the Golfo Borromeo and its islands. It became a popular holiday destination in the 18th century, and its popularity grew in the 19th century. Many of the hotels and villas on the esplanade were built in the early 20th century, often in a sophisticated Art-Nouveau style.
Facing the lake, in the spacious *Piazza Marconi*, where the boat jetty is located, is the neo-classical *Parish church of S. Ambrogio* (1790).
It contains some good statues and paintings of the 17th-century Lombard School. Just beyond the church is *Villa Ducale* (1770), where, in 1855, the philosopher Antonio Rosmini died. It now houses a small *museum* about his life. South of the town, on the road to Arona, is the magnificent **garden of Villa Pallavicino***, with wonderful views down to the lake. This botanical garden is very famous because it has an enormous variety of species: splendid *magnolia grandifloras*, cedars of Lebanon, rhododendrons, azaleas and camellias. The garden is also a kind of zoo, where many of the animals roam freely. They include roe deer, llamas, Tibetan goats, rheas, ferrets, zebra, kangaroos, macaques, flamingoes and tortoises.

VERCELLI

The area around Vercelli is also known as the 'rice plain' because it is completely flat and dominated by rice farms. Rice-farming came to the Vercelli area in medieval times thanks to Benedictine and Cistercian monks. By the early 16th century, rice was already being exported from this area. Subsequently, large-scale canal-building programs ensured that there was a regular supply of water to the rice-farming area. Today, Vercelli is Europe's main rice-producing area. The rectangular fields are separated by low mud banks which retain the water. From March to October the rice-fields are flooded. In spring they look like a lagoon of geometric shapes with the occasional stand of poplars. The area has a rich historic and artistic heritage. Vercelli, situated on Sesia River, began as the Roman town of Vercellae. The town's medieval prosperity can be seen in the church of S. Andrea. The old center is still intact, surrounded by tree-lined avenues which follow the lines of the town's medieval walls. Famous architects, including Filippo Juvarra, Benedetto Alfieri, Bernardo Antonio Vittone and Ignazio Amedeo Galletti introduced Vercelli to the severe, elegant lines of Piedmontese Baroque.

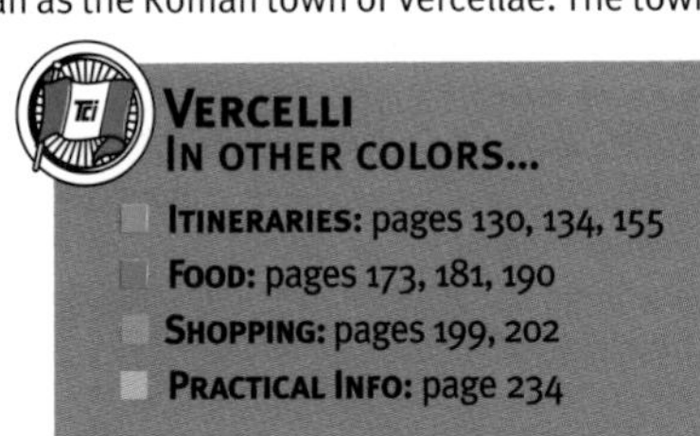
VERCELLI
IN OTHER COLORS...
ITINERARIES: pages 130, 134, 155
FOOD: pages 173, 181, 190
SHOPPING: pages 199, 202
PRACTICAL INFO: page 234

Basilica di S. Andrea ❶

The Basilica of S. Andrea, Vercelli's most important monument, built between 1219 and 1227, incorporates both Gothic features (rampant arches, doors with deep embrasures, Gothic capitals) and others associated with the Romanesque style of Lombardy and Emilia (small hanging arches, blank walls). The result is a building of rare beauty and majesty. The facade, framed by two tall bell towers, has three doorways with deep embrasures. Above the central door is a lunette depicting the **Martyrdom of**

Vercelli 1:18 000 (1 cm = 180 m)

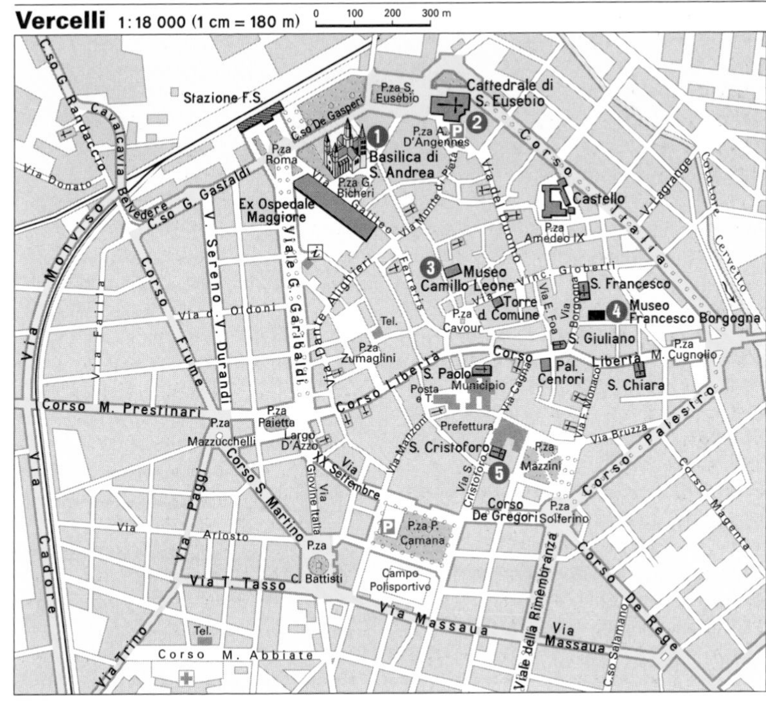

St Andrew (c.1220) and a rose-window. At the top are two rows of superimposed blind arcades. On the right-hand side, slender rampant arches spring up from the buttresses to rest on the sides of the nave. Above the crossing of the transept is an octagonal tiburium and a small tower with a spire. To the right is a bell tower, built between the end of the 14th century and 1407. The interior is built in the form of a Latin cross with a nave and two side-aisles in the Gothic style. There are clusters of piers with two sets of *capitals* supporting the ribbed vaulting. The top of the tiburium is decorated with a carving depicting the *Evangelists*. At either end of the transept is a large Baroque *confessional* dating from the 17th century. The *choirstalls* (1511) in the apse are decorated with marquetry work. To the left of the building is what is left of the *abbey*. There is a beautiful *chapter-house* with vaulting supported by four central columns and *frescoes*. From the **cloister**,

Basilica of S. Andrea

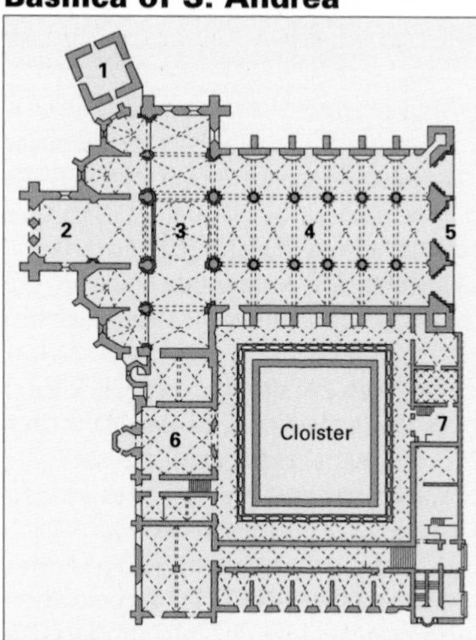

1 Bell tower (1407)
2 Apse
3 Tiburium
4 Nave
5 Main doorway
6 Chapter-house
7 Cloister entrance

TCI HIGHLIGHTS

Golf

Surprisingly, Piedmont has 49 golf-courses. They include some of Italy's best courses, both in terms of the nature of the course and their natural setting. They can be found in all kinds of landscape: by lakes, on hills and in the mountains. The courses all have different characteristics and each has plenty to offer golfing tourists, whatever their level of expertise.

Many of the courses are associated with a high-quality hotels and other facilities which, in many cases, benefited from restructuring carried out in view of the approach of the Turin Winter Olympics in 2006.

For information about the courses in Piedmont, we suggest you consult the website www.federgolf.it and select the region which interests you.

Many golf-courses are situated within a radius of about 15km on the west side of Lake Maggiore. They include the Alpino di Stresa Golf Club (see photo), one of Italy's first golf-courses: 9 holes, built in 1924 taking advantage of the natural landscape, at an altitude of 700m; the Golf Club des Iles Borromées, 18 holes, set in a birch wood, with breathtaking views of the five lakes and their islands, the Arona Golf Club, 9 holes, open all year, the Golf & Sporting Club Verbania, an informal, friendly club where the 9-hole course and executive course are open year-round, thanks to the local micro-climate; the Piandisole Golf Club, a typical mountain course, at an altitude of 1,000m, is surrounded by an old forest, with considerable height differences which pose a serious challenge. The Circolo Golf Bogogno, situated in the undulating countryside between Lake Maggiore and Lake d'Orta was voted best Italian golf-course 1997. It has two 18-hole courses, each one slight different. The Castelconturbia Golf Club, with its three 9-hole courses set in hilly landscape, has twice hosted the Italian Open and, in 2004, was voted best course in Italy. Another course which has benefited from this title several times is the Golf Club Biella Le Betulle. Its 18-hole course takes advantage of its inimitable natural landscape, with very few man-made additions.

with its 13th-century stone basin, there are lovely views of the church. Opposite the church, the portico with pointed arches belongs to the old *Ospedale di S. Andrea* (1224), a vast complex with a lovely 15th-century *hall*.

Cattedrale di S. Eusebio/ Cathedral of St Eusebius ❷

The cathedral dedicated to St Eusebius, Vercelli's first bishop, was built on the site of an earlier church and has been altered many times. The bell tower is all that remains of the medieval church. The presbytery and the apse date from 1572-78, but the front of the church dates from the 18th century (B. Alfieri built the neo-classical pronaos). The dome dates from the mid-19th century. The majestic, somber interior is arranged in the form of a nave and two side-aisles, separated by rows of pillars with paired columns. Above the altar is a majestic silver-plated **Crucifix***, made between 999 and 1026.

Museo Camillo Leone ❸

The museum was created at the wishes of a local notary, Camillo Leone, who left all his collections to the Istituto di Belle Arti. These are now housed in two buildings, each of which has an interesting history. The 15th-century *Casa Alciati* (where the original painted decoration has been restored) and a connecting wing added during the Fascist era contain an interesting archeological collection with finds from the Paleolithic and Neolithic eras, Roman amphoras and sarcophagi, Greek, Apulian, Messapian and Etruscan vases, Etruscan bucchero-ware, Cypriot ceramics, Egyptian grave-goods, glass-ware, Roman and Christian inscriptions, parts of an **11th-century mosaic floor** and **sculptures** from the cathedral. There is an important **stele** known as the *stone of Acisio*, found in the bed of the Sesia River. Each side is engraved with an inscription, one in Latin and one in Celtic characters. This and the two *sarcophagi* of young women all date from the 1st century BC.

Around Turin there are two courses which have been voted best course in Italy: at Fiano Torinese, the **Circolo Golf Torino La Mandria**, where there are two 18-hole courses, set in an area which was once part of the royal La Mandria estate and which has hosted the Italian Open, and the **Golf Club I Roveri**, with 36 holes. At Stupinigi, south of Turin, the **Golf Club Stupinigi** has a 9-hole course, open year-round.
At Carmagnola there are two fine 18-hole courses in a hilly setting: the **Golf Club I Girasoli** and the **Golf Club La Margherita**.
Between the Langhe hills and the Alps, in the Province of Cuneo, the **Golf Club Cherasco** has an 18-hole course laid out at a range of altitudes.
Golf-courses in the Monferrato include the **Golf Club Villa Carolina**, at Capriata d'Orba (Alessandria), with a 27-hole course set in an ancient park, and a club house in an 18th-century villa; the brand new **Golf Feudo di Asti**; the **Margara Golf Club** at Fubine (Alessandria), a 36-hole course with an extremely demanding championship course, and the **Golf Colline del Gavi**, an 18-hole and a 9-hole executive course at Tassarolo, on the slopes of the Ligurian Apennines. Piedmont can also claim to have Europe's highest golf-course, the **Sporting Club Sestrieres Circolo Golf**, an 18-hole course at 2,035m above sea-level.

The Baroque *Palazzo Langosco* (now beautifully restored) contains collections of the applied arts, paintings, costumes, ceramics and furniture. Highlights include three caskets (12C-15C), some 15th-century frescoes and pulpits, and splendid *majolica*, *bronzes*, *porcelain*, *glass-ware*, and *silver-ware*.

Museo Francesco Borgogna ❹

The elegant neo-classical Palazzo (1836) which now houses the collection was bought in 1882 by a local lawyer, Avvocato Antonio Borgogna, with the aim of creating a museum in memory of his father. The gallery was created thanks to the private collections of the founder, a philanthropist with a passion for collecting works of art. The collection has gradually grown over the years. On the ground floor: Rooms 1-4 contain detached frescoes from churches in the Vercelli area; Room 5: **paintings** of the Italian School; Room 6: 16th-century Venetian **works** (including a *Deposition* by Titian); Room 7: *diptychs* attributed to late 15th-century painters from southern France and other fine **works** by Piedmontese painters. Rooms 11 and 12 contain more fine paintings, and Rooms 13 and 14 contain *frescoes*. On the first floor, Rooms 4 and 6 contain **works** by Flemish, German and Dutch painters.

S. Cristoforo ❺

The church of S. Cristoforo was built in 1515. The apse and the tiburium date from this period, whereas the rest of the building was altered in the 18th century. The inside is organized in the form of a nave and two side-aisles. The most interesting features are in the chapels in the apse, which are decorated with **paintings*** by Gaudenzio Ferrari (1529-34), one of the finest expressions of Renaissance art. At the back of the apse is the altar-piece of the **Madonna of the Orange Tree**, while, in the right transept, the chapel dedicated to St Mary Magdelene is frescoed with a wonderful and painfully expressive **Crucifixion** and scenes from the life of the saint, including the **Arrival of Mary Magdalene, Lazarus and Martha at Marseilles**. The chapel of the Blessed Virgin contains an *Arrival of the Magi,* a marvelous and intense **Assumption** and some interesting gray monochrome *grotesques*.

DAY TRIPS

SACRO MONTE OF VARALLO [55 km]

In 2003, the pilgrimage site of the Sacro Monte of Varallo was designated a UNESCO World Heritage Site. Situated on a rocky spur above the town at an altitude of 608 m, the pilgrimage complex is set in the **Riserva Naturale Speciale del Sacro Monte di Varallo**, a park laid out in the Renaissance style with a beechwood and ancient box, yew, holly and field elm trees. The Sacro Monte was conceived as a religious complex with a message. Built between 1486 and 1491, its purpose was to enable pilgrims who could not make the journey to the Holy Land to see all the most important pilgrimage sites associated with the Life of Christ. The master entrusted with giving concrete form to the evangelical ideas of Bernardino Caimo, the monk who founded the complex, was Gaudenzio Ferrari, who worked here as painter, sculptor and architect from 1507 to 1528. During the following centuries, additions and changes were made, until the 'New Jerusalem' had a fine church and 45 chapels, either isolated in the vegetation of the park or incorporated within the main complex. The **Basilica dell'Assunta**, the main focus of the Sacro Monte, was begun in **1641** and completed in **1728**. Its white marble facade dates from 1896. It has a single nave lined with side-chapels and a dome above the high altar containing an astonishing Baroque rendering of the *Assumption,* with 142 polychrome terracotta statues and 514 painted figures. The 45 **chapels** are decorated with frescoes and groups of highly expressive, life-size, polychrome wooden and terracotta figures depicting episodes in the Life of Christ.

VARALLO [62 km]

This is a prosperous little town situated at the confluence of the Sesia River and the Mastellone Stream. On a rocky promontory above Piazza Vittorio Emanuele II is the **Collegiate church of S. Gaudenzio**, an impressive building surrounded by a loggia, rebuilt in the 18th century on the site of a 13th-century

Sacro Monte of Varallo

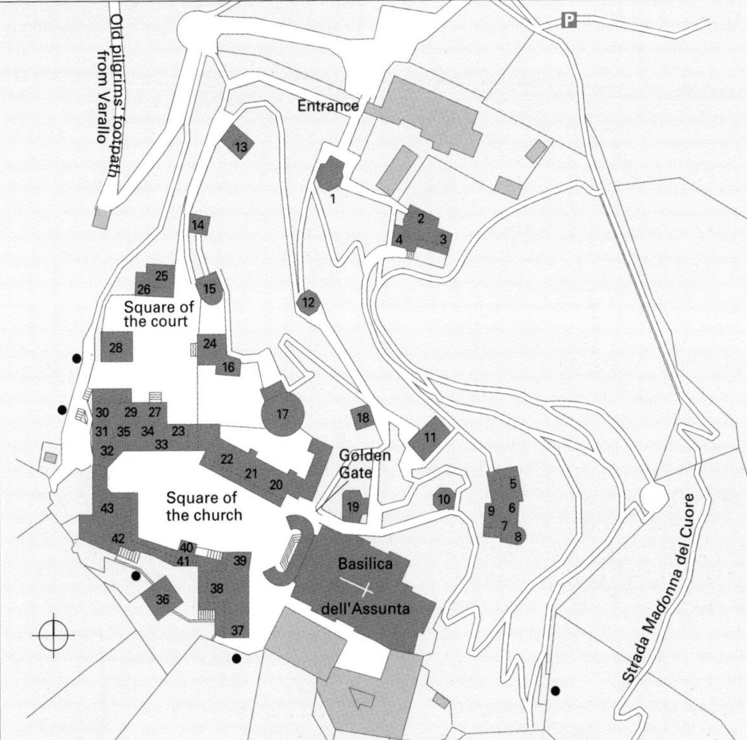

1 Adam and Eve
2 The Annunciation
3 Mary visiting Elizabeth
4 Joseph's first dream
5 The Adoration of the Magi
6 The Nativity
7 The Adoration of the Shepherds
8 The Presentation of Jesus at the Temple
9 Joseph's second dream
10 The Flight into Egypt
11 The Slaughter of the Innocents
12 The Baptism of Jesus
13 The Temptation of Jesus
14 Jesus and the Good Samaritan at the Well
15 The Healing of the Cripple
16 Jesus brings the widow's son back to life
17 The Transfiguration of Jesus on Mount Tabor
18 The Raising of Lazarus
19 The Entry into Jerusalem
20 The Last Supper
21 Jesus in the Garden of Gethsemane
22 Jesus waking the Apostles
23 The Arrest of Jesus
24 Jesus is brought before Annas
25 Jesus before Caiaphas
26 Peter's Atonement
27 Jesus is brought before Pontius Pilate
28 Jesus is brought before King Herod
29 Jesus returns to Pontius Pilate
30 The Flagellation of Jesus
31 The Mocking of Jesus
32 Jesus is brought before the Magistrate
33 Jesus is shown to the people
34 Pontius Pilate washing his hands
35 Jesus is condemned to death
36 The Ascent to Calvary
37 Jesus is nailed to the Cross
38 The Death of Jesus
39 The Deposition
40 Mary mourning the Dead Jesus
41 Jesus is wrapped in the Shroud
42 Altar of St Francis
43 Jesus is placed in the Tomb

● Viewpoints
P Car park

church. Inside, the single nave is decorated with polychrome marble altars and, in the apse, a **polyptych** by Gaudenzio Ferrari (1520-22). Walking south from the piazza along Corso Roma, you come to the **church of S. Marco**. Built in the Romanesque style and altered since, this is one of the oldest churches in the valley. It contains 16th-century frescoes by the school of Gaudenzio Ferrari. **Palazzo dei Musei**, in Via Maio, houses both the **Pinacoteca**, with a fine collection of paintings, frescoes, stuccoes and furnishings, and the **Museo Pietro Calderini**, with its mineral, paleontological, ornithological, ethnographical, numismatic and archeological collections. On Piazza Gaudenzio Ferrari is the **church of S. Maria delle Grazie**, built between 1486 and 1493. Inside, the back wall of the church is covered with a spectacular fresco cycle of 21 panels depicting the **Life of Jesus*** painted by Gaudenzio Ferrari in 1513. Marvelous from the point of view of composition and color, the center of the cycle is dominated by a solemn *Crucifixion*. Gaudenzio Ferrari also painted the grotesques and the frescoes in the chapel on the left in 1507.

The spectacular mountains of Piedmont and the Valle d'Aosta, including some of Europe's highest and most beautiful peaks, offer a wide range of runs: from difficult runs for more experienced skiers to the long, broad runs which sweep down valleywards through the pine trees. Wherever you go, you can be sure to find excellent accommodation (in many cases you can ski right up to the front door of the hotel). For those who prefer peace and quiet, there are still places where the silence, the fresh mountain air and the unspoiled scenery make it seem like another world. At many ski resorts, thanks

Ski

to modern, well-designed ski-lifts and cables cars, and a multitude of runs, you can ski on various mountain slopes without ever repeating the same run twice.

Highlights

- Sestriere, a skier's paradise.
- Sauze d'Oulx, with spectacular views over the Susa valley and 400km of runs.
- The Indian Park at Breuil-Cervinia, excitement at high altitude.
- Glorious skiing on long, broad runs at Gressoney.

Inside

96 **Valle d'Aosta**
109 **Piedmont**

La Thuile

Lifts and related facilities: open from November to April

The last ski resort before the French border, La Thuile stands in the centre of a vast bowl trapped between the Venoise and Mont Blanc massifs and within sight of the majestic outline of the Testa del Rutor. It is one of the most popular winter resorts in the Vallée area, with good accommodation and modern facilities. However, the hamlet has maintained its traditional mountain identity, with a welcoming and pleasant feel that has helped it to earn three Alpine stars from

SKI RUNS
Downhill skiing
98 km, including 22 covered by artificial snow spraying
blue **13** red **17** black **6**
Cross-country skiing
35 km

LIFTS
Cable cars 1
1 La Thuile-Les Suches 1466-2176
Chairlifts 10
2 Bosco Express 1471-2088
4 La Combe 2176-2326
5 Chalet Express 2084-2345
6 Chaz Dura 2301-2576
7 Chaz Dura Express* 2164-2564
10 Argillien Express 2001-2397
11 Arnouvaz 1937-2238
12 Belvedere* 2323-2612
13 Fourclaz Express 2015-2488
14 Piccolo S. Bernardo Express 2188-2531
Ski-lifts 6
3 Piloni 2030-2174
8 Les Suches 2153-2296
9 Gran Testa 2297-2394
15 Edelweiss 1472-1500
16 Baby 1476-1490
– Magic carpet*

* These lifts have been altered or enlarged.

Legambiente. The skiing is on the southern slopes of Chaz-Dura and is part of one of the largest ski areas in the Alps. The valley enjoys a microclimate that, with constant low temperatures, practically guarantees good snow, although there is also artificial snow spraying as needed. The cross-border link to the French resort of La Rosière means it is possible to ski on two sides of the Alps with a single skipass. Indeed, there are 67 routes, ranging in difficulty and altitude (from about 1,470 up to 2,612 m at the top of the Belvedere cableway). The most beautiful ski runs are route no. 7 (11 km), which goes from Chaz-Dura (2,579 m) down to La Thuile (1,441 m) past various refuge huts and through thick fir forests with occasional, stunning views of Mont Blanc, and the more demanding route

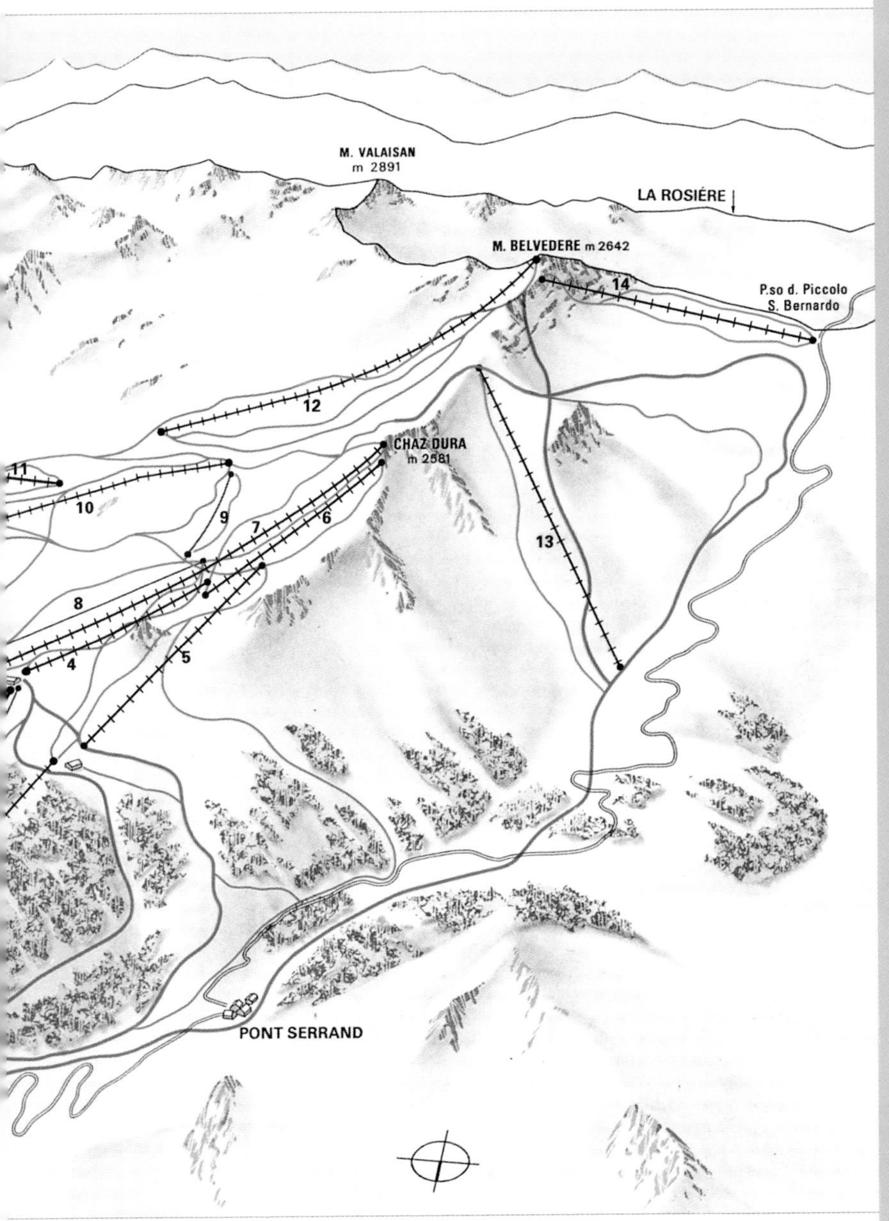

no. 3 (3,5 km). The latter is used in international downhill skiing competitions and runs from Chaz-Dura down to the resort, entering the wood at Les Suches.
In total, including both the Italian and French sides, there are 150 km of ski runs, accessible via a series of modern lifts. In addition, there is a free 'skibus' (shuttle service) and children can enjoy themselves either at the 'baby park in the snow' or the 'miniclub'. La Thuile also has something for cross-country skiers. Besides the training area, there are four trails (of 3, 5, 7.5 and 10 km) near the resort and in the Petosan bowl that head through thick woods and across sun-drenched plateaus where one can enjoy the majestic view of Mont Blanc.

SKI RUNS
Downhill skiing
100 km, including 18.6 covered by artificial snow spraying
blue **6** red **13** black **4**
Cross-country skiing
46.2 km of trails of varying difficulty

LIFTS
Chécrouit-Val Veny
Cable cars 4
1 Val Veny 1293-1912
2 Courmayeur 1208-1702
3 Youla 2363-2624
4 Arp 2620-2755
Chairlifts 8
6 Pra Neyron 1689-2024
7 Maison Vieille 1703-1960
8 Dzeleuna 1892-2080
9 Peindeint 1664-2030
10 Zerotta 1520-2080
11 Bertolini 1767-2247
12 Plan de la Gabba 2055-2334
13 Aretù 1921-2250
Cable cars 1
5 Checrouit* 1704-2260
Ski-lifts 3
15 Chiecco 1707-1790
14 Le Graye I 2008-2298
16 Tzaly 1955-2000
Magic carpets 1
– Dolonne 1212-1697
There is a new lift not marked on the map.

*This lift has been changed.

Courmayeur/Chécrouit-Val Veny

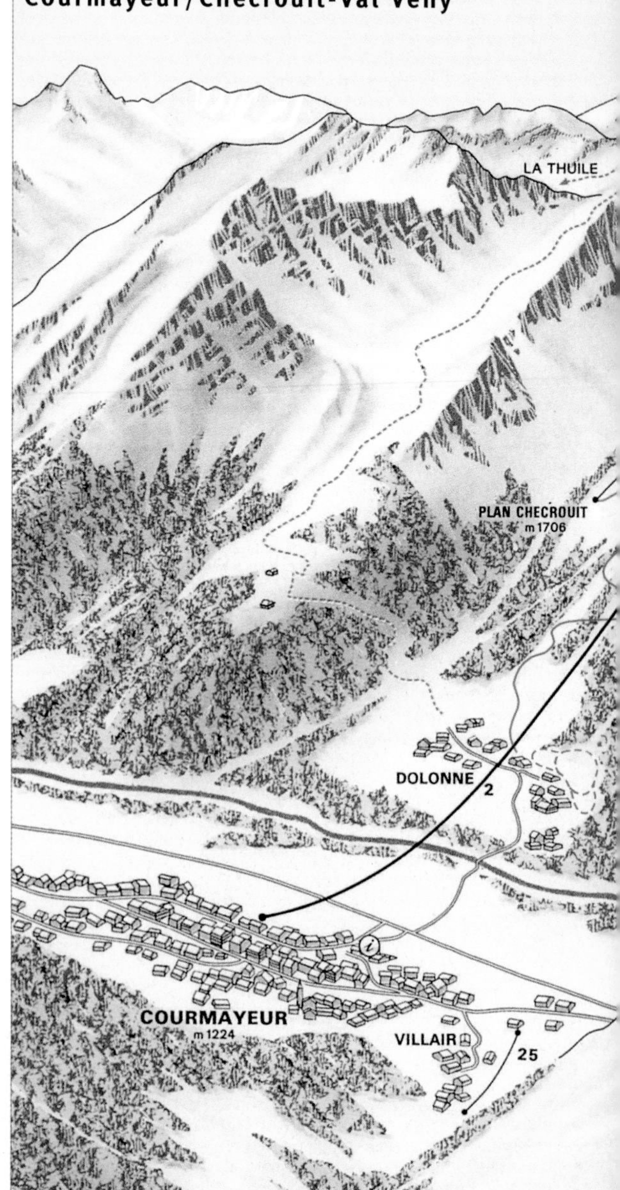

The ski-mountaineering routes are also excellent and the heli-skiing service makes it easy to reach the best surrounding peaks. The most notables routes are those that start from Testa del Rutor (3,486 m) or the Rutor ice-falls, and the climb to Miravidi (3,051 m) followed by the descent to La Thuile. These excursions are possible in February and March, but only with an Alpine guide.

Courmayeur

Lifts and related facilities: open from December to April

This elegant ski area at the foot of Mont Blanc has been awarded three Alpine stars from Legambiente. It sits in the shadow of four soaring mountains, Grand Golliaz, the Léchaud point, Aiguille des Glaciers and Mt Dolent, and runs along the two deep valleys of

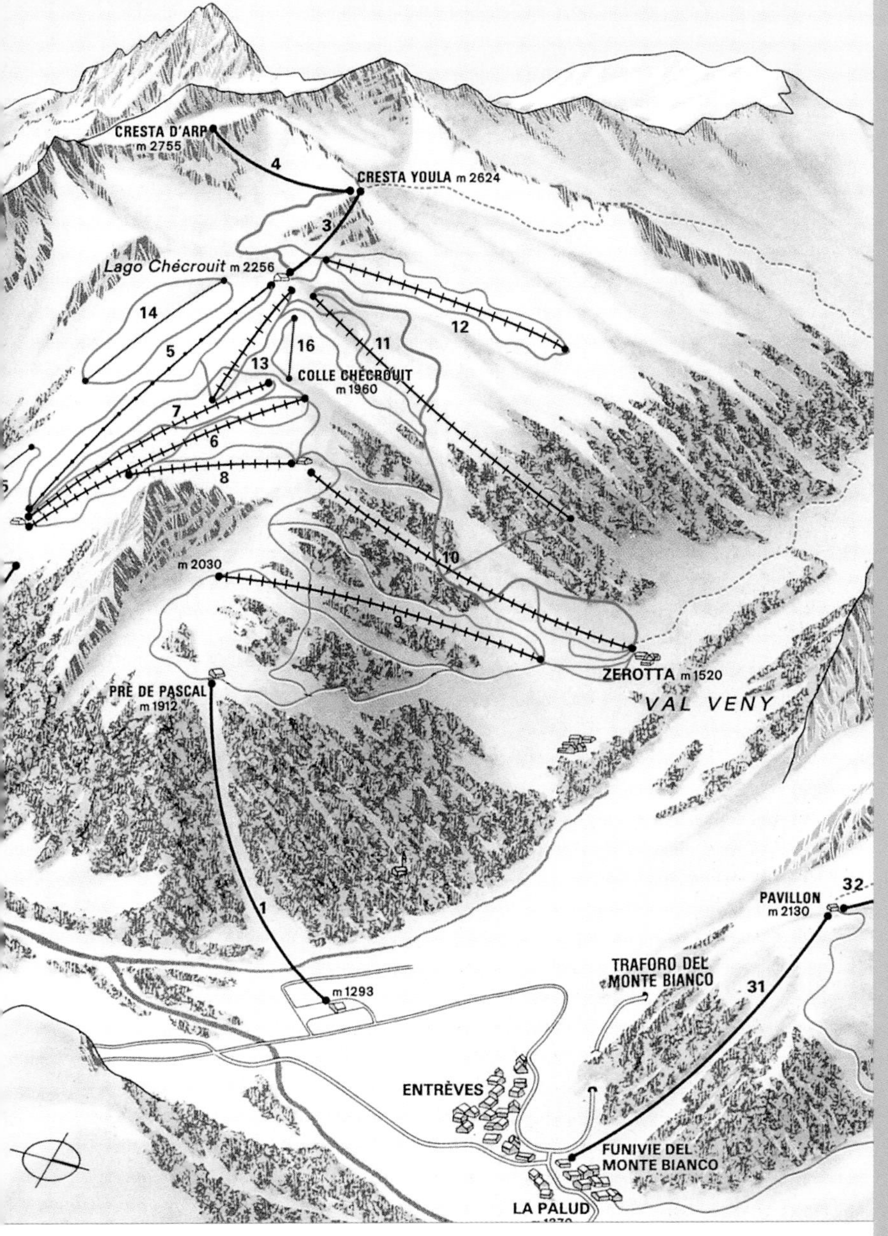

TCI HIGHLIGHTS

Legambiente

Legambiente, Italy's most diffuse environmental organization, and the Touring Club of Italy have undertaken a project aimed at protecting mountain environments. In this context, Legambiente has chosen and classified a series of mountain hamlets in terms of environmental protection, and quantity and quality of accommodation and tourist infrastructure. On this basis, they have uncovered places where modern tourist development happens hand-in-hand with safeguarding the environment. The chosen centers, awarded from one to five "Alpine stars", are then noted for their commitment to sustainable environmental management, the quality of the landscape and the town centers, the protection of the local artistic and cultural heritage, and the suitability of the place and the services to humans.
As such, the goal of this "sign" of environmental tourist quality is to encourage public and private operators to undertake actions that will improve quality in such a way as to improve the quality of the place for both residents and visitors.

Veny and Ferret, where there are six large glaciers. It is one of the most famous ski resorts in the world, largely because of the spectacular, varied ski runs and lifts, and the high standard of the accommodation. This ski area in the Mont Blanc valley includes La Salle, a relaxing hamlet where there is good downhill skiing and lovely excursions, Morgex, which has some lovely cross-country skiing trails in the Arpy valley, and Pré-Saint-Didier, home to one of the most spectacular ravines in Valle d'Aosta. It is easy to enjoy yourself on the 23 well-groomed runs that cover a 100 km, including roughly 20 km that are part of a well-organized artificial snow-spraying program. The network of lifts is vast, with the Arp cableway reaching an altitude of about 2,750 m. The skiing is on two slopes, both with different characteristics: Veny has wide, wooded runs while Checrouit cuts across vast, grassy plateaus. It is also possible, with an appropriate guide, to undertake some thrilling off-piste adventures. These run through the 24 km of the Vallée Blanche: starting from the Helbronner point, on the Gigante glacier, you then head down the slopes of Mer de Glace to Chamonix, across the steep walls of the Toula glacier, and then once more along the trails that lead into the Veny valley or to La Thuile. The Alpine guides of Courmayeur also organize special off piste and snowboard 'ski' schools. Indeed, lovers of the snowboarding can try a special cross-border run at Plan de la Gabba: 500m of cambered turns, jumps and moguls. The surrounding woods are also a good place for off-piste boarding, with some natural jumps. Plan-Pincieux lies in the Ferret valley, at the foot of Grandes Jorasses, and is the start point for four cross-country circuits (3, 5, 10 and 11 km) that lead to Lavachey and Arnouvaz. There are also three other circuits (3, 3.2 and 11 km) departing from Dolonne, Entrèves and Arpy. For lovers of heli freeriding, Courmayeur has a range of heliski and heliboarding options on Mont Blanc.

A section of the Pra Neyron run.

Breuil-Cervinia

Lifts and related facilities: open from October to April

Lying at the foot of the pyramid-shaped granite mass of Cervino (the Matterhorn), Breuil-Cervinia is one of the best known ski resorts in the Alps, a white expanse that runs from 3,480 m at Plateau Rosà, touches the 3,883 m of Piccolo Cervino and climbs the 4,478 m of the summit of Cervino. Breuil-Cervinia, a trendy, modern and innovative skiing capital, has an excellent network of lifts.

The Breuil-Cervinia ski area is one of the most beautiful in the Alps, with 60 snow-covered, well-groomed runs (many are covered by artificial snow spraying) that wind for over 350 km across the Breuil bowl, Valtournenche and Zermatt in an area straddling the Swiss-Italian border. The modern network of lifts makes it possible to get from Plan Maison to the Bontadini-Colle del Teodulo area and Plateau Rosà. From here, it is possible to take the Klein Matterhorn cableway, the highest in Europe, to Zermat, or to head to Piccolo Cervino. From Plateau Rosà, more advanced skiers can head back to Breuil-Cervinia via the 11km-long Ventina run, with plenty of walls and thrilling fast, straight sections. From the Cime Bianche saddle, the Goillet chairlift takes you to the runs in the Valtournenche ski area, while the Bardoney and Cieloalto chairlifts take you up to some wonderful runs. Next to the Fornet di Plan Maison is the Indian Park, a true fun park on the snow that is aimed at snowboarders who love grooving to music. It is nearly 1km long and has an area with three different-sized kickers, boardercross with a halfpipe and jumps, as well as a track for speed and slalom events. There is a 3 km cross-country skiing circuit, at 2,050 m, in the shadow of the splendid Grandes Murailles and Cervino. Alternatively, at Valtournenche (Champlève), there is a 4.8 km circuit. The heli-skiing service makes it possible to take on some thrilling off-piste runs. The ski-mountaineering is also notable, with some good full day itineraries that explore the pristine, fresh snow. Finally, Cervinia has a proud history of professional, experienced Alpine guides and these are the ideal people to help you learn about mountaineering in winter and ice-climbing.

The Breuil-Cervinia ski area.

Valtournenche

Lifts and related facilities: open from December to April

This ski resort is dominated by the imposing, easily identifiable bulk of Cervino (the Matterhorn) and the Grandes Murailles mountain chain. Since the 19th century, Valtournenche has been closely tied to some major mountain-climbing exploits: it was the starting point for the discovery of various, memorable routes to scale Cervino. The resort slowly became an increasingly important downhill skiing resort and, today, it is one of the largest ski areas in Valle d'Aosta and, along with Breuil-Cervinia, it has been awarded three Alpine stars by Legambiente.

The skiing is in the vast bowl between Mt Roisetta and Gran Sometta, with the routes generally being easy or moderate. The useful skibus (shuttle) makes access to the lifts easy. Valtournenche has numerous runs, but there is also the link from the Superiore (upper) hill of Cime Bianche to the snowfields and lifts of Breuil-Cervinia and Zermatt, on the Swiss side of Cervino. Taken all together, this is one of the largest skiing zones in the Alps and makes it possible to spend entire skiing holidays without ever repeating a run. In addition, if you want to get in some summer skiing, you should head to the the Italian-Swiss Plateau Rosà glacier. For off-piste skiing, you can try, with an Alpine guide or ski instructor, the delightful route that goes from the Inferiore (lower) and Superiore hills of Cime Bianche, crosses the deep Courtod valley and then leads to Saint-Jacques, in Val d'Ayas. The options for ski-mountaineers are plentiful: there are routes to the Falinère point (3 hrs), Petit Tournalin (6 hrs) and Mt Roisetta

LIFTS
Breuil-Cervinia
Cable cars 4
10 Breuil-Plan Maison II 2032-2557
12 Laghi Cime Bianche-Plateau Rosà 2825-3478
9 Breuil-Plan Maison 2030-2555
11 Plan Maison-Laghi Cime Bianche 2557-2911
Chairlifts 10
13 Cieloalto 2112-2480
14 Bardoney 2028-2475
16 Plan Maison 2545-2876
17 Fornet 2865-3048
18 Bontadini 3041-3332
19 Rocce Nere 2534-2870
20 Rocce Bianche 2542-2923
21 Plan Torrette 2471-2676
27 Pancheron 2633-296528
28 Lago Goillet 2691-3090
Ski-lifts 5
15 Baby La Vielle 2538-2595
22 Cretaz I* 2010-2212
23 Cretaz II* 2010-2127
25 Cretaz V* 2212-2498
26 Cretaz VI-Gran Roc* 2490-2685
Magic carpets 1
24 Cretaz IV (Baby Cretaz) 2011-2023

* These lifts are now chair-lifts.

Valtournenche
Cable cars 1
1 Valtournenche Salette 1562-2281
Chairlifts 2
3 Becca d'Aran 2229-2443
4 Roisette 2391-2874
Ski-lifts 5
2 Baby Salette 2269-2283
5 Motta 2270-2455
6 Bec Carrè 2421-2832
7 Du Col 2830-2898
8 Gran Sometta 2866-3100
A new lift goes from Valtournenche to Breuil-Cervinia

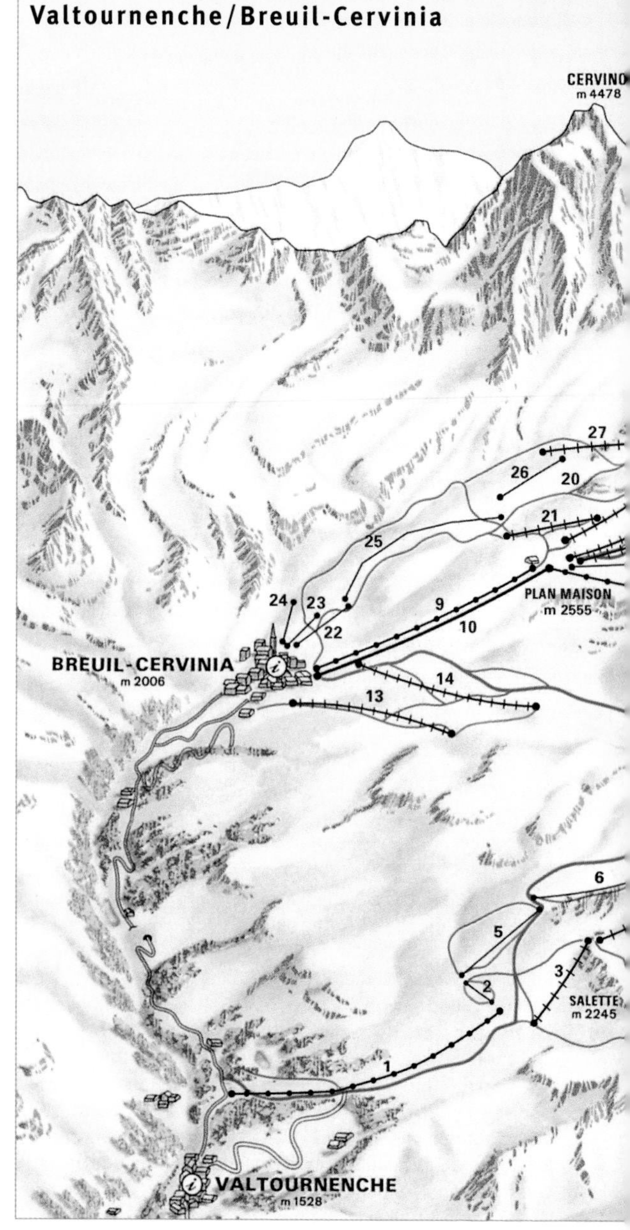

(5 hrs). There are two cross-country skiing circuits at Maën (6.5 km) and Champlève (4.8 km), as well as a trail in the Cheneil bowl, which can only be reached on foot or by skiing and offers stunning views of Cervino and the surrounding peaks: Becca d'Aran, Mt Roisetta, Mt Molar, Becca Trecaré, Grand and Petit Tournalin and the Falinère point.

Val d'Ayas

Lifts and related facilities: open from December to April

Val d'Ayas is dominated by the Monte Rosa mountain chain and has 14 peaks that soar over 4,000 m. As you head up the valley, you come to Brusson, home to international cross-country skiing competitions, the village of Antagnod, famed for its wide, sunny

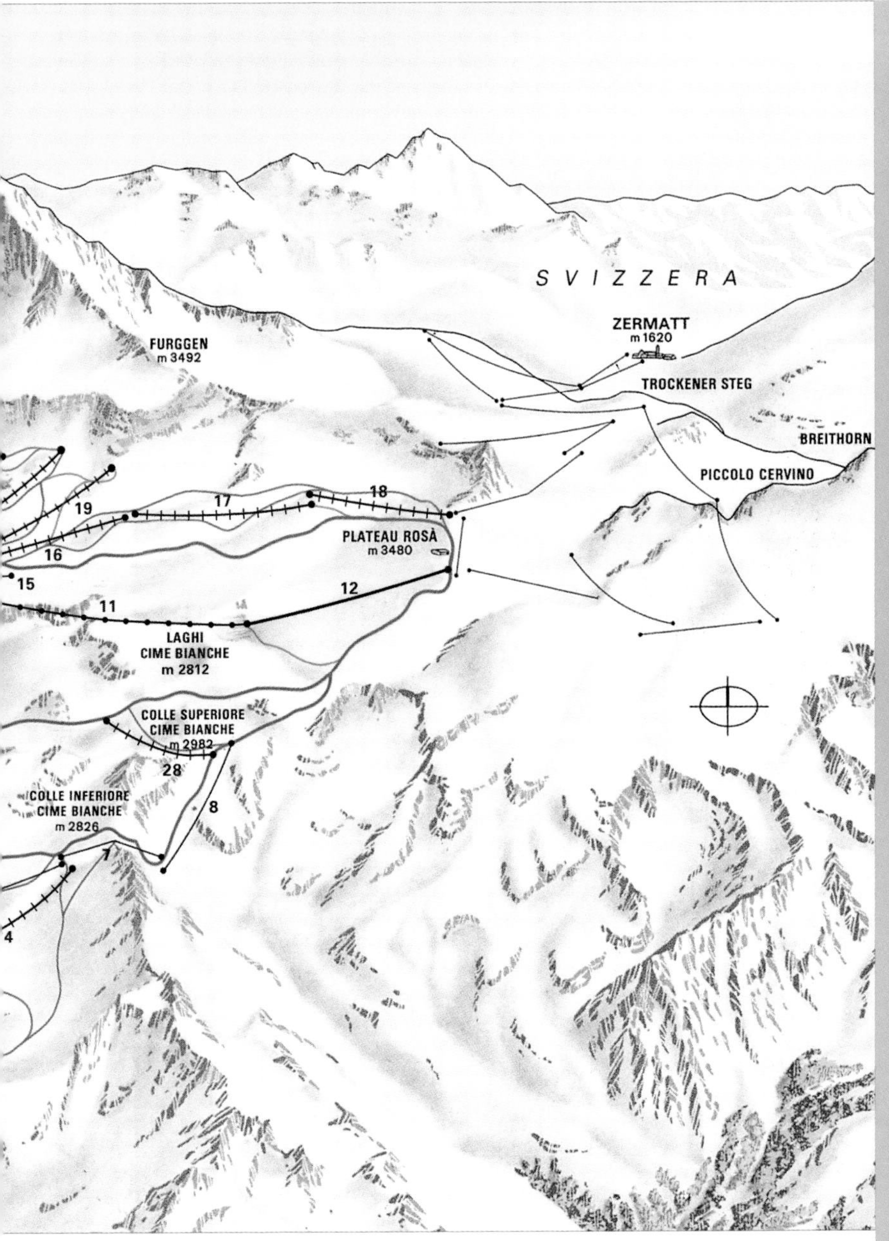

runs, and Ayas, which has been awarded 4 Alpine stars by Legambiente. Champoluc, the last village in the Evançon valley, stands in a lovely bowl in the shadow of the Monte Rosa massif. The skiing at Champoluc-Frachey is on the western slope of the Bettaforca hill, which has numerous runs, including the Contenerey one and the taxing Larici. Beyond the hill lies the Gressoney valley, and then Staffal. In addition to the Champoluc lifts, there are the Palasinaz ski runs, at Brusson, and the Antagnod lifts. There are many ski-mountaineering trails, especially on the Palasina point, which can be reached using the Estoul lifts, not far from Brusson. The glaciers in Val d'Ayas are the setting for the famous Trofeo Mezzalama, the oldest race in the whole Alps. For cross-country lovers, there are eight circuits, covering roughly 60 km: Brusson, which is also home to the well-equipped Foyer du Fond sport and accommodation complex, has the international Trois Villages circuit (10 km), one of the best in the world, Arcesaz (7.5 km) and the scenic Extrepieraz (7.5 km), as well as

SKI RUNS
Downhill skiing
74 km (53 in Gressoney-la-Trinitè and 21 in Gressoney-Saint-Jean) including 33 in Gressoney-la-Trinité and 7 in Gressoney-Saint-Jean covered by artificial snow spraying
blue **7** red **22** black **5**
Cross-country skiing
28.5 km (25 km in Gressoney-Saint-Jean and 3.5 in Gressoney-la-Trinité)

LIFTS
Antagnod
Chairlifts 2
- Boudin 1726-1878
- Antagnod-Pian Pera 1735-2304

Magic carpets 2
- Antagnod I and II 1767-1895

Brusson
Chairlifts 1
- Champeille-Litteran 1730-2230

Ski-lifts 2
- Estoul Baby 1803-1880
- Palasinaz I and II 1805-2090

Champoluc
Cable cars 1
1 Champoluc-Crest 1580-1993

Chairlifts 8
3 Crest Ostafa I and II 1995-2412
4 Ciarcerio-Belvedere 2217-2307
5 Ostafa-Colle Sarezza 2410-2703
6 Frachey-Ciarcerio 1623-1992
7 Pian di Tzeccon 1965-2009
8 Alpe Mandria 1971-2457
9 Bettaforca 2290-2701

Magic carpets 2
2 Fontaney I and II 1975-2000

Gressoney-la-Trinité
Cable cars 3
11 Staffal-Sant'Anna 1830-2150
12 Staffal-Gabiet 1819-2325

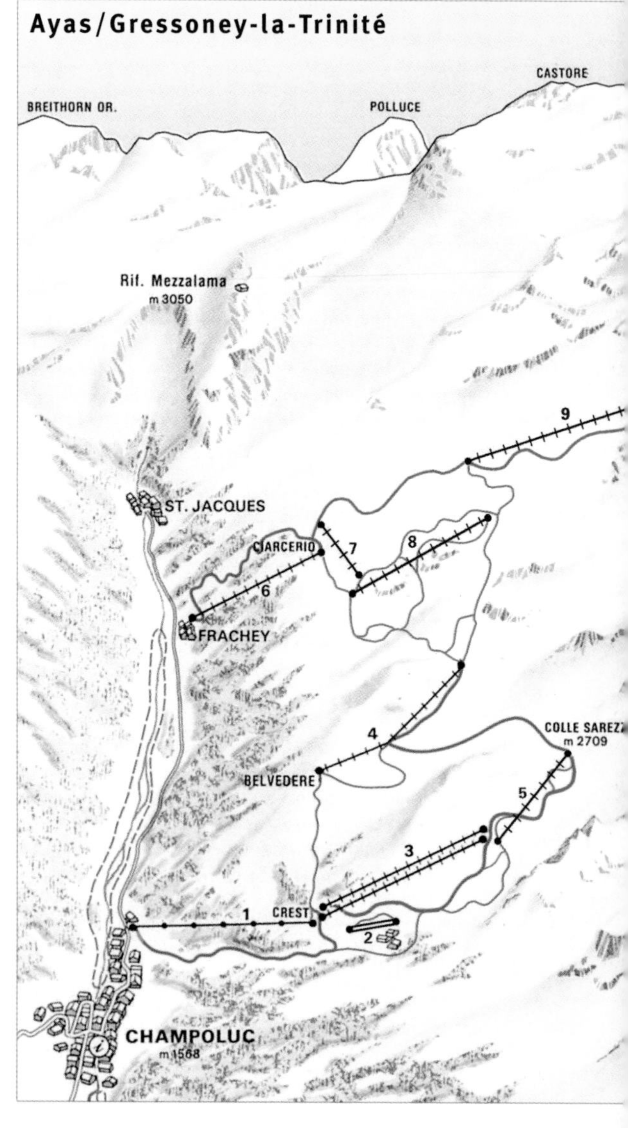

a training circuit; the Ayas municipality has Mentenc-Periasc (7.5 km), Barmasc-Antagnod (5 km), Varasc-Champoluc (6 km) and the easy Villy-Champoluc (3 km).

The Gressoney valley

Lifts and related facilities: open from December to April

The Gressoney valley, also known as the Lys valley, is located at the foot of the imposing Testa Grigia and surrounded by a glacier. It is also the central valley in the vast Monterosaski ski area. There are two main resorts: Gressoney-la-Trinité, at the head of the valley and awarded three Alpine stars by Legambiente, and Gressoney-Saint-Jean, which achieved fame as early as the last century and was chosen by Queen Margherita of Savoy as the setting for her castle. The Gressoney-la-Trinité resort has 53 km of runs, including some covered by artificial snow spraying; there are modern lifts on the Bettaforca hill (connection to Val d'Ayas), the Gabiet slope and the Jolanda point, leading up to 3,000 m at the Salati pass, which is the

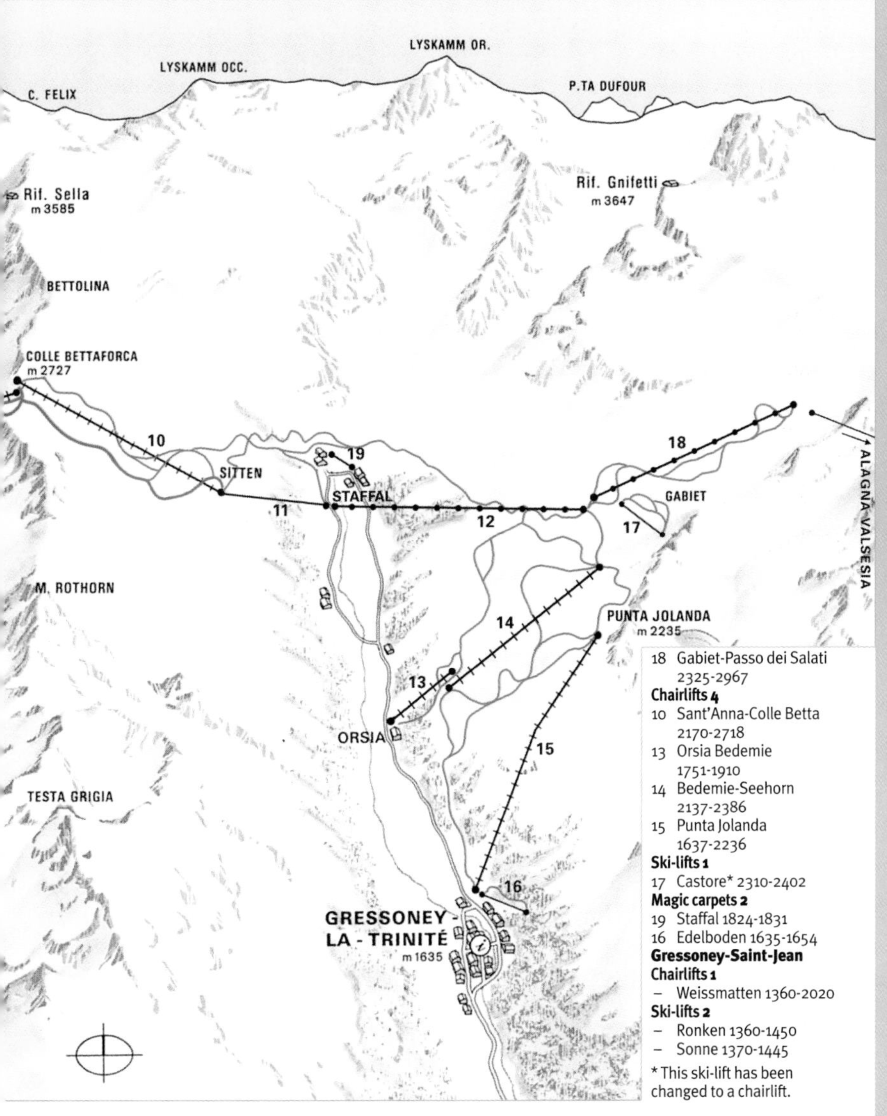

TCI HIGHLIGHTS

MONTEROSASKI

This is one of the largest ski areas in the Alps. It lies at the foot of Monte Rosa massif and between the peaks and hills of three valleys: Ayas and Gressoney, in Valle d'Aosta, and Valsesia, in Piedmont. This vast area has 200 km of ski runs, connected with modern, efficient lifts, thus ensuring a range of trails for all types of skiing. There is also a network of 56 runs that takes in the major towns and villages, such as Champoluc, Gressoney-la-Trinité and Alagna Valsesia, and the more compact resorts of Brusson, Gressoney-Saint-Jean and Antagnod.

starting point for the link to the Alagna Valsesia lifts. The off-piste skiing is between La-Trinité, Zermatt and Saas Fee or on the Monte Rosa massif, where there is also a heli-skiing service as well as numerous ski-mountaineering trails. There are three cross-country skiing circuits, creating a combined total of 10 km, and, from Staffal, a cable car takes you up to the

Pila

PUNTE DELLA VALLETTA
m 3090
m 2252
LA NOUVA
m 2309
m 2280
3
2
9
PILA
m 1790
10
11
Aosta
12

SKI RUNS
Downhill skiing
70 km, including 15covered by artificial snow spraying
blue **3** red **18** black **4**
Snowboarding
1 Snowpark

LIFTS
Cable cars 4
1 Gorraz-Grand Grimod 1869-2245
– Aosta-Les Fleurs 579-1373
– Les Fleurs-Plan Praz 1373-1540
12 Plan Praz-Pila 1540-1801
Chairlifts 9
2 Chamolè 1765-2309
3 La Nuova 1925-2252
4 Grimondet 1978-2348
5 Leissè 1871-2381
6 Couis I 2163-2705
7 Couis II 2157-2612
8 Grimod 2122-2257
9 Pila-Gorraz 1801-1877
10 Baby Gorraz 1832-1866
Ski-lifts 1
11 Baby Pila 1750-1780

3.5 km circuit near Lake Gabiet. There are 21 km of runs in the Gressoney-Saint-Jean ski area: the most notable is the black L. David, a favorite among skiers on the World Cup circuit. It starts from Weismatten and heads down through centuries-old Swiss stone pines and frozen lakes. Staffal is the starting point for thrilling ski-mountaineering trails (and off-piste skiing) that go up Monte Rosa to the Gnifetti point and the Regina Margherita refuge hut, the highest in the Alps. Alternatively, you can take a helicopter to the Lys hill and then head down the Swiss side of Zermatt. Saint-Jean has one of the longest cross-country skiing routes in Valle d'Aosta: 25 km divided into the five subsections of Dresal (8 km), Castello (7.5 km), Mulino (4 km), Woald (2.5 km) and Champsil (3 km).

Pila

Lifts and related facilities: open from December to April

The Pila bowl lies in a delightful natural setting, amid endless larch and fir forests. Many of the main mountains in the western Alps are visible: Mont Blanc, Grand Combin, Cervino (more commonly known outside of Italy as the Matterhorn) and Monte Rosa. The bowl is almost like a natural balcony overlooking the charming town of Aosta from beneath a chain of mountains that includes Mt Emilius, the Valletta point and the Tza

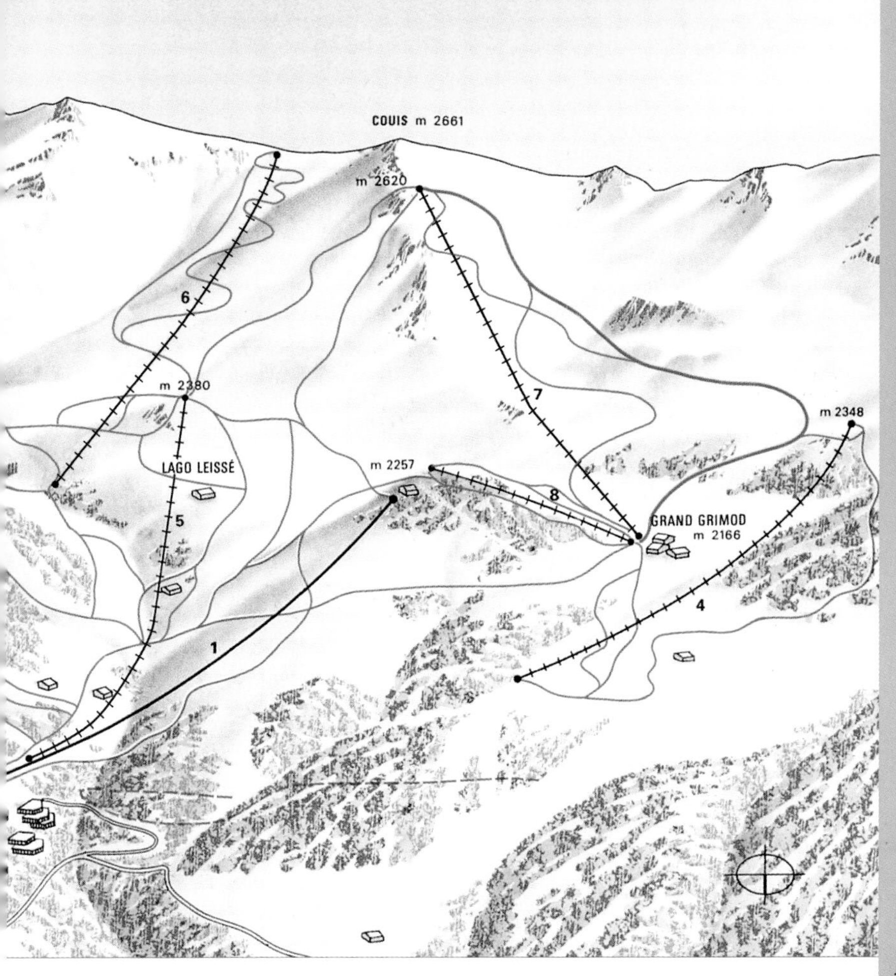

A wide open section of the Chatelaine run with delightful panoramic views.

Setze Couis and Drinc hills. This winter resort was built specifically for skiing, that is, it was created basically from scratch as a ski resort, and has various forms of accommodation (hotels, self-catering apartments and other resort accommodation) right behind the ski runs. It is also continually being modernized to ensure all aspects are up to date. The 70 km of well-groomed runs make this a skiing paradise. There are 25 runs encompassing most levels of difficulty: Baby Pila, Baby Gorraz and Grimod are for beginners, Leissé and Nuova are for amateurs, while experts can take on Couis 1 and 2, which have the added bonus of fantastic panoramic views of the peaks that enclose the Vallée area to the north, from Mont Blanc to Monte Rosa. In addition, there are comfortable lifts and snow cannons, ensuring artifical snow can be sprayed, if needed. Pila is also an ideal location for skiers who love carving (Bosco, Bellevue run) and for those who are fans of telemarking or boarding. For expert skiers, there is also a timed slalom section with gates and photocells at the end as well as a range of off-piste options that charge thrillingly through the woods, especially those starting from Pointe de la Pierre. For those who are just starting or who are looking to improve, instructors, specializing in various disciplines, are available and offer group or individual lessons. There are some ski-mountaineering trails, of varying difficulty and length, that start from the hermitage of S. Grato or the slopes of Mt Emilius. For snowboards there is a snowboard park with a funbox, rails and jumps for daring acrobatic flights as well as slides and a spectacular halfpipe made with permanent structures dug into the ground. Cross-country skiing is also catered for at the villages in the central Saint-Nicolas valley (2 circuits), Introd and Vetan, where the skiing area is at about 1,800 m.

The Chatelaine refuge hut.

PIEDMONT

Sestriere

Lifts and related facilities:
open from December to April

Around the world, Sestriere is largely synonymous with skiing, which is no surprise since this hill saw the creation of one of the first Italian ski resorts in the 1930s. Indeed, the resort was specifically built for this winter sport and is dedicated to what could be termed a 'complete skiing experience', perhaps explaining why it has been awarded 2 Alpine stars from Legambiente. The key elements for the creation of the resort were the notable altitude (2,035 m), the natural ski runs where it was easy to design pistes without pulling down hundreds of trees and the vast open views. In addition, the resort has been something of an international model for other resorts.

The location of the hill is also favourable: it is surrounded by peaks that soar over 3,000 m, such as Fraitève and Banchetta. The zone also has a solid tradition of involvement with sport at the highest level, hosting the Arlberg Kandahar skiing competition, World Cup events, the World Championships in 1997 and, most notably, the Torino Winter Olympics in 2006. Sestriere is at the heart of the largest ski area in Italy, the Vialattea, which also includes Sauze d'Oulx, Sansicario, Cesana Torinese, Claviere and Montgenèvre (France), amounting to an impressive total of 400 km of ski runs and over 80 lifts. This is a true skiing paradise, with ski runs for first-timers and average skiers, who can choose from an array of moderate runs, as well as some of the best black and competition level runs in Europe. The comprehensive artificial snow-spraying program ensures skiing even when there is minimal snow. The best area for beginners is the section between Borgata and the hill; at the summit, on the Sises slope, there are some lifts for young children. The options are endless for the average skier. Imagine immense, snow-covered hills that invite you to 'carve' them up. The entire Banchetta area, which is accessible from Borgata, is wonderful and was host to the men's speed skiing (downhill and SuperG) at the Winter Olympics in 2006. The show piste for the races was the Kandahar Banchetta-Giovanni Nasi, a challenging technical run that goes from the top of Banchetta down to the village, passing walls, sharp turns and spectacular jumps. The technical events for the men and women were held on the slopes of Sises, where the floodlit Giovanni Alberto Agnelli ski run is one of the best in the world for the special slalom. Those taking on the Giant Slalom had to start from higher up, at the Sises summit. This includes a super wall, but it should only be attempted by more advanced skiers. There are also some notable runs towards Sauze d'Oulx and Sansicario, which can be reached via the Triplex cable car from Borgata. An interesting option for relatively good skiers is to head down from here towards Sansicario, along the ski runs used for the women's races at the 2006 Winter Olympic Games, and then up to the Fraitève summit and on towards Jovenceaux along the lovely red 12 ski run. The total vertical drop for this route is over 1,000m. To head back up from Jovenceaux towards Col Basset, you cross the Sauze d'Oulx ski area, which is one of the largest in Vialattea. Finally, there are 10km of circuits for lovers of cross-country skiing.

The unmistakable towers of Sestriere.

SKI RUNS
Downhill skiing
400 km, including 100 covered by artificial snow spraying
blue **52** red **117** black **42**
in the whole ski area
Cross-country skiing
10 km
Snowboarding
1 Snowpark

LIFTS
Monte Fraitève-Col Basset
Cable cars 1
1 Col Basset 1846-2471
Grangesises
Ski-lifts 2
4 Clos dei Fiori 1857-2224
5 Clos dell'Acqua 2140-2380
Monte Sises
Cable cars 2
3 Garnel 1988-2286
6 Cit Roc 2029-2353
Chairlifts 4
2 Principi 2020-2107
7 Baby I and II 2052-2141
8 Sises 2305-2610
9 Jolly 2027-2054
Monte Banchetta
Chairlifts 1
11 Chisonetto-Banchetta 1934-2594
Ski-lifts 1
10 La Motta 2438-2838
Borgata Sestriere
Chairlifts 4
12 Nube 1840-2231
13 Anfiteatro 2080-2509
17 Capret 1850-2049
18 Trebials 1853-2124
Ski-lifts 3
14 Nube d'Argento 1840-2231
15 Orsiera 2090-2430
16 Combetta 1825-1910

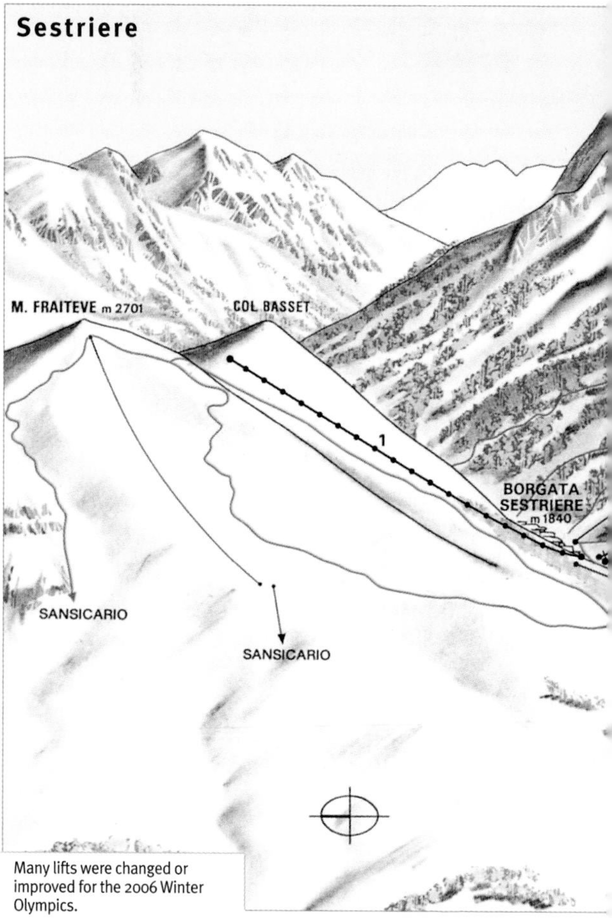

Sestriere

M. FRAITEVE m 2701
COL BASSET
1
BORGATA SESTRIERE m 1840
SANSICARIO
SANSICARIO

Many lifts were changed or improved for the 2006 Winter Olympics.

Sansicario

Lifts and related facilities: open from December to April

Sansicario was born out of nothing to become a ski resort and, although 40 years later, it followed the same model as nearby Sestriere. Once again, the plan was to create an ideal ski resort, although this time it was designed to meet the needs of more modern skiers and to cater for the advances in skiing. The result was a resort where the ski runs end right in the village and the preferred means of getting around is walking, or using escalators, rather than the car or some similar form of transport.

Sansicario owes much of its success to its location on a sunny, scenic balcony overlooking the Susa valley. The slopes that loom above the resort lead to the summit of Mt Fraitève and are covered by a large ski area with notable vertical changes. Despite the plentiful sunlight, the altitude and the position ensure good snow for skiing. Sansicario is an integral part of the Vialattea ski area and is largely on the northern side of Mt Fraitève, between 2,700 and 1,700 m. The majority of lifts are chairlifts. The nature of the slopes, where the gradient changes and wooded areas alternate with open fields, means there are wide, enjoyable ski runs. Most of the runs are of moderate difficulty, but there are some easier ones that glide down the sun-drenched slopes. The resort is also the ideal place for children to learn more about winter sports, especially at the "fun park", which has a special conveyor lift that is ideal for the youngest learners. For more advanced skiers, two runs are particularly notable, nos. 21 and 72. The former, which leads right into town

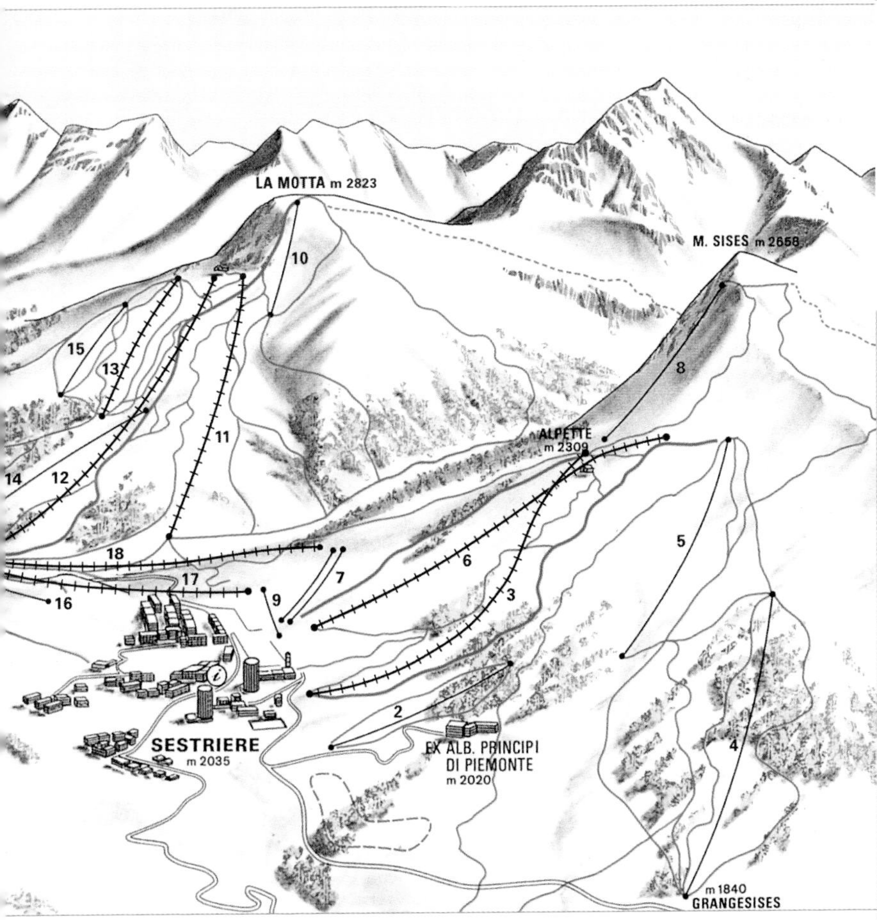

LA MOTTA m 2823
M. SISES m 2658
ALPETTE m 2309
SESTRIERE m 2035
EX ALB. PRINCIPI DI PIEMONTE m 2020
m 1840 GRANGESISES

with a vertical drop of around 1,000 m, starts off as a truly challenging black run above the forest on a steep slope. It then levels out somewhat, becoming a moderately difficult and then easy run, although the succession of curves, walls and false plateaus maintain the interest, especially if done at speed. No. 72, where the difficulty ranges substantially across the different sections and the vertical change is 750 m, is easier than no. 21 at first, but the section in the wood is more taxing as the trail is tight. After this tough part, it comes out of the wood directly into the resort. These slopes where used for the women's downhill and SuperG during the Winter Olympics in 2006. The skiing links to Sestriere and Sauze d'Oulx take just a few minutes and open up a range of options; the lifts can also be used to get to Cesana Torinese and then head up the opposite slope of Mts Luna and Claviere. The main ski runs are covered with artificial snow spraying if necessary. For cross-country skiers, there is a 10 km circuit.

A scenic ski run with a view of Mt Chaberton.

Cesana Torinese

Lifts and related facilities: open from December to April

Cesana Torinese is strategically located in one of the most important hubs of the Vialattea, which is a massive ski area where you can go to Sestriere, Sauze d'Oulx, Sansicario, Cesana, Claviere and Monginevro, without ever removing your skis. The resort has, along with San Sicario, been awarded three stars by Legambiente and is one of the most unique villages in the

The Soleil Boeuf refuge hut.

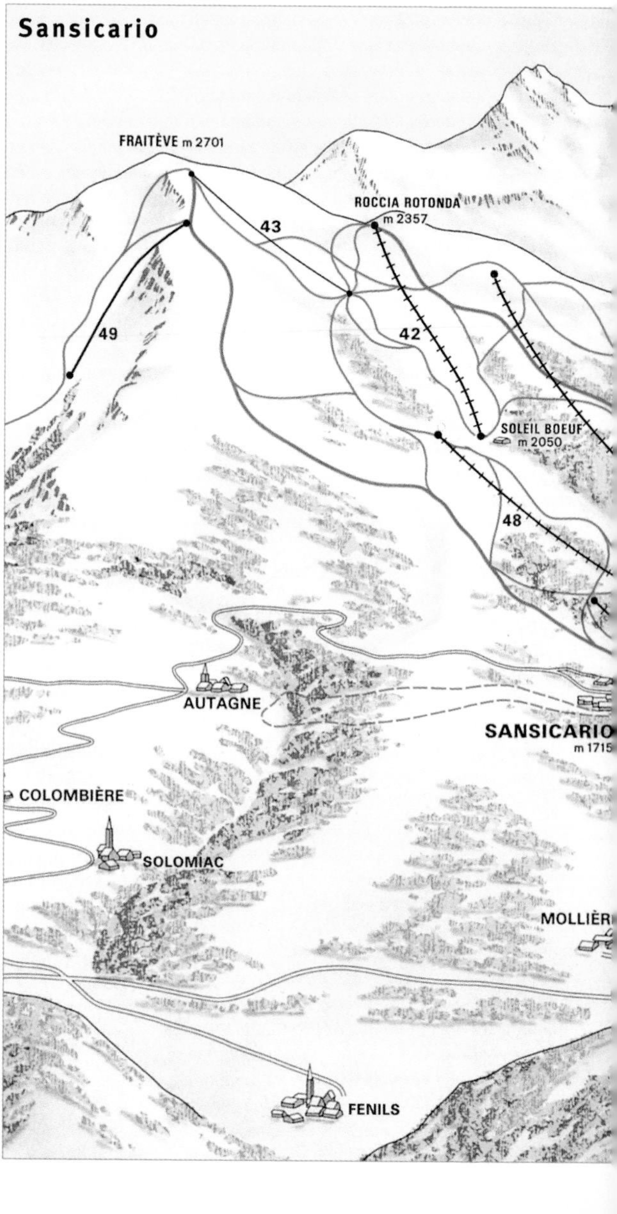

Sansicario

FRAITÈVE m 2701
43
ROCCIA ROTONDA
m 2357
42
49
SOLEIL BOEUF
m 2050
48
AUTAGNE
SANSICARIO
m 1715
COLOMBIÈRE
SOLOMIAC
MOLLIÈR
FENILS

SKI RUNS
Downhill skiing
400 km, including 100 covered by artificial snow spraying
blue **52** red **117** black **42** in the whole ski area
Cross-country skiing
10 km

LIFTS
Chairlifts 7
41 Ski-Lodge 1726-2253
42 Roccia Rotonda 2062-2486
44 Baby Sansicario 1704-1816
45 Pariol *
46 Forte *
48 Rio Envers 1708-2071
61 Rafusel 1359-1538
Ski-lifts 3
43 Fraitevé 2415-2671
47 Monterotta *
49 Nero Sansicario 2288-2610

Many lifts were changed or improved for the 2006 Winter Olympics.

area. It has a bob, skeleton and sledge track, which made it a key destination during the Winter Olympics in 2006. Two chairlifts upstream of the village climb towards Sansicario and the Monti della Luna area, one of the best options for people looking for a ski holiday on the move. By heading towards Sansicario, you reach the Sauze d'Oulx/Sestriere sector: a large area with a rich array of ski runs for everybody. The climb towards the Monti della Luna and the Claviere/Montgenèvre ski area is equally interesting. A series of lifts takes you up to 2,293 m at the Bercia hill: from here, you head back down towards Claviere and Montgenèvre, via the pass with the same name.
The Monti della Luna/Clavière/Montgenèvre ski area is one of the best for panoramic views and has numerous red and blue runs for average skiers, first-timers and those who are still finding their skiing legs. There are also some interesting black

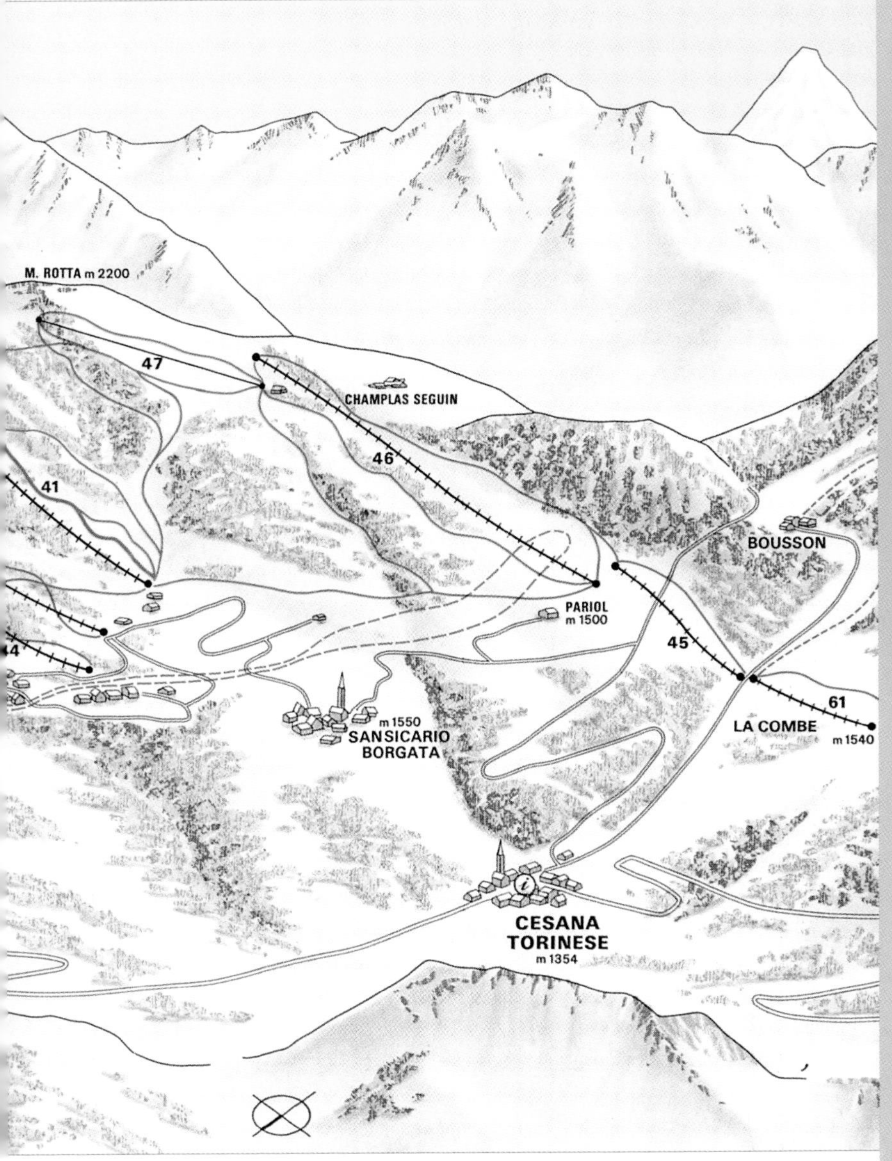

runs. One of these, for example, connects France and Italy by heading down from Colletto Verde at 2,560 m. Alternatively, to cross the border you can take an easy blue run at a lower altitude. The runs accessible using the Col Saurel chairlift are also worth trying. For lovers of cross-country skiing, there are 22 km of trails to be explored.

Claviere

Lifts and related facilities: open from December to April

Claviere has been awarded two Alpine stars by Legambiente and is the final village before the French border. As the resort is in the heart of the Monti della Luna/Montgenèvre ski area, it is an ideal base for exploring the Vialattea skiing zone, which has

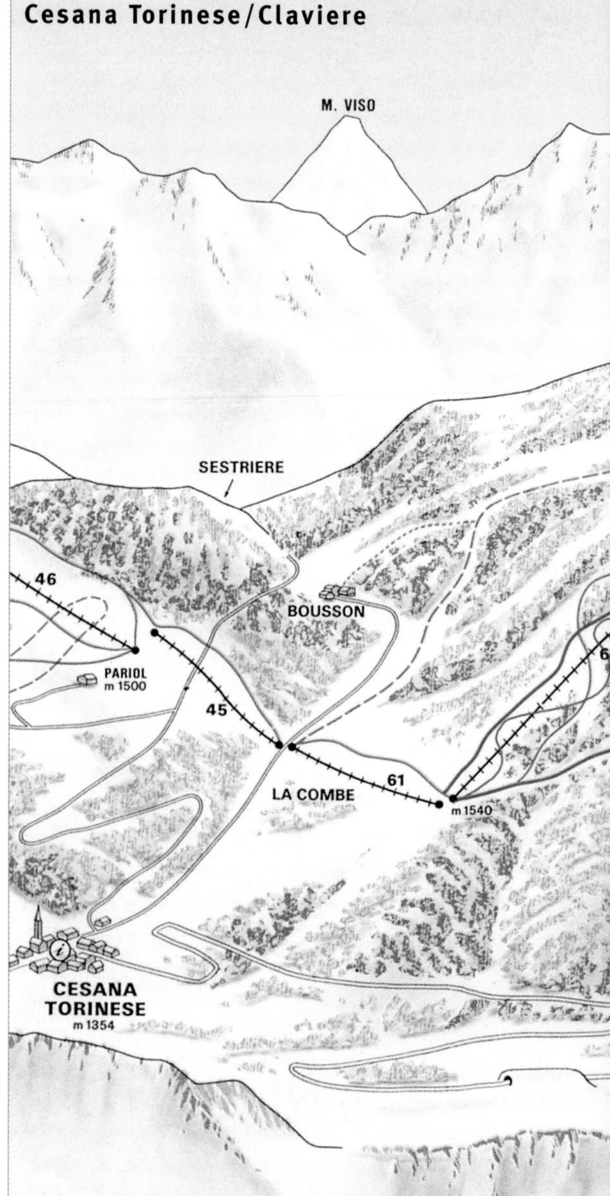

SKI RUNS
Downhill skiing
400 km, including 100 covered by artificial snow spraying
blue **52** red **117** black **42**
in the whole ski area
Cross-country skiing
16 km of trails of medium difficulty

LIFTS
Chairlifts 8
45 Pariol *
46 Forte *
61 Rafusel 1357-1536
62 Sagna Langa 1540-2029
63 Montanina 2000-2220
67 La Coche 1736-1947
70 Col Sounel 2065-2409
71 Col Boeuf 1750-2011
Ski-lifts 5
64 Bercia 2198-2284
65 Gimont I and II 2054-2297
66 Serra Granet I and II **
68 Baby Claviere 1731-1787
69 Baby Clot 1980-2073

Many lifts were changed or improved for the 2006 Winter Olympics.

over 80 lifts and 400 km of runs.
To reach the Sestriere/Sauze d'Oulx/Sansicario sector of this zone, you need to pass through Cesana Torinese and take two chairlifts that do not provide access to any particular runs. A ski-touring itinerary!
There are two chairlifts and one for younger children starting from the resort and leading to some lovely runs, including two black trails and a long blue one that heads all the way back to the resort. From the lower section of the ski area, you can reach France along a link that includes a red run and some lifts. The ski area runs as far as the Bercia hill, which is the point where you meet the lifts that go from Cesana to Col Saurel, at 2,409 m, and it is also one of the loveliest spots in

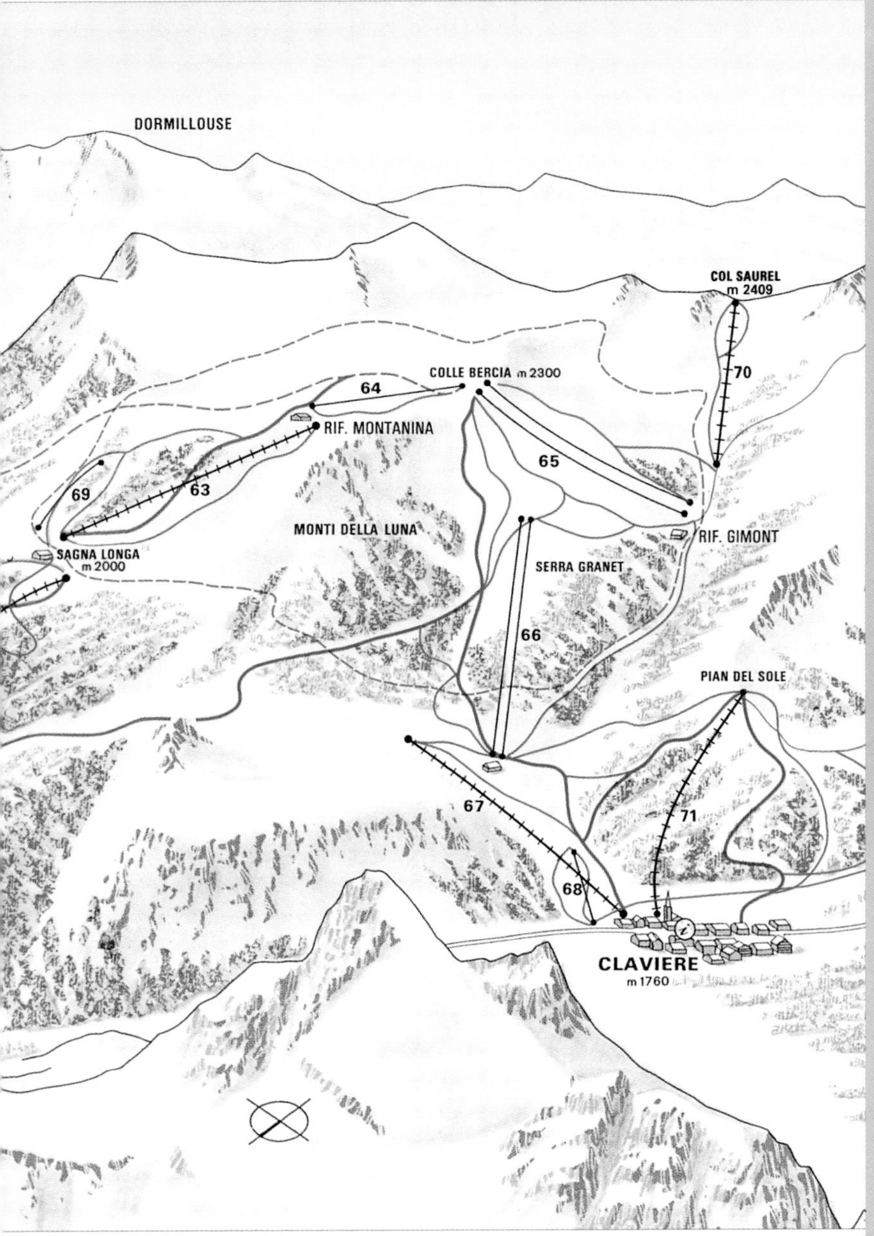

the Vialattea. The upper section tends to have moderately difficult ski runs, but there is also a simple run that takes you down into the valley from the Gimont refuge hut. The only section without any blue runs is the final one, near the Bercia hill and Col Saurel. By taking the red run that links this area to the French side of Montgenèvre, you find a series of easy numerous willow trees in the area. This scenic natural balcony overlooks the Susa valley and is dominated by the peaks of Genevris, Moncrons and Triplex. The location makes Sauze an ideal ski area, with various runs in both open and wooded stretches, wide-open panoramas and many hours of delightful sun. It is also home to some of the most formidable runs in the

SKI RUNS
Downhill skiing
400 km, including 100 covered by artificial snow spraying
blue **52** red **117** black **42** in the whole ski area
Cross-country skiing
13 km

LIFTS
Chairlifts 11
1 Clotes 1542-1731
3 Pian della Rocca 1720-2201
4 Sportinia 1565-2135
5 Jouvenceaux-Sarnas* 1392-1907
6 Sarnas-Sportinia* 1907-2158
7 Rocce Nere I 2134-2420
8 Rocce Nere II 2134-2420
9 Gran Comba 1500-1890
15 Triplex 2070-2450
16 Treceira 2412-2470
17 Basset 2170-2481
Ski-lifts 11
2 Baby Roch 1586-1700
10 Costapiana 2215-2288
11 Chardonnet I and II 1879-2296
12 Baby Genevris 1872-1987
13 Tuassieres 2178-2472
14 Moncrons 1948-2469
8 Rio Nero Sauze 2183-2450
19 Chamonier 2125-2456
20 Bourget 2123-2405
21 Mini Sportinia 2125-2150

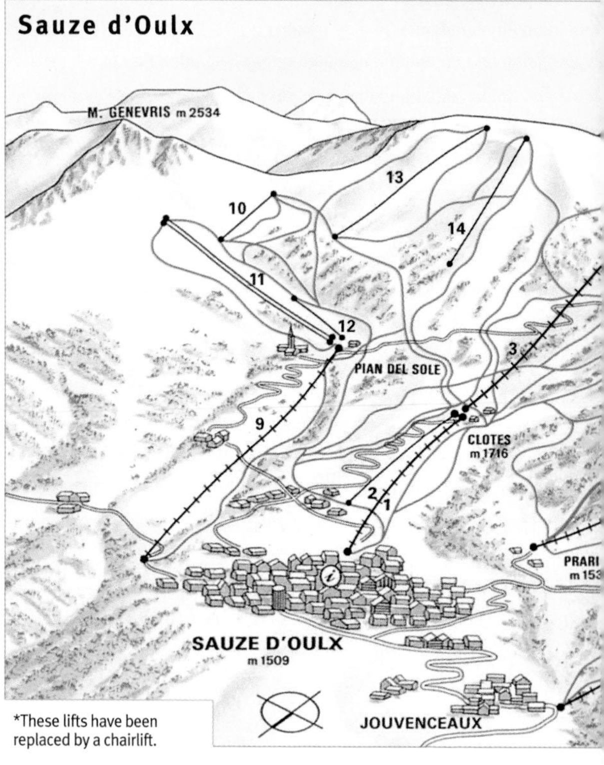

*These lifts have been replaced by a chairlift.

runs in the Prarial and Col de l'Alpet sections. This part of the Vialattea gets some of the best snow, thanks to the location, and the main runs in the lower half of the ski area are also covered by artificial snow spraying, if needed. Claviere is a good destination for cross-country skiers: a charming 16km circuit takes you to Montgenèvre and then back to the resort. The altitude ensures good snow even beyond the season's end.

Sauze d'Oulx

Lifts and related facilities: open from December to April

The name seems to have come from the

Vialattea and, during the 2006 Olympics, these were used for the freestyle events. This ski area is also in the heart of the main sector of the Vialattea, that is, the area around Mt Fraitève, and so has a wonderful array of ski runs and lifts. It is possible to reach, without having to remove one's skis, Sestriere and Sansicario. From Sansicario, it is then possible to reach the Monti della Luna area and Claviere, although this link is much longer and is better for a ski-touring holiday than a single run. The Sauze ski area has a total vertical drop of over 1,000 m, with the main lifts being chairlifts and draglifts. The location together with the

use of artificial snow spraying on some of the main runs (and at most altitudes) ensure good snow conditions throughout the season.
If the two black runs, that is 34 and 33, are not included in the equation, then this ski area is ideal for average skiers and beginners, with red runs and long blue trails connecting just about everywhere in the ski area. try out some of the 400 km of runs. From Col Basset, you head towards Sestriere on a red run, while from Fraitève, you would need to head to Sansicario along the taxing route 21, which is one of the loveliest in the entire Vialattea area, or on one of the interesting red trails. For lovers of cross-country skiing, there are 13 km of trails.

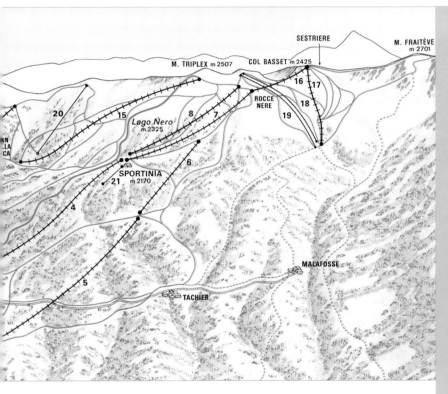

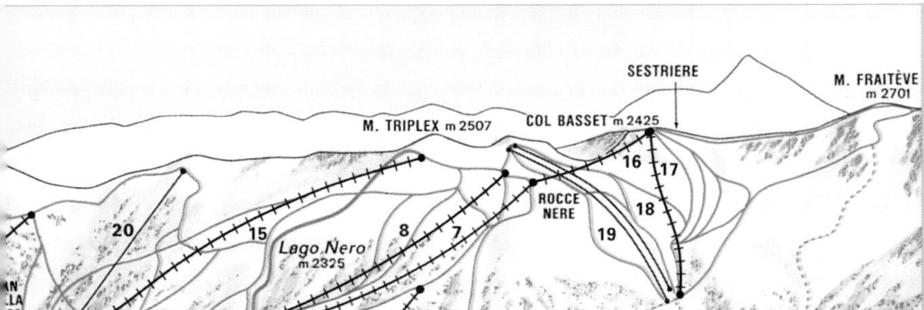

SESTRIERE
M. FRAITÈVE m 2701
M. TRIPLEX m 2507
COL BASSET m 2425
16
17
ROCCE NERE
18
19
20
15
Lago Nero m 2325
8
7
6
SPORTINIA m 2170
21
4
5
MALAFOSSE
TACHIER

Two consecutive chairlifts, with the first leaving from the center of the resort, take you up the mountains and then you can, for example, return to the resort on either red or blue runs. It is also possible to get back to the resort from the Col Basset area using only blue trails. More generally, the whole sector between Sauze d'Oulx, Sportinia and Jovenceaux is covered with exciting red runs. One of these, which is definitely worth trying, is no. 12, starting from Jovenceaux: a long, varied run with a notable vertical drop. Of course, Sauze d'Oulx is one of the best bases for a excursion towards Sansicario or Sestriere, where you can

A view of Sauze d'Oulx.

Bardonecchia

Lifts and related facilities:
open from December to April

Bardonecchia is a pleasant village that has been awarded two stars by Legambiente and can be seen as the birthplace of Italian skiing. It is home to 21 lifts and 110 km of runs. The ski area is large and divided into two parts: Jafferau and Mélezet-Colomion. At Jafferau, the vertical drop is greater, with skiing between 1,300 and 2,800 m, and the slopes face west. In the other section, the vertical drop is around 1,000 m and the slopes face north. There is something for all levels of skier, with some notable trails in the wood that are ideal for average skiers. The easiest runs are found at Campo Smith, Mélezet and in the middle of the Jafferau section. There are also some challenging trails for advanced skiers, such as the interesting ones reached on the Clos, Chesal-Selletta, Chesal-Seba and Mélezet-Colomion lifts as well as the one accessible via the Fregiusia-Plateau and Testa del Ban chairlifts at Jafferau. The altitude and the exposure ensure the skiing is good, and the use of artificial snow also helps when needed. The nature of the Bardonecchia runs has made them very popular with snowboarders. Indeed, this ski area was chosen for the Torino Winter Olympics in these events, with runs 23 and 24 of Mélezet being used. Run 23 is ideal, in terms of width and vertical drop, for a parallel giant slalom event: the run is wide and fast with gentle changes in slope. Run 24, by contrast, is best used as a halfpipe.

SKI RUNS
Downhill skiing
110 km, including 23 covered by artificial snow spraying
blue **18** red **18** black **2**
Cross-country skiing
9 km of trails of medium difficulty
Snowboarding
1 Halfpipe

LIFTS
Campo Smith Colomion
Chairlifts 4
1 Smith I 1279-1539
2 Smith 4 1273-1551
3 Prà Reymond 1506-1884
4 Pian del Sole 1526-1635
Ski-lifts 2
5 Colomion 1554-2037
6 Baby Scuola 1285-1309
Les Arnauds
Chairlifts 1
7 Les Arnauds 1337-1605
Ski-lifts 1
8 Del Clos 1591-2078
Mélezet-Valle Stretta
Chairlifts 1
9 Mélezet-Chesal 1375-1819
Ski-lifts 6
10 Baby Gavard 1376-1597
11 Chesal-Selletta I and II 1380-1416
12 Chesal-Seba 1788-2168
13 Del Bosco 1783-2118
14 Vallon Cros 2100-2395

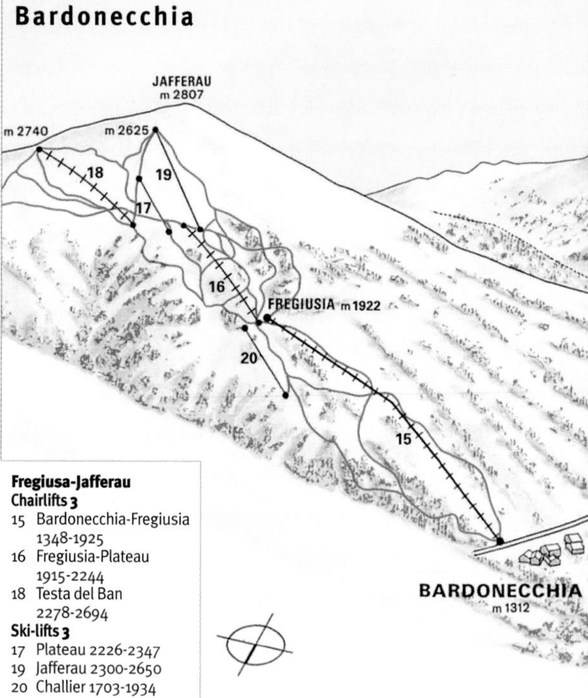

Fregiusa-Jafferau
Chairlifts 3
15 Bardonecchia-Fregiusia 1348-1925
16 Fregiusia-Plateau 1915-2244
18 Testa del Ban 2278-2694
Ski-lifts 3
17 Plateau 2226-2347
19 Jafferau 2300-2650
20 Challier 1703-1934

Macugnaga

Lifts and related facilities:
open from November to May

The resort of Macugnaga is protected by the imposing east face of Monte Rosa, which could be called the Hymalyan Alp because of its vertiginous drops and the sheer size of the expanses. The resort, moreover, is one of the most intact in the Alps and it has been awarded an impressive four Alpine stars by Legambiente.

The Macugnaga ski area is divided into two sectors: Alpe Burky and Monte Moro. Both have an interesting range of runs that are given an extra special touch because of the panoramic views you can enjoy. The roughly 40 km of runs are equally divided in terms of difficulty and thus there is something for just about everyone. From Pecetto, two consecutive chairlifts take you to Alpe Burky, which lies right under the imposing wall of Monte Rosa. Here, there are various long and enjoyable blue runs: the Belvedere run, over 3 km long, will satisfy even more demanding skiers. The other sector, namely Monte Moro, is connected to Macugnaga by two cableways. In this section, if you ignore the higher runs accessible by the S. Pietro lift

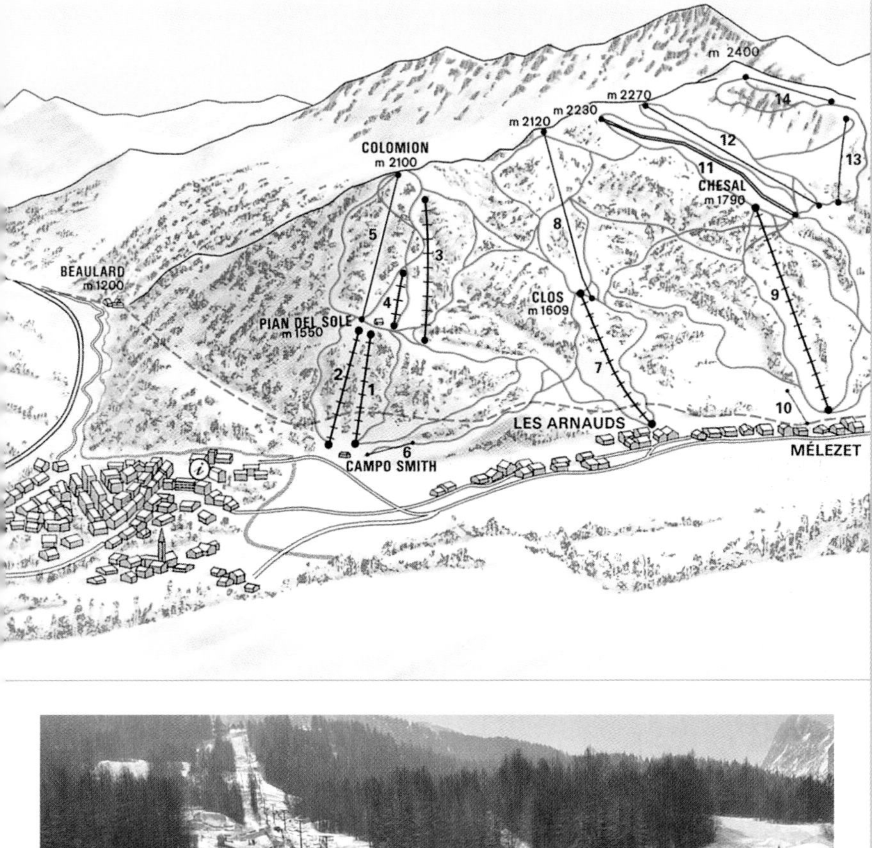

A view of some of the Bardonecchia lifts.

(also giving access to a "snowpark" for snowboarders), the trails are largely for moderate to good skiers. Some of the red and black runs that head down into the valley are 7.5 km long with an impressive vertical drop of over 1,000 m. The most notable are the black Roccette, and the red Ruppenstein, Lado and Meccia. The altitude ensures good snow cover and Alpe Burky can also rely on artificial snow spraying, if needed.
For lovers of cross-country skiing, there are about 20 km of trails, with the most notable probably being the circuit through the various districts that takes you past old Valais houses (that is, the interesting houses built by former inhabitants of Canton Valais in Switzerland) and through some woods. For those looking for the thrill and excitement of off-piste skiing, then there are helicopter rides to take you to the best spots for powdery snow: you head to the east face of Monte Rosa and then down towards the bottom in the direction of the distinctive Cervino (normally known as the Matterhorn outside of Italy).

SKI RUNS
Downhill skiing
42.6 km, including 9.5 covered by artificial snow spraying
blue **6** red **6** black **2**
Cross-country skiing
21.5 km of trails of varying difficulty
Snowboarding
1 Snowpark

LIFTS
Belvedere
Chairlifts 2
1 Pecetto-Alpe Burky 1390-1600
2 Alpe Burky-Belvedere 1600-1932
Ski-lifts 1
3 Burky 1 1470-1620
Monte Moro
Cable cars 2
4 Macugnaga-Alpe Bill 1327-1700
5 Alpe Bill-Passo Moro 1700-2900
Chairlifts 1
6 Ruppenstein 2350-2630
Ski-lifts 5
7 Joder
8 San Pietro 2850-2970
9 Smeraldo
In town
10 Tambach* 1320-1410
11 Vecchio Tiglio 1480-1530

* This lift has been replaced by a magic carpet.

The old church and, in the background, Pizzo Croce.

Artesina-Prato Nevoso

Lifts and related facilities:
open from December to April

The ski resorts of Prato Nevoso and Artesina lie in the upper Val Maudagna, in the heart of the Maritime Alps, where the damp air from the sea meets the colder air from the plain, resulting in plenty of snow. They are connected to the Mondolé Ski ski area, without having to take your skis off. Both of these centers were created specifically for skiing. The former stands on a sunny balcony with a scenic view at 1,500 m; the other, dominated by the Gaviot summit, is at 1,300 m. Mt Mondolé rises above the ski runs. These plateaus actually enjoy a mild microclimate with short, heavy snowfalls and wonderful vegetation with rhododendrons and, beech and fir trees. The resorts are, though, quite different. Prato Nevoso is based on the idea of a chalet, with large buildings with sloping roofs lining the ski runs. When the sun shines, the bowl becomes a natural solarium. Artesina has north-west facing houses that are more like medieval manor houses: tall cement towers spaced narrowly. Mondolé Ski is one of the best ski areas in Piedmont and, thanks to the connection (without having to take your skis off) with the nearby Frabosa Soprana, it has over 130 km of runs. Mondolé Ski alone has 90 km of runs, a total vertical drop of just under 800m and over 20 lifts, including some chairlifts. Various runs on both slopes are within range of the artificial snow cannons ensuring good skiing conditions throughout the season. There are all levels of runs, with a good range of blue and red routes and some interesting black ones, which tend to be on the Artesina side. All this adds up to varied, fun skiing. The most notable easy run at Prato Nevoso is Uno, while the Verde and Rossa chairlifts lead to some interesting red runs. At Artesina, the Turra lift takes you to some lovely runs that are easy and moderate, but with superb

SKI RUNS
Downhill skiing
90 km, including 12 covered by artificial snow spraying
blue **13** red **18** black **6**
Cross-country skiing
7 km easy circuits
Snowboarding
2 Snowparks

LIFTS
Artesina
Chairlifts 3
22 Colletto 1380-1624
27 Mondolé 1624-1951
31 Castellino
Ski-lifts 9
21 Costabella 1395-1427
23 Mirafiori 1 1307-1607
24 Mirafiori 2 1307-1607
25 Pogliola I 1602-1734
25 Pogliola II 1602-1734
28 Cima Durand 1951-2065
29 Turra I and II 1745-2085
30 Rocche Giardina 1601-1937
Plus 2 new chairlifts

Prato Nevoso
Chairlifts 3
3 Blu
5 Verde
6 Rossa 1562-1928
Ski-lifts 6
1 Arlecchino I 1468-1512
2 Arlecchino II 1468-1565
8 Argento 1592-1780
7 Rosa 1537-1696
9 Bianca
10 Celeste
Magic carpets 2
4 Arcobaleno
11 Pratolandia
Plus 1 new chairlift

Artesina/Prato Nevoso

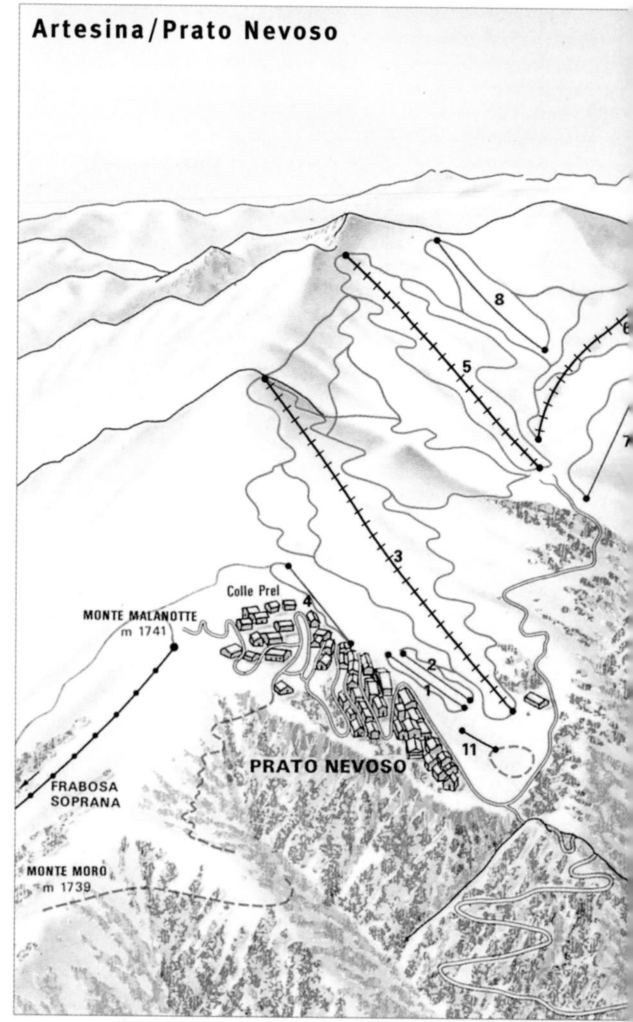

A panoramic view from the Rocche Giardina ski run in Artesina.

panoramas. The chairlift from Artesina to Turra provides access to a lovely black trail. The run down from Colla Bauzano is another taxing run. Prato Nevoso and Artesina have facilities for younger children and, for snowboarders, well-equipped "snowparks". By heading across Mt Malanotte, near Prato Nevoso, you can reach the Frabosa Soprana ski area. For those who favor cross-country skiing, there are two circuits, one at Prato Nevoso (3 km) and one at Artesina (4 km).

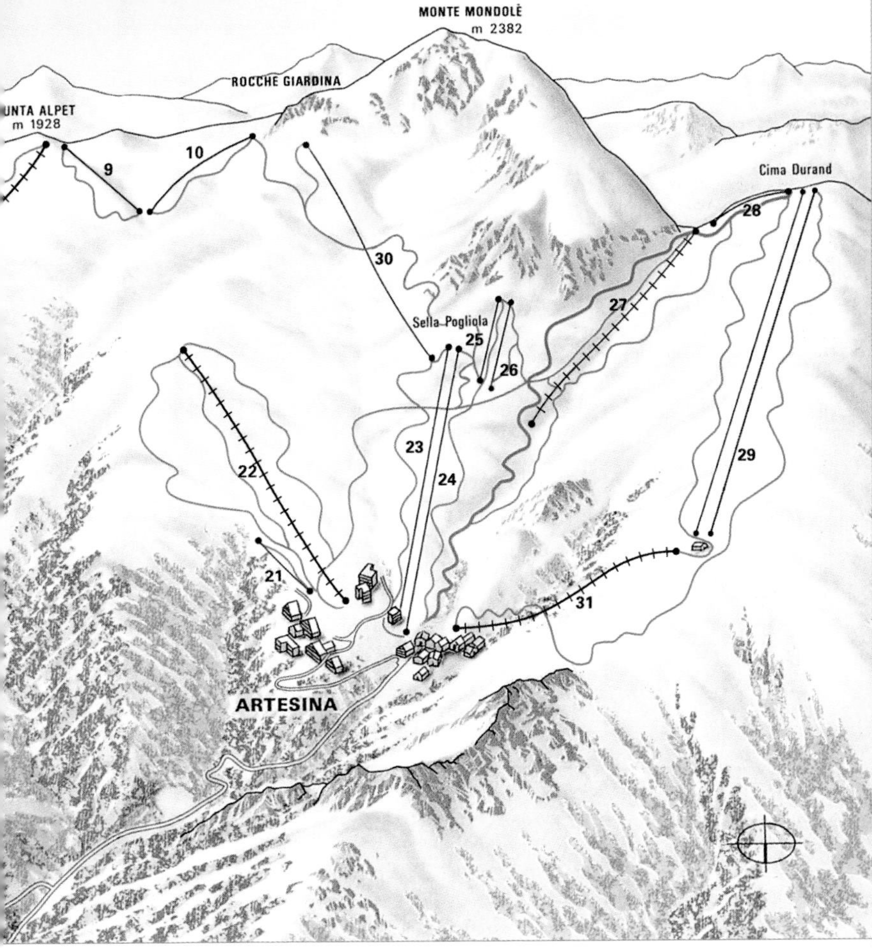

Limone Piemonte and a winter view.

Limone Piemonte

Lifts and related facilities:
open from December to April

Located at 1,009 m above sea level, Limone Piemonte is the main resort in Val Vermenagna (or the Vermenagna valley). This valley starts out as open and gently rolling, but then becomes more Alpine in appearance and shape. In the early years of the 20th century, this village was the setting for some of the very first skiing in the Alps and it soon became a winter resort. Since those early days, it has grown in fame and now boasts 2 Alpine stars from Legambiente. Indeed, this gracious resort is at the top of the ranks of Italian ski resorts and it plays host to World Cup skiing events. A true highlight is the Riserva Bianca

SKI RUNS
Downhill skiing
80 km, including 40 covered by artificial snow spraying
blue **7** red **27** black **5**
Cross-country skiing
6 km
Snowboarding
1 Snowpark

LIFTS
Chairlifts 9
1 Gegia 1088-1156
3 Sole 1046-1528
6 Alpetta 1593-2025
12 Cabanaira 1375-1966
13 Carosello 1386-1462
14 Colle di Tenda 1405-1835
15 1400 Morel 1400-1581
16 Limone Morel 1347-1581
17 Alpe 1380-1508
Ski-lifts 11
2 San Secondo 1060-1090
4 Punta Buffe 1525-1525
5 Sole 2 1525-1775
7 Belvedere 1365-1705
8 Panice 1355-1625
9 Gherra 1575-1855
10 Pian del Leone 1575-1868
11 Rancani S and D 1840-2050
18 San Lorenzo 1505-1628
19 Del Colle 1624-1876

Some lifts have been changed or improved.

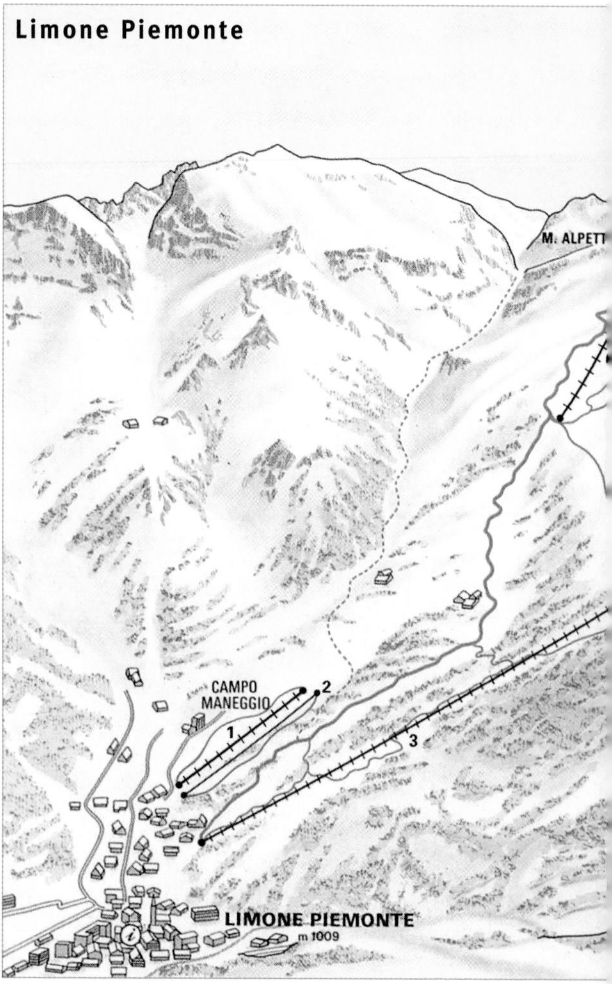

Limone Piemonte

M. ALPETT
CAMPO MANEGGIO
1
2
3
LIMONE PIEMONTE
m 1009

ski area. This is one of the best such areas in the world with carefully chosen, snow-covered runs. This formidable ski area has 80km of runs and is ideal for average skiers, although there is also plenty for people who love more trying runs that test one's technique. There are also options for true first-timers or relative beginners, with a nice training slope in the town. For those who have just left the training slopes, though, the options are limited, even though run 36, in the Limonetto area, is long and entertaining, making it possible for those still progressing. Despite the upper limit being 2,000 m, the climate remains relatively mild. In addition, Riserva Bianca receives plenty of snow thanks to the microclimate and it often has good skiing conditions right throughout the season. Should there be limited snow, then there is a substantial network of artificial snow spraying that keeps the main runs open as well as the connections with the main hubs in the lift network. The best run, which is one of the most charming in the Italian Alps, is the Olimpica: set between 2,014 and 1,042 m, it offers 4km of thrills. The upper and lower sections are red, while the middle stretch is black, making it ideal for competitions. The other notable runs are Macchetto, Cabanaria and Giorgio Armand. For those who like snowboarding, there is a "snowpark", while cross-country skiers can make use of the 6 km of runs.

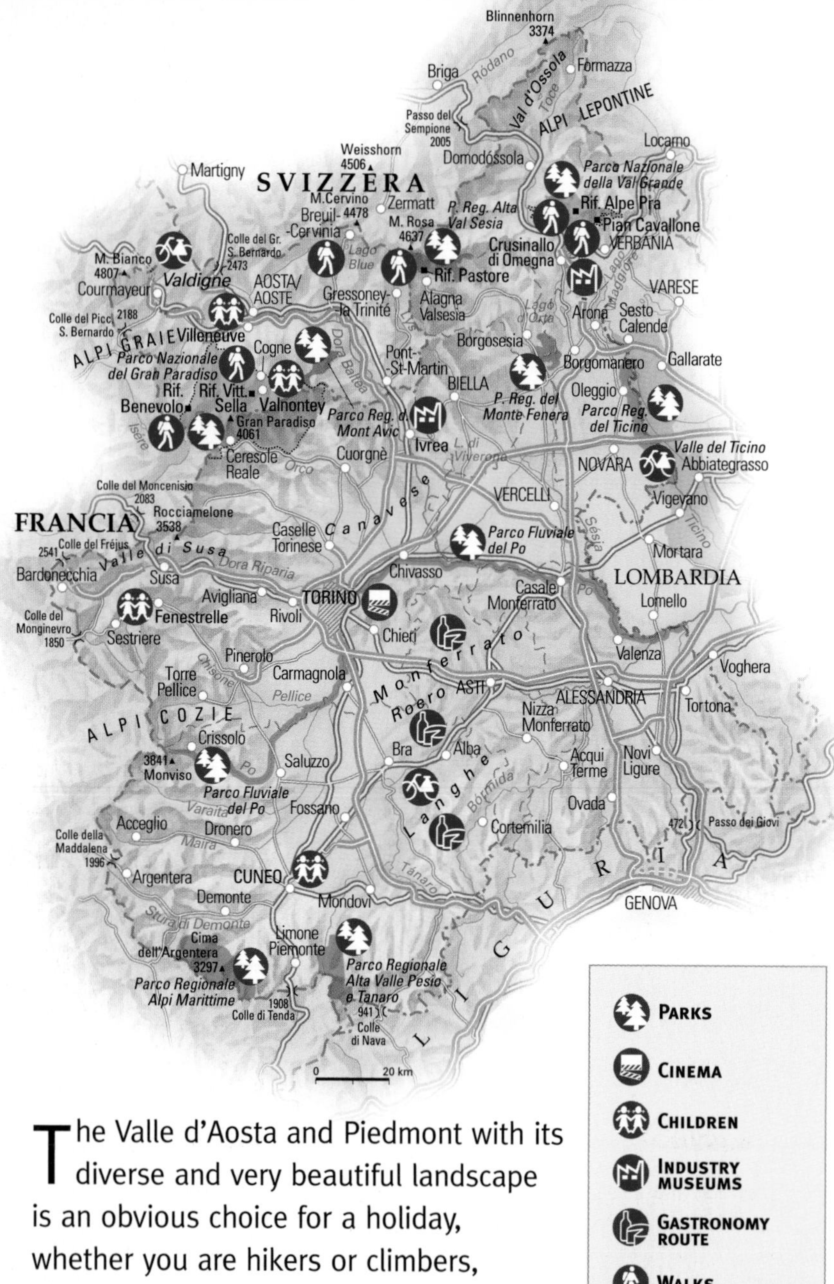

The Valle d'Aosta and Piedmont with its diverse and very beautiful landscape is an obvious choice for a holiday, whether you are hikers or climbers, wildlife enthusiasts, culture vultures or food-and-wine buffs.Thanks to the shape of the valleys, many holiday resorts are also ideal places from which to admire some of the most famous mountains in the Alps, an unforgettable sight. Wherever you go, and whatever your passions, in winter or summer, there is plenty to choose from in terms of accommodation and interest: parks for small kids, art and architecture, biking holidays in unspoiled landscape, skiing or hiking in magnificent Alpine scenery. A perfect place to recharge the batteries, where you can enjoy the diverse and gratifying aspects of an enchanting corner of Italy.

Itineraries

Highlights

- Admire the marvelous scenery and wildlife in the national and regional parks.
- Go hiking in breathtaking mountain scenery.
- Visit Forte di Fenestrelle, Europe's largest fortified Alpine complex.
- Enjoy the food and wine of the Langhe, the Roero and the Monferrato: a paradise for gourmets.

Inside

128 **Parks**
132 **Children**
134 **Cinema**
137 **Industry museums**
139 **Gastronomy route**
146 **Walks**
153 **Biking routes**

PARCO NAZIONALE DEL GRAN PARADISO/GRAN PARADISO NATIONAL PARK

PROVINCES OF AOSTA AND TURIN

AREA: 70,318 HECTARES. INCLUDES THE MOUNTAINS OF THE GRAIE ALPS AND THE SURROUNDING VALLEYS SLOPING DOWN TO THE DORA BALTEA AND ORCO RIVERS.

HEADQUARTERS: ENTE PARCO NAZIONALE GRAN PARADISO, VIA DELLA ROCCA 47, TORINO, TEL. 0118606211

VISITORS' CENTERS: NOASCA TOWN HALL, PARK TOURIST OFFICE (OPEN ALL YEAR ROUND), TEL. 0124901070

WEB SITE: WWW.PNGP.IT

Seldom has a name, Great Paradise, been so apt in describing this imposing slice of mountain scenery with its spectacular glaciers, one foot in Piedmont and the other in the Valle d'Aosta region. It was the first, and perhaps the most famous, Italian national park. Over 70,000 hectares of untrammelled and mainly mountainous nature hedged by four valleys. The southern limits of the park are marked by the long Valle dell'Orco, to the east the well-wooded slopes of Val Soana, to the north the Val di Cogne (with the Vallone dell'Urtier), and to the west the Val di Rhêmes, while the Valsavarenche is driven like a wedge between the other two Aosta valleys and lies completely within the park. The snow-covered Mt Gran Paradiso peak (4,061m) occupies pride of place, surrounded by a halo of equally impressive peaks and glaciers.

3,000 m from head to toe

The park covers a vast area with a dramatic altitude difference of over 3,000 m from its peaks to its valleys. The valleys themselves are well-wooded with evergreen larch, spruce, Scotch pine and the occasional silver fir extending to the tree line at just over 2,000m. Higher up the woods give way to Alpine pastures, the lonely 'hanging valleys' (basins of glacial origin suspended at the head of many alpine valleys) and sweeping scenery against the dramatic

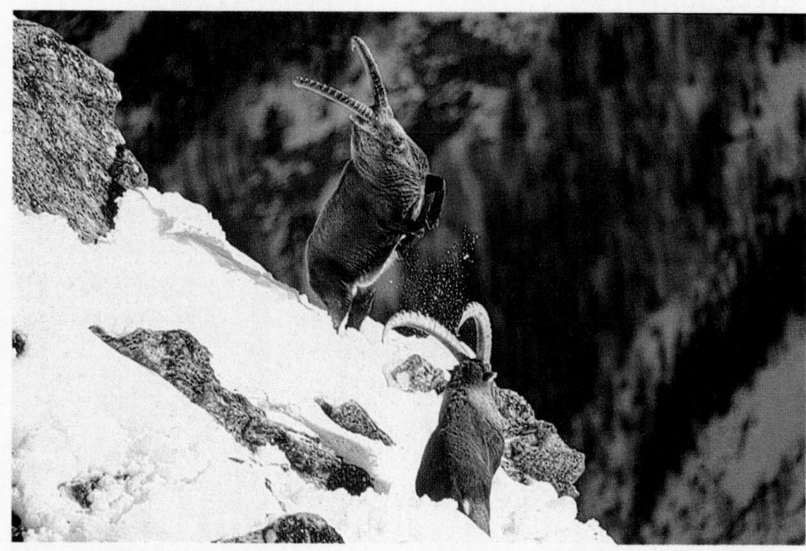

Two adult males challenge each other on a snow-covered rocky slope to decide who will be the leader of the herd and earn the right to mate with the females.

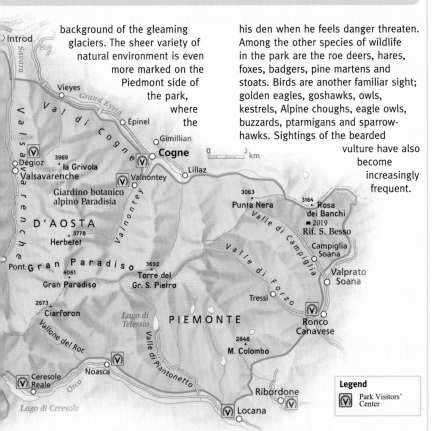

background of the gleaming glaciers. The sheer variety of natural environment is even more marked on the Piedmont side of the park, where the boundaries dip down to below the 1,000m mark and include deciduous woods of chestnut trees, ash, maple and beech. Water is one of the park's signature tunes, with a wealth of rushing streams that have carved out whole valleys, waterfalls and lakes, some of them with dams to produce hydroelectric power.

The easiest place to catch a glimpse of the normally shy, but supremely elegant, chamois are the quiet valleys towards Canavesa. The true symbol of the park, the majestic ibex, is much easier to spot: they graze peacefully all over the park, including its more popular parts, supremely indifferent to parties of eager camera-toting tourists. The ibex are the uncrowned kings of the pastures and the peaks, mountain goats whose cloven hooves are perfectly adapted to rock climbing. Another animal that can often be spotted in the park is the marmot, a born lazybones who only rushes into his den when he feels danger threaten. Among the other species of wildlife in the park are the roe deers, hares, foxes, badgers, pine martens and stoats. Birds are another familiar sight; golden eagles, goshawks, owls, kestrels, Alpine choughs, eagle owls, buzzards, ptarmigans and sparrow-hawks. Sightings of the bearded vulture have also become increasingly frequent.

Introd
Savara
Vieyes
Grand Eyvia
Val di Cogne
Épinel
Gimillian
Cogne
0 3 km
Lillaz
Valsavarenche
3969 la Grivola
Dégioz
Valsavarenche
Valnontey
Giardino botanico alpino Paradisia
Valnontey
D'AOSTA
3778 Herbetet
Pont
Gran Paradiso
4061 Gran Paradiso
3692 Torre del Gr. S. Pietro
2673 Ciarforon
Vallone del Roc
Lago di Telessio
Valle di Piantonetto
PIEMONTE
3063 Punta Nera
3164 Rosa dei Banchi
2019 Rif. S. Besso
Valle di Campiglia
Campiglia Soana
Valle di Forzo
Valprato Soana
Tressi
Ronco Canavese
2848 M. Colombo
Noasca
Ceresole Reale
Orco
Lago di Ceresole
Ribordone
Locana
Legend
Park Visitors' Center

The controversial road between lakes Agnel and Serrù leading to Colle del Nivolet.

PARCO NAZIONALE DELLA VAL GRANDE/VAL GRANDE NATIONAL PARK

PROVINCE OF VERBANO-CUSIO-OSSOLA

AREA: 14,598. COVERS THE MOUNTAINS AND VALLEYS OF THE SOUTHERN LEPONTINE ALPS.

HEADQUARTERS: ENTE PARCO NAZIONALE DELLA VAL GRANDE, VIA SAN REMIGIO 19, VERBANIA PALLANZA (VB), TEL. 0323557960

VISITORS' CENTERS: ALL THE PARK FACILITIES ARE OPEN DURING THE SUMMER. FOR FURTHER INFORMATION AND OPENING TIMES CONTACT THE PARK HEADQUARTERS TEL. 0323557960. VISITORS' CENTER "ANIMALI DELLA NOTTE" (NOCTURNAL ANIMALS), INTRAGNA; VISITORS' CENTER "LE ROCCE RACCONTANO" (THE ROCKS' TALE), PREMOSELLO CHIOVENDA; BUTTOGNO VISITORS' CENTER, SANTA MARIA MAGGIORE: "CICOGNA" VISITORS' CENTER, CICOGNA.

WEB SITE: WWW.PARCOVALGRANDE.IT

This is the most important wilderness area in Italy. An untouched, fertile, wooded valley lying in silent splendor between its guardian mountain peaks, dark ravines and harsh rocky spurs. A stark, lonely, natural island of metamorphic rock sculpted by time and glaciation, with its lower reaches shaped by the moraines and alluvial deposits of the Quaternary period into terraces ideal for building villages and summer grazing. This splendid valley, so geomorphologically

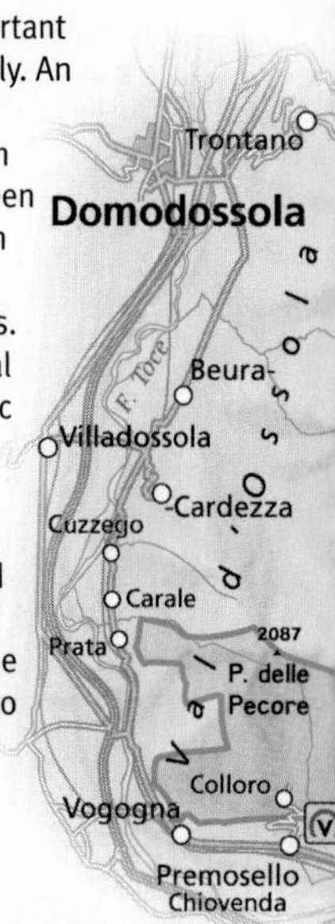

TCI HIGHLIGHTS

VALLE D'AOSTA AND PIEDMONT, THE GREEN KINGDOMS

The Valle d'Aosta is a lodestone for mountain and alpine sports enthusiasts alike. Here lies the Alps' oldest national park and the Mont Avic regional park, a vast pine forest with a patchwork of lakes and peat bogs along the upper reaches of the Chalamy Stream, home to some of the most characteristic wildlife species native to the Alps. The region also boasts another 9 nature reserves, making it a treasure trove of natural resources. Piedmont is a leader in nature conservation in Italy, apart from the two national parks described above, it also has forty regional parks and nature reserves that illustrate the region's remarkable biodiversity and variety of landscape. Glaciers, wetlands, woods and hills plus plenty of cultural attractions. A good example of careful landscape management is the Po River Park, a project that aims to protect Italy's most important river in its entirety, and has welded 17 separate nature reserves into a single park, stretching from the source of the river at Pian del Re on the French border, down to Lombardy as the Po is transformed from an Alpine stream into a mature valley river, home to a wealth of wildlife. Among the many Piedmontese parks is the Valle del Ticino, part of the MAB area (Man and Biosphere, an important United Nations project) along the banks of the Ticino River from its birthplace in Lake Maggiore to where the river crosses the border with Lombardy, where it passes under Lombard jurisdiction. The Maritime Alps Park in the province of Cuneo has been awarded a European Environmental Diploma by the Council of Europe; here ibex, chamois, wolves, boar and numerous birds of prey, among them golden eagles and bearded vultures, make their homes in the midst of the austere mountains criss-crossed by rushing streams and dotted with alpine lakes. Another park well worth a visit is the Alta Valsesia park, in the province of Vercelli, home to a wide variety of alpine wildlife, where the impressive Monte Rosa glacier is framed by vast evergreen forests. The Monte Fenera Park, near Orta Lake, has a system of caves with interesting remains of prehistoric animals (bears, rhinocerous), and traces of ancient human settlement. Another attraction, especially for the adventurous, is the Alta Valle Pesio e Tanaro Regional Park to the south of Cuneo, which has 150 km of unexplored caves, a wealth of flora and fauna and the unusual feature of numerous springs where the underground rivers surface.

varied, has been magically preserved, probably because it is flanked by more favorable environments for human settlement. On one side are the hospital Mediterranean shores of Lake Maggiore, and on the other the Val d'Ossola, with its slow-winding Toce river, while to the north lie the gentle Val Vigezzo and Val Cannobina hugging the contours of the Val Grande mountains. These form a chain that is not particularly high, just topping the 2,000m mark, but is harsh, steep and impenetrable. The dramatic cliffs of the Corni di Nibbio, plunging down to the flat Ossola valley floor, are easily visible from the main Sempione road. Behind them lie Val Grande and its neighbouring Val Pogallo: two mountain torrents named after the valleys they have carved over the centuries that join forces at the Casletto bridge to form the San Bernardino, which in turn flows down to the nearby Lake Maggiore.

The woodlands heritage

Beyond the Casletto bridge Val Grande is completely uninhabited, while its slightly tamer sister valley, Val Pogallo, has one small village, Cicogna, at its mouth. The wealth and variety of this woodland heritage are jealously guarded by the park rules and regulations. Chestnut trees, yews, alders, willows, white ashes, turkey oaks, ashes and, above all, beeches weave a rich tapestry of woodland variety. This kingdom is ruled by the chamois and the eagle, with an assortment of roe deers, foxes, badgers, weasels, hedgehogs, stone and pine martens, marmots, hares and numerous other small rodents. Vipers are also extremely common.

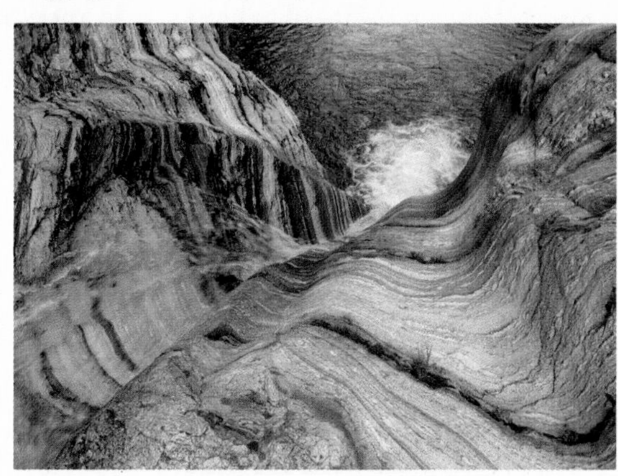

A mountain stream gushes down the La Piana alp. In Val Grande water erosion has produced spectacular effects on sculpted layers of different rock types.

GIARDINO BOTANICO ALPINO PARADISIA/PARADISIA ALPINE BOTANIC GARDENS

VALNONTEY (AOSTA), TEL. 016574147

OPENING TIMES: JUNE AND SEPTEMBER: 10AM – 5.30PM; JULY AND AUGUST: 10AM – 6.30PM

ADMISSION: FULL PRICE € 2.50; REDUCTIONS (CHILDREN UNDER 12 AND SENIOR CITIZENS OVER 65) € 1.

GETTING THERE:
BY CAR: TAKE THE AOSTA EST (AOSTA EAST) HIGHWAY EXIT GO THROUGH AOSTA AND FOLLOW THE DIRECTIONS FOR COGNE.

Set in stunning scenery at a height of 1,700 m in the Parco Nazionale Gran Paradiso, the gardens owe their name to a white lilly, the *Paradisea liliastrum*, found in the Alpine meadows and pastures. The gardens cover 10,000m², with natural dips and valleys that have been used to recreate several different Alpine environments. Around 1,500 species of plants are grown at the Paradisia, some of them from the Alps and others from faraway mountain ranges such as the Himalayas and the Andes. Visitors can also learn about lichens, which are not plants but associations of fungi and algae or bacteria which blaze a trail so that other plants can colonize rocks.

PARCO AVVENTURA/ ADVENTURE PARK

CHAVONNE, VILLENEUVE (AOSTA), TEL. 016595082, WWW.PARCOAVVENTURA.COM

ADMISSION: GREEN PATH FOR CHILDREN (5-8 YEARS OLD ACCOMPANIED BY AN ADULT) € 8; BLUE PATH (MINIMUM HEIGHT 1.40M, UNDER 14S) € 6, (OVER 14S) € 8; RED PATH (COMPLETE FORMULA) € 19.

FACILITIES: HARNESS, DOUBLE SAFETY LINES, SAFETY HATS, WINCHES. WEEKEND PACKAGES AVAILABLE INCLUDING RAFTING, HYDROSPEED, ADVENTURE PARK AND OVERNIGHT CAMPING.

GETTING THERE:
BY CAR: TAKE THE AOSTA OVEST (AOSTA WEST) HIGHWAY EXIT FOR SAINT PIERRE, TO COGNE; AT THE AYMAVILLES TURN-OFF THERE IS A HAIRPIN BEND TO THE LEFT WITH A CHURCH PERCHED ABOVE IT, TURN RIGHT FOR CHAVONNE 2 KM AWAY.

This is a great day out for the whole family, with carefully constructed trails for all ages. The adventure park runs through a wood of pine trees, poplars and chestnut trees. Visitors make their way along adventure paths at various heights moving from one tree to the next in complete safety thanks to a harness and double safety lines hitched onto an overhead cable. Villeneuve has two alternative paths: the blue path for children over 10 (minimum height 1.40 m), that runs through the trees at a height of 3-4 m above ground over rope bridges, logs and Tarzan-style lianas (woody vines); and the red path for adults, which is technically more demanding and reaches heights of 13 m at some points, with log bridges, stirrup climbs and tyrolese ropes. Safety is always a priority because younger children are supervised from the ground by members of the staff. If you need to cool off, Rafting Aventure organises river activities on the Dora Baltea River, including junior rafting, rafting for full and half days, hydrospeed, orienteering and a summer camp for 4 to 13 year olds.

FORTE DI FENESTRELLE/THE FENESTRELLE FORTIFICATIONS

STRADA DEL FORTE, FENESTRELLE (TORINO), TEL. 012183600, WWW.FORTEFENESTRELLE.COM

OPENING TIMES: OPEN ALL YEAR ROUND

ADMISSION: THE ROYAL WALKWAY, FULL PRICE € 12, REDUCED (7-12 YEARS OLD) € 10, FAMILY TICKET (2 ADULTS + 2 CHILDREN 7/18 YEARS OLD) € 30, FAMILY TICKET (2 ADULTS + 1 CHILD 7/18 YEARS OLD) € 27 (€ 6 FOR EVERY ADDITIONAL CHILD); WITH IN THE WALLS, FULL PRICE € 7.50, REDUCED (7-12 YEARS OLD) € 6, FAMILY TICKET (2 ADULTS + 2 CHILDREN 7/18 YEARS OLD) € 20, FAMILY TICKET (2 ADULTS + 1 CHILD 7/18 YEARS OLD) € 18 (€ 3 FOR EVERY ADDITIONAL CHILD); SHORT TOUR, € 5; THE TALE OF THE ANCIENT WALLS (BOOKING REQUIRED), EVERY SECOND SATURDAY OF THE MONTH, € 7, TOUR STARTS AT 9AM

GETTING THERE:
BY CAR: TAKE THE SESTRIERE SS 23 ROAD AT STUPINIGI FROM THE TURIN FLYOVER OR THE NONE EXIT ON THE ORBASSANO-VOLVERA HIGHWAY.

With their 43 km of walls and strongholds running along the mountains, the Fenestrelle fortifications are the largest Alpine defence works, an impressive bastion in stone and brickwork. Built at the beginning of the 18th century they were never actually besieged and were never the scene of a battle, but they did their job as a deterrent. During the Napoleonic wars they were one of France's most important defences. During the WW II they formed the backdrop to partisan forays and today, after years of neglect, they have become a symbolic monument. There are three different tours available. The Passeggiata Reale (the Royal Walkway) takes visitors up all the 400 steps with marvelous views to a height of 1,800 m and the valley fort. The tour within the walls takes you round the San Carlo fort, the covered part of the steps to a height of 1,300m, the Tre Denti fort and the 'devil's lookout'. The western Tenaglie tour includes the San Carlo fort parade ground and buildings. For the first 2 tours, sensible walking cloths and boots are advisable and an electric torch may be useful.

TRENO DELLE MERAVIGLIE/ THE WONDER TRAIN

CUNEO, WWW.TRENITALIA.COM

OPENING TIMES: OPEN ALL YEAR ROUND; SEE RAILWAY TIMETABLE

ADMISSION: CHECK THE TRENITALIA WEBSITE

FACILITIES: BICYCLES CAN BE LOADED ON BOARD (EXTRA CHARGE); THEMED TOURS AND NATURE HIKES AVAILABLE FROM DEIK CULTURA E TURISMO, TEL. 0172717185

GETTING THERE:
BY CAR: A6 HIGHWAY TORINO-SAVONA, FOSSANO EXIT.

BY TRAIN: CUNEO RAILWAY STATION.

It is known as the Wonder Train for two reasons: firstly because it goes through the Valle delle Meraviglie (Wonder Valley), famous for its rock carvings, and secondly because the line itself is a masterpiece of railway engineering, with daring viaducts and corkscrew tunnels. The ride starts in Cuneo, and then runs through the beautiful Vermenagna, Roya and Bevera river Alpine valleys, touching several places of historical, cultural and natural. Interesting stopovers include: the Cuneo and Tenda museums, and the Notre Dame des Fontaines chapel 4 km outside La Brigue.

Cinema

Avant-garde and 'retrò'

Turin is a must for visitors interested in the history of Italian cinema, it was here that the first Italian film studios were built at the end of the 19th century and today it is home to the National Cinema Museum. Obviously Turin, with its long history so closely interwoven with that of Italy itself, its links to the Risorgimento, to the flood of immigration from the south, to industrialisation, tends to be the focus of Piedmontese film making, and Italian cinema has dealt with its dominant themes from several different perspectives and in numerous films. However other areas of this vast region have also played their part, especially in films made during the post-war period: the rice paddies of Vercelli and the Monferrato area formed the background to many a Resistance struggle by the partisans, and still echo with scenes from literature and the cinema. The haunting song of the female paddy workers, like the heroine in *Riso Amaro* (1949), Silvana Mangano (see photo), who became an icon of Italian cinema. Foreign film-makers have also used the Turin studios and Piedmont to make films, going back to the joint Italian-Hollywood production of *War and Peace* (1956) by King Vidor.

The golden age of the Turin's cinema

The start of the 20th century saw the birth of a flourishing film industry in Turin, helped by local readiness to invest in technology. Producers built imposing studios and laboratories and summoned directors, actors, screenwriters and technicians.
In 1919 the huge FERT (acronym of Fiori Enrico Roma Torino) studios opened in Viale Lombardia, but after the First World War the film industry in Turin was already in decline, due partly to the economic crisis and to a great extent to the advent of Fascism.
The Fascist regime saw the cinema as an important propaganda mechanism and decided to concentrate resources on Rome, fostering the birth of Cinecittà, which marked the end of film-making in Turin.
However the city itself, thanks to its architectural merits, remained a favorite setting for films. For example the film version of Tolstoy's novel *War and Peace* made by the American King Vidor in 1955 with Audrey Hepburn, Henry Fonda and the native Mario Soldati behind the camera in the role of assistant-director coordinating the crowd scenes and the battles.
The film was shot in Turin and the surrounding countryside, using the Stupinigi royal residence, the Valentino castle, scene of the Tilsit meeting between Napoleon and the Tsar Alexander. Sestrière did duty as the Russian steppe during the retreat, while Pinerolo became Austerlitz.
In *The Italian Job* (1969) by Peter Collinson, with Michael Caine, Raf Vallone and Rossano Brazzi, Turin, with the hurch of Gran Madre di Dio, the dome of the Palazzo Vela and its 18th-century streets, was the background to a daring robbery in a fleet of Minis. In more recent times, *La Puttana del Re (The King's Whore)* (1990) by the Austrian Axel Corti, deals with the story of the Duke of Savoy's (Vittorio Amedeo I) favourite at the end of the 17th century, and was filmed between Rivoli, Stupinigi and Palazzo Carignano in Turin. Tom Tykwer, one of the better-known contemporary German directors, recently shot *Heaven* (2002) in Turin, the story of a tenacious teacher's fight against a drug pusher.

The castle at Racconigi was the scene for the third and final episode of *Tulse Luper Cases*, a sophisticated and ambitious example of experimental film-making from the English director Peter Greenaway presented at the Venice Film Festival in 2003. In the ironic, sophisticated *The Emperor's New Clothes* (2001) by Alan Taylor, with a superb Ian Holm as Napoleon Bonaparte "in incognito", Turin is magically transformed into Restoration Paris. Over the last few decades several well-known Italian authors have also dedicated some of their works to Turin.
However Turin still maintains its links with the world of the cinema through a series of events, such as its numerous festivals during the year, the most famous being the Turin Film Festival, the most important film festival in Italy after the Venice Film Festival. Finally, over the last few years the industrial area of the erstwhile FERT studios, have been transformed into the Virtual Reality & Multimedia Park, a technology park that aims to promote and develop the cultural, economic and technological contents of the multimedia, with particular reference to virtual reality applications, in some ways the third millennium version of cinema.

Museo Nazionale del Cinema/ The National Cinema Museum

Turin was the cradle of the film industry in Italy, so it is hardly surprising that a cinema museum was founded here back in 1941. In its current guise the museum is housed in the building that is the very symbol of Turin, the Mole Antonelliana, now transformed into an amazing vertical museum, a real treat for cinema buffs. Its impressive collection includes a rich array of 12,000 films (both mute and with soundtrack), 750,000 photographs, 9,000 items of viewing apparatus and art objects, 341,440 posters and other advertising material, over 26,000 books, 3,400 magazines, 1,500 film soundtracks and a huge collection of important historical documents. The tour round the museum starts with the first, fascinating magic lanterns, which go back to the 17th century and the prehistory of the so-called 'seventh art', and ends up with some of today's most spectacular special effects. The objects, memorabilia and documents displayed are extremely representative of the whole collection. And this is very much a hands-on museum where visitors do not just look at things, they are encouraged to try them out too, experimenting with the joys of shadow theatres, new worlds and magic lanterns. The tour continues through the area dedicated to the mechanics of film-making: visitors see how a production is transformed into entertainment and everything that is actually present on the set, but which audiences never see in the final image on the screen when the final cut has been made.
This part is laid out in a fascinating series of alcoves each with a detailed display of memorabilia, documents, photographs, sketches and costumes. The Temple Hall, the huge space under the

Inside the National Cinema Museum in the Mole Antonelliana.

dome, is the heart of the museum, with its 'chapelles' dedicated to the great themes of cinema history. Visitors lie on comfortable red *chaises longues* and watch films projected on mega screens. At regular intervals the roof of the dome suddenly appears to open to reveal the stars, racing clouds and magic lantern images, all courtesy of the illusion of the projected image. The winding ramp that wends its way up the sides of the dome around the temple hall and the gallery on the second floor tell the story of the cinema through an extensive series of wall posters. At the bottom of the ramp the last stage of the exhibition is housed in 6 alcoves illustrating the relationship between cinema and television. One final touch that definitely adds to the museum's already considerable charm is the panoramic lift that allows visitors to glide through part of the exhibition and go through the roof of the dome for a visit to the external temple, where they can admire a marvelous view of the city against its majestic backdrop of Alps. Among the vast number of exhibits the most popular items from over "a century of cinema" have been Rudolf Valentino's costume in *Blood and Sand*, Charlie Chaplin's famous bowler hat, the costume and the egg from *Aliens* by James Cameron, the head of the most frightening predator ever seen on the big screen, the shark in Steven Spielberg's *Jaws*, and Darth Vader's black helmet in *The Empire Strikes Back* by Irvin Kershner. Other precious exhibits include the original screenplays for masterpieces such as Orson Welles' *Citizen Kane*, *Psycho* by Alfred Hitchcock, *La caduta degli dei* by Luchino Visconti, *The Godfather - Part II* by Francis Ford Coppola and, just as a reminder that cinema also means the personality cult of figures who have become icons for a whole generation, some of Marilyn Monroe's shoes, jewels and one of her corsets.

Posters in the Temple Hall of the National Cinema Museum.

Museo Nazionale del Cinema
Fondazione Maria Adriana Prolo
Mole Antonelliana
Via Montebello 20, Torino
Tel. 011 8138511
www.museocinema.it

TCI HIGHLIGHTS

The Turin Film Festival, work in progress

**The Turin Film Festival «is a meeting place and a test area for the new international cinema with all its different points of view and artistic tendencies.
A place where emerging styles and the young can be sure of a warm welcome.
The competitive sections promote and encourage the viewing of films by new authors experimenting with new styles and forms». With these words the critic and cinema historian Gianni Rondolino introduced the Turin Film Festival, its artistic aims and the essence and the spirit that was behind its conception 23 years ago. The event aims to be a research laboratory to help discover emerging authors in the new realities of contemporary cinema by providing a showcase for all forms of cinema, regardless of where they are from, how long the work is, what format it is in and what technology it uses.
In line with this spirit of research and rediscovery the festival office also organizes seasons dedicated to chosen authors and retrospectives.**

www.torinofilmfest.org

MUSEO ALESSI/ THE ALESSI MUSEUM

GENERAL INFORMATION:
VIA PRIVATA ALESSI 6, CRUSINALLO DI OMEGNA (VERBANO-CUSIO-OSSOLA)

TEL. 0323868611, WWW.ALESSI.COM

HOW TO GET THERE:
A26 VOLTRI-GRAVELLONA TOCE HIGHWAY, GRAVELLONA TOCE EXIT, THEN FOLLOW DIRECTIONS FOR OMEGNA.

OPENING HOURS:
VISIT BY PRIOR APPOINTMENT ONLY FOR GROUPS OF NOT MORE THAN 15 PEOPLE, TOURS AVAILABLE IN ENGLISH; CLOSED SATURDAYS AND SUNDAYS.
FREE ENTRY.

How the museum began

The Alessi philosophy means that its designers are constantly experimenting and developing new products, and over the years this has built up into a substantial, fascinating collection of prototypes and drafts, that have been rounded off by objects from all over the world to give visitors a balanced view of the history of the development of household goods and accessories.

What's inside

The museum is housed in the Alessi headquarters and has an interesting display of prototypes, drafts, project dossiers, catalogues and other objects, both from the company itself and other companies, as well as photographs, press cuttings, books and magazines. Exhibits are in mobile showcases where they are arranged by type (saucepans, trays, cutlery, sculptures etc) and, more generally, by operational sequence (preparation, consumption and presentation of food and drink, personal hygiene).

Aims

The museum serves a dual purpose. It is both an effective archive that can be constantly referred to by the company's own staff to guide product development and policy and it is also a museum of applied art that aims to preserve and promote the heritage value of the collection itself, as well as carrying out scientific research and promoting cultural events.

Activities

The museum organises temporary exhibitions and workshops with university students and pupils from design schools. It also organises lessons and seminars for universities and research institutes who are interested in Alessi's work, the museums and the history of the company. It provides support for students doing dissertations or researchers who want to study the company or who are working on the theme of corporate museums.
In the field of research and scientific activity it promotes projects aimed at studying the history of the company.

Kitchen utensils and tableware by Philippe Starck, 'hung' to one side.

ASSOCIAZIONE ARCHIVIO STORICO OLIVETTI/THE OLIVETTI HISTORICAL ARCHIVE ASSOCIATION

GENERAL INFORMATION:
VILLA CASANA, VIA DELLE MINIERE 31, IVREA (TORINO) TEL. 0125641238, WWW.ARCOLIV.ORG
PARTIAL ACCESS FOR THE DISABLED

HOW TO GET THERE:
A5 TORINO-AOSTA HIGHWAY, IVREA EXIT.

OPENING HOURS:
BY PRIOR APPOINTMENT ONLY FROM MONDAY TO FRIDAY, 9-12AM AND 2-5PM; CLOSED ON SATURDAYS AND SUNDAYS. FREE ENTRY.

How the museum began

The Olivetti Historical Archive was set up during the second half of the 1980s in order to research, select, organize and preserve the documentation on the history of Olivetti and the entrepreneurs who founded and guided it. The Olivetti Historical Archive Association collects, catalogues and transfers to data storage the huge and varied documentary and multi-format heritage of the company.

What's inside

The library contains thousands of books ranging over a wide variety of categories: exhibition catalogues, and restoration notes, collections of books on Olivetti themes and on the history of the company, original company publications such as diaries, gift editions of books, calendars and monographies. The newspaper and periodical library carries hundreds of titles, including some historical magazines. The cinevideo collection contains a wealth of material, much of it original, with material going back to the 1940s, unique in terms of filmed company documents. The audio collection is extremely valuable in historical terms and contains recordings of meetings and debates. The important computer and photographic sections have interesting collections of posters, advertising campaigns and other images. There are also the thousands of manuscripts, pictures, documents, notes and projects that belong to the archive of the Olivetti family. The museum also houses an extensive collection of machines once produced by Olivetti; the company records; a huge collection of documents linked to production, cultural services and social services; interesting studies carried out by the company psychologists and sociologists; the original section dedicated to gift items

A 1912 poster for the M1 model, created by Teodoro Wolf Ferrari.

and material linked to training and the commercial department.

Aims

The Olivetti Historical Archive Association's aim is to collect, maintain and promote the huge archive legacy of Olivetti and the Olivetti family.

Activities

The Olivetti Historical Archive Association's aim is to sort through the huge amount of documentation in its possession, and perform multiform cultural and editorial tasks in order to enhance the collection. The association has promoted cultural events and initiatives through conventions, exhibitions, conferences, plays, film shows, most of which are attested to by the promotional material produced at the time. It has also published a quantity of material.

Gastronomy route

Langhe, Roero and Monferrato: enchanting castles, towns and ru wine connoisseurs. Langhe, Monferrato and Roero, landsca and castles. There is no doubt that this triangle formed by Turin, As has a great deal to offer tourists, especially when it comes to foo stretches from the banks of the Po to the Apennines and the foothil etable farms and fruit plantations in the valleys to the vineyards o high grazing land. It is the cradle of typical local produce of th sophisticated cuisine which is enhanced even further by the regi ly the reds. Here, the Nebbiolo grape finds its most sublime expression in wines of absolute excellence, Barbera is also well-known, and the fame of Asti's sparkling Moscato wines has traveled the world. We propose various itineraries which, based on the area's most famous wines, visit the main towns of the areas where they are made and, while we are at it, tell you about the typical local produce and the specialties of the local cuisine.

The Monferrato

The Monferrato is the name given to the broad expanse of hills stretching into the south-east corner of Piedmont. The Tànaro River divides the area into two parts, the Alto and Basso Monferrato, which reflect the differing nature of the land, something that is also reflected in its wines. We have suggested five itineraries in the Basso Monferrato and three in the Alto Monferrato, taking the line of Chieri-Asti-Alessandria as the dividing line. Between these two areas are the hills of Asti, a world of wine unto itself.

The wineries of the **Basso Monferrato**, which lies between the towns of Casale Monferrato and Asti, produce mainly Barbera and Grignolino. On the palate, these two wines have an instant, warm rapport which gives them a particular status within the daunting list of otherwise rather dry Piedmont reds.

Our **first itinerary** looks at the main centers of production of **Barbera del Monferrato DOC**. It travels through landscape dominated by hills and vineyards, through the medieval town of Castagnole Monferrato, Vignale Monferrato, with its wine-cellars dug out of the tufa in its hills, and site of the Enoteca Regionale del Monferrato, Rosignano Monferrato, arranged picturesquely on the slope of a spur of tufa, with steep, narrow streets, and Casale Monferrato, which has a complex history, with buildings dating mainly from the medieval, Renaissance and Baroque periods.

The **second itinerary**, which unfolds in the territory of **Grignolino d'Asti DOC**, visits the town of Portacomaro. Its medieval tower houses the Bottega del Grignolino and it has an *osteria* attached, a stronghold of good food and wine. We visit the little town of Scurzolengo with its rustic castle, the pretty town of Casorzo surrounded by vineyards, the charming medieval center of Grazzano Badoglio, Moncalvo, with its many churches and palaces, prime truffle country, and Serralunga di Crea, with its fine medieval castle and the nearby sanctuary of Crea. The **third itinerary**, in the lands of **white Freisa**

A typical Piedmontese wine-cellar.

(in the hills near Turin), begins at Chieri, whose undulating hills are home to some remarkable religious and civic buildings. We proceed to Castelnuovo Don Bosco, where Malvasia di Castelnuovo Don Bosco DOC is made, and Pino d'Asti, a beautiful town surrounded by vineyards, the starting-a panoramic road to gnano, deep in vine country. The st part of the itinerary visits Cocconato, an old hill-top town with wonderful views, and Moncucco Torinese, with its 15th-century castle and excellent Bottega del Vino.

The **fourth itinerary** takes us south of Asti, into the exceptional vine-growing area of the **Colli Astigiane**, where the landscape is dominated by vines, famous for its Moscato and Barbera d'Asti. It's also home to Asti Spumante, invented here a few centuries ago. The route starts at the provincial capital, and travels in a circle around the towns where Barbera d'Asti DOC is made. In Asti, the red-brick and yellow-tufa medieval houses and towers are interspersed with imposing Baroque palaces. From here, we go to Isola d'Asti, a typical country town where the vegetables are cultivated down in the valley and the hills are planted with vines. Next is San Damiano d'Asti, famous for its truffle harvest and its elegant porticoes. The town of Celle Enomondo owes its name to its ancient wine-cellars (called 'celle'), whereas Costigliole d'Asti, a charming hill-top town dominated by its Gothic castle (the magnificent setting of the Cantina Comunale) has some historic vineyards. Nizza Monferrato is a town with lots of atmosphere. It has a main street with narrow porticoes and a Town Hall with a medieval tower. It has made a name for itself by growing local produce produce, a really remarkable range of gastronomic delights. Mombaruzzo, with its medieval clock tower and fine Gothic church, is famous for its *amaretto* biscuits and good food. Rocchetta Tànaro lies in the shade of an old castle while, on the other side of the Tànaro River, is Castello di Annone, a place known for its excellent Grignolino and its pretty countryside. The vineyards here are worth a fortune. We move on to Montegrosso d'Asti ideally situated for growing vines, where the castle with two round towers dominates the valley. Agliano Terme is situated in a marvelous position, on top of a hill planted with vines, and has a reputation for making excellent Barbera. The **fifth itinerary** explores the **Colli Astigiane** where **Moscato** is made. Here, between Monferrato and Langa, the sheer variety of food and wines is amazing. The fulcrum of this tour is Canelli, which has many old wine-cellars. Surrounded by vineyards, this town, dominated by Castello Gancia, is regarded as the capital of Spumante. All around the hill, cellars dug out of the tufa sell local food and wines and offer tastings. We move on to San Marzano Oliveto, where, in summer, gastronomic evenings are organized around the local wines, truffles and salami. We go to Calamandrana, a secluded little town overlooked by its castle, and Sessame, where the landscape heralds the rough beauty of the Langhe. A bridge over the Bòrmida and a fortified monastery resulted in the town of Monastero Bòrmida, whereas Bubbio is built on a spur. Walking up through its narrow streets, you eventually come to its grand Baroque Parish church and its 15th-century castle. This area is

Gavi: vineyards of the famous Gavi wine on the way to Novi Ligure.

renowned for its wines, salami, truffles, cheese, honey and nougat. Loazzolo, an enchanting town, has charming cobbled streets overlooked by rustic stone houses. The local red DOC wine has a longstanding reputation for quality. One of the sanctuaries of Moscato is Santo Stefano Belbo. The Enoteca Regionale di Mango, a town situated on a ridge between the Valle del Tinella and the Valle del Belbo, makes about 150 types of wine, as well as cakes, candies and other local delicacies, while, at Neviglie, truffles are drunk with local Moscato. The itinerary ends at Calosso, with its fortified gate, old houses and castle, a well-preserved medieval town.

The **first itinerary** through the steep slopes and rough valleys of the **Alto Monferrato** travels through the **land of white Cortese**. It starts at Gavi, situated in the gentle landscape of the Valle del Lemme with an ancient fortress which dominates the town, and continues to Serravalle Scrivia. Here, a footpath leads to the excavations of the Roman town, with its ruined theater, amphitheater houses and roads. Further on we come to Novi Ligure, surrounded by splendid hills with vineyards, castles and medieval towns which, as well as being a wine town, is also renowned for its excellent confectionery, especially chocolate. Other stops on the tour include Pasturana, Capriata d'Orba, San Cristoforo, Bosio and Voltaggio, small, enchanting medieval towns, each with its castles and churches, scattered around countryside of environmental importance. Our **second itinerary** zig-zags through hills and towns on the **trail of Brachetto**, the famous fizzy red which is well suited to aging a light, bubbly, robust wine. We begin at Acqui Terme, where they produce a famous Dolcetto DOC and we can visit the Enoteca Regionale del Brachetto. We move on from here to the small town of Quaranti, which organizes various events for wine tourists, Fontanile, which has a very old wine-making tradition, and Maranzana, whose walls and imposing castle conceal excellent wines and truffles. With its scenic piazzas and striking buildings, Cassine, nestling among rolling hills planted with vines, is one of the most interesting towns of the Alto Monferrato. We end at Castelnuovo Bòrmida and Strevi, with its ancient castle, wide-ranging views over the valley and a number of noble villas, where the fame of Brachetto vies with that of its dry sparkling wines.

From the Monferrato to the Langhe, the **third itinerary** on the **Dolcetto trail** stops first at the town of Ovada, famed for its truffles and local cookies, as well as for its Dolcetto. The next town is Tagliolo Monferrato, where the 13th-century castle has been converted into a delightful residence-cum-wine-cellar. Castelletto d'Orba is famous for its *agnolotti al vino*. Montaldo Bòrmida is a small town in the hills between the Bòrmida River and the Orba Stream where Dolcetto and Barbera are produced. Diano d'Alba is dominated by its castle and has unforgettable views

Vineyards in autumn near Diana d'Alba.

over the Langhe hills. Not only do they make Barolo here, but also a Dolcetto which is justly famous. The last towns on the itinerary are Montelupo Albese, set on a hillside, the small hill-top town of Roddino, and Dogliani, an aristocratic, noble little market town whose name is linked to Dolcetto. With regard to typical local products, we should mention the *krumiri* of Casale Monferrato, one of Piedmont's most famous cookies. Another specialty of the area is the cardoon produced around Nizza Monferrato: an unusual vegetable and one of the vital ingredients of *bagna cauda*, one of the local cuisine's most typical dishes (raw vegetables dipped in a hot anchovy and garlic sauce).

The Langhe

In the local dialect, the term *langa* refers to the gentle hills which make up the landscape of this area of Piedmont. In the Middle Ages, castles, churches and abbeys were built in the Langhe, and, during the following centuries, noble villas, palaces, towns and cottages. Today, they attract tourists who are not only after culture but also enjoy good food and wine. The Langhe are in the Province of Cuneo. The principal wine towns here are Alba, Barolo and Barbaresco. Here, the Nebbiolo grape, which already enjoys a high reputation in other parts of Piedmont, achieves its finest expression in the two wines named after these towns. To complete the wine scenario of the Langhe, the area produces a Moscato d'Asti of the highest caliber, along with a host of excellent reds such as Nebbiolo, Barbera d'Alba and four Dolcetto wines from four famous wine towns. The **first itinerary** visits the eleven towns of the area which makes **Barolo DOCG**. This is one of the wine sanctuaries of the world and the concentration of enotecas and gourmet restaurants has to be seen (and tasted) to be believed. In addition to the road itinerary, there is a network of delightful walks which meander through vineyards and along winding lanes. Beautiful hills surround the old town of Barolo, with its fine castle, narrow streets and interesting corners. This town has the honor of being the capital of a wine district which is quite unique. As a result, many food and wine events are staged here and the activities of the Enoteca Regionale del Barolo are hosted in the Falletti castle. The itinerary continues to Castiglione Falletto, with its huge medieval castle, and Serralunga d'Alba, famous for its excellent Nebbiolo, with a splendid 13th-century castle at the top of the town. Further along is Monforte d'Alba, a medieval town built into the hillside with an intricate network of tiny steep streets leading up to an ancient bell tower with lovely views at the top. Next on our itinerary is La Morra, which has some interesting churches, Verduno, which has the exclusive right to produce DOC wine from the Pelaverga grape, and Grinzane Cavour, which has not only the Enoteca Regionale with a restaurant attached within the walls of its castle, but is also the headquarters of the distinguished Confraternity of the Knights of the Truffles and the

TCI HIGHLIGHTS

Enoteche Regionali and Botteghe del Vino

Piedmont has a sophisticated network of Enoteche Pubbliche (Regional Wine Promotion Centers) and Botteghe del Vino (private wine outlets) which has no equal anywhere else in Italy. Both play a decisive role in promoting the region, but they differ in terms of size and aims. The larger 'enotecas', often located in historic buildings, promote the wines of a whole area, while 'botteghe', which tend to be small outlets representing local consortiums of wine-producers, sell the wines of that particular town and specialize in those alone.
The wine itineraries suggested here refer to only a few of the myriad wine outlets scattered around Piedmont's numerous wine-making areas.

Enoteca Regionale Acqui, Piazza A. Levi 7, Acqui Terme - Tel. 0144770273
Enoteca Regionale Colline Del Moscato, Piazza XX Settembre 19, Mango - Tel. 014189291
Enoteca Regionale Del Barbaresco, Piazza Municipio 7, Barbaresco - Tel. 0173635251, www.enotecadelbarbaresco.it
Enoteca Regionale Del Barolo, Piazza Falletti, Barolo - Tel. 017356277
Enoteca Regionale Del Monferrato, Piazza Cardinal Callori 7, Vignale Monferrato - Tel. 0142933243
Enoteca Regionale Piemontese Cavour, Via Castello 5, Grinzane Cavour - Tel. 0173231120-0173 262159-0173230078
Bottega del Grignolino, Piazza Marconi 16, Portacomaro - Tel. 0141202666
Bottega dei Quattro Vini, Palazzo Comunale, Neive - Tel. 017367110 (Municipio)
Bottega del Vino, Via Mosso 6, Moncucco Torinese - Tel. 0119874765

Barolo, the historic wine-cellars of the Marchesi di Barolo.

Wines of Alba. Above the confluence of the Stura di Demonte and the Tànaro is the picturesque little town of Cherasco, with broad porticoed streets and elegant buildings. Cherasco is famed for its snails. The last town on our itinerary is Roddi, whose castle has splendid views.

Our **second itinerary** unfolds in the rectangle where **Barbaresco** is produced: it may not be a very long itinerary but there are good reasons for stopping at every turn. There is another itinerary for walkers 'From Barbaresco to Moscato to the Langa di Fenoglio', which sets off through the vineyards, passing Neive, Barbaresco, Treiso and Alba, and continues to Neviglie, Trezzo Tinella and Mango. At Barbaresco, another Nebbiolo paradise, the Torre del Bricco, the town's symbol, stands as tall as a lighthouse. (Be sure to visit the Enoteca Regionale located in the former church of S. Donato). The town of Neive forms concentric circles around its old *ricetto*, a kind of rustic fortress where the town's inhabitants withdrew in times of danger. The Bottega dei Quattro Vini (the four wines in question being Barbaresco, Moscato d'Asti, Barbera and Dolcetto d'Alba) is located in an 18th-century palazzo in the historic center. Treiso has some of the highest vineyards in the area and some prime truffle-hunting reserves. Alba, capital of the white truffle, was once associated with Barbaresco and has maintained its role as the production center of this famous wine. This town, with its reputation for sublime tastes and aromas, continues to impress food connoisseurs. Alba lies in the triangle formed by the confluence of the Cherasca Stream and the Tànaro River. Its circle of walls still surrounds the medieval town, with its umpteen towers and tower-houses, and its Romanesque, Gothic and Baroque buildings. Around it lie the gentle hills of the Bassa Langa, which gourmets know for their venerable wines and the noble white truffle. When the area produces such noble stimuli for the palate, it is hardly surprising that the local cuisine is of a rare level of sophistication. The noble wines made here go particularly well with the extraordinary range of locally-made, top-class cheeses, another treasure of this land. Castelmagno is the cheese *par excellence* of the upper and middle reaches of the Valle Grana, in the Province of Cuneo. The excellent Raschera cheese comes from the Alta Langa. The famed Robiola di Roccaverano is produced in various towns in the provinces of Asti and Alessandria. Murazzano is named after the town in the Province of Cuneo where the Valle del Belbo, the epicenter of its area of production, is located (for a more detailed description, please refer to the section on Cheese).

The Roero

The Roero is an area of hills covered with meadows, vineyards, extensive peach-tree plantations, chestnut woods and strawberry fields. The ridges of the hills are dotted with fortresses and the slopes of the hills are furrowed with deep, narrow gorges which reveal the stratification of the land. This wine area comprises about 20 towns situated on the left bank of the Tànaro River, opposite Alba, and its principal towns are Bra and Canale. Like the Langhe, it is devoted to Nebbiolo, but, increasingly, it owes its fame to two white grapes: Arneis and Favorita. The itinerary starts in Bra, the most important town in the area, and travels along the valleys of the Tànaro River and the Bòrbore Stream, encountering a succession of old towns and castles *en route*. Bra is essentially a Baroque town where it's worth stopping to sample its variety of good food and wines. But it is also of cultural interest. The town has given its name to a famous semi-fat cheese, one of the most important cheeses of the Cuneo area from the point of view of quality and quantity. Santa Vittoria d'Alba, perched on a panoramic ridge overlooking the broad valley of the Tànaro, is a picturesque little town where a visit to Cinzano, the famous producer of sparkling wines, vermouths and aperitifs, is a must. The underground cellars used to age its produce reach deep into the heart of the hill, covering an area of 3,000 m². They are quite extraordinary in terms of extent and atmosphere. Guarene has some fine Baroque churches and Castello Provana, a grand building with luxurious 18th-century decoration inside, in a panoramic position and surrounded by a large garden. The plain of the Tànaro is also renowned for its excellent vegetables. The itinerary continues towards Castagnito, in the heart of Roero, an area which produces many smooth, fruity wines (but also fruit and hazelnut plantations). The medieval town of Castellinaldo, clinging to its 13th-century castle, appears in the beautiful hilly landscape separating the waters of Tànaro and the Bòrbore, whereas the high bell tower of the

TCI HIGHLIGHTS

Turin's historic cafés

Turin's porticoes are a characteristic feature of the city, an outward expression of the civilized elegance and the discreetness of its people. Turin has many luxurious historic cafés which have been preserved like treasured antique caskets. Oozing with elegance and charm, these cafés are traditional meeting-places for politicians and intellectuals. They offer tourists the chance to experience not only a charming facet of the city but also the chance to taste some of its delicacies. Under the porticoes of Via Po, Abrate (10 Via Po) has a coffered ceiling and the original walnut counter. The mahogany shelves and mirrors, the tastefully arranged window with its jars of sweets, and the charming old terracotta and pale stone floor create a romantic, elegant atmosphere. Al Bicerin (5 Piazza della Consolata, Tel. 0114369325, www.bicerin.it), which opened in 1763, has conserved its old-fashioned aura. The wooden paneling, the red velvet benches and the white marble tables generate warmth and create a special, intimate, welcoming ambience. The ideal place to sample the original recipe of Turin's traditional 'bicerin', made with hot chocolate, espresso coffee and cream of milk. Under one of the porticoes overlooking Piazza Castello, for more than a century, Baratti&Milano (27 Piazza Castello, Tel. 0114407138) has maintained its old-fashioned, aristocratic charm. The walls are decorated with marquetry and gilt wooden ornaments which 'light up' the splendid interior. The main room has a long wooden counter and looks out onto the Galleria Subalpina. It is renowned for its brightly-colored sweets, delicious gianduiotti (made with chocolate and Piedmont hazelnuts), melt-in-the-mouth chocolate creams (all hand-made and of the highest quality), and its own blends of coffee, always including Arabica and exclusively wrapped. Between Piazza Castello and Piazza Vittorio Veneto, also under the porticoes of Via Po, is Caffè Fiorio (8 Via Po, Tel. 0118173225-0118170612). Beyond the entrance are semi-circular counters in yellow Siena marble. Behind, gleaming mirrors form a backdrop for the rows of bottles of liqueurs. In contrast to the classic note of this ambience, the other rooms are decorated with warm velvet furnishings, wallpaper with floral motifs, soft curtains and polychrome glasses. Together with the parquet floor they recreate the warm, elegant atmosphere of days gone by. Upstairs, small sitting-rooms and separés help to create a more secluded, romantic, muffled atmosphere. Fiorio is famed for its own blends of coffee,

Parish church of Priocca can be seen from miles away. As well as coming here to taste its wines, many people come to sample its *fritto misto alla piemontese* (mixed fry). In the upper reaches of the valley of the Bòrbore, Canale d'Alba is famed for its wine and its peaches, whereas Montà d'Alba, situated in hills supporting vines and fruit plantations, has some fine churches and a late- Renaissance castle, the Castello dei Morra, set in a splendid park. Cisterna d'Asti with an interesting medieval castle stands in a panoramic position in the south-west Monferrato hills. Here, as well as sipping Bonarda, you can sample all the typical local produce of the area. Built on two hills near a branch of the Bòrbore Stream, Monteu Roero is overlooked by the imposing Castello dei Roero, richly decorated and frescoed in the 16th and 17th centuries. The local farms produce not only superb wines, but also strawberries that have a wonderful perfume. Santo Stefano Roero, whose castle is now reduced to a ruined but imposing tower, focuses on the Parish church of S. Maria del Padio (which contains precious 17th-century marquetry work). The cuisine here revolves around truffles and dishes where wine is an important ingredient, such as *risotto all'Arneis* and *lasagne alla Bonarda*. Finally, the picturesque ruins of a tower overlook Vezza d'Alba, the starting-point for the hiking route called 'Sentieri del Roero' (Paths of Roero). This town is not only famous for its wines, but also for its truffles.

ice-cream and spectacular ice-cream cups. Caffè San Carlo (156 Piazza S. Carlo, Tel. 0115617748-011532586) embodies all the charm of Turin's historic cafés. Decorated like a Renaissance palace, it has two series of flower frescoes above the cornice, mirrors galore, columns set into the walls and a glorious technicolor marble floor. And, hanging in the center of the main room, as if to reinforce the uniqueness of the place, a vast chandelier in blown glass from Murano. Have a peek at the little dining-room called the 'Chinese room', with its Corinthian columns and capitals, niches with statues and gilt friezes. The café, which first opened in 1822, sells excellent blends of coffee and tea, but what it's most proud of is its candies and cakes. A rival, on the same side of the square, Caffè Torino (204 Piazza S. Carlo, Tel. 011545118) opened in 1903. It has several rooms, all decorated with flowery wallpaper, gilt mirrors and carved wooden fireplaces which add a touch of homely elegance to the place. Caffè Mulassano (9 Piazza Castello, Tel. 011547990), which opened four years later, is a delightful, petite café, richly decorated with colored marble, large mirrors, and carved gilt bronze and wooden decor. Because it is so unusual, this luxurious ambience was used as a film-set three times between 1940 and 1971. In addition to having a reputation for special liqueurs, the café also takes a pride in its exquisite sandwiches (or 'tramezzini'). Another historic venue not to be missed is the cake-and-coffee shop Platti (72 Corso Vittorio Emanuele II, Tel. 0115069056, www.platti.it), with a refined yet relaxed atmosphere. Here, you can gorge on chocolates or sip cocktails, surrounded by Louis XIV-style furnishings, huge antique mirrors, pastel-colored walls and ceilings and gilt stuccoes and friezes.

The Valle d'Aosta, the roof of Europe

Situated in the heart of the western Alps, the Valle d'Aosta is, not surprisingly, associated with the majestic peaks located in its territory: Mont Blanc, Monte Rosa and Gran Paradiso. These mountains are monuments of rock that carve up the sky while the valleys that lead up to the ridges linking them form a unique background, transforming even the simplest of walks into a truly memorable experience because of the magnificent scenery. The valleys that you encounter along course of the Dora Baltea offer a great deal to hikers. This very stark, picturesque area is largely unspoiled and consequently a source of immense plesure for naturalists. The local people are friendly and extremely hospitable. Whether you enjoy simple walks or go in for more energetic pursuits such as rock-climbing, this area has something for everyone to enjoy. But for anyone who visits the Valle d'Aosta, the memory they are most likely to take away with them is of its spectacular scenery.

Vittorio Sella refuge hut

Height difference: 920 m
Time: 2 hours and 30 minutes
Period: From June to October
Difficulty: None, some training is required
Altitude: 2,584 m
Location: Loson
Open: from Easter to end of September, Tel. 016574310

The hike to the Vittorio Sella refuge, found in the Parco nazionale del Gran Paradiso, which is immersed in an environment characterized by grassy slopes and dense forests, offers a magnificent view of the glaciers of Valnontey, where the ibex reigns as lord of the park.

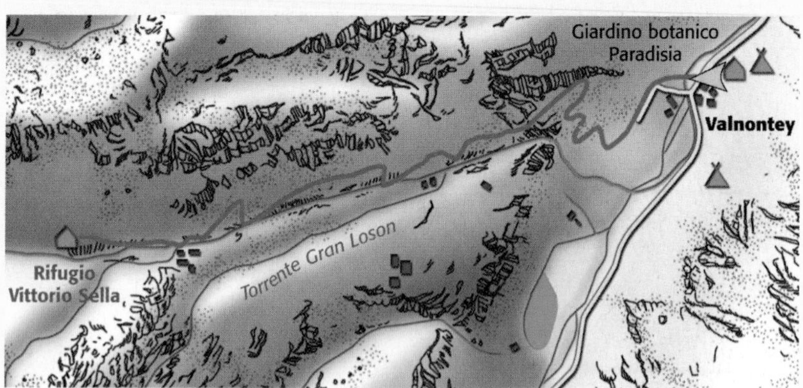

The itinerary

From Valnontey, a hamlet of Cogne found at 1,666m, follow the path (yellow sign) that goes along the Paradisia Botanical Garden and enter into the dense larch forest, where you easily reach a high altitude climbing the winding roads. As you go up, the view broadens allowing you to admire the impressive summits like the Torre del Gran San Pietro and the Mt Roccia Viva that form the head of Valnontey. Towards the valley, you can see the Garin peak and Tersiva, the pyramidal peak. Near the winding road, where the rushing torrent of Gran Loson flows, continue on the left, crossing the torrent and going past a steep forest zone, until you get out of the bushes. Continue up the steep rise going along the stream in order to make your way down to the pebbly riverbank, which you cross over a bridge. Then, go up only a few meters bringing yourself back to the mule track that you left at the fork. With some more winding roads, you pass an area that is often populated by ibex, which are used to the presence of people and allow you to admire them from nearby. Continuing the hike on flat ground, you reach the park building near the Sella refuge. This refuge dominates the wide plateau, found at 2,584m, where you can enjoy an excellent view of the group of the Gran Serra.

Panorama on the plateau where the Sella refuge is located.

Extending the hike

By sleeping at the refuge and starting out fresh the next day, it is possible to brave the climb up to the Loson hills (3,296m). The path does not present any particular difficulty but because of the high altitude and the danger that some of the stretches pose, it is recommended only for expert hikers. From the refuge, continue following the indications on the yellow signs and the triangular trail mark of Alta Via no.2 until you reach the adjacent plateau. Then, start going up the steep winding roads until you have almost reached the summit where, a little before the hills, the last couple of meters (equipped with metal cords) require great attention during a short unprotected stretch. The view of the mountains in the park, the bordering Valsavarenche, and the group of Monte Rosa towards the north-east, is extraordinary. Near the valley that is home to the refuge, you can find the small Lake Loson, a small expanse of water among the rocks, reachable in about 40 min.

Reflections in the water of Lake Loson.

Reaching the starting point

From Aosta follow the signs for Courmayeur until you arrive at Saint-Pierre where, before coming to the developed area, turn to the left towards Aymavilles. From here, continue along state road no.507 in the direction of Cogne. Then, bend to the right towards Valnontey until you come to the end of the street, where you reach a wide parking lot with yellow signs that indicate the road for the Vittorio Sella refuge.

Benevolo refuge hut

Height difference: 417 m
Time: 1 hour and 30 minutes
Difficulty: None whatsoever
Period: From June to September
Trail mark rods with signs and park information tables
Altitude: 2,285 m
Open: From June to September, Tel. 0165936143

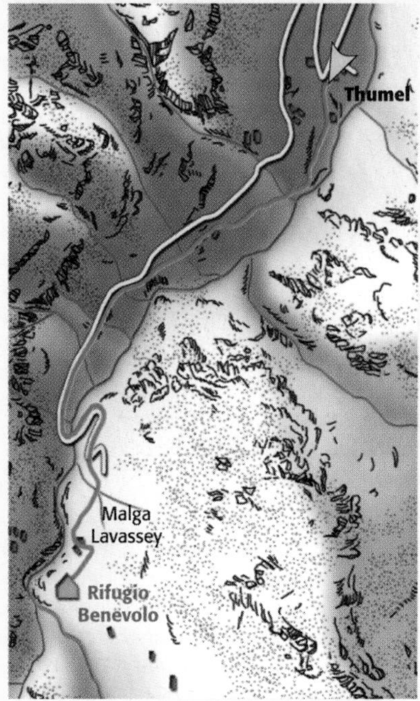

The Rhêmes valley, the westernmost part of the Parco nazionale del Gran Paradiso, is crossed by a torrent that creates the border between the protected area, to the left of the mountain ranges, and the protected area to the right. The absence of ski slopes has allowed for an exemplary preservation of the nature and the villages, as in the case of the village of Chaudannaz.

The itinerary

The hike begins at the end of the road, which is open to private vehicles, and where the last asphalt stretch continues until it arrives at a panel near some chalets. Get onto the easy mule track that crosses a larch forest during the first stretch and continues until it arrives near the Park house. Move ahead while remaining on the valley floor along path no.13 that follows the mountain range on the right and runs parallel to the Dora di Rhêmes. Keep on the same path as it alternates between streches that are clearly sloping and others that seem flat, but are actually slightly inclined. The view here takes in the valley floor and the imposing Grande Traversière. Cross the bridge and continue on the right, where you find a wooden board that indicates the direction of the refuge. The paved mule track goes up the valley until the fork, where it cuts to the left and you take the path towards Col Bassac on the right. Continue passing along the foot of a rock fortification and on the remains of a mountain pasture, after which you can see the eastern wall of the Granta Parei. Go up along the gorges, where you can catch a glimpse of the silhouette of the refuge. To the right, you can admire the flow of the waterfall that springs from the gorge above and continues until the farm road. Now, bend to the left towards the bridge and go up on the right cutting across two winding roads of the mule track. Then, get back onto the mule track and continue until you reach the Lavassey pasture. Here turn to the right along a track beside the small canal and go ahead until you come to the Benevolo refuge that is found on 2,285 m high plateaus, surrounded by rocky ridges at the high part of the Rhêmes valley. As an alternative for the climb, you can walk the entire road, which is open to cars. Although it is longer because of its narrow curves, it makes for an easier climb. This time, the majority of the uphill is covered along two series of continuous, winding turns. Beyond these turns, the road remains at the same altitude offering a broad view of the valley floor and the path that runs along the torrent.

The waterfall below the last part of the walk up to the mountain refuge.

A splendid view of the small mountain tarn of Lake Bleu.

Extending the hike

The climb to Lake Goletta is an interesting and easy way to extend your trip, offering a scenic and naturalistic route.
Leaving the refuge, go to the right of the plateau, cross the torrent using the bridge, and turn right again (path no. 13 D). Going up the slope crosswise, go past the crest and find your way onto the last glacial terrace, occupied by the basin and the Goletta glacier.

Reaching the starting point

From Aosta continue in the direction of the Monte Bianco tunnel until Villeneuve where you leave the main street and turn to the left to get to Introd. From here, continue uphill and take a right at the fork, heading towards Rhêmes, and drive along the valley until you get to Thumel where you find a parking lot.

Lake Bleu

Difference in height: 426 m
Time: 1 hour and 30 minutes
Difficulty: None whatsoever
Period: From June to October
Trail mark: Signs and marks in yellow paint
Note: The lake can also be reached by mountain bike. In Blanchard, instead of going past the bridge on the left, walk along the mule track on the right before crossing the river.

There is a multitude of expanses of water found in this section of the Alps. Lake Bleu, which is located in the Val d'Ayas, did not receive its name by chance, but because of its very particular color.

The itinerary

From Saint-Jacques square (1,689m), follow the road that arrives at the houses of Blanchard, after passing the church. After a small bridge (yellow signs), go right along the edge of the stream until you arrive at the village of Fiery, where the path goes up into a dense larch forest. When the vegetation thins out the road leads you to the plateau on the lower part of Verra, which is dominated by the massive of Monte Rosa, with a scenic view of the Gobba di Rollin and the Castore and Polluce mountaintops. After crossing the plateau and following the signs near the wooden bridge, take the path on the left. In about 20 minutes, you arrive at Lago Bleu, 2,215 m high, which is surrounded by a moraine from the Verra glaciers and dominated by the immense size of Roccia di Verra.

Reaching the starting point

From Verrès, follow the signs for Champoluc that you pass while driving along the val d'Ayas, until you get to Saint-Jacques. On the left of the small church, there is an asphalt road that leads to Blanchard, where you can leave the car.

Piedmont, crowned with mountaintops

Piedmont literally means the foot of the mountain and it is a good indication of the type of landscape that abounds in these parts. On a clear day, the mountains are visible from the plain, forming a majestic natural frame and offering some spectacular views. In south-west section of these mountains, the valleys are almost in a radial pattern with Turin in the center, while to the north, they tend to be slightly less regular and more Alpine, adding to the overall glacial appearance. To the south, by contrast, the Maritime Alps are located close to the Mediterranean coast, but are not lacking in soaring mountains. This is truly the type of destination loved by hikers and those who enjoy superb landscapes. In addition, there are plenty of relatively unknown stunning spots with excellent views, ensuring this is a genuinely pristine natural area.

Casa dell'Alpino refuge hut

Difference in height: 571 m
Time: 1 hour and 30 minutes
Difficulty: None whatsoever
Period: From April to November
Trail mark: Signs and marked stones
Altitude: 1,303 m
Location: Pra Alps
Open: summer and weekends,
Tel. 032353326

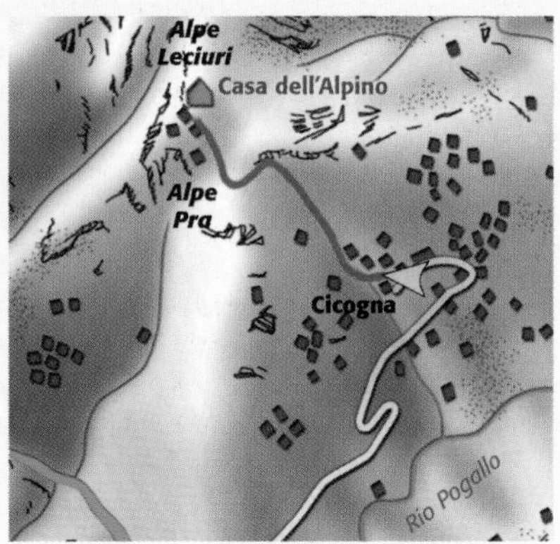

Near Lake Maggiore, you can find the most vast wilderness in Italy. In a unique valley, encompassed by silence, nature becomes sovereign with deep, steep, narrow valleys and gorges protected by an overhanging rock-face at the bottom, from which clear water runs. The hike enters into the territory of the Parco nazionale del Val Grande along a nature trail and continues among forests and pastures until it reaches the grassy summit, where the Casa del'Alpino refuge is found.

The itinerary

The path departs from a small parking lot in the populated village of Cicogna. After a few meters on the right, you find a wooden board that shows the park territory with its paths. On the way up, there are eight information panels and four signs in place that show the main aspects of the site. A little further on, a sign on the left indicates the direction to follow for the Pra Alps. Go past the last chalets, and follow the tracks up the side again entering into a chestnut forest. Continue to go up the path that climbs with a winding road as you are surroundeded by thick vegetation that hides the landscape. The track, at this point in the underwood, begins to look like a mule track, such as in the very first

The Casa dell'Alpino refuge.

leg of the itinerary. The vegetation thins out widening the view of Lake Maggiore and Lake Mergozzo. After you pass the other winding roads that are noticeably inclined, you arrive at the last side road and pass from the grassy summit to the Casa del'Alpino, from whose terrace you can enjoy a wide-open view.

Extending the itinerary

It is possible to go beyond the Pra Alps by continuing along the crest until you reach the Leciuri Alps, which are 1,311 m high. From here, continue going down along the ridge until you reach the small center of Pogallo. Now, walk keeping to the right and get on the path once the Pogallo Stream below is visible. This stream has a unique way of bringing the water to life in its spectacular movements in the narrow and rigid valley. Although the changes in altitude are minimal, the route is notably long as it takes at least two hours to make the return trip back to Cicogna by making a loop.

Reaching the starting point

By car, drive along the Milano-Laghi highway until the Gravellona Toce exit. From here, follow the signs to Verbania by turning to the left towards San Bernardino Verbano, before reaching the developed area. Along this road, which goes uphill, turn to the left again when you see the Cicogna sign. The road becomes rather narrow and goes up the Val Grande, running along the San Bernardino Stream for a long stretch. We suggest avoiding this in a camper. There are very narrow stretches with protruding rocks, and about 3 km from Cicogna, there is a tunnel that prohibits the entrance of vehicles taller than 2.7 m. Along the road there are very few chances to stop.

Pian Cavallone refuge hut

Difference of height: 500 m
Time: 1 hour and 30 minutes
Difficulty: None whatsoever
Period: From March to November
Trail mark: Signs and marked stones
Altitude: 1,530 m
Location: Pian Cavallone
Open: Last week in July to August,
Tel: 03234022852

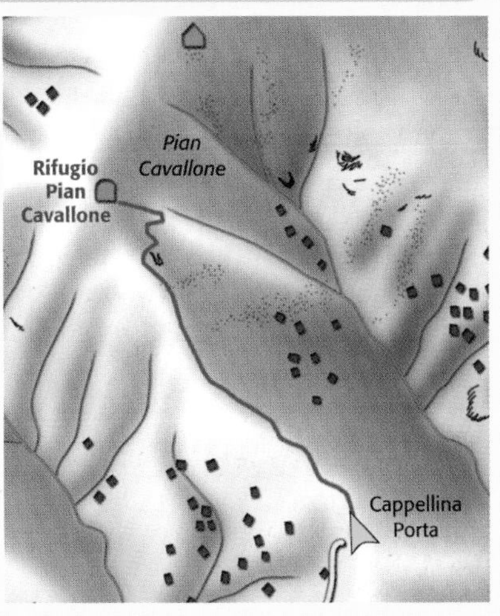

On the grassy slopes of Mount Todano, on the eastern boundary of the Parco nazionale del Val Grande territory, the rise of Pian Vallone forms a natural balcony that overlooks Lake Maggiore. The Pian Cavallone refuge stands above the dense forests that cover the crests all the way to the villages below.

The itinerary

The starting point is located near a little chapel called Porta, in the Caprezzo mountains. The path has been equipped by the park authority and offers a route, mostly in the forest, guided by explanatory boards and educational tables. The path alternates between short, but steep stretches uphill and side roads on flat ground. During some of the stretches, pay attention to the trail marks so you don't lose the route. You arrive at the small chalet of the Cornala Alps, after a fair bit of climbing, go around the side of the mountain on the long contour path, along the flat ground that leads you out of the forest, in sight of the Mt Todano crest. Further along, the track which becomes a gravel road goes up with few narrow winding roads until it reaches Pian Cavallone. From here, one last climb gets you to Pian Cavallone, a grassy rise between the Pogallo and Intrasca valleys, where there is a small votive chapel. You arrive, then, at a cross at the top, where you can enjoy the wide-open view of Lake Maggiore.

Reaching the starting point

From Gravellona Toce continue towards Verbania, turning at San Bernardino Verbano, before reaching the developed area. Along the road, turn to the left towards Caprezzo, and after arriving in the square, continue uphill until you get to the parking lot with the small chapel called Porta.

View of Alm Pile and the visitors' center.

Pastore refuge hut

Difference in Height: 271 m
Time: 30 minutes
Difficulty: none whatsoever
Period: from March to November
Pastore Refuge
Altitude: 1,575 m
Location: Pile Alps,
Opening: from May to September,
Tel. 016391220
Crespi-Calderini Refuge,
Altitude: 1,829 m
Location: Bors Alps,
Opening: August,
call Pastore Refuge

The path in the Parco Nazionale dell'Alta Valsesia territory, the highest park in Europe, unwinds in a mild environment in the presence of the Monte Rosa massif.

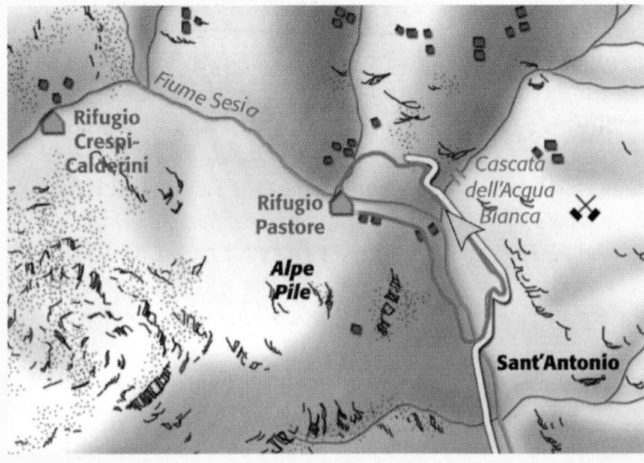

The itinerary

From the first waterfall of Acqua Bianca, you take a path that goes into a fir woods. Once you pass two small bridges, you arrive on foot at a flight of stone steps that lead to an open area, marked off by a net, where you can admire the beautiful waterfall of Pissa that allows you to see a rainbow when the sun is shining. Now, the path alternates between flat stretches and other steep steep uphill until you get to a deviation that is clearly marked. Go down on the left towards the river and then over a wooden bridge that overhangs a small gorge and leads to a field in the Pile Alps, where you find the Pastore refuge. Here you can appreciate the classic Walser architecture, which becomes the backdrop to the southern part of Monte Rosa. For the return to Alagna, you can opt for a different path that crosses the Alps and turns into a small street going towards Sant'Antonio. You walk downhill along narrow curves until you get to the pebbly riverbank and the small church of S. Antonio that you reach after a flat stretch of land. With a turn to the left, cross the bridge over the Sesia River to return to the starting point at the waterfall.

Extending your trip

From the Pastore refuge, leave in the direction of the Crespi-Calderini refuge on the path with the trail mark no. 6, passing through pastures with huge boulders. The hike develops in front of the massif of Monte Rosa, which remains in sight from the Parrot and Gnifetti mountaintops. After you cross the bridge over the torrent, go up the steps on the left which take you to the refuge.

Reaching the starting point

From Varallo drive along the entire valley in the direction of Alagna along highway no. 299. Continue going along the river until you reach the waterfall of Acqua Bianca where you find a parking lot.

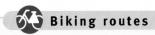

VALDIGNE

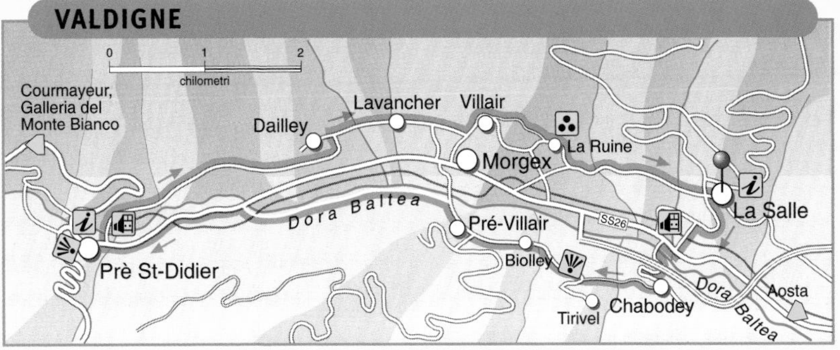

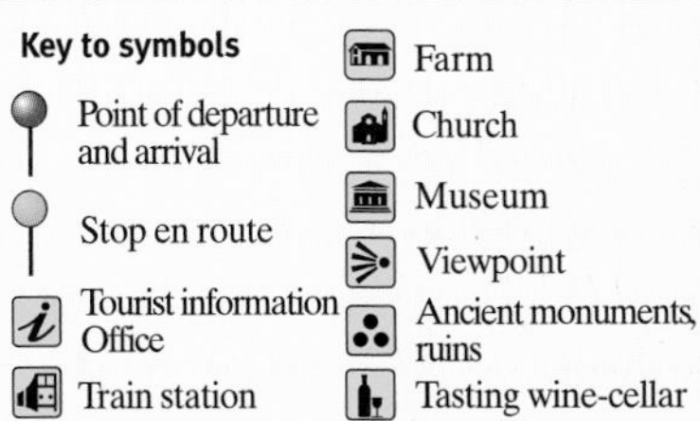

Route: about 20 km (14 km asphalt, 6 km dirt road): La Salle - Pont de La Salle - Chabodey - Tirivel - Morgex - Pré-Saint-Didier - Dailley - Villair di Morgex - La Salle.

Difficulty: easy to bike, not rugged, and suitable for cycle tourism. Can be cycled from Spring to the end of Fall.

Bike service: Cicli Benato, Via Lostan 106, Arvier, Tel. 016599131.

M.B. Aventure, Villair 15, La Salle, Tel. 3472417667, www.mbaventure.it

TOURIST INFORMATION

AIAT Mont Blanc, Piazzale Monte Bianco 13, Courmayeur, Tel. 0165842060.

On the valley floor that smells of wine

Valdigne is the zone in the north-western part of the Valle d'Aosta that starts from the valley of La Salle and Morgex and continues towards Pré-Saint-Didier as far as Courmayeur, which is found at the foot of the Mont Blanc massif and La Thuile. Leave from La Salle, on the sunny side facing the south, which is famous for its rural Alpine architecture. After crossing the SS 26 road, go up towards the hamlet of Chabodey. Pedal along the short stretch of the asphalt road passing under the highway, and shortly after, get onto the right side of the road going uphill.

A short pause beside the Dora Baltea.

Turn immediately to the right, following the wooden sign indicating Tirivel.
From Tirivel, continue towards Morgex, which lies at the bottom of the valley and is surrounded by the highest thick white grape vineyards in Italy, from which the famous DOC, 'Blanc de Morgex et de La Salle', is made. Once you reach Morgex and the bridge over the Dora Baltea, turn left and pedal uphill along the right of the Dora. The short stretch of asphalt road turns into a dirt road, and after passing a narrow gorge, you arrive at Pré-Saint-Didier, a small center where you can enjoy one of the most beautiful landscapes in the Monte Bianco area. At Pré-Saint-Didier, continue on the right following the signs that indicate the railway station and then cross the Dora Baltea. At this point, continue along one of the most charming and fascinating roads of the valley that winds through the vineyards stated above. After passing the campsite, turn left and head towards the village of Dailley. Right after arriving, take a right downhill towards Villair di Morgex. Go through the village while staying on right, and go up to the point along the road paved with cobblestones that extends into the vineyards.
The latter part of the itinerary goes on to La Salle, the starting and arrival point, without presenting any difficulty.

LE LANGHE

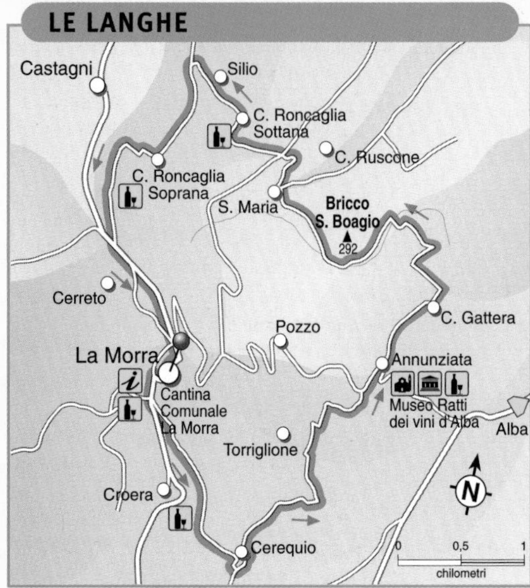

Route: 14 km: La Morra - Cerequio - Pelorosso - Torriglione - Rocchette - Annunziata - Monfalletto - Tetti Santa Maria - Silio - Roncaglia Soprana

Difficulty: The altitude of the path changes from time to time. The course covers mainly dirt roads, so a mountain bike is a must. Untrained cyclists may also attempt the course. There are a few steep climbs and they can be covered on foot. The path can be walked all year round. Best not to attempt after strong rains because the end of the road may be muddy.

Bike Service: Cicli Gagliardini, Via Ospedale 7, Alba, Tel. 0173440726

Idea Bici Dogliani, Via Cappa 59, Dogliani, Tel. 017371129

TOURIST INFORMATION

Atl Ente Turismo Langhe Monferrato e Roero, Piazza Risorgimento 2, Alba, Tel. 017335833, www.langheroero.it

Comune di La Morra, Piazza Municipio 1, La Morra, Tel. 017350105 www.la-morra.it

The Barolo path in La Morra

The relaxing atmosphere of Langhe with its rolling hills allows you to immerse yourself in your surroundings while pedaling through a charming landscape, where man and nature have made geometrically perfect vineyards. Mount your bike in front of the La Morra winery continuing on the path that leads to the medieval wall, known as Bastioni, then follow the sign for Cerequio-Fontanazza. Veer right at the fork between Fontanazza and Cerequio, and after a stretch along the crest, continue downhill until you reach Cerequio. The dirt road follows a contour line passing under the houses of Fontanazza. Carry on towards Pelorosso, where you take a left downhill towards the bottom of the valley. After passing under the houses of the small village of Torriglione (on the left), head towards the vineyards. The path then crosses the Gallinotto Stream, passing the vineyards of Giachini and Bricco Rocca. Get onto the road and pass near the church of Annunziata – with baroque facade and Romanesque bell tower – and a winery of the former monastery of the monks of Marcenasco. Shortly after, leave the town heading into the country until you reach Monfalletto. Near the monumental cedar of Lebanon, the road bends left and connects to a road that runs along the mountain of San Biagio and arrives at Santa Maria. The course continues along the hillside, which is plowed by the Porretta River, almost to the valley floor, and soon after begins to go up the side of the hill, where you reach Tetti di Santa Maria. At this point, continue on the county road until you reach the church of Madonna di Plaustra and take the road to Silio, where the road bends to the left towards La Morra. In the vineyard of Roncaglie, take a right up a steep hill to the Madonna di Loreto plateau.

View of the village of La Morra.

PARCO DEL TICINO

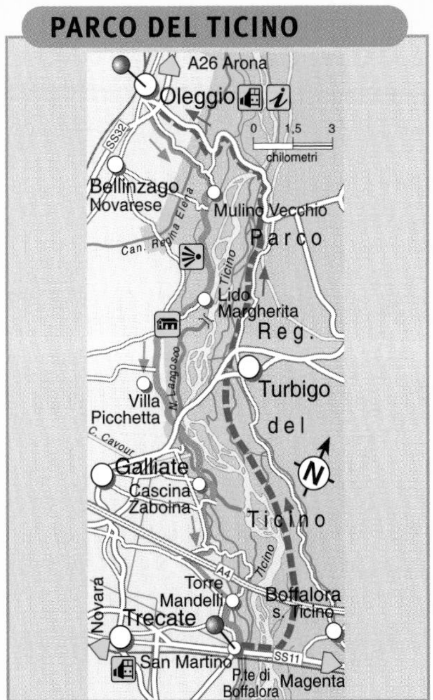

Route: 30 km: Oleggio - Mulino Vecchio di Bellinzago - Lido Margherita - cascina Galdina - Villa Picchetta - Vecchia Dogana - Villa Fortuna - Sette Fontane picnic area- Torre Mandelli - San Martino - ponte di Boffalora - Trecate

Difficulty: None whatsoever. Tour within range of everyone, very charming, and for the most part on special cycle paths. Accessible all year round.

Bike + Train: You reach the zone by train from Turin. Oleggio is on the Novara-Domodossola line; Trecate is on the Torino-Vercelli-Novara-Milano line.

Bike Service: Milani, Via Novara 80, Oleggio, Tel. 0321992208

Miglio Ezio, Via Libertà 95 Bellinzago Novarese, Tel. 032198424

TOURIST INFORMATION

Ente Parco naturale della Valle del Ticino, Villa Picchetta, Cameri, Tel. 0321517706, www.parcodelticino.pmn.it

Consorzio Parco Lombardo della Valle del Ticino, Via Isonzo 1, Ponte Vecchio di Magenta, Tel. 02972101, www.parcoticino.it

Along the cyclists' river

The Parco del Ticino offers many cycle paths that wind through the protected area. It is a true paradise for bicycle lovers. The itinerary departs from Oleggio and crosses the bypass, where you pedal towards the church of San Giovanni continuing in the direction of Molino Vecchio di Bellinzago, which you reach after having crossed the Regina Elena canal. Take the bicycle path going south, and go along the Molinaria irrigation ditch (14C), until you arrive at Lido Margherita (about 10 km from Oleggio) there is a refreshment stand. You arrive near the Galdina farmhouse, where there is a scenic view of the Cameri oxbow. From the small bridge that comes before the uphill stretch towards the farmhouse, you may continue on foot until you get to the Cameri oxbow, where there is a bird-watching hide. About 3 km from Lido Margherita, you arrive at Villa Picchetta (16C), a residential estate. At this point, the cycle path goes deep into a forest with trees as high as 30m. The road goes under the railway and crosses the SS 341 before passing near Cava Dogana and reaching the Vecchia Dogana. Here, you find another refreshment stand. Continue pedaling along over the bridges that pass over the Naviglio Longosco and the Cavour canal, passing near Villa Fortuna (16C, on the right). After passing the Ticinazzo canal and the 'Sette Fontane' picnic area, the

The scenic riverside cycle path.

route continues towards Galliate. Just after crossing the Naviglio Longosco, bend to the left towards Torre Mandelli and San Martino. Here, after the Boffalora bridge, you may continue by bike and head up the river along the towpath of Naviglio Grande through Boffalora, Turbigo, and over the Oleggio bridge, until you reach Oleggio. Or you may go to Trecate by taking the SS 11 (by train from Oleggio about 30 min). The Valle del Ticino is worth noting, as it forms a part of the Man and Biosphere areas, greatly recognized by the Assembly of the United Nations. Oleggio, Marano Ticino, Pombia, and Varallo Pombia are immersed in the greenness of the park, and offer paths suited to all cyclists.

The unmistakable excellence of the cuisine of Piedmont and the Valle d'Aosta stems from the blending of simple, genuine ingredients with the imaginative cuisine from beyond the Alps and the culinary legacy of the House of Savoy. Dishes vary from one area to another and have distinctive flavors and smells, ranging from the tasty products of the mountains, notably hams, salami and cheese, to the freshwater fish of the lakes, the noble white truffle, star of Piedmont cuisine, and the traditional rice

- Pasta
- Hams and Salami
- Cheese
- Wine
- Cakes

Food

dishes of the Po Valley. But the cuisine is also excellent because it is served with superb local wines. The famous wines of Piedmont are an important part of its heritage. Not to mention the wondrous art of pastrymaking which, in Turin's historic cafés, reaches dizzying heights.

Highlights

- Traditional Alpine flavors, Fontina and Fromadzo, jambon de Bosses and lardo di Arnad.
- Caffè Valdostano and Turin's exquisite chocolates and pastries.
- Genepì, a liqueur with the scent of Alpine flowers.
- Longstanding traditions and superb quality: the wines of Piedmont.

Inside

160 Pasta
163 Hams and Salami
168 Cheese
174 Wine
182 Liqueurs
185 Cakes
191 Food Festivals

VALLE D'AOSTA

After tourism, agriculture and livestock rearing are the main pillars of the economy of the Valle d'Aosta, a region which has made defending tradition into a political and economic principle. In the kitchen, the people of the valley reason like their ancestors in terms of knowing what it means to live in the mountains. The Valle d'Aosta has a range of typical local produce which few other regions in Italy can match. Fruit plantations and vineyards occupy the valley floor and the lower slopes of the mountains. The higher slopes are covered with vast expanses of woodland and pastures where the indigenous red-spotted Valdostana cows graze. One of the maximum expressions of this combination is Fontina cheese, but there are many types of local cheese. The same applies to hams and salami, one of the highlights being *jambon de Bosses*, a local type of raw ham, and *lardo di Arnad*, lard with a wonderful flavor and aroma, at its best with local rye bread and a drizzle of honey, *mocetta*, made from the leg of a goat or chamois, possibly the most typical of all the valley's preserved meats.

Mountain cuisine

As for the cuisine, one of the most traditional dishes is *soupe*, a wholesome soup which varies from one valley to another, but which contains all the flavors of the mountains: rye bread, cheese, meat stock, and local vegetables, anything from potatoes to cabbage. The range of *primi piatti* includes *zuppa d'orzo* (soup made with barley, another common mountain cereal), *polenta grassa*, flavored with butter and cheese, and *gnocchi alla Fontina*. Then come the meats, cooked with cheese in the famous *costoletta alla valdostana*, or marinated or cooked in red wine with juniper berries and other mountain flavorings. One example is the *carbonade*, particular for its sweet, oniony flavor, and game dishes, often made with roebuck or chamois meat.

Castello di Aymavilles.

The wines are the result of heroic efforts by the valley's farmers, who have painstakingly built terraces on the south-facing slopes of the mountains. The grape varietals have Franco-Piedmontese names (Petite Arvine, Vien de Nus, Picoutener (also called Picotendro) are some of the most common) and produce wines which are peculiar to this area. The best-known reds are made at Donnas and Chambave and go particularly well with meat cooked in the Valle d'Aosta style. The whites, such as Chardonnay and Pinot Grigio, have a stronger flavor here in the mountains. Blanc de Morgex, grown on the slopes of Europe's highest mountain, also makes superb sparkling wine. About 20 wines are produced in the valley overall. To find them you have to go from one winery to another, because they are hard to find outside the area where they are made.

At the end of a meal, apples and chestnuts tend to rule the roost. The pastry shops specialize in *tegole di Aosta* (wafer-thin, crunchy, round cookies made with almonds and hazelnuts, and sometimes chocolate), and *torcetti di Saint-Vincent* (buttery cookies, excellent when dunked in sweet wine). Finally, a fitting end to a meal is *caffè alla valdostana*, piping-hot espresso coffee generously flavored with grappa and ritually served in the *coppa dell'amicizia* (cup of friendship), a wooden bowl with several spouts, embodying the spirit and the fortitude of this area.

Red-spotted Valdostana cows grazing.

PIEDMONT

The word Piedmont conjures up images of Turin, with its history of the Savoys, its symbol, the Mole Antonelliana, and the hills of Langa and Monferrato, with their vineyards and castles. The figures confirm that the largest number of visitors who come to Piedmont, whether for cultural or food and wine tourism, come to explore the triangle formed by Turin and the towns of Asti, Alessandria and Cuneo. This large area, stretching from the right bank of the Po River across to the Apennines and up to the Alps, has a variety of scenery: the valleys with their vegetable and fruit farms, the hills with their vineyards planted on the sunnier slopes, and the rough grazing land higher up. The great variety of raw materials resulting from this diversity of landscape ennobles the cuisine of domestic kitchens, and makes it sumptuous in the extreme when chefs turn patrician houses into gourmet restaurants.

Steeped in tradition

If we look at a traditional menu, we can see that the cuisine is multi-faceted. Among the starters, two sauces deserve special mention: *bagna cauda* and *finanziera*. The first is made with olive oil, garlic and salted anchovies (thelatter were brought for centuries from Liguria along the old Salt Route), and eaten with the vegetables typically produced in the area of the Monferrato, especially the 'cardo spadone' (cardoon). These are dipped raw into the piping hot sauce. The *finanziera* is a dish combining the spirit of the peasantry, who use ingredients such as chicken combs, livers and giblets, and the spirit of the aristocracy, so that it became a favorite with the bankers of Turin (hence its name). Now it is the turn of egg-pasta dishes, the real test of a good cook: first *tajarin*, pasta rolled flat and cut into very fine strips. Often they are served with the juices from roasts, or flakes of the noble white truffle, a feature of many excellent Piedmontese dishes. Here, *agnolotti* are filled with 'magro', that is, spinach and ricotta, or with strongly-flavored stewed meat. Rice grown in the Po Valley deserves a special mention. Risotto is made *all'onda* (meaning quite liquid and creamy), with truffles, and with beans in the Novara classic, *paniscia*.

Having reached the meat course, the first mention goes to the 'fat-thighed ox' of the Piemontese breed, the pride of the Langhe. They provide the raw material for unforgettable *bollito misto* (braised beef) and produce a marvelous flavor when cooked with Barolo. Another famous dish is the *fritto misto* (mixed fry), consisting of different meats, vegetables and even apple slices and amaretto cookies, all disguised in a thin veil of batter. Frogs and snails also feature on the traditional menu.

Cheese in Piedmont is an enormous subject. Some of the most renowned are Bra, Castelmagno, Murazzano, Raschera and Roccaverano, with their DOP labels. Up in the mountain pastures, cheeses have different flavors, made with recipes brought from the other side of the Alps by people who settled in the Piedmontese mountains centuries ago: the Occitans, the French from Provence in the western valleys, and the Walser on the slopes of Mt Rosa. Lastly, we come to the desserts, where chocolate has pride of place, and that typically Turin invention, the *gianduiotto* (a smooth blend of chocolate and Piedmontese hazelnuts), not to mention *marrons glacés* and many other sweet specialties.

A great deal remains to be said about the wonderful wines that accompany these dishes, especially the reds. Here, the Nebbiolo grape reigns supreme and Barbera is also a favorite with many wine connoisseurs, but we must also mention the sweet white Moscato d'Asti, which is world-famous.

Sheep- and goat-rearing makes an important contribution to Piedmontese cheese-making.

PASTA IN THE VALLE D'AOSTA

Isolated by the high massifs of Mt Cervino (the Matterhorn), Mt Rosa and Mt Blanc, the Valle d'Aosta has developed its own culinary traditions based on local products. As in all mountainous areas, under *primi piatti*, we find many soup and polenta dishes. Even pasta has succeeded in carving a tiny niche for itself in Valle d'Aosta cuisine. In addition to pasta shapes and recipes from the nearby Piedmont, we find a wide range of dishes with gnocchi, made either with boiled potatoes or pumpkin, and served either with the classic Fontina or other excellent local cheeses. Serving dishes with cheese or *fonduta* (cheese fondue) is the Valle d'Aosta's main contribution to the field of pasta. In fact, there is an endless list of recipes prepared in this way, called *alla valdostana*. Pasta povera ('poor' pasta), which comes from the rustic cuisine of the Walser minorities, whose culture is close to German culture and is made with chestnuts or buckwheat, has been pounced upon by many restaurateurs.

Fettuccine di castagne/ Chestnut pasta ribbons

Once upon a time white flour was a rarity and white bread was made only on special occasions. The habit of using other types of flour to make bread and pasta is still very common. Take fettuccine di castagne, a specialty of Saint-Vincent.
The dough, which usually contains some white flour nowadays, is rolled very thin and then cut into *fettuccine* (long, thin strips). When they have been boiled, they are traditionally served with a sauce made with pork ribs, cut into pieces and cooked with Savoy cabbage, white wine and vegetable stock.

Gnocchi

In the Valle d'Aosta, as in many mountainous areas, the cuisine contains many variations of gnocchi. The dough is made either with or without potatoes, and before the potato was introduced to Europe, they had to rely on other vegetables. Gnocchi di zucca are typical of the Valle d'Aosta and Piedmont, and are made with common wheat flour and boiled pumpkin flesh, bound with an egg. The gnocchi are baked in the oven with melted butter flavored with sage and Fontina.
Other gnocchi are made with buckwheat flour, according to an old Walser recipe.
In Gressoney, they flavor them with speck and chopped aromatic herbs.
In the Valle d'Aosta and Piedmont, the traditional recipe for potato gnocchi involves taking small lumps of dough, giving them a slightly concave shape, boiling them briefly and serving them piping hot with cubes of Fontina and grated parmesan cheese.

AOSTA

COURMAYEUR

Pastificio Gabriella

Via Roma 90, Tel. 0165843359
This artisan workshop makes dried pasta (short pasta shapes and spaghetti, dried in traditional drying rooms), and fresh pasta. As well as traditional egg pasta, they make pasta that is colored and flavored with cuttlefish ink, chili, basil or nettles. Their cocoa pasta is very unusual.

Pumpkin gnocchi, a Valle d'Aosta specialty.

Check Out Receipt

BPL- North End Branch Library
617-227-8135
http://www.bpl.org/branches/north.htm

Monday, August 27, 2018 5:06:47 PM

Item: 39999059257996
Title: Authentic Piedmont and Aosta Valley
.
Material: Book
Due: 09/17/2018

Item: 39999071132417
Title: Italian ways : on and off the rails from Milan to Palermo
Material: Book
Due: 09/17/2018

Total items: 2

Thank You!

PASTA IN PIEDMONT

In Piedmont, pasta recipes are either very sophisticated, a legacy of the Savoy court and a well-heeled bourgeoisie, or stem from the farming tradition, and are based on simple ingredients and basic recipes. From *agnolotti*, the pride of bourgeois families who jealously guard the secret of their umpteen versions, to the *tajarin* of the Langhe, made with lots of eggs. Since egg pasta was only served on special occasions, many country recipes were invented based on cheese and the products of the earth, from pumpkin to nettles or *erbette*, spinach-like greens still collected today in the fields. When combined with common wheat flour, these ingredients made unusual dishes oozing with flavor. There are many different types of gnocchi and *gnocchetti*. Many delicious-smelling recipes come from the Occitan valleys with their Provençal culture, for example *ravioles*, which are really gnocchi, made with only Toma cheese and potatoes. As far as sauces are concerned, as well as *ragù* (a classic meat and tomato sauce) and vegetable sauces, they serve *agnolotti* with the cooking juices of *brasato* (braised beef) or Alba's famous *tartufo bianco* (white truffle). They also grate it generously over tajarin, provided they are not already flavored with an old-fashioned *ragù* made with giblets or mushrooms.

In the gentle landscape of Piedmont, over the years, a prestigious gastronomic tradition has evolved in which pasta has become an important ingredient.

Agnolotti

This shape of filled pasta is made with squares or rectangles of fresh egg pasta. Like *tajarin*, *agnolotti* are one of Piedmont's standard pasta shapes. They are found all over the region and are made with fillings which vary in terms of ingredients and richness, depending on the area. *Agnolotti* are usually fairly small, about 2-3 cm long. Although, in the Monferrato around Casale and around Turin, the filling is usually made with beef and pork (as it is in Asti) and pieces of ham or brain, in the Lower Canavese, the filling also contains sausage and Savoy cabbage. Cooking this vegetable with meat is also common in and around Cuneo, whereas, around Alessandria and Tortona, it is made with beef braised in a robust red wine, and the cooking juices are poured over the *agnolotti* before serving. During the truffle season, *agnolotti* are often served with grated white truffle. *Agnolotti al plin*, which look vaguely like little boats, are a variation on the traditional *agnolotto*. Generally they are filled with veal and pork meat. *Plin* is a dialect word for the pinch given to the top of the *agnolotto* to seal in the filling. *Agnolotti* are particularly common in the area of the Langhe, where they are usually served with sage cooked for a few minutes in melted butter or with the juices from roast meats.

Corzetti

A specialty of Novi Ligure (Alessandria), *corzetti* are thin disks of flat egg pasta which are cut out using a wooden mold. The pictures on the molds are imprinted on the pasta. Once every family had its own pasta mold, usually depicting a particular symbol or the family crest.

Gnocchi della Val d'Ossola

The enormous variety of gnocchi in Italy is due to the fact that there are different ways of making the dough, variations in the shape, the size, the filling, and what they are served with. As well as the classic potato gnocchi, in the Val d'Ossola they are made from pumpkin flesh and chestnut flour. Usually they are served with a mushroom and onion sauce and a smattering of Piedmontese cheese.

Ravioles are made with boiled potatoes and Toma cheese bound with egg, and served with melted butter.

Ravioles or raviolas

These large cheese and potato gnocchi, served with melted butter, are typical of the Vallone di Bellino in the Val Varaita (Cuneo). The dough is made with potatoes and Toma cheese, bound with egg. The dough is made into small, ciabatta-shaped 'loaves', which are then cut into long strips. These are rolled on a flat surface until they are long thin rolls with a diameter of about 1cm. These are made into spindle-shaped *raviolas*, about 4 cm long.

Tajarin

This is a form of fresh egg pasta, long and very thin with a square or rectangular cross-section. Invented in the areas of the Langhe and Monferrato, *tajarin* have been common all over Piedmont since at least the 15th century. Once the pasta has been rolled thin, it is rolled up and cut with a large knife into thin strips no wider than 2.5-3 mm. The sauce they are served with varies depending on the area. The most famous is a *ragù* made with giblets, known as *comodino*, typical of the Langhe, but *tajarin* are also excellent with mushrooms or truffles and a dash of extra-virgin olive oil (*tajarin alla trifula*). At Roaschia, near Cuneo, *tajarin* are served with a sauce made by cooking *pancetta* (local bacon) and onions in red wine.

BIELLA

Pastissima

Via Pietro Micca 5, Tel. 01521982

This pasta shop is renowned for its *agnolotti al plin*.

CUNEO

Pastificio Boetti

Corso Soleri 2, Tel. 0171692466

Here the fresh pasta is made with flour from common and durum wheat. Typical pasta shapes include: *ravioli al plin*, gnocchi and classic *tajarin* made with flour and eggs.

TURIN

AVIGLIANA

Emilio Maldera

Via Quarto Inferiore 56, Tel. 0141293715

Artisan pasta made with flour from local common and durum wheat: many different kinds of *agnolotti*, especially good agnolotti al plin and freshly-made *tajarin*.

The humble potato is often used to make gnocchi.

HAMS AND SALAMI IN THE VALLE D'AOSTA

In the heart of the Alps, in a microcosm which is still fairly wild and has been a crossroad of different cultures for centuries, the Valle d'Aosta takes pride in its hams and salami, part of its highly unusual mountain tradition. Products like *jambon de Bosses* and *lardo di Arnad* have rightly been added to the list of foods that must be protected. *Mocetta*, *teuteun* and *boudin* are other typical charcuterie products of the Valle d'Aosta, whose magnificent flavors are achieved through refining processes which involve spices, wild berries and aromatic herbs. The hams and salami of the Valle d'Aosta should be eaten on their own or accompanied by genuine farmhouse products.

Boudin

Individual towns in the valley have various traditional ways of making this sausage. The most typical recipe uses potatoes and/or beet, pork lard, spices, garlic marinated in wine and, occasionally, blood. The mixture is fed into natural gut so as to obtain sausages of an opaque red color with large grains of fat and potato.
The blood sausage is then dried or matured. The dried sausages are eaten raw, while the matured version is boiled, after which it is either eaten as it is, grilled or fried.

Jambon de Bosses DOP

Made exclusively within the municipality of Saint-Rhémy-en-Bosses, at an altitude of 1,600 m, this raw ham is made from the leg of adult pigs of prized breeds reared according to the DOP rules of production. The process involves pickling the meat in salt flavored with sage, garlic, rosemary, juniper berries, thyme and bay leaves. After this, the ham is left to mature in a dark, cool, well-ventilated room for 12 to 18 months. During the maturing period, the hams are usually moved into *rascards*, the typical hay barns of the high mountains of the Valle d'Aosta. When cut, the meat is a deep winey-red, whereas the fat should be white, and sometimes pinkish near the edge. It has a slightly salty, delicate flavor with an aromatic flavor resulting from the mixture of mountain herbs and berries, and an after-taste with a slight hint of game. Jambon de Bosses is branded with a trade-mark proving that it has been controlled by the Consortium.

Lardo di Arnad DOP

This famous lard is first mentioned in the registers of the refectory of the monastery of Sant'Orso in Aosta in 1570. Produced in the towns of the municipality of Arnad, it is made with the shoulder and back of pigs that are at least one year old, weighing 160 kg. The lard is cut into pieces and put into special containers which

TCI HIGHLIGHTS

Products with the DOP and IGP labels

Protecting food production is the first step to safeguarding a heritage which is not only of economic significance, but also, and more importantly, of cultural importance. It is an act which confirms and aims to preserve the quality of a product. The DOP and IGP labels protect a product's environment, the human input and its quality. Products carrying the DOP (Protected Designation of Origin) label are products which, first, must comply with a strict set of production regulations, based on the local tradition, which specify what raw materials must be used and how they are processed. Secondly, they must be produced in a particular geographical area, although the "typical production area" may extend beyond the territory of a town and refer to a whole region. Products carrying the IGP (Protected Geographic Indication) label are protected in a similar way to DOP products (in terms of complying with production regulations and the particular area in which it may be produced) but the processing and packaging may be conducted in a wider area. The IGP label is the form of protection most often applied to fruit and vegetable products and their derivatives.

are gradually filled up with alternating layers of lard and salt mixed with pepper, slices of garlic, bay leaves, sage, rosemary, cloves, cinnamon, juniper berries, nutmeg, yarrow and water. Finally, it is covered in brine. Lardo di Arnad is left to mature for a minimum of 3 months and sometimes more than a year. The final product has a wonderful perfume and an unforgettable taste--it melts in the mouth--which recalls the many herbs and spices used in this traditional recipe.

Lardo di Arnad, rye bread, walnuts and honey.

Mocetta or motzetta

This cured meat is common throughout the valley. It is made using the muscle or thigh of a cow, sheep or goat, flavored with salt, pepper, garlic, juniper berries, thyme, sage, bay leaves, rosemary, winter savory and other mountain herbs, and kept under salt. The product is then left to dry for at least a month. Mocetta releases its flavors best when eaten with slices of rye bread spread with fresh farm butter, and a drizzle of honey.

Teuteun

This unusual kind of cured meat is made with the teats of red-spotted Valdostana cows. The teats are cut into small pieces and soaked in brine with a mixture of bay leaves, rosemary, sage, juniper berries, garlic and salt. When the mixture is removed from the brine, the teuteun is pressed and hung in special rooms to dry before being steamed. When cut, the slices are pink and have a delicate flavor. Usually it is served with a 'salsa verde' made with parsley, olive oil, and garlic.

AOSTA

La Bottega degli Antichi Sapori
Via Porta Pretoria 63, Tel. 0165239666
Their range of products includes selected artisan salami, hams and *lardo di Arnad*; also cheese.

ARNAD

Macelleria Renzo Cretier
Extraz, via Nazionale 11, Tel. 0125966212
Here you will find traditional local hams and salami: lardo di Arnad, *pancetta alle erbe*, *mocetta*, Valle d'Aosta hams, *boudin* and *teuteun*.

Salumificio Bertolin
Champagnolaz 10, Tel. 0125966127, www.bertolin.com
A longstanding producer of traditional Valle d'Aosta salami and cured meats, where you can buy excellent *lardo di Arnad*, *mocetta* and *teuteun*.

COGNE

Macelleria Marco
Via dottor Grappein 38, Tel. 016574632
This butcher has top-quality meat, from Valdostana or Piedmontese Fassone herds. The finest ingredients for traditional products such as *boudin*, Valle d'Aosta sausages, *teuteun*, beef *mocetta* and *lardo di Arnad*.

GIGNOD

Salumificio Gignod
Plan Chateau 1/D, Tel. 016556007
The hams and salami produced in this meticulously professional butcher's include *teuteun* and *mocetta*.

LA SALLE

Macelleria Salumeria Ottoz
Via Gerbolier 1, Tel. 0165861165
Here you can be sure to find typical local hams and salami, especially *lardo*, *boudin* and *mocetta*.

SAINT-RHÉMY-EN-BOSSES

Cooperativa Jambon de Bosses
Saint-Rhemy, Tel. 0165780842, www.jambondebosses.it
The cooperative was formed by the artisans who produce this prized DOP ham, pickled in a mixture of juniper berries and mountain herbs and matured in hay.

HAMS AND SALAMI IN PIEDMONT

Piedmont produces great wines and truffles, and has an ancient and much-revered cheese-making tradition. But it is also known for its expertise in processing meats to produce hams and salami. The sheer variety of such products reflects the diversity of its landscape, which ranges from mountain pastures to the unique microcosms of the Langhe and the Monferrato, and the area around the lakes. Here, typical local produce are not just a matter of artisan skills but also a matter of pride. In the field of salami this has resulted in niche products and a profusion of hams and bresaolas made in different ways in different valleys, according to local variations and customs. The meats produced here go excellently with the area's famed local wines (Barbera, Grignolino, Nebbiolo, Dolcetto....), and are sometimes used by butchers to add a particular flavor to the other ingredients. As well as being served as a starter, marinated or cooked, hams and salami are also used to enhance many specialties of Piedmontese cuisine, such as *salsicce all'uva* (sausages with grapes) and *bollito misto* (mixed boiled meats).

Bresaola from the Val d'Ossola

In the Val d'Ossola, making cured beef is an ancient tradition. It is also sometimes called *carne salata*. Salted meat is pickled in pepper, cinnamon, nutmeg, thyme, rosemary, cloves, bay leaves, sugar and white wine, and then transferred for 3 to 4 months to special cool, dry, well-ventilated maturing rooms. *Bresaola* is usually almost round and the meat is bright red and uniform with very faint striations of fat. It is eaten raw, having been dressed with a little olive oil, pepper and lemon-juice.

Mortadella di Fegato or 'Fidighin'

This salami made with pure raw pork is a typical product of the area of Novara and Vercelli, and of the eastern edge of the region. It comes both 'cotta' (cooked) and 'cruda' (raw). The cooked version contains pork liver, cheek, *pancetta* (bacon) and chopped pork fat, while the raw version contains pork liver, pork rind and *pancetta*.

Salam d'la Duja

A typical product of Novara, Vercelli and Biella and the southern part of the Val Sesia, this is pure pork salami preserved in pork lard. Once the small salami have been dried and matured, they are put into a 'duja' (a terracotta jar) and covered with rendered lard which, as it solidifies, keeps them soft and enables them to keep longer. They are matured in lard for at least 8 or 9 months, a process which gives them a slightly tangy flavor.
Salam d'la duja is a key ingredient in the typical Piedmontese bean risotto, *paniscia*, or can be sliced and eaten raw.

Salame cotto

This salami is one of the ingredients of a traditional *gran bollito alla piemontese* (Piedmont's classic dish of boiled meats). It is a large sausage made with prime pork meat, lard, pancetta and herbs which vary depending on the recipe (salt, pepper, cinnamon, winter savory, mint, cloves and wine: usually Barbera but Bonarda, Arneis or Marsala are also used).
The cooked salami, produced mainly around Alessandria and Asti, is eaten when it is fresh, either warm or cold. When sliced, the salami is dry and pink with large grains of lard.

Salami cotto, an ingredient of the traditional bollito alla piemontese, resembles its more famous cousin from Emilia, mortadella.

Salsiccia di Bra

Produced in Bra and the surrounding area, this sausage is visibly leaner than other sausages because it is made mainly with meat from a year-old calves. When the meat has been minced and processed to form a uniform paste, it is flavored with salt, freshly ground pepper, cinnamon, nutmeg, wild fennel seeds, mace, wine and grated mature Toma cheese from the Langhe. The sausage can also be eaten raw when fresh, but is also excellent cooked.

Sausages from Bra.

Violino di Capra

This small raw ham is a typical product of the Alpine Chain. It is made using the leg of goats from local farms. It is flavored with salt, pepper, garlic, cinnamon, bay leaves, rosemary, thyme and juniper berries. It is then washed, dried in the open air, and left to mature for about 2 or 3 months in a warm, ventilated room. Some versions use lamb and chamois meat.

ALESSANDRIA

Il Salumaio

Via dei Guasco 20,
Tel. 0131253624
Has a wide range of selected Piedmontese artisan cheeses.

ASTI

AGLIANO TERME

Salumeria Truffa

Via Mazzini 1,
Tel. 0141954047
Artisan production with a broad range of specialties including *salame al tartufo*, *salame al Barolo* and *salame al Barbera* (salami made with truffle, Barolo and Barbera) and *pancetta alle erbe* (bacon flavored with herbs).

CASTELLO DI ANNONE

Gastronomia Fungo

Via Roma 90,
Tel. 0141401696
An artisan butcher's selling the best of the region's hams and salami: raw and cooked ham, *prosciutto cotto al vapore* (steamed ham), classic *lardo* and *lardo* flavored with herbs.

COCCONATO

Salumificio Ferrero

Via V. Veneto 5, Tel. 0141907186,
www.salumificioferrero.it
This butcher's makes an all-Piedmontese prosciutto crudo using pigs he rears and butchers himself. Products on sale include: *pancetta* (bacon), *lardo*, cooked salami and raw salami flavored with truffles.

BIELLA

COGGIOLA

Salumeria Marabelli

Via Garibaldi 15, Via Roma 35,
Tel. 01578294
This artisan pork butcher's makes top-quality, little-known hams and salami, such as *salsiccia con le patate* (sausage containing potatoes) and *paletta*, a sort of miniature cooked ham.

CUNEO

Salumeria Ariano

Via Pascal 2, Tel. 0171693522
Everything sold in this shop is delicious: lard flavored with *herbes Provençales*, *salame cotto d'oca* (cooked goose salami), *salame di suino alle castagne* (chestnut salami), *salame alle lumache* (salami with snails) and *pancetta al Barolo* (Barolo-flavored bacon).

BOVES

La Bottega delle Carni

Via Roma 7, Tel. 01713802070,
www.martinicarni.com
This shop carries a wide range of local meats. They include *lardo speziato* (lard flavored with spices), cooked hams and salami, *pancetta* and *bresaola*.

BRA

Macelleria Aprato

Corso V. Emanuele II 162, Tel. 0172426334
This is the capital of *salsiccia di vitello* (veal sausage), but also has classic local hams and salami.

CASTIGLIONE FALLETTO

Cooperativa Carni Valle Belbo

Via Alba-Monforte 10, Tel. 014188250, www.carnivallebelbo.com
Products on sale include: *salsiccia al vino bianco* (sausage made with white wine), Barolo-flavored wild-boar salami, ham cooked in a wood oven, *salame crudo* and *salame cotto* made with hand-cut lard.

CORTEMILIA

Macelleria Robino Giuseppe

Via Cavour 20, Tel. 017381075
This butcher makes the great Piedmontese classics: *salame delle Langhe*, *salame al Barolo* and *salame cotto*, *cotechino* and little salami.

The distinctive flavor of beef from free-range cattle is enhanced even more when cured.

TURIN

Baudracco Maurilio & C.

Corso V. Emanuele 62, Tel. 011545582
Here everything is home-made: *prosciutto cotto al rosmarino* (ham flavored with rosemary), raw and cooked salami, sausages and *cotechino*. They have a wide range of DOP cheeses from the region and a splendid deli counter.

Macelleria Curletti

Corso Moncalieri 47, Tel. 0116602177
One of Turin's oldest butchers, this shop still has its original furnishings and a magnificent white marble counter.

Salumeria Steffanone

Via Maria Vittoria 2, Tel. 011546737, www.steffanone.com
Traditionally one of Turin's most important food shops , where you can find hams and salami, truffles, regional specialties and Piedmontese DOP cheeses.

CAVOUR

Macelleria Salumeria Silvio Brarda

Via Peyron 28, Tel. 01216295
Home-made specialties here include salami with Nebbiolo, products made with ox meat, salted and smoked meats, lard with rosemary and cooked salami.

Rolfo Elio

Piazza Sforzini 3, Tel. 012169091
This shop sells only its own products. Its specialty is a rare salami called *batiur*, meat cured in a pig's bladder, cleaned and treated with vinegar.

IVREA

Macelleria Salumeria Gastronomia Fratelli Giordano

Corso Cavour 78, Tel. 012549037
Specialties of this butcher's include *lardo alle erbe* (lard flavored with herbs), *salsicce al finocchio* and *salsicce al peperoncino* (sausages flavored with fennel and chili), *salame di patate* (potato salami), *salame d'la duja* and beef *mocetta*. These products can also be sampled at the restaurant next-door.

RIVOLI

Macelleria Scaglia

Bruere, Via Artigianelli 71/7, Tel. 0119573808
This butcher rears and butchers his own pigs and cattle from selected breeds using natural methods. In addition to excellent fresh meat, he also makes *salame* cotto, classic small salami, *lardo* and *pancetta*.

SUSA

San Giuliano

San Giuliano, Tel. 012232722
This butcher's shop makes hams and salami that have virtually disappeared, such as *mica*, a small salami with a wonderful smell left to mature in rye flour, and *carne concia* from the upper Valle di Susa, which is pickled, matured meat.

VERBANO-CUSIO-OSSOLA

SANTA MARIA MAGGIORE

Salumeria Bonardi

Via Matteotti 80, Tel. 032494781
Here they make incredible ham flavored with Alpine herbs, dry-smoked over a fire of beech, pine and juniper wood, and matured for 18 months.

CHEESE IN THE VALLE D'AOSTA

'The Valle d'Aosta, where the cheese is delicious and there is excellent grazing land...The cheeses are medium-sized and melt when cooked on the fire or used to flavor food.' It may sound like an excerpt from a Valle d'Aosta tourist brochure but the description comes from '*Summa Lacticinorum*', a book about cheese written in 1477. So we know that the cheese-making tradition here is extremely old. The milk used to make Fontina comes from one breed, indigenous to the valley, the red-spotted Valdostana cow. It feeds on Alpine pastures in the summer and on hay in winter. The milk is processed immediately after each single milking and the cheeses are matured in natural caves, washed with brine and regularly brushed. The result is a wax-yellow, smooth cheese with scattered eyes and a distinctive taste. It is often served as a fondue, but also accompanies polenta or gnocchi.

Fontina DOP

A register of the Great St Bernard Pilgrims' Hospice, dated 1717, is the earliest document mentioning Fontina officially, but the tradition of making this famous mountain cheese is very much older. The DOP production rules, some of the strictest in the entire Italian cheese-making scenario, defines Fontina as a semi-cooked cheese with a minimum fat content of 45%. The milk must be full-fat cow's milk from a single milking, only from indigenous Valdostana cows. It may be made anywhere in the Valle d'Aosta region. The round, flat cheeses must weigh between 8 kg and 18 kg. They are matured for an average of 3 months in dark storage rooms in natural environments with constant temperature and humidity.
At the same time, the microflora in such environments favors the formation of a thin, compact rind, which turns from straw-yellow to reddish-brown. When cut, the body is elastic, fairly soft and fondant with a few small eyes. It melts in the mouth and is usually a pale straw-yellow color, becoming a darker yellow in summer.

Fontina, with the label showing that it is protected.

Formaggio di Capra a Pasta Molle/Soft goat's cheese

Made with raw, full-fat goat's milk. A round cheese, matured in cellars or natural caves for between 20 and 25 days.

Formaggio di Pecora o Capra a Pasta Pressata/Pressed ewe's or goat's cheese

This cheese can be made with raw, full-fat ewe's or goat's milk. It is round and comes in various sizes. It is usually matured in cellars or natural caves. The words 'di alpeggio' (that is, produced in a mountain dairy) should feature on the label.

Formaggio Misto/Mixed milk cheese

Made with milk from raw, full-fat milk from Valdostana cows, goats and ewes. Usually round in shape, it is matured in cellars or natural caves for between 60 and 90 days. The words 'di alpeggio' (that is, produced in a mountain dairy) feature on the label.

Fromadzo DOP

Mentioned in early descriptions of the valley, this cheese was the traditional alternative to Fontina whenever the other was scarce. According to the DOP production rules for Fromadzo, it must be made with cow's milk from at least two milkings. The maturing process can last from 60 days to 8-10 months. In time, the straw-yellow rind of these round, firm cheeses changes to reddish gray. The body is firm and elastic with scattered faint eyes. It has smells of buttermilk and has a pronounced hint of grass in summer. The flavor is semi-mild when fresh, and slightly salty and tangy when mature. It is sometimes flavored with juniper berries, cumin or wild fennel seeds.

Reblec (Reblèque)

A fresh cheese made with full-fat milk from Valdostana cows, usually eaten with salt. Reblec da Crama is a similar cheese, regarded more highly because a greater amount of cream rises to the surface.

Salignoùn

This is a special kind of Séras with a uniform body flavored with salt, oil, vinegar and herbs. There is also a spicy version containing chili.

Fromadzo DOP.

Séras

A cheese made with Valdostana cow's, goat's and ewe's milk. The words 'di alpeggio' (that is, produced in a mountain dairy) feature on the label.

Toma di Gressoney

Produced in the lower Valle d'Aosta from raw, skimmed or semi-skimmed cow's milk. A small quantity of goat's milk is sometimes added. This round cheese is matured in cellars or natural caves for beetween 3-4 months and 2-3 years.

AOSTA

L'Angolo del Formaggio
Via Trottechien 13, Tel. 0165230817
The place to go for local cheeses, including Fontina and goat's cheeses.

Maison de la Fontine
Via Monsignor De Sales 14, Tel. 0165235651
This shop sells matured home-made Fontina and other Valle d'Aosta cheeses, local hams, salami and wines.

Institut Agricole Régional
La Rochère 1/A, Tel. 0165215811, www.iaraosta.it
This agricultural school is famous. During the summer months, the students learn how to make Fontina and Fromadzo at the dairy in Rhêmes-Notre-Dame.

ARNAD

Caseificio Cooperativo Evançon
Glair, via Nazionale 7, Tel. 0125966261
This dairy sells Fontina and Fromadzo DOP, Reblec, Salignoùn and fresh milk.

CHAMBAVE

Champagne Società Cooperativa
Champagne, Tel. 016646360
This dairy specializes in Fontina, Fromadzo and other typical local cheeses.

CHÂTILLON

Società Cooperativa Latte Châtillon
Via Rimembranza 10, Tel. 016661681
Production at this dairy focuses on Toma flavored with spices, Reblec and fresh cheeses.

COURMAYEUR

Fratelli Panizzi
Via Circonvallazione 41, Tel. 0165843041, www.panizzicourmayeur.com
Here you will find regional specialties such as Reblec and Salignoùn.

DONNAS

Pietro Vallet
Via La Balma 18, Tel. 0125807347
Specializes in artisan cheeses such as Fontina, Salignoùn and local cheeses.

NUS

Maison Rosset
Via Risorgimento 39, Tel. 0165767176
This dairy makes remarkable cheeses using natural processes, without any chemical additives. Cheese is also sold at their mountain dairy.

SAINT-CHRISTOPHE

Cooperativa Produttori Latte e Fontina
Croix Noire 10, Tel. 016535714, www.fontinacoop.com
Here you can buy Fontina and Fromadzo.

SAINT-PIERRE

Azienda Agricola Les Ecureuils
Homené Dessus, Tel. 0165903831, www.lesecureuils.it
This company, based at a farm at an altitude of 1,500 m, makes goat's cheese.

VALTOURNENCHE

Cooperativa Fromagerie de la Vallée du Marmore
Evette, Tel. 016692132
This cooperative sells Fontina, Reblec, cow's milk cheeses, milk and butter.

CHEESE IN PIEDMONT

On 23 September, 218 BC, Hannibal was making his way down the Alps, bound for Rome. He stopped at Susa (others say at Taurasia, now Turin) but not for military purposes: it was to build up his army with 'toma'. But milk-production in Piedmont dates back much further. It was introduced by Indo-European peoples who migrated here in about 5000 BC. When they arrived with their herds of cows, they already knew how to process milk. That ancient tradition continues today. Castelmagno, Murazzano, Raschera and Seirass are just a few of the long list of Piedmontese cheeses. Cheeses made from cow's and goat's milk, hard, soft, fresh or matured cheeses, ricottas and Tomas. Many are made with milk from indigenous breeds, many are famous, others hardly known at all, but are equally interesting. Overall there are about 30 main types. About 80% of all Italian cheese comes from mountainous regions and the art of Italian cheese-making is at its most creative in Piedmont. Cheese is the basis of the popular *fonduta*, it's used in risotto, poured melted over *gnocchetti*, used in the fillings of fresh pasta, grated over *carpaccio*, eaten as cheese, tasted with sublime wines and incorporated into desserts. Its scope is infinite.

Bra DOP

The name comes from the town in Roero which, in the past, was the main market for this cheese made in the Cuneo Alps. Bra is a semi-fat cheese made with cow's milk, especially from the White Piemontese breed. It is round, with a diameter of 30-40 cm and weighs 6-8 kg. There are two types, depending on how long it is matured. The Tenero (soft) version is matured for a minimum of 45 days, has a thin, straw-white, elastic rind, and a straw-white, soft, mild-tasting body. Bra Duro (hard) is matured for more than 6 months, has a firm, dark rind and a firm, yellow-ochre body, a mild smell and a slightly tangy taste. The words 'd'alpeggio' (that is, produced in a mountain dairy) feature on the label of cheese made in the summer.

Castelmagno DOP

This is an Alpine, semi-fat, semi-hard blue cheese made mainly from cow's milk. Documented since at least the 13th century, the cheese is produced in a tiny area of the Cuneo Mountains in the municipalities of Castelmagno, Pradleves and Monterosso Grana. The round cheeses weigh 2-7 kg. They are matured for between 2 and more than 5 months in the traditional way, in natural caves or mountain farms facing the summit of Mt Parvo. During maturation, the rind, which is initially thin and reddish-yellow, becomes thicker, more wrinkled and brown. The body, which is crumbly, changes from white to yellow, with blueish-green marbling. The flavor changes from delicate to strong. The development of the characteristic blue mould stems from a unique combination of natural factors, in which the quality of the pasture and the maturing conditions play a fundamental role.

The Swiss Saanen breed produces some of the finest goat's milk for making into cheese.

Gorgonzola DOP

The most famous of all Italian blue cheeses originated in Lombardy, in a town situated between Milan and the Adda River. However, with the passing of time, the area of production has spread to the provinces of Novara, Vercelli and Cuneo and to Casale Monferrato (Alessandria).

Murazzano DOP

The name comes from the town in the Valle del Belbo which is the epicenter of production, but it is also made in various parts of the High Langa. It is a fat cheese with a smooth body, made from pure ewe's milk or mixed ewe's and cow's milk. The round cheeses have a diameter of 10-15 cm. The thin rind acquires a straw-yellow patina when matured. The body is white and soft, has a refined flavor, a delicate perfume and is slightly tangy when matured for more than the statutory 10 days.

Ossolano

The name refers to the area of the Ossola and Formazza valleys (in the Province of Verbano-Cusio-Ossola). The raw material of this mountain-dairy cheese is whole or semi-skimmed cow's milk, almost exclusively from the Bruna Alpina breed. The flat, round cheeses weigh 5-6 kg and are matured for 60 days. By then the body is scattered with small eyes and is white or straw-white. The taste is mild with a characteristic hint of mountain grass. Cheeses made in the municipalities of Baceno, Formazza and Premia (in the Province of Verbano-Cusio-Ossola) have the words 'Bettelmatt' or 'Ossolano d'Alpe' or 'Grasso d'Alpe' (other names for the same cheese) printed on the label.

Raschera DOP

This denomination refers to the whole Province of Cuneo where this semi-fat cow's milk cheese originated. Sometimes ewe's or goat's milk is added, making the flavor either milder or tangier. Raschera is round or square and weighs 7-10 kg. The minimum maturing period is 30 days, but is sometimes extended to 3 months. In the first case, Raschera has a white body and a delicate taste. In the second, the color is yellowish and the flavor is stronger. The words 'di alpeggio' appear on the label of cheeses made in the High Langa above 900 m.

Robiola di Roccaverano DOP

19 towns in the Monferrato produce this cheese (10 in the Province of Asti, including Roccaverano, while the others lie in the Province of Alessandria). It has a fresh, tender, firm body and is made with up to 85% cow's milk mixed with varying proportions of ewe's and goat's milk. Robiola is usually round, with no rind. The body is milk-white, has a fragrant smell and a delicate,

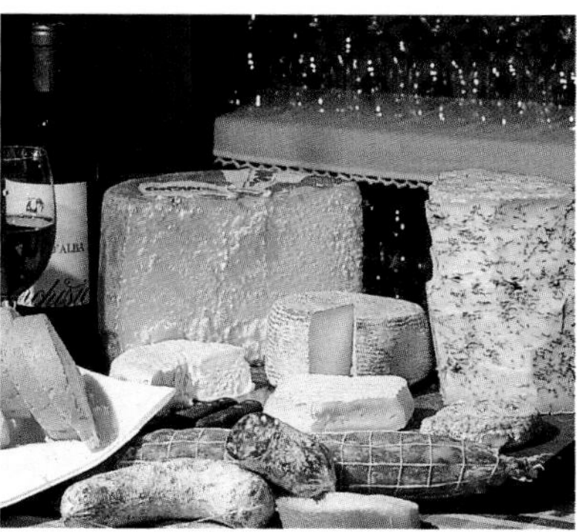

Cheese, an important part of Piedmontese gastronomy.

pleasantly acidic taste, with hints of thyme and other herbs. Some robiolas are made with goat's milk, matured for a short period and are slightly tangy. It is often preserved under oil with aromatic herbs.

Seirass or Sairass di Latte

Produced throughout the Piedmontese Alps, this fine-grained cheese is obtained from whole cow's and ewe's milk. The whey from daily cheese-making is curdled and left to drain in cone-shaped cloths. Other varieties include 'Seirass del Fen', a ricotta made from whey deriving from the process used to make Toma, wrapped in hay; 'Seirass di Siero di pecora' (made from ewe's-milk whey), which is cone-shaped, and 'Seirass Stagionato' (matured Seirass), which is matured for between 20 and 90 days and smoked over a juniper-wood fire.

Toma piemontese DOP

The typical area of this semi-cooked cow's milk cheese is vast, and includes most of the Piedmontese Alps. However, almost half the production comes from the Province of Turin, and in particular, the Valle di Susa, the Val di Lanzo and the Canavese. There are two types, made from whole and semi-skimmed milk. They can be distinguished by the rind, which is smooth and elastic in the first and more rustic in the second, but particularly by the body, which has fewer eyes and is firmer in the cheese made with semi-skimmed milk. The cheeses are round, have a diameter of 15-35 cm and weigh 2-8 kg. Maturing takes place in natural caves, or in store-rooms that are similar in terms of humidity and temperature, for 15-60 days, depending on the weight and the desired consistency. The body of younger tomas is soft and almost white, while more mature cheeses are semi-hard, a yellowish color, and have a stronger smell and taste. There are many different types of toma and 'tomini' (small toma) resulting from local traditions in the various areas of production.

ASTI

Fucci Formaggi
Piazza Statuto 9, Tel. 0141556343
This shop carries a range of more than 200 cheeses, including Raschera DOP, Castelmagno and Bra from Piedmont.

This selection of cheeses gives an idea of the richness of the Piedmont cheese industry.

ROCCAVERANO

Azienda Agricola Buttiero e Dotta
San Gerolamo 23, Tel. 014493183
An organic farm which makes the famous Robiola di Roccaverano.

Caseificio Sociale di Roccaverano
Tassito 17, Tel. 014493068
Here you can buy Robiola di Roccaverano and Toma piemontese.

Gianfranco Nervi
Via Cascina Caramello 14, Tel. 014493155
Here they sell locally-made Robiola di Roccaverano.

BIELLA

Giovanni Mosca
Via S. Filippo 16, Tel. 01523181
Sells cow's-milk and goat's-milk cheeses, including the rare Bettelmatt.

CUNEO

La Bottega del Formaggio
Via Grandis 2, Tel. 0171634428
Here you can find Robiola di Roccaverano, Raschera, Bra and Murazzano.

ALBA

Adriano e Doriana
Via V. Emanuele 29, Tel. 0173440118
Here you can find Raschera, Testun, Bra and Castelmagno.

BAGNOLO PIEMONTE

La Tominera
Via Bibiana 86, Tel. 0175391350
Here they make and sell Toma, Seirass del fen, Castelmagno, Raschera and Bra.

BRA

Giolito Fiorenzo
Via Monte Grappa 6, Tel. 0172412920, www.giolitocheese.it
This traditional dairy sells excellent Bra, Raschera and Castelmagno.

CASTELMAGNO

Dove Osano le Aquile
Via Matteotti 4, Tel. 0171986160
One of the best local producers of Castelmagno.

FEISOGLIO

Luciana Camera
Sprella, Tel. 0173831234
Produces Murazzano and Toma. In summer, the cheese is made up at the mountain dairy.

MARENE

Caseificio Sepertino
Via Reale Nord 2, Tel. 0172742575
Since 1930, this dairy has been making, maturing and refining Bra, Raschera, Castelmagno and Toma.

MELLE

Azienda Agricola Roggero

Via Provinciale 36, Tel. 0175978197
This farm produces and sells home-made Toma and 'tomini'.

SALUZZO

I Formaggi

Piazza XX Settembre 6, Tel. 0175248262
This shop carries a wide range of Piedmontese cheeses including Seirass del fen and Toma.

NOVARA

Costa Mario

Corso Vercelli 3, Tel. 0321452376, www.mariocosta.it
At this dairy you will find mild and strong gorgonzola.

ARONA

Guffanti Luigi

Via Milano 140, Tel. 0322242038, www.guffantiformaggi.com
This shop matures its own Castelmagno, Bra, Raschera, Toma and Gorgonzola.

CAMERI

Latteria Sociale di Cameri

Via per Novara 67, Tel. 0321518224
Known for its mild gorgonzola and natural gorgonzola without any added enzymes.

TURIN

Gastronomia Barbero

Via Fratelli Carle 6, Tel. 0115683474
A well-stocked shop selling local delicacies, including Raschera and various kinds of Toma.

La Baita del Formaggio

Via Lagrange 36, Tel. 0115623224, www.castagno.it
One of the best-stocked shops in the city where you can find all the DOP cheeses of the region.

BOBBIO PELLICE

Franco Durand Canton

Borgata Gentogna 1, Tel. 0121957836
Home-made artisan cheeses including Seirass del fen and Toma.

CANTALUPA

Azienda Agricola Cascina Rosa

Strada Pero, Tel. 0121352013
Unusual artisan cheeses including various types of Toma, 'tomini' and Seirass del fen.

SAUZE D'OULX

Consorzio V. Vezzani

Via Richardette 63, Tel. 0122858060
At this dairy you can buy top-quality products such as Toma and Seirass del fen.

VERBANO-CUSIO-OSSOLA

BACENO

Adolfo Olzeri

Via La Torre 27, Tel. 032462140
Artisan production of Bettelmatt and butter. In summer the cheeses are made up at the mountain dairy at Crampiolo, at Alpe Devero.

CREVOLADOSSOLA

Azienda Agricola Bravi

Via del Ponte 5, Tel. 0324338355
Bettelmatt cheese processed in summer in the mountain dairy of the same name in the Val Formazza.

VERBANIA

La Casera

Intra, Piazza Ranzoni 19, Tel. 0323581123, www.formaggidieros.it
This well-known refiner of cheeses carries a wide range of cheeses from the Ossola valleys.

VERCELLI

Marucchi

Via Gioberti 14, Tel. 0161253241
A cheese shop with more than 500 varieties.

PIODE

Caseificio Alta Val Sesia

Via Varallo 5, Tel. 016371154
A traditional dairy specializing in Toma and fresh 'tomini'.

WINE IN THE VALLE D'AOSTA

In the Valle d'Aosta vines are cultivated on the lower slopes of Mt Blanc. The continuing, persevering efforts of local farmers to tame the lower slopes of the mountains has resulted in some exceptional wines. A land of contrasts, the valley has persuaded even the vine to submit and acclimatize. The low range of its habitat are Pont-Saint-Martin, at an altitude of 300 m, where the rocks strongly reflect the sun's rays, and Morgex where, at 1,200 m, vines grow between larches and fir trees on the slopes at the foot of Mt Blanc.

The challenge of growing vines in the Valle d'Aosta lies in the fact that they have to adapt to fairly infertile soil, which is only possible in special climatic conditions. First, because vines have to be grown almost exclusively on south-facing slopes, where, in the central hours of the day, the sun's rays hit the slopes perpendicularly, thus releasing maximum energy into the soil. However, even here, further selection has ensured that vineyards are planted only where they are well sheltered from the wind. They must be well watered, too, because, since the valley is enclosed by mountains which intercept most of the clouds, it has one of the lowest rainfalls in Italy. This area is so special that it is even out of the reach of the fungi are so common elsewhere, and rarely need to be sprayed against parasites.

In this miracle of Alpine wine-making, merit must go to the farmers of the valley, who have succeeded in exploiting every possible corner of cultivable land by building terraces, transforming the landscape. The drystone walls, created to protect the slopes from erosion and to clear cultivable land from rubble, also play an important part in the plant cycle of the vines. The stones capture the heat of the sun and retain it for a long time, protecting the soil from rapid falls in temperature at night. Pergolas on columns support the vines in their constant struggle against the wind. The farmers have also selected grape varietals which are particularly resistant to the extreme conditions here. The most hardy is Blanc de Morgex, which holds the altitude record for producing grapes. But there are also more than 20 indigenous varieties which, having been selected over the centuries according to the type of terrain, orientation, and altitude, play an important role in the regional wine scenario, producing a remarkable variety of very good wines.

The production regulations unite some of these products under a single DOC label, Valle d'Aosta DOC or Vallée d'Aoste DOC, with 9 wines named after the grape and 6 with a geographical specification. Some wines can be produced throughout the region while others may only be grown in certain sub-zones. The former, in addition to the general regional denomina-

A vineyard in the Valle d'Aosta, with its distinctive columns and drystone walls.

tion, are specified as 'Bianco' (white), 'Rosso' (red) or 'Rosato' (rosé) or carry the name of the particular grape varietal. The latter are named after the specific area of origin, such as Donnas, Arnad-Montjovet, Chambave, Nus, Torrette, Arvier and Morgex-La Salle.
However, although the region has a great variety of wines, in terms of quantity, it produces very little. On a national scale, wine from the Valle d'Aosta is a niche wine at the bottom of the national table in terms of production. However, penalized though they may be by the roughness of the terrain, the wines of the valley are at the top in terms of quality and rarity. The fact that they cannot produce large quantities has led to a quality of product which has enabled wines produced in the valley to withstand the challenge of the market. A tiny miracle, when you consider that, with the exception of a few specialized farms in the middle of the valley, vines are cultivated using traditional farming methods.
However, this limiting factor is compensated by the existence of wine cooperatives which stand forward as a benchmark in terms of technology, selling and promoting the products, and encouraging wine tourism.
But behind it all is the work of the farmers, which is significant from an environmental point of view. The vineyards contribute significantly to defending the hydrogeological structure of the valley. From the point of view of vine-growing, the valley can be divided into three main areas: the Lower Valley, from Pont-Saint-Martin to Montjovet, where they grow the local variety of Nebbiolo, called Picoutener; the Middle Valley, from Saint-Vincent to Arvier, where Petit-Rouge, Fumin, Vien-de-Nus and Moscato di Chambave predominate; and the Upper Valley, near Morgex-La Salle, with the highest vineyards in Europe, more than 1,000m above sea-level, the exclusive domain of Blanc de Morgex.

Valle d'Aosta Arnad-Montjovet DOC

Produced south of the Dora Baltea River, in the municipalities of Arnad, Verrès, Issogne, Challant-Saint-Victor, Hône, Montjovet and Champdepraz, this red wine made with Nebbiolo/Picoutener/Picotendro is a bright ruby-red color with hints of garnet.
It has a refined bouquet with a hint of almond, while the flavor is dry, with a slightly bitter, smooth, harmonious after-taste. It goes particularly well with grilled, roasted or barbecued red meat.

Valle d'Aosta Blanc de Morgex et de La Salle DOC

This white wine comes from vineyards in the territory of Morgex and La Salle. Made from pure Blanc de Morgex, it goes excellently with starters and fish. It has a slightly greenish straw-yellow color, and a delicate bouquet with a hint of mountain herbs.
It has a dry, slightly acidic flavor and is slightly fizzy. There is also a Spumante version.

Valle d'Aosta Chambave DOC

This wine is made in the municipalities of Chambave, Saint-Vincent, Pontey, Châtillon, Saint-Denis, Verrayes and Montjovet in the following versions: Rosso (red), Moscato (white) and Moscato Passito (white).
The Rosso has a dry, harmonious flavor and is an excellent table wine.
The straw-yellow Moscato accompanies desserts and has an intense bouquet and a delicate, aromatic flavor.
The Moscato Passito has a golden yellow color verging on amber.
The flavor is medium-sweet and aromatic, a wine suitable for drinking at the end of a meal.

TCI HIGHLIGHTS

Wine categories

Three labels define Italian wines according to quality. The top label is DOCG (Guaranteed and Controlled Origin Denomination); there are around 20 DOCG wines in Italy, 6 in Tuscany. DOC (Controlled Origin Denomination) indicates conformity to regulations for a given area of origin, and production and maturation procedures. IGT (Typical Geographic Indication) guarantees vine cultivation according to certain regulations. VDT is for table wine with an alcohol content of at least 10%.

Valle d'Aosta Donnas DOC

This wine is produced in a small mountainous area spanning the Dora Baltea River, in the municipalities of Donnas, Perloz, Pont-Saint-Martin and Bard. It has a bright red color, smells slightly of almonds, and the flavor is dry and smooth with plenty of body. Excellent with red meat.

Valle d'Aosta Enfer d'Arvier DOC

This red table wine is made in Arvier. It smells of almonds and has a dry, smooth flavor with plenty of body.

Valle d'Aosta Nus DOC

Production of this wine is restricted to Nus, Verrayes, Quart, Saint-Christophe and Aosta. It is made in the following versions: Rosso, Malvoise and Malvoise Passito. The Rosso, an excellent table wine, has a dry, smooth, slightly herby flavor. The Malvoise, an amber color with hints of gold, is a table wine with a harmonious, balanced taste. The Passito, a dessert wine, is a deep coppery yellow with a medium-sweet taste and an after-taste of chestnuts.

Valle d'Aosta Torrette DOC

Made in the municipalities of Quart, Saint-Christophe, Aosta, Sarre, Saint-Pierre, Charvensod, Gressan, Jovençan, Aymavilles, Villeneuve and Introd, this wine smelling of wild roses accompanies stewed meats or meats with sauces. It has a bright red color with hints of violet and a dry, smooth, well-rounded flavor with a slightly bitter after-taste.

AOSTA

AYMAVILLES

Cave des Onze Communes

Urbains 14, Tel. 0165902912, www.caveonzecommunes.it

● D.O.C. Valle d'Aosta Torrette
● D.O.C. Valle d'Aosta Torrette Superieur

CHAMBAVE

La Crotta di Vegneron

Piazza Roncas 2, Tel. 016646670, www.lacrotta.it

● D.O.C. Valle d'Aosta Nus
○ D.O.C. Valle d'Aosta Chambave Moscato
○ D.O.C. Valle d'Aosta Chambave Moscato Passito

MORGEX

Cave du Vin Blanc Morgex-La Salle

Chemin Des Iles - La Ruine 31, Tel. 0165800331, www.caveduvinblanc.com

○ D.O.C. Valle d'Aosta Blanc De Morgex Et De La Salle
○ D.O.C. Valle d'Aosta Vini Estremi Blanc De Morgex Et De La Salle

Vitivinicola Pavese Ermes

La Ruine, strada Pineta 26, Tel. 0165800053, www.vievini.it

○ D.O.C. Valle d'Aosta Vin Blanc De Morgex Et De La Salle
○ D.O.C. Valle d'Aosta Vin Blanc De Morgex Et De La Salle Nathan

QUART

Maison Vigneronne Freres Grosjean

Ollignan 1, Tel. 0165775791, www.grosjean.vievini.it

● D.O.C. Valle d'Aosta Torrette
● D.O.C. Valle d'Aosta Torrette Superieur Vigne Rovetta

Wine legend

Wines are listed with symbols which indicate their type

● red
○ white
● rosé
◐ sweet or dessert

WINE IN PIEDMONT

The Langhe and the Monferrato are the most important wine areas in this region which has succeeded in safeguarding its traditions while adopting leading-edge technology. With 43 DOC and 7 DOCG wines, Piedmont is one of Italy's most prestigious wine areas. A land where the vineyard is synonymous with culture, hard work and an artisan tradition centuries old, where producers hope to create new opportunities around the wineries to develop and safeguard the environment. But what lies behind the success of Piedmont's wines? First, a particularly favorable environment, namely the hills which cover one third of the territory. Production can be divided into two main areas. The most important is the south-east sector, which extends from the Monferrato, on the right bank of the Po River, as far as the Langhe, crossed by the Tànaro River, in the Provinces of Asti, Alessandria and part of Cuneo. The second area corresponds to the strip of land around the edge of the Alpine foothills, from Cuneo across the Provinces of Turin, Biella, Vercelli and Novara to Verbano-Cusio-Ossola. The hills of the Monferrato and the Langhe are formed of sedimentary deposits which are ideal for growing vines, whereas the Alpine foothills tend to be rocky, like the mountains higher up, or formed by moraines where the valleys fan out, where only a few areas are suitable for growing vines. In the Monferrato and the Langhe, the unusual combination of pedological (the type of terrain, orientation, altitude, and so on) and climatic factors have resulted in exceptional wines: reds like Barolo, Barbaresco, Nebbiolo d'Alba and others, and whites, especially the wines of Asti. If we divide the vine-growing area into three sections, we can see that it is extremely adaptable. The warmest area stretches from the plain of the Tànaro up to 250 m-300 m above sea-level. This area is suited to vines with a longer natural cycle which have higher thermal requirements, such as Barbera, Nebbiolo and, to a lesser extent, Grignolino. This is where red wines which require a long period of aging are grown. In the area situated between 300 m and 400m above sea-level, where there is a wide temperature range and less humidity, we find mainly vines that make red and white fruity, aromatic wines. This is the large area where Moscato d'Asti, Brachetto and Dolcetto vines are grown.
Vine-growing is widespread in vast areas of the foothills of the Piedmontese Alps. These areas generally have high average temperatures, a wide temperature range, and plenty of sunlight. This is certainly a more selective area, where land suitable for vine-cultivation is fairly limited, but where vines can be grown, they tend to produce excellent results. We are talking about the areas of Caluso, Carema, Gattinara and Ghemme whose names are associated, intentionally, with excellent, and, in some cases, superlative wines.
The Piedmontese grape *par excellence* is Nebbiolo, a varietal mentioned in medieval times and the origin of Piedmont's most famous wines, in particular the four with DOCG status: Barolo, Barbaresco, Gattinara and Ghemme. The prize for the most widespread vine goes to Barbera. Other reds include Dolcetto, Freisa, Bonarda, Brachetto, Grignolino and Malvasia, all of which have a great following. As for white wines, Moscato predominates, and holds the regional record.

A farm between Rosignano Monferrato and Terruggia.

Barbaresco DOCG
The area of production includes the town of the same name and other towns in the Province of Cuneo. This red wine made with Nebbiolo goes well with red meat. It has an intense bouquet and a dry, robust, full-bodied, harmonious flavor.

Barolo DOCG
Barolo is made in a very restricted area from grapes grown exclusively in the 11 municipalities of Barolo, Castiglione Falletto, Cherasco, Diano d'Alba, Grinzane Cavour, La Morra, Monforte d'Alba, Novello, Roddi, Serralunga d'Alba and Verduno. It is garnet-red in color and has an intense bouquet. Its dry, full-bodied, robust flavor makes it particularly suitable for drinking with red meat and mature cheeses. Locally it is regarded as a 'vino da riflessione' (a wine for contemplation).

Brachetto d'Acqui DOCG
Produced around Asti and Alessandria, this dessert wine is made with grapes from the vine of the same name. It is grown and concentrated in the High Monferrato, and on the hills around Acqui Terme and Nizza Monferrato. It is usually a ruby-red wine, sometimes pale-red or even rosé. It has a very delicate, vaguely musky bouquet. Its sweet, smooth flavor makes it ideal for drinking with cakes, cookies and fruit salads containing fruits of the woods.

Gattinara DOCG
This red wine is often considered the equal of great Piedmont reds such as Barolo and Barbaresco. Gattinara, named after a town in the Province of Vercelli, is made with Nebbiolo grapes. However, in this case, small quantities of Bonarda grapes may be added. It is garnet-red, verging on orange and, like all Nebbiolo wines, has an intense scent of violets. It has a dry, slightly bitter flavor and must be aged for at least three years in wood. It should be accompanied by traditional dishes such as stews and roasts, red meat and mature cheeses.

Gavi DOCG
Made with Cortese grapes, this white wine is straw-yellow in color. It has a delicate bouquet, a dry, harmonious flavor, and is ideal as an aperitif, with fish or a light meal.

Ghemme DOCG
This red wine is named after the town in the Province of Novara where it is made, an area with very longstanding wine

Classic Piedmontese scenery: rolling hills covered with vines.

traditions, some of which date back to the 1st century AD. Ghemme is another of Piedmont's great Nebbiolo wines, although, in this particular area, the regulations permit the addition of Vespolina and Bonarda Novarese. It is ruby-red with hints of garnet, has a delicate bouquet of violets, and a dry flavor with a bitter background taste. It is sold after 3 years of aging. Excellent with red meat and matured cheeses.

Moscato d'Asti DOCG

This wine from the Provinces of Asti, Cuneo and Alessandria is an aromatic, sweet, fizzy wine made from the partially-fermented must of Moscato grapes. It has a straw-yellow color and a fragrant perfume. Its delicately sweet, aromatic flavor makes it ideal for drinking with desserts, cookies or on its own.

Barbera DOC

Barbera is the most widespread red grape varietal in the region. It is a vine that needs little care and grows profusely; resulting in a large number of bunches on each vine. It is also less susceptible than others to changes in climate, parasites and moulds. A robust wine with lots of character, Barbera is the classic red table wine. It ages well, and, if made and stored in wood, improves considerably. In Piedmont, three Barbera wines have official DOC status: Barbera d'Alba, Barbera d'Asti and Barbera del Monferrato.

Collina Torinese DOC

This DOC label applies to red table wines made in the Province of Turin, such as Bonarda and Barbera, a Malvasia Rossa dessert wine and Pelaverga or Cari, another dessert wine.

Dolcetto DOC

The area where Dolcetto d'Alba is produced lies in the provinces of Cuneo, Alessandria and Asti. The denomination is associated with the area of production and 7 have DOC status: Alba, Dogliani, Asti, Diano d'Alba, Acqui, Ovada, and Langhe Monregalesi. Despite its name, Dolcetto is not a sweet wine, but is named after the Dolcetto grape. It has a ruby-red color with hints of purple, and purplish froth and a faint bouquet with hints of violet. It has a dry, rounded, persistent flavor with a pleasant hint of bitterness. It may be drunk throughout a meal, but goes particularly well with hams and salami, roasts, white meat and cheese.

Erbaluce di Caluso DOC

This dry, white wine goes well with starters and fish. The 'Passito' version also goes well with strong cheese.

Freisa DOC

Freisa is a red wine and has been given DOC status in wineries of Asti and Chieri. It has a fine, delicate bouquet reminiscent of raspberries, and a dry flavor which goes excellently with hams and salami, *primi piatti* and white meat.

Grignolino DOC

This ruby-red wine, which verges on orange when aged, has a delicate bouquet and a pleasantly bitter flavor with a persistent after-taste. The denomination is associated with the area of production and includes two DOC wines: Asti and Monferrato Casalese.

Malvasia DOC

The Malvasia wines made in Piedmont are sweet, fragrant, slightly aromatic red wines. Two have DOC status: Malvasia di Casorzo d'Asti and Castelnuovo Don Bosco. Malvasia di Casorzo is ruby-red while the wine of Castelnuovo Don Bosco is a cherry-red. The sweet flavor goes well with desserts.

Nebbiolo d'Alba DOC

This ruby-red wine of varying strength is made with grapes from Nebbiolo vines grown in an area of the Province of Cuneo. It has a faint, delicate bouquet reminiscent of violets. The taste is dry, with the right amount of tannin and a delicate, slightly bitter after-taste. The rules of production stipulate two types: Spumante (sparkling) and Secco (dry). The latter must be aged for at least one year. The dry version may accompany any part of a meal, while the sparkling version should accompany the dessert.

Roero DOC

Roero is a ruby-red wine with a distinctive, delicate, fragrant, fruity bouquet. It has a dry, rounded flavor. Arneis is a superb white wine produced in the Roero area with Arneis grapes, especially at Baldissero, Montaldo Roero, Santo Stefano Roero and Vezza, in the Province of Cuneo. Straw-yellow in color with hints of amber, it has a delicate, herby smell and a dry, bitter flavor which makes it particularly suitable for accompanying starters and fish.

ALESSANDRIA

OLIVOLA

Bricco dei Guazzi

Via Vittorio Veneto 23, Tel. 0422864511

- D.O.C. Barbera d'Asti
- D.O.C. Barbera del Monferrato
- D.O.C. Grignolino del Monferrato Casalese

VIGNALE MONFERRATO

Accornero

Ca' Cima, Tel. 0142933317, www.accornerovini.it

- D.O.C. Barbera del Monferrato
- D.O.C. Malvasia di Casorzo
- D.O.C. Grignolino del Monferrato

ASTI

NIZZA MONFERRATO

Bersano

Piazza Dante 21, Tel. 0141720211, www.scarpavini.it

- D.O.C. Barbera d'Asti
- D.O.C. Dolcetto d'Acqui
- D.O.C. Nebbiolo d'Alba

Rocchetta Tanaro, the Marchesi Incisa della Rocchetta winery.

Scarpa
Via Montegrappa 6, Tel. 0141721331, www.bersano.it
○ D.O.C.G. Moscato d'Asti
● D.O.C. Barbera d'Asti

Scrimaglio
Strada Alessandria 67, Tel. 0141721385, www.scrimaglio.it
● D.O.C. Barbera d'Asti
● D.O.C. Barbera del Monferrato

CUNEO

ALBA

Adriano Marco e Vittorio
San Rocco Seno d'Elvio 13A, Tel. 0173362294, www.adrianovini.it
● D.O.C.G. Barbaresco
● D.O.C. Barbera d'Alba
○ D.O.C. Moscato d'Asti

A wine-cellar at Costigliole d'Asti.

BARBARESCO

Albino Rocca
Strada Ronchi 18, Tel. 0173635145, www.roccaalbino.com
● D.O.C.G. Barbaresco
● D.O.C. Barbera d'Alba
● D.O.C. Dolcetto d'Alba

LA MORRA

Agricola Gian Piero Marrone
Annunziata 13, Tel. 0173509288, www.agricolamarrone.com
● D.O.C.G. Barolo
● D.O.C. Nebbiolo d'Alba

NEIVE

Paitin
Via Serra Boella 20, Tel. 017367343, www.paitin.it
● D.O.C. Barbera d'Alba
● D.O.C. Dolcetto d'Alba
● D.O.C. Nebbiolo d'Alba

NOVARA

FARA NOVARESE

Bersano
Via Cesare Battisti 21, Tel. 0321829252, www.cantalupo.net
● D.O.C.G. Gattinara
● D.O.C.G. Ghemme
● D.O.C. Nebbiolo Colline Novaresi

GHEMME

Antichi Vigneti di Cantalupo
Via M. Buonarroti 5, Tel. 0163840041, www.dessilani.it
● D.O.C.G. Ghemme
● D.O.C. Nebbiolo Colline Novaresi

TURIN

Franco M. Martinetti
Corso Filippo Turati 14, Tel. 0118395937
● D.O.C.G. Barolo
● D.O.C.G. Gavi
● D.O.C. Barbera d'Asti

AGLIÈ

Cieck
San Grato, Tel. 0124330522, www.cieck.it
○ D.O.C. Erbaluce di Caluso
○ D.O.C. Erbaluce di Caluso Passito

SAN GIORGIO CANAVESE

Orsolani
Corso Repubblica 5, Tel. 012432386, www.orsolani.it
○ D.O.C. Erbaluce di Caluso
○ D.O.C. Erbaluce di Caluso Passito

VERCELLI

GATTINARA

Nervi
Corso Vercelli 117, Tel. 0163833228, www.gattinara.nervi.it
● D.O.C.G. Gattinara

Travaglini Giancarlo
Via delle Vigne 36, Tel. 0163833588, www.travaglinigattinara.it
● D.O.C.G. Gattinara

LIQUEURS IN THE VALLE D'AOSTA

Remote mountain areas have a tradition of producing liqueurs to keep out the cold during the long winter months, and the little Valle d'Aosta is no exception. Its traditional liqueurs and distillates are made with local herbs and berries, from recipes that have been handed down from one generation to another. Of all the recipes still used today, the most famous is Genepì, a vital ingredient of the drink which symbolizes the Valle d'Aosta: *caffè valdostano*. These traditional drinks, often artisan-made, can be tasted in bars and restaurants throughout the valley.

Genepì/Alpine herb liqueur

Genepì is a liqueur made in the mountainous areas of the region. The name refers to the modern names for several Alpine herbs: *Artemisia mutellina* (*genepì maschio* or spiked wormwood), *Artemisia glacialis* (*genepì femmina* or Alpine wormwood) and other similar species. These plants are first dried and then left to soak in alcohol for 40 days. The mixture is then distilled and diluted with water and sugar. The resulting liqueur is a straw-yellow color verging on pale green. It has an unmistakable, full, slightly bitter taste, with an alcohol grade of between 30% and 42% and has to be aged to bring out its organoleptic properties. Making genepì is very common in the Western Alps. The recipe has been handed down for generations by spice merchants and pharmacists because of its tonic and digestive properties.

Ratafià/ Sour cherry liqueur

A liqueur made from the small round black cherries of the *Prunus cerasus* (of the *Rosaceae* family). As a fruit it is not very popular because of its acidic flavor, but it is often used to make syrups, jams and liqueurs. Today, the liqueur is still made according to the traditional recipe. The cherries are selected, washed in water, dried, and squeezed to extract the juice. The cherry-juice is filtered and mixed with water, alcohol, sugar and herbs and left to amalgamate. The liqueur tastes strongly of cherries, and has the sweet-sour flavor of the fruit, an intense cherry scent and a moderate alcohol grade (26°). It can be drunk neat at room temperature, after a meal or at any other time, served with ice and garnished with cherries or cherry leaves as a refreshing drink, or used to flavor desserts, fruit salads or ice-cream.

TCI HIGHLIGHTS

CAFFÈ VALDOSTANO: A RITUAL TO SHARE WITH FRIENDS

Served piping hot in the traditional "coppa di amicizia" (cup of friendship, a low, bulbous, carved wooden bowl with several spouts from which each person at the table takes a sip and passes it on) is the perfect end to a meal in the Valle d'Aosta and is a must for anyone visiting the valley. Very hot espresso coffee is mixed with lemon- or orange-zest, grappa and genepì, and a few spices, such as cloves or cinnamon, after which it is set alight. Sugar is sprinkled over it just before replacing the lid. The host takes a sip and it is passed around the table. There is a tradition that it should not be put down until it is finished.

LIQUEURS IN PIEDMONT

In the region which can claim to have some of Italy's most prestigious and noble wines, the typical local liqueurs include many made by infusing herbs in hydro alcoholic solutions, an Alpine tradition, and various recipes for 'amari' (bitter digestives) and elixirs. They all involve particular mixtures of medicinal herbs, and natural herbs and spices, and are often used as digestives or tonics.

Amaro alle Erbe Alpine delle Montagne di Cesana/ Alpine Herb digestive from the Cesana Mountains

This typically Piedmontese product is made by distilling spices and medicinal herbs gathered in the high mountains of the Valle di Susa. Once the medicinal herbs (including Alpine yarrow, angelica, absinthe, marjoram, thyme and clary sage) and the cloves and gentian root have been carefully selected, they are left to soak in a cold mixture of ethyl alcohol and water, without adding any other flavorings or artificial colorants, after which the infusion is filtered several times. The result is a bright-green liqueur with an alcohol grade of about 35°, with a pleasant, intense fragrance of herbs and a moderately bitter flavor. The 'amaro' is drunk especially as a digestive and as a tonic, because of the properties of the herbs it contains.

Arquebuse or Alpestre/ Alpine herb digestive

Typical throughout Piedmont and especially the area of Carmagnola, near Turin. This distillate contains more than 30 herbs, including wormwood, valeriana, verbena, sage, mint, camomile, lemon, arnica, gentian and hyssop. The herbs are left to soak in a hydroalcoholic solution for about two days and the resulting liquid is distilled with steam stills and put into oak casks to mature. Arquebuse is straw-yellow in color, has an alcohol grade of 45°, and tastes and smells pleasantly of herbs. It is drunk especially to aid the digestion, sometimes adding it to boiling water and sweetening it with sugar or honey. It is also used to 'correct' coffee.

Elisir del Prete/ Strong herb liqueur

This very concentrated liqueur of medicinal herbs comes from an old tradition of artisan liqueurs and distillates based on natural essences for domestic use. This practice is common in the Alpine valleys near Pinerolo, in the Province of Turin. As well as medicinal herbs, such as gentian, Roman absinthe, gentianella, coriander, mint, wormwood and china, the recipe contains spices such as cloves and cinnamon. When the herbs have been gathered, they are left to soak in a mixture of alcohol and water at room temperature. The mixture is then filtered several times until it reaches the desired level of intensity, after which it is added to alcohol again to bring the alcohol grade up to 50°. The result is a concentrated brown liqueur tasting and smelling strongly of herbs. Because of its high concentration and alcohol grade, it is not drunk neat, but used to 'correct' coffee or diluted with hot water. Sometimes it is poured onto a sugar cube and sucked until it dissolves.

Elisir d'Erbe Barathier/ Herb and spice liqueur

A digestive made exclusively by Barathier, near Pomaretto (Province of Turin). Seven types of natural herbs and flowers are left to soak in water and alcohol, including angelica, liquorice and walnut. Once they have been picked by hand, the herbs are dried. They are put into a glass or steel non-porous container in a solution of water and alcohol for about 35-40 days. Then spring water, alcohol and crystallized sugar are added. The elixir has an alcohol grade of 20°. Its unusual, refined flavor is bitter at first but then the bitterness attenuates (the effect of the angelica) to a flavor with hints of walnut and liquorice.

Garus Susino/Exotic spice liqueur

This drink, obtained from exotic spices, is made in the Valle di Susa, in the Province of Turin. The ingredients include myrrh, cinnamon, nutmeg, cloves, aloe, maidenhair fern, raw cane sugar, orange-flower water and saffron, many of which first came to the Valle di Susa when trading began with the East in medieval times. The recipe is quite complicated because some of the spices and plants are infused in alcohol and in slow stills, while the rest are put into a raw cane-sugar solution. When the infusion and the distillate are ready, they are mixed with the cane-sugar solution and saffron is added. The liquid is then aged in steel containers and then filtered and bottled. The alcohol grade varies between 20° and 40°. It is transparent and colorless, with a complex, varied taste and smell. Garus is served neat at room temperature, at the end of a meal.

Liquore d'Erba Bianca/ Alpine yarrow liqueur

This traditional liqueur is made in the Val d'Ossola, in the north of Piedmont. It is made with Alpine yarrow (*Achillea moscata*), which grows on stony ground and on rocks in the Alps between 1,400 m and 3,000 m. When it has been dried, it is left to soak in large glass tanks full of pure alcohol for about two months. When it is ready, water, sugar and alcohol are added. The temperature of the resulting liqueur is reduced to below 0°C for a few days so that the essential oils are deposited on the bottom of the tanks. Finally, it is bottled at room temperature. It has a transparent amber color, an alcohol grade of 35°, a bitter flavor, typical of yarrow, and an intense scent of the essential oil of the plant. It can be served as an aperitif or a digestive and has diuretic properties.

Liquore di Genziana/ Gentian liqueur

This liqueur used to be made in the middle and upper Valle di Susa (in the Province of Turin) for domestic consumption. To make the liqueur, gentian roots are dried, washed, dried again, chopped finely and left to infuse in ethyl alcohol for about 40 days. Then a sugar solution is added to the mixture, and it is filtered and bottled. The result is a liqueur with a very unusual scent, due mainly to the sugars contained in the gentian root. It has a pleasantly sweet flavor which then becomes very bitter. It has a low alcohol grade (16°) and, because of the typical properties of the gentian, is used especially as a digestive.

Nocciolino di Chivasso/ Hazelnut liqueur from Chivasso

Originally from Chivasso and the surrounding area of the Province of Turin, this sweet liqueur is made by infusing hazelnuts. The hazelnuts are shelled and left to infuse in alcohol to extract the essential oils. Water, alcohol, flavorings, and other infusions are added to this liquid and mixed together. When cold, the liquid is then filtered and bottled. Nocciolino has an alcohol grade of 24°, is pale-brown and transparent, with a rounded taste with hints of hazelnut, and a varied scent dominated by hazelnut. Drunk after a meal as a liqueur for contemplation.

Rosolio

The classic recipe for this liqueur is based on roses, but it may be made with other ingredients such as bay leaves, angelica, aniseed, oranges, absynthe, cocoa, coffee, cinnamon, blackcurrants, quinces, celery, vanilla, tea and so on. A typical product of the Province of Turin, the first phase involves infusing the ingredients in alcohol. The infusion is then filtered. Now water and a high percentage of sugar is added which may be as much as 50% of the product. The result is a rather dense and very sweet liqueur with a low alcohol grade (25-28°), with the color, flavor and smell of the original ingredients. It can be drunk on any occasion and is served at room temperature.

Vermut/Vermouth

Vermouth is a liqueur-like wine flavored with infusions of various plants and herbs, including absynthe (*Artemisia absinthium*) which gives it a particular hint of bitterness. The alcohol grade, between 17.5° and 21°, is achieved by adding alcohol or brandy. This drink (which is used to make various cocktails) is normally served in a small chilled cocktail glass or with ice and lemon- or orange-zest. It is often used in cooking and pastry-making.

CAKES IN THE VALLE D'AOSTA

The Valle d'Aosta is a unique region in terms of appearance and history, a triangle of very high mountains and an ancient route of transit. The Romans called it the Road to Gaul, for medieval pilgrims it was the *Via Francigena*, after which it constituted a link between Piedmont and Savoie, and the kingdoms of Italy and France, generating all kinds of gastronomic and other repercussions. Having said this, we can also begin to describe the sweet side of the valley's gastronomy. First of all, the raw ingredients, which are the ingredients of the high mountains, milk, cream, chestnuts, honey, Reinette apples and Martin Sec pears – with whatever else was brought across the Mediterranean to countries north of the Alps and viceversa: almonds and spices, chocolate and coffee. As for the recipes, these range from country cuisine, deliciously simple cakes and puddings, to the traditions of the castles, where, amongst other things, the ritual of *caffè alla valdostana* originated, a relic from the time when medieval knights ended every banquet by passing a cup of friendship around the table.

Blanc Manger

A traditional milk pudding originally from Savioe. The ingredients are simple: milk, sugar and vanilla.

Ciambelline aostane/ Doughnuts Aosta style

Small round cakes with a hole in the middle, baked in the oven.
Made with corn meal, sugar, butter, white flour and eggs, flavored with lemon-juice.

Mont Blanc

A delicious mound of sieved boiled chestnuts mixed with sugar, cocoa, milk and rum, then topped with whipped cream. There is a quick version which involves sieving *marrons glacés* and mixing them with rum.

Pere Martin Sec al Vino/ Pears cooked in wine

This old variety of small, dark pear is cooked in the oven in red wine and flavored with cinnamon, nutmeg and cloves. Served with medium-sweet or sweet wine.

Tegole di Aosta

Tegole are made with sweet and bitter almonds, hazelnuts, sugar and egg-white. The mixture is rolled out and circles are cut out and put in the oven to dry. At this point, the wafer-thin cookies should be left on

The art of making cakes and candies in the Valle d'Aosta is a longstanding tradition, as this painting in the castle at Issogne proves.

The classic tegole from Aosta are curved like traditional terracotta tiles.

a rolling-pin or a similarly curved surface to give them their distinctive Roman pan-tile shape. For reasons of practicality, this manual operation is now often omitted. So the *tegole* remain flat, "like the slates on the roofs of the baitas" as they are described in dialect, so that tradition is not too severely offended. The *tegole* are also made in a richer version, covered in chocolate. They are delicious eaten on their own (they melt in your mouth) but often they are served with whipped cream flavored with grappa and sugar. Tegole are often accompanied by local *passito* (sweet) wines.

Torcetti di Saint-Vincent

The *torcetti* of Saint-Vincent, are small, sugar-coated twists of short pastry, a typical souvenir of this town situated below Colle di Joux. The ingredients are simple: flour, yeast, butter and sugar. Their twisted shape gives them their name (or sometimes they are curved like a horse-shoe, a sign of good luck) with overlapping ends. They should be eaten fresh with a sweetish white wine, zabaglione, milk or tea.

Delicious buttery torcetti, a typical specialty of Saint-Vincent.

AOSTA

Caffè Boch

Piazza E. Chanoux 22, Tel. 016535606
This traditional pastry shop is almost 100 years old and sells traditional cakes such as *tegole*.

Chuc

Via S. Anselmo 102, Tel. 016540829
A venue in the Valle d'Aosta style, where you can sample artisan cakes and cookies.

Nazionale

Piazza Chanoux 9, Tel. 0165262158
Almost an institution, this café serves many traditional Valle d'Aosta specialties.

CHÂTILLON

Dal Santo

Via R. Pellissier 1, Tel. 016661376
Home-made cakes including *tegole* and *torcetti*.

COURMAYEUR

Caffè della Posta

Via Roma 51, Tel. 0165842272
This café specializes in croissants and other yeast-baked specialties for breakfast, jam tarts, apple and chocolate cakes, all home-made.

Mario Il Pasticcere

Strada Regionale 8, Tel. 0165843348
The only pastry-shop which makes *tegole* without using flour.

NUS

Buzzi

Via Risorgimento 16, Tel. 0165767000
This traditional venue sells lots of traditional Valle d'Aosta pastries.

SAINT-VINCENT

Morandin

Piazza E. Chanoux 105, Tel. 0166512690
Here they specialize in confectionery, chocolates and sweets, based on traditional and modern recipes.

VILLENEUVE

Dupont

Piazza Assunzione 8, Tel. 016595014
Here they make Valle d'Aosta torcetti rolled by hand, fresh fruit tarts and the classic tegole.

CAKES IN PIEDMONT

The heart of Piedmont's candy and chocolate industry is Turin. This city with its fine monuments, which was once the capital of the Savoy kingdom, also has an extraordinary legacy of pastry-making and confectionery reflecting the centuries of contact with the royal houses of France and Spain. You only need to enter one of its historic cafés with their antique mirrors and velvet chairs to understand this (see p. 144-145). Even today café windows are full of exquisite displays of candies and chocolates, tiny cakes, chocolate pralines, sugar candy and candied violets. Every town in the province follows suit in its own way, with mountains of *amaretti, canestrelli* and *baci di dama*. Cuneo, a serious mountain town, is famous for its chestnuts. Once the valley-dwellers made them into bread, but now their specialty is *marrons glacés*. The Tondo Gentile halzelnuts of the Langhe, often preserved in honey, are turned into a *gianduja* (chocolate and ground halzelnuts) cream. On a par with its pastries are Piedmont's dessert, sweet and sparkling wines: Moscato d'Asti, Brachetto d'Acqui and the delicious rosé Malvasia wines of the Monferrato.

Amaretti
These little biscuits from the area of Asti and Alessandria are made with sweet and bitter almonds, sugar and egg-whites. The ones from Gavi, Ovada and Mombaruzzo are famous and the latter also contain apricot seeds.

Amaretti smell and taste of almonds.

Baci di dama
These are very common around Alessandria, especially near Tortona. They consist of two half spheres made with a mixture of ground almonds, flour, sugar, butter and liqueur, held together with a chocolate-and-almond cream.

Biscottini di Novara
These feather-light sponge fingers are made with a few simple ingredients: flour, sugar and whole eggs. They are light, spongy and fragile and can be eaten at any time, for breakfast or for afternoon tea, but also at the end of a meal with a good sweet passito wine.

Bonet
The Piedmontese dessert *par excellence*, *bonet* is a sort of pudding made with amaretto biscuits, cocoa and, in the original recipe, a drop of Fernet digestive. The name refers to a typical item of Piedmontese headgear, similar in color and shape to a beret. It is traditionally offered at the end of a proper Piedmontese meal.

Canestrelli
These traditional cakes are common around Ivrea and the Canavese, but also in the Valle di Susa (Province of Turin). They are made in the shape of a little basket, hence their name. The *canestrelli* made in Biella are little cakes consisting of two thin wafers filled with a chocolate cream, while *canestrelli* of Novi Ligure and Ovada (Province of Alessandria) are soft, dry, ring-shaped biscuits.

Caramelle di Torino
The Italian word 'caramella' (meaning 'sweet') was invented in Piedmont. In the early days of confectionery, while it was molten, the flavored sugar was put "into a small copper spoon with a very long spout, which was used to pour the

Brightly-colored candies from Turin.

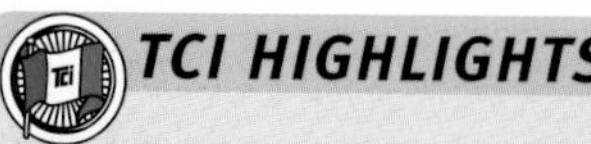

Ferrero and the Italian Chocolate Miracle

Behind the Italian chocolate boom is the extraordinary figure of Pietro Ferrero. This enterprising man, born in 1898, left his home town of Farigliano and went to Dogliani (both towns are in the Province of Cuneo) to learn the art of pastry-making. In this small town near Mondovì, in 1923, he opened his first cake shop and, three years later, moved his business to Alba. Having spent some time in Africa and in Turin, Ferrero returned to his workshop with the intention of making a sweet that could replace more economic foods in the diet of the poor. With this in mind, he shut himself in his workshop and began to use a new technique to mix the most classic ingredients of Piedmontese chocolate-making: cocoa and hazelnuts. By blending them in just the right proportions with sugar and palm oil, he obtained a nutty chocolate paste, a sort of "poor man's chocolate", to use the words of his son Michele. It was a semi-solid block that could be cut with a knife and eaten with bread. What's more, it was much cheaper than ordinary chocolate. In 1946, the Ferrero sweet factory was founded. The new discovery was christened Giandujot (pronounced "Jan-doo-yot"). Its namesake, the famous clown of Turin, was depicted on the label. It was an immediate success. In 1949, the Giandujot became Supercrema, a cream that could be spread on bread rather than cut into pieces. On April 20, the name was changed again, this time to Nutella, as part of a clever plan to expand sales. But Ferrero went on to produce many more successes, culminating in the Ferrero Rocher in 1982. This irregularly-shaped chocolate praline, filled with Nutella with a whole hazelnut in the center, has topped world chocolate sales and, as such, may be described as the world's most popular chocolate.

sugar drop by drop onto a marble surface. This led to the formation of round 'pills' the size of a small coin. As the sugar cooled they became transparent and extremely hard." Turin became famous for its candy. After the first barley-sugar pastilles, recommended for "soothing a cough", they moved on to making candy with fruit pastes and natural extracts: pineapples, oranges, cherries, lemons, pears, Reinette apples, strawberries, blueberries, aniseed and mint. In the mid-19th century, candy began to be eaten by the masses and confectioners which had once supplied only the nobility were forced to step up production. Candy made in Turin include the multicolored, flat, crunchy sugar candy. They used to be called 'bottoni da prete' (priest's buttons) and were sucked. The fore-runner of the lollipop also came from Turin. They were large, flat, round candies on a hexagonal stick.

Gianduiotto

The *gianduiotto*, the unique, smooth, hazelnut-flavored chocolate, is the Turin chocolate par excellence. It is extraordinary for many reasons: its ingredients, cocoa, sugar and the famous Tondo Gentile hazelnuts of Piedmont, toasted and finely-ground; its incredibly smooth consistency; its long triangular shape, and the fact that it is wrapped in golden paper, giving it a touch of class. Turin's most famous chocolate, perhaps, but by no means the only one. The *cremino* consists of two layers of *gianduia* held together with a layer of chocolate paste flavored with hazelnuts, coffee or lemon.

The cremino, an exquisite, mid-19th-century invention.

Krumiri

This specialty comes from Casale Monferrato. These biscuits were invented in 1878 in honor of Vittorio Emanuele II of Savoy. The king had a handle-bar moustache and the shape of the biscuit is supposed to resemble one. Made with a sort of sweet short pastry, they contain flour, butter, sugar, fresh eggs and vanilla.

Lingue di Gatto/Cats' tongues

These delicious biscuits are made with flour, icing sugar, liquid cream, egg-whites and vanilla essence.

Marrons glacés of Cuneo

For centuries, Cuneo has been famous for its chestnuts. There are more than 20 different types, each with its own special application. The candy which best represents this legacy is the *marron glacé*. Having been washed and selected, the best chestnuts are soaked in water for nine days, which helps to stabilize the starch, reduce the tannin and improve the flavor. Once they have been matured, the *marrons* are measured and shelled. Then they are boiled and then put into a syrup obtained by adding sugar and vanilla to the cooking water. Finally they are dipped into icing sugar, which crystallizes in the oven, giving them a transparent sheen. In the hierarchy of *marrons glacés*, the best are called 'fioroni'. Three or four of them weigh 100 g. If you've never tasted them, try *marrons glacés* with candied violets.

Marrons Glacés from Cuneo, a symbol of the region.

Nocciolini di Chivasso

These candies from Chivasso in the Province of Turin were invented in the early 20th century. Today they still have only three ingredients: toasted, ground Piedmontese hazelnuts, sugar and egg-whites.

Pesche Ripiene/ Stuffed baked peaches

For this dessert, *spiccagnola* peaches are used. The flesh can be easily removed from the stone. They are cut in half, some of the flesh is removed, then they are filled with the peach flesh mixed with crushed amaretti, cocoa, sugar and a dash of Moscato wine. They are baked in the oven and can be served hot or cold.

Torcetti

Typical of the Valli di Lanzo (Province of Turin), these cookies are made with natural yeast, flour, butter and sugar. Lengths of the mixture are sprinkled with sugar and the ends are pressed together before baking. Ideal with tea or hot chocolate, or dipped in white wine.

Torrone di Nocciole/ Halzelnut nougat

This nougat is sold under the name Torrone d'Asti and Torrone d'Alba e delle Langhe. Hard but crumbly, its ingredients include Piedmontese hazelnuts, especially the special Tondo Gentile hazelnut of the Langhe, and locally-produced polyflora or acacia honey.

Violette Candite/Candied violets

These candied violets are a tradition of Borgo San Dalmazzo (Province of Cuneo), and are made with fresh violets dipped in sugar syrup according to a traditional recipe.

ALESSANDRIA

CASALE MONFERRATO

Pasticceria Krumiri Rossi

Via Lanza 17, Tel. 0142453030, www.krumirirossi.it
This is where *krumiri* were invented in 1878.

ASTI

Giordanino

Corso Alfieri 254, Tel. 0141593802
Here you can buy typical local cakes and candies.

G.N.B.

Via Malta 24, Tel. 0141557291
Traditional and local candies.

BIELLA

Confetteria Bianchi

Via Italia 42, Tel. 01521418
This confectioner's dates from 1875 and sells the typical *canestrelli*.

Ferrua
Via Italia 43, Tel. 01522485
This café sells local pastries including *canestrelli*.

Fratelli Coggiola
Via Delleani 13/F, Tel. 01520655, www.pasticceriacoggiola.com
Try the local type of canestrelli and the drunken pear cake with ratafià.

Jeantet
Piazza V. Veneto 16, Tel. 01530211, www.canestrellobiellese.com
A broad range of typical local pastries.

CUNEO

Confetteria Arione
Piazza D. Galimberti 14, Tel. 0171692539
A historic pastry-shop. Specialties of the house include *cuneesi al rhum* (chocolates with a rum filling).

ALBA

Antico Caffè Calissano
Piazza Risorgimento 3, Tel. 0173442101
Not just coffee, also a wide range of local pastries and chocolate.

Cignetti
Via V. Emanuele 3, Tel. 0173440218
Stop here and try their *amaretti speziati* (amaretti flavored with spices) and nougat.

BRA

Converso
Via V. Emanuele II 199, Tel. 0172413626
For more than a century, the Converso has been selling cakes and chocolates.

NOVARA

Premiata Pasticceria Bertani
Corso Cavour 5, Tel. 0321629811
A pastry-shop with typical local pastries.

TURIN

Baratti & Milano
Piazza Castello 27, Tel. 0114407138
A historic café, their specialty here is *gianduiotto*, also coffee-flavored.

Caffè Confetteria Al Bicerin
Piazza della Consolata 5, Tel. 0114369325, www.bicerin.it
A café with a long history where you can taste the typical Turin *bicerin*, made with espresso coffee, chocolate and cream of milk.

Caffè Gelateria Fiorio
Via Po 8, Tel. 0118173225
Mirrors and stuccoes, velvet and crystal, with an atmosphere of days gone by.

Caffè San Carlo
Piazza S. Carlo 156, Tel. 0115617748
A historic café where they make traditional Turin cakes and desserts.

Confetteria Avvignano
Piazza Carlo Felice 50, Tel. 011541992
A historic confectioner where they make typical Turin specialties, including *gianduiotti*.

Confetteria Stratta
Piazza S. Carlo 191, Tel. 011547920, www.stratta1836.it
Gianduiotti and *marrons glacés*, plus a vast assortment of pralines and candies.

Il Vero Cioccolato Stroppiana
Via P. Paoli 51, Tel. 0113190460
Very special artisan pralines.

The traditional bonet.

CHIVASSO

Pasticceria Bonfante
Via Torino 29, Tel. 0119102157, www.nocciolini-bonfante.it
An elegant venue where you can find the best of Piedmontese pastries.

VERBANO-CUSIO-OSSOLA

VERBANIA

Casa del Dolce
Intra, Via XXV Aprile 54, Tel. 0323402555
In the historic center, this artisan pastry-workshop has a shop attached.

VERCELLI

Taverna&Tarnuzzer
Piazza Cavour 27, Tel. 0161253139
In the historic center of Vercelli, a place where you can sample typical cakes and sweets.

Festivals in the Valle d'Aosta

JULY

↘ The Sunday before or after 27 July
SAGRA DELLA SEUPA À LA VAPELENENTSE
Valpelline
Comune, Tel. 016573227 (www.comune.valpelline.ao.it - www.valpelline.com)
On the Sunday closest to 27 July (the festival of the town's patron saint, St Pantaleon), the people of the Valpelline celebrate in the evening with dancing, games and open-air dinners based on a local specialty: *seupa Vapelenentse* (Valpelline soup). This traditional soup of the mountain people of the Valpelline is made with alternate layers of stale bread and thin slices of Fontina, covered with stock and cooked in the oven.

AUGUST

↘ First Sunday of August
SAGRA DEL JAMBON ALLA BRACE
Saint-Oyen
Aiat del Gran San Bernardo Tel. 016578559 (www.gransanbernardo.net)
Each year, in the Valle del Gran San Bernardo, at Prenoud, there is a festival where they barbecue large quantities of ham, giving it a slightly smoky flavor. The hams are cooked on enormous open grills and are served with a sauce made of white wine and cognac, and sprinkled with chopped garlic and aromatic herbs (bay, rosemary and sage). The ham is served on the plate with beans or polenta. In the evening there is music and dancing.

↘ 15. August
FESTA DELLA FONTINA
Oyace
Pro Loco
Tel. 0165730914
The festival of Fontina, the Valle d'Aosta's renowned DOP cheese, starts a few days before with an open-day up at the mountain farm where it is produced (just over an hour's walk). You can visit the store-rooms where the cheeses are left to mature. You can also see Fontina being made and, after lunch, watch the cows being milked. On Ferragosto (15 August, the festival of the Assumption) the proper festival begins, with various dishes based on Fontina and other produce like *polenta concia* (polenta with butter and cheese), meat from the Valle d'Aosta and rye bread. In the evening, there is dancing and local bands give concerts.

↘ Weekend after 15 August
FËTA DOU TETEUN E FESTA DEL TURISTA
Gignod
Aiat del Gran San Bernardo Tel. 016578559 (www.gransanbernardo.net)
Every year, at Gignod, there is a festival based on the local specialty called *teteun*, a dish made with the udders of the Valdostana cow, cut into small pieces and pickled in brine with spices and herbs. It is served sliced, usually with vegetables. The Friday is the "festa del turista" (tourist festival), with musical entertainment. Saturday is the festival proper with food and dancing, building up to a climax on Sunday, when more entertainment is laid on.

↘ Last weekend of August
FËTA DE LA TRIFOLLE
Allein
Aiat del Gran San Bernardo Tel. 016578559 (www.gransanbernardo.net)
Trifolle the Valle d'Aosta dialect word for 'potato'. During this festival you can taste various specialties, including the unusual *sorsa di Allein*, a dish made with stock, beans, haricots, carrots, pears, apples and rye bread—and potatoes, of course. They put up a marquee in one of the villages of Allein where you can taste dishes made with potatoes or join in the games organized for the festival.

↘ Last weekend of August
FËTA DOU LAR
Arnad
Organizzazione della Sagra Tel. 0125966443 (www.festalardo.it)
The area of Arnad is famous for its magnificent flavorsome lard, made in the Lower Valle d'Aosta between Verrès and Bard. During the lard festival, the producers offer tastes to passers-by, arranging tiny pieces of this delicious food on beautifully embroidered cloths, and displaying it in typical wooden houses decorated with flowers especially for the occasion. They also offer warm chestnuts cooked in butter. The festival starts with tastings of typical local delicacies and races, with various other competitions in the afternoon. You can also watch demonstrations of traditional craft activities or participate in 'laboratori del gusto' (food workshops). In the evening there is more entertainment: theatrical performances, dancing, and music.

SEPTEMBER

↘ Last weekend of September
SAGRA DELL'UVA
Chambave
Comune
Tel. 016646106 (www.regione.vda.it)
This festival, during which the vignerons of the area display and offer tastings of their most delicious grapes and the best wines in the region, began in the 1950s. The festival starts on the Friday with an open-air ball and the traditional 'gara delle botti' (barrel-rolling contest) between the various wine-producing areas of the valley, namely Aosta, Aymavilles, Chambave, Donnas and Morgex.. In the evening, the old wine-cellars of the town open their doors to offer tastings of their best wines. On Sunday there is a competition for the most beautifully decorated basket of grapes. The jury awards marks both for the quality of the grapes and for the composition as a whole. There is also a scare-crow exhibition and town bands and folk groups provide musical entertainment.

Festivals in Piedmont

JANUARY

↘ 2. January
FAGIOLATA DI SAN DEFENDENTE
Castiglione d'Asti (Asti)
Pro Loco Tel. 0141206061 (www.atasti.it)
A few days before the festival, people go from door to door collecting offerings of beans. These are then cooked in 48 copper cauldrons suspended from long wooden beams above wood fires, usually in the main square. This tradition seems to have started in the 13th century, when, to celebrate the peace settlement between the clergy and the nobility, a dish of beans was distributed to the poor. Beans have always been considered a 'poor man's dish'.

MARCH

↘ Second Sunday of March
SAGRA DEL POLENTONISSIMO
Monastero Bormida (Asti)
Comune
Tel. 014488012
This festival has been held since the early 19th century and has a historical basis. During the terrible famine of 1573, some hungry itinerant tinkers were given a dish of *polenta e frittata* (polenta and omelet) by Marquis Della Rovere. To thank him they presented him with a large copper cauldron.
The festival includes demonstrations of old craft skills and a procession of about 100 people in costume, accompanied by folk groups and town bands. One ton of polenta is cooked in the main square, along with large quantities of sausages and an onion omelet weighing 40kg.
The food is later distributed to the populus and is washed down with copious quantities of wine.

APRIL

↘ Second-last Sunday of April
SAGRA DEL POLENTONE
Ponti (Alessandria)
Comune
Tel. 0144596142
(www.comunediponti.it)
Every year, 800 kg of polenta is made and served with *frittata e merluzzo* (omelet and cod), and accompanied with local wine. Before the Sagra, there is a historic procession of townsfolk dressed in medieval costume. The entertainment includes music, folk dancing, stalls selling local produce and exhibitions of vintage photographs.

MAY

↘ Second Sunday of May
SAGRA DEL CANESTRELLO
Vaie (Torino)
Comune
Tel. 0119649020
(www.comune.vaie.to.it)
This festival celebrates the *canestrello*, a typical cookie of the Province of Turin. All sorts of entertainment is laid on: concerts, musical performances and exhibitions. The streets of Vaie are filled with stalls selling products from the Valle di Susa.

JUNE

↘ Third Sunday of June
SAGRA DELLE CUCINE MONFERRINE
Moncalvo (Asti)
Comune
Tel. 0141917505
(www.comune.moncalvo.asti.it)
At this festival you can sample the typical delicacies of the area. There are tastings of *primi piatti*, meat dishes, dishes with truffles, and desserts. The food is naturally accompanied by local wines, such as Barbera.

AUGUST

↘ 15 and 16 August
SAGRA DEL RASCHERA E DEL BRUSS
Frabosa Soprana (Cuneo)
Comune
Tel. 0174244024
(www.frabosasoprana.com)
As part of the celebrations for Ferragosto (the Festival of the Assumption) there is a festival devoted to two cheeses made here: Raschera and *brüss*, which is obtained by fermenting the waste from the Raschera process. There are stands offering menus based on cheese, stalls selling local products, an exhibition of local produce organized by the dairy, and cheese-tastings. Events are organized all over the town: music, folk dancing, games for kids and a historic procession of people dressed in medieval costume. The procession, accompanied by town bands and flag-throwers, ends in the square in front of the Town Hall, where the festival is officially opened. After the ceremony, the festival continues with theatrical performances, cabaret, street artists and Occitan musicians and dancers.

↘ Last Friday of August
SAGRA DEL PEPERONE QUADRATO
Carmagnola (Torino)
Comune
Tel. 0119724222
(www.comune.carmagnola.to.it)
A wonderful food and wine market is set up below the old bastions and in the historic center for the festival devoted to the square pepper, a typical product of the area. For 10 days, this humble vegetable remains in the limelight, as an ingredient of traditional dishes, and tastings organized in its honor by local producers, who sell it fresh, pickled or under oil. A special competition is held for the occasion, with prizes for the heaviest pepper and the heaviest group of peppers. All sorts of entertainment takes place in the streets of the town: side-shows, concerts, folk dancing, cabaret and games for kids. In the evening, after a dinner for 1,800 people, where the menu is based on square peppers, there is a marvelous firework display in the football ground.

SEPTEMBER

↘ First Saturday of September
COCCO-WINE
Cocconato (Asti)
Comune
Tel. 0141907007
(www.comune.cocconato.at.it)
This wine and food festival provides opportunities for

tasting the wines and typical foods of the area of Asti. In particular, you can taste the dish called *riso e gallina* (rice and chicken), a typical Cocconato dish which apparently dates back to Roman times. From late afternoon until the evening more than 30 stalls line the main streets of the town, of which about 20 represent local wine producers, providing an opportunity to taste the local wines. On the previous day, there is a 'wine test', a meeting of wine producers and wine connoisseurs, when prizes are awarded for the best wines of that year.

➘ First half of September
SAGRA DELL'UVA
Borgomanero (Novara)

Comune
Tel. 0322837711
(www.comune.borgomanero.no.it)
The grape festival is a tradition dating back more than 50 years and is still going on today with the aim of promoting local wines. Various events are associated with the festival: concerts by town bands, theatrical performances and tastings of local specialties. On the last Sunday, there is a historic procession in costume through the town. Parallel with the festival is a trade fair of artisan and industrial produce from the Novara area.

➘ Second Sunday of September
FESTIVAL DELLE SAGRE
Asti

Ufficio Comunicazione ed eventi, Tel. 0141535262
(www.festivaldellesagre.it)
Asti celebrates its farming origins with a festival devoted to specialties of the Asti area and the Piedmont region, including DOC wines. In Piazza Campo del Palio a typical country village is set up for the occasion so that local cultural action groups (called *pro loco*) (more than 100 of them) can promote their products. The miniature houses are surrounded by tables where you can sit down and have a meal. Great care is taken in the reconstruction of the miniature brick village, which has traditional roofs and gutters, hay-barns and bread ovens, even hand-embroidered curtains, and rare and antique farm equipment. The aim of the reconstruction is to recreate the values and the atmosphere of a farming culture which is gradually disappearing under the onslaught of the industrial society. With this in mind, on the Sunday morning, there is a procession of locals dressed in medieval costume, a living museum re-evoking a world which is fast disappearing. To liven things up, the *pro loco* (village action groups) participate in a contest to decide which one best represents the food and wine culture of the Asti area. They are subjected to five tests each is awarded marks for its procession, its cuisine, its service, and quality of the products and how they are displayed. Other events at the festival include games, music and old side-shows from fun-fairs (such as a shooting range, a stall where you can win a goldfish, and so on).

OCTOBER

➘ Every weekend of October and the first weekend of November
FIERA NAZIONALE DEL TARTUFO BIANCO D'ALBA
Alba (Cuneo)

Ente Fiera
Tel. 0173361051
(www.fieradeltartufo.org)
The festival starts with the Palio degli Asini (donkey race) and the Giostra delle Cento Torri (Joust of 100 Towers, a humorous procession in costume). This is the best time to visit the town which, more than any other, is associated with the white truffle. Alba has acquired international fame as the white truffle capital of the world. To show its gratitude, the town devotes this long festival to the noble white truffle, with its magical scent and exquisite taste, the best in the world. After the opening ceremony, the events associated with the fair begin: exhibitions, conferences and guided tastings with experts. Throughout the fair, you can also buy and taste typical local products, such as wine (especially Barolo), cheese (including Robiola di Alba), hams and salami, at the stand called 'oltre il tartufo' (beyond the truffle), while top chefs prepare dishes with this magnificent tuber.

➘ Last two weekends of October
FIERA DEL TARTUFO DI MONCALVO
Moncalvo (Asti)

Comune, Tel. 0141917505
(www.comune.moncalvo.asti.it)
The Moncalvo truffle fair, which began in the early 20th century, is an important event for truffle enthusiasts. As well as being a gastronomic event where you can taste typical local delicacies, it is also an exhibition of local artisan products, with other events such as flag-throwing displays, folk dancing, music, exhibitions and conferences.

➘ Third Sunday of October
LA CASTAGNA
Venasca (Cuneo)

Comune
Tel. 0175567353
This festival is a showcase for all the artisan food and craft produce from the Val Varaita. The fair occupies many of the streets, and is divided into three main areas: one focusing on agricultural produce, one for craft skills and another for tasting local delicacies. Here you can find artisan produce made of wood, iron, glass and stone as well as typical local food produce such as hams and salami, cheese, wine, chestnut cakes and candies. In the morning, a prize is awarded to the best producer of organic farm products, while the rest of the day is devoted to various other pursuits: painting and photographic exhibitions, book exhibitions, but also entertainment in the squares with street artists and concerts. The whole festival is about chestnuts. There are even conferences on the subject and, throughout the month of October, on Monday and Thursday, there is a chestnut market.

An outward expression of the extraordinary cultural richness of Piedmont and the Valle d'Aosta, the typical products you can purchase here reflect the enormity and diversity of the artisan traditions of these two regions. The famous lace of Cogne and the ceramics and jewelry of Piedmont are just two examples. In this part of Italy, artisan products are known for their quality and craftsmanship and, near the mountains, an unmistakable Alpine style. Modern, hi-tech companies, like FIAT in the automotive sector,

Shopping

produce sophisticated, first-class products. Inside the many artisan businesses, longstanding traditions continue. Many of them, wood-carving for example, represent a distinctive feature of an exquisitely local culture which takes advantage of the typical raw materials of the area.

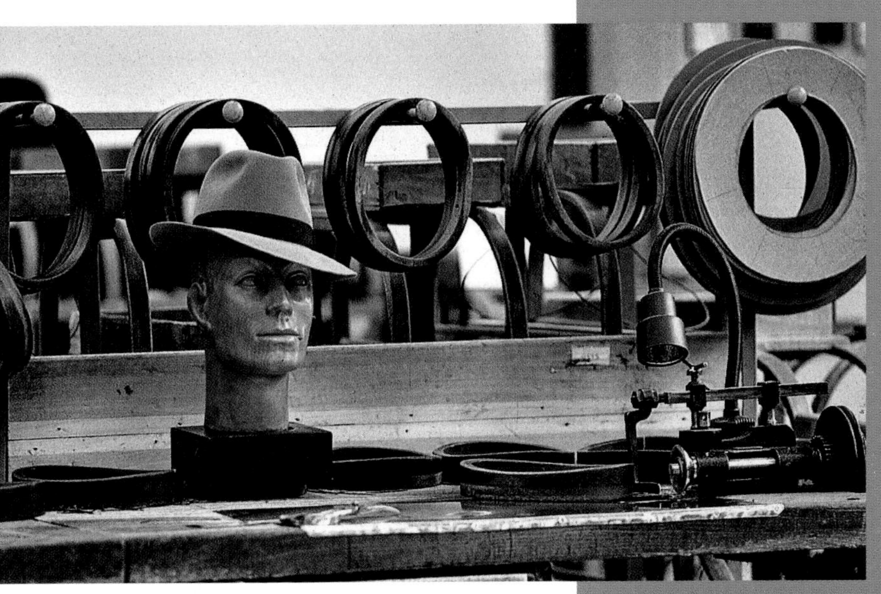

Highlights

- Intricate embroidery and exquisite lace from Cogne.
- Top-quality artisan gold, silver and jewelry from Valenza Po.
- Elegant artisan ceramics from Castellamonte, Villanova Mondovì and Chiusa di Pesio.
- The Fiera di S. Orso in Aosta and its absorbing antiques and craft markets.

Inside

196 Arts & crafts
200 Markets
203 Fashion

ARTS AND CRAFTS IN THE VALLE D'AOSTA

The traditional lifestyle that has characterized the farming civilization of the Valle d'Aosta for centuries has driven the inhabitants of these mountains to diversify their own skills and become resourceful, self-taught artisans, capable of making up for the lack of those products which one could only find at very high prices in the markets in distant towns. From that point on, the need to produce the tools necessary for field work and domestic use, at one's own house, became essential. Throughout the centuries, countless generations of farmers-craftsmen have acquired multiple skills and have refined their technical capabilities.

Wood

Most of the craftsmen from the Valle d'Aosta employ techniques refined to such an extent that throughout the centuries they often have crossed the thin line between art and crafts. Wooden sculptures are witness to this. One of the distinguishing elements of the wooden crafts and their cultural roots is found in the wide variety of types of wood used. All types are derived from forests in the area and are used to make valuable furniture, domestic furnishings, such as the traditional wine glasses (*grolla*, wooden cup) or *coppe dell'amicizia* (friendship cups), and objects used in daily work and handiwork in which the artistic aim prevails. Among the most distinguishing are the *sabots*, solid and inexpensive shoes suitable for mud and the winter in the Alps, and toys, almost all taking the form of an animal (the *cornailles*, which are stylized cows, are classic). The ornamented chests furnished with several compartments, otherwise referred to as *artson*, are among the different types of furniture that deserve attention. These chests are, in some cases, clever hiding places. Finally, there are small cradles that are lifted off of the ground by their foot which are joined by small boards to ensure rocking.

Examples of the traditional wooden grolla.

Iron

Iron crafts have already encountered prosperity in the past as can be noted in the elegant wrought iron balconies of Aosta and of the villages in the Valle d'Aosta. Over the last several decades, there has been a vigorous resumption of this trade, concentrated in the southern part of the Valle d'Aosta, thanks to the market's renewed interest in rustic furniture. The trade that has been resumed is based on the production of artistically made locks, chandeliers, umbrella stands, hatstands, street lamps, fences, and signs.

Lace

Among the costumes that stand out in the region are those from the Cogne valley because of their rich embroidery and marvellous make. Since the 1600's, the manufacturing of lace pillows has been widespread in the Cogne valley. The elaborate lace of Cogne, known by its dialectal name *dentelles*, is made with either white linen or linen in its natural color, without the help of designs or models but by reproducing from memory the patterns passed down from mother to daughter. The lace, still made today using the original technique, is put together to make tablecloths, sheets, towels, bedspreads, centerpieces, and collars. The recurrent decorative features draw their inspiration from an agricultural setting by reproducing flowers, animals, and commonly-used objects. The dentelles also shows originality from a technical point of view, as it is made with unique stitches and marked by unusual names in local dialect. In Cogne, it is possible to see and buy different types of lace at the Mostra dei Pizzi al Tombolo at 50 Via Grappein.

Fabric

The ancient traditions of weaving wool and cloth have been maintained in

Valgrisenche, where the distinctive 'drap', or broadcloth, is produced. The drap is a furniture fabric that blends well with rustic-style furniture. Hemp weaving, however, is limited to the Champorcher valley, where it is used to make shirts, drapes, towels, and table linens. In the Lys valley, in Gaby, felt-soled and hemp-soled slippers referred to as *sock* are still produced today with recycled fabric that is embellished with needlework.

Pietra ollare

The *pietra ollare* is considered the best material for the construction of stoves, still used today in the Champorcher, Ayas, and Valtournenche valleys. The *pietra ollare* is able to accumulate much more heat that other materials, whether they are natural or artificial. As a result, it has always been used to make objects and structures linked to heating and maintaining heat. In addition, the *pietra ollare* possesses a property that makes it ideal for being sectioned, carved, and lathed. Therefore, besides embellishing the stoves with refined decorations, the artisans from the Valle d'Aosta use the stone for making statues, pots, jars, finely-made boxes, and sculptures.

Leather

The significant availability of hides has allowed the leather craftsman to prosper and transform himself from an ordinary craftsman into an artist. However, the classical products manufactured in leather, such as knapsacks, leather bags, and flasks, have become rarer over time while factories that produce objects linked to the farming tradition have maintained their activity in the valleys. Such objects are artistically-decorated collars for animals, ornaments, and *socques*, traditional clogs with the upper part made from leather and the sole from wood. In the last few years, the production of clothing accessories, such as belts, bags, wallets, and shoes has greatly developed.

Ceramics

In recent years, ceramics from the Valle d'Aosta have become very successful. Of particular importance is the production of stoves and fireplaces that has allowed this sector to carve itself a space in the group of craftsmen in the Valle d'Aosta.

Agricultural tools

Even though it is inspired by the local craft forms, agricultural tool production is a completely separate category with deep local roots and is an extremely precise art. An incredible range of tools is still used in agriculture today, in addition to vats, barrels, and various tools used at the grape harvest and in the cellar, as well as a large variety of 'vannerie', including baskets, *gerle* (rustic baskets with straps used for carrying hay), and handmade hampers.

AOSTA

Torchio Marina Studio Ceramico
Regione Chabloz 20, Tel. 0165552559
Artistic ceramics

Jaccod
Via M. Solarolo 5, Tel. 016544585
Pietra ollare production

CHAMPORCHER

Cooperativa Lou Dzeut
Località Chardoney 42, Tel. 012537327
Fabric

PONT-SAINT-MARTIN

Ferrari F. & C.
Via Nazionale per Carema 34, Tel. 0125804166
Pietra ollare production

SAINT-PIERRE

Cooperativa La Grolla
Località Cognein 44, Tel. 0165903403
Wooden articles

SAINT-VINCENT

Robert Chiurato
Località Champcillien 8, Tel. 0166511441
Wooden sculptures

VALTOURNENCHE

Fratelli Varisellaz
Via degli Artigiani 11, Tel. 0125929474
Artistic ceramics

Luciano Savin
Via degli Artigiani 5, Tel. 0125929374
Wrought iron production

ARTS AND CRAFTS IN PIEDMONT

The farming spirit of Piedmont has persisted and survived with such vigor that it has obstinately led traditions, lifestyles, and trades over time. Therefore, it is not surprising that the ancient craft business, even with its many cultural and ethnic roots, has stood the test of time in spite of the influence of the social environment that continually looks towards the future. The region, which has been politically unified for centuries, does not show a sense of cultural unification that one would expect. This region, which has managed to reconcile industrialization with traditional culture, has persistently preserved its many different roots, linked to a great range of artisan trades.

Metals

The production of copper objects for use in daily life was widespread in Piedmont. Following the migration of artisans from craft workshops to factories, especially car factories, this had the positive effect of creating a market niche for the few diehards who were able to continue with their traditional craft activities, mainly in the Cuorgnè, Pont Canavese, and Alpette (Turin) areas. Strong activity and high quality is still noted in the production of wrought iron, today, in some centers of the Cuneo province and the territory of Rivarolo Canavese (Turin). These characteristics extend to Vernante, where the artisan production of *vernantini* (handmade jack-knives with a horn-handle) has been maintained.

The goldsmith's art

Thanks perhaps to the continuity of the House of Savoy and the noble court, the artistic production of precious metals has always found a thriving market in Piedmont, developing especially in the provinces of Vercelli and Alessandria. Today, this craft is concentrated in Valenza Po (Alessandria), where the gold and silver production, nearly the only economic source for its people, is exclusively based on artisan skill. There are over 1,300 experts working on the gold and silver production as well as on precious stone production.

Silver

In Alessandria, silver production is the most common craft and has a long history here. Over the years, the artisans have acquired substantial technical knowledge, turning Alessandria into one of the main Italian centers for silver crafts.

Wood

Wood production has always been an typical activity of the mountain population, practiced especially during the winter months when one can take advantage of the abundant raw material and the idleness induced by the cold winters. Wood finds its use in domestic furnishings, in the tools for field work, in the cellar and the stall, and in objects of artistic and religious inspiration. Similar trades still exist in the Vasesia, Valstrona and Viù valleys. Thanks to the closeness of richer markets, these craft forms have evolved into the production of rustic furniture with carved ornaments in Valsesia, Val Varaita, and Pinerolo (Turin), while in Saluzzo (Cuneo) valuable wood and antique-style furniture is made.

Musical tools

The production of musical tools in Piedmont has popular and elite origins, tied to the nobility of the Turin Court. Around the mid-1600's, in order to respond to the demands of the Court, French lute-makers arrived, bringing production techniques that conditioned the style of the Piedmontese lute-makers, differentiating their art from the Italian tradition. Today, expert craftsmen have escaped certain extinction, thanks to their high level of specialization. This is the case in Centallo and Piasco (Cuneo), where the production of organs and harps prospers. Other examples are found in Leinì (Turin), where accordions are produced, and in Quarna (Verbano-Cusio-Ossola), where wind instruments are made. Lute-makers can also be found in Rosignano Monferrato and in Solero (Alessandria).

Ceramics

Castellamonte, in Canavese, is the epicenter of ceramic crafts where the tradition has been preserved for centuries. The diversification of production is great, ranging from commonly used items and furnishing objects, to tiles, architectural elements, statues, busts, fireplaces, and rounded pots with small handles. The fame of Castellamonte, however, is owed to the great glazed ceramic heaters.
Traditional production continues in the areas of Mondovì, above all in Villanova Mondovì and Chiusa di Pesio (Cuneo), where tableware, small religious statues, decorative tiles, and hand-painted plates are manufactured. Instead, in Vinovo (Turin), handmade bricks and architectural elements in baked clay obtained by ancient wooden forms are produced.

Stone

Verbano-Cusio-Ossola is rich in marble, where the quarries have yielded the pink granite of Baveno, the green stone of Mergozzo, and the marble of Candoglia been extracted for centuries. This zone has contributed to the development of an age-old artisan and sculptor school, primarily in Baveno, Gravellona Toce, Mergozzo, and Ornavasso. The teaching is still active today and is diversified in a wide range of productions, from classical artistic productions to decorative objects for the house and garden.

Fabric

The towns of Caraglio (Cuneo), where refined and precious, thin and thick silk cloth is produced, and Pella, on Lake Orta, where hemp is manufactured by a handloom, are havens for traditional handiwork. The most precious examples of fabric craftwork are found in Asti, in Ugo Scassa's tapestry, which is housed in the Certosa di Valmanera, and the Montalbano tapestry, located in the old town center, inside the striking rooms of Michelerio.

Lace

In Valsesia, the refined art of *puncetto*, a cotton lace formed by small slip-knots connected by stitches, flourishes. This production, which has always been used for enriching the 'bottom drawer', met its moment of splendor in 1800, when it was discovered by Queen Margherita of Savoy. *Puncetto* then became one of the most fashionable ornaments among the ladies-in-waiting .Today, it is used for fringes, doilies, and decorations.

ASTI

Arazzeria Scassa
Via dell'Arazzeria 60, Tel. 0141271352
Tapestry

NOVARA

Pellicceria Giroli
Via Zandonai 29, Tel. 0321431122
Fur shop

Bottega della cornice
Viale Piazza d'Armi 14, Tel. 0321463580
Wooden frames

Vetraria
Via Caimi 20, Tel. 0321694878
Artistic glass windows

TURIN

L'Artigiano dell'Ottone
Via Vanchiglia 24, Tel. 0118172813
Brass work

Atelier d'Arte Orafa
Via dei Mercanti 15/C, Tel. 0115627680
Jewelry shop

Redivivus
Via Bava 32, Tel. 0118171667
Lute shop

Rocca Arte Vetri e trafilati
Corso Regio Parco 34, Tel. 011854937
Artistic glass windows

VERCELLI

Cooperfisa
Via Donato Francesco 15, Tel. 0161392115
Accordions

MARKETS IN THE VALLE D'AOSTA

The particular and striking farming traditions of the population from the Valle d'Aosta emerge in a spontaneous way from many of the craft products that that tell of the ancient social traditions of the area. There is so much craftwork, both in terms of variety and quantity, that it is possible to find it in wood, leather, iron, and ceramics at local markets.

AOSTA

Fiera di Sant'Orso

30-31 January

At Sant'Orso, the largest, oldest, and most well-known regional fair is celebrated in honor of St Ursus, the patron saint of the craftsmen, with the first fair dating back to 1243. Over the centuries, Sant'Orso has gradually assumed the responsibility of becoming the meeting point in the world of local crafts. Today, just as before, the fair gathers nearly all the craftsmen in the region, giving rise to an extraordinary display of local productions. The exhibitors assemble in the old village of Sant'Orso, in the square that extends to the foot of the Porta Pretoria, where wooden agricultural tools (that is, the most antique handiwork traditions) and artistic products of recognized mastery are displayed. Via S. Anselmo and Via Porta Pretoria are also filled with booths selling wooden products, as well as hemp, lace, wrought iron, and *pietra ollare* (soapstone). It provides a cheerful atmosphere as the Fiera di Sant'Orso is not only an exhibition, but also a party, brightened by music, dancing, and masks.
Information: Tel. 0165236627, www.fieradisantorso.it

Foire d'été

The Saturday before the mid-August holiday

The Foire d'été tallies nearly 500 exhibitors who present traditional craftwork. The competitive exhibition of local crafts from the Valle d'Aosta takes place between the end of July and the beginning of August, on dates that vary from year to year. An event that allows one to appreciate local crafts.
Information: Tel. 0165236627, www.regione.vda.it

COURMAYEUR

Mercatino d'Antiquariato

Every Monday in July and August

Small, picturesque Entrèves is home to a local street market where 50 exhibitors sell antiques and second-hand objects, such as agricultural tools from the past, local clothing and hats, prints, and toys, etc. The market is worth a visit.
Information: Tel. 0165831311, www.comune.courmayeur.ao.it

DONNAS

Fiera del Legno

Third week in January

This fair is dedicated to the carving and craft production of wood and it exhibits sculptures, furnishings, and diverse traditional objects at Sant'Orso di Donnas.
Information: Tel. 0125807515

PONT-SAINT-MARTIN

El mercà del ghett

Second Sunday in July and August

This local street market has natural, handcrafted products and takes place in an old area facing the Lys Stream, also called *Ghett* because of the *Bourg* (town) on the right bank.
Information: Tel. 0125804843

PRÉ-SAINT-DIDIER

Foire des Glaciers

30 December

This local crafts fair includes nearly 80 exhibitors. Examples of the traditional handiwork presented are wrought iron, sculpture, carving, and bobbin lace products, along with objects produced from *pietra ollare*. Information:
Tel. 0165236627, www.regione.vda.it

VERRÈS

Petit Marchè des Brocanteurs

First Sunday of the month May to Sep

This important local street market, with good bargains, allows people to trade antiques. Three-hundred exhibitors offer diverse objects from the late 1800's, such as farming tools, furniture, antique prints, books, papers, and maps, as well as various gifts and fancy goods.

MARKETS IN PIEDMONT

The many markets that Piedmont has to offer give visitors the chance to browse around the booths in search of old things, among which rare objects, furnishings, and high-quality furniture are frequently hidden. The markets are often combined with farmers' stands offering local produce under the arcades in the square.

ALESSANDRIA

CASALE MONFERRATO

Mercatino dell'antiquariato

2nd weekend of the month, except August
The local antiques market is one of the most prestigious events of its kind in Piedmont. About 220 exhibitors offer furniture from different periods, wooden doors with valuable inlays, wrought-iron gratings and gates from the 1800's, old books, illustrated magazines, old newspapers, vintage telephones.
Information: Tel. 0142454757, www.entemanifestazioni.it

GABIANO

Mak Bosk

First Sunday in June
Mak Bosk commits itself to handing down the old tradition of wood production. Here it is possible to find wicker objects, baskets, clogs, and true works of art by sculptors and woodcarvers.
Information: Tel. 0142955018

ASTI

Mostra mercato dell'antico e dell'usato

Fourth Sunday of the month
Along the streets under the arcades of the old center, one can discover this market presenting antiques and second-hand products such as gifts and fancy goods, gold and silver, and agricultural tools put out by nearly 200 exhibitors.
Information: Tel. 0141355861

CUNEO

CHERASCO

I Grandi Mercati di Cherasco

From April to December
Cherasco dedicates one Sunday each month to different markets, such as the Antiques and Collectors Market- three times a year the Ceramics and Glass Art Market - June, the Antique book Market - July, and the Antique Toy and Bargain Model-making Market- October.
Information: Tel. 0172488552, www.cherasco2000.com

A typical antiques and collectors' market.

MONDOVÌ

Mostra dell'Artigianato

Mid-August Holiday
This craft show highlights the ceramics tradition from Mondovì, which is characterized by the recurrent depiction of very colorful roosters and has been kept alive by two craft shops that produce traditional pieces.
Information: Tel. 0174559300, www.comune.mondovi.cn.it

SALUZZO

Mostra di Antiquariato

The last two weeks in May
In this antique furniture exhibition that takes place in the splendid 17th-century setting of the royal stables, it is possible to find tapestries, silverware, paintings, sculptures, porcelain and also unusual objects. There are also many antique dealers and restorers from Saluzzo present, who specialize in cabinet-making and inlaid work.
Information: Tel. 017543375, www.comune.saluzzo.cn.it

Mostra Nazionale di Artigianato Artistico e Tipico

The last two weeks in September

This event urges the expansion of high-quality craftwork, especially that tied to wooden art. About 50 exhibitors present all types of furnishing objects.

Information: Tel. 0175433375, www.comune.saluzzo.cn.it

SAVIGLIANO

Quintessenza

Second Sunday in May

Herb, spice, and medicinal plant show. Countless stands along the street in the village sell herb-derived products, such as infusions, essences, distillates, and cosmetics.

Information: Tel. 0172712536, wwww.entemanifestazionisavigliano.com

TURIN

Fiera del Gran Balôn

Second Sunday of the month

The Balôn is the oldest market of its kind in Italy and it owes its origins to the city authorities, who wished to regulate the phenomenon of reselling old things. Today, this village fair, which takes place at Porta Palazzo, presents antiques and collections of modern art obtained by nearly 200 exhibitors in the maze of alleys lined with junk dealers, antique dealers, and restorers.

A wide range of antiques at Gran Balôn.

Information: Tel. 0114369741, www.balon.it

PANCALIERI

Viverbe

Third weekend in September

Pancalieri, known as 'isola d'erba' by Italians (literally herb island), produces the majority of herbs in Italy. The collection of nurseries and medicinal herbs put on an herbalist, cosmetics, and natural nutrition market, including essential oils, liqueurs, pharmaceuticals, and mint, otherwise known as the *regina di Viverbe* (literally the queen of Viverbe).

Information: Tel. 0119734102, www.comune.pancalieri.to.it

PONT CANAVESE

Mostra dell'Artigianato

First weekend in June

Under the arcades on Via Caviglione, one can discover a crafts show where wood, wrought iron, copper, stone, glass, and fabric handiwork is on display.

Information: Tel. 0124862511, www.comune.pontcanavese.to.it

VERBANO-CUSIO-OSSOLA

MACUGNAGA

Fiera di San Bernardo

First weekend in July

This fair is an occasion which promotes the Walser culture through meetings, exhibitions, markets, and events. It takes place at Staffa and the exhibitors are exclusively Alpine and Walser craft sculptors.

Information: Tel. 032465119 www.comune.macugnaga.vb.it

VERCELLI

VARALLO

Alpàa

Second Saturday to third Sunday in July

This market exhibition involves picturesque log cabins in a splendid park and the participation of many exhibitors and over 40 craftsmen from various parts of the region. The main characteristic that this market exhibits is the *in diretta* (live) demonstration of local handiwork from the Valle d'Aosta. Examples include the production of *puncetto* (lace) and *pietra ollare (soapstone)*, as well as many other articles.

For further Information:

Tel. 3474188583, www.alpaa.com

FASHION IN THE VALLE D'AOSTA AND PIEDMONT

Many consumers can see the success of the outlet phenomenon in Italy, which originated about twenty years ago in the United States and spread rapidly to other parts of the world. Savings and high quality are both guaranteed. In this way, one can make a good purchase without spending a great amount of money. Besides outlets, one can find shopping centers that include a group of businesses that sell their products directly from their stores and allow you to make good buys.

AOSTA

QUART

Nike Factory Store

Amerique 125, Tel. 0165775149
Clothing, shoes, and sports items for men, women, and children. Accessories are also available.

ALESSANDRIA

SERRAVALLE SCRIVIA

Blunauta

SS 35 Bis dei Giovi, Tel. 0143601129
www.blunauta.it
A vast assortment of clothing and accessories for men and women.

McArthur Glen Designer Outlet

Via della Moda 1, Tel. 0143609000
www.mcarthurglen.it
A shopping village with ca. 150 shops of the most important brand names, offering shoes for all, as well as housewares and gifts. The labels found range from sports brands and casual clothing to high fashion.

BIELLA

Lanificio Fratelli Cerruti

Via Cernaia 40, Tel. 015351144
www.lanificiocerruti.com
High quality men's and women's clothing for every occasion.

CUNEO

BORGO SAN DALMAZZO

Nike Factory Store

Via Cuneo 72, Tel. 0171268022
www.nike.com
Clothing, shoes, and sports items for men, women, and children. They also sell various sports accessories as well as a range of items for the gym and for swimming.

NOVARA

CALTIGNAGA

Sergio Tacchini Factory Store

SS 229, km 8, Tel. 0321651800
www.sergiotacchini.com
Clothing, shoes, and accessories. Casual and sports clothing for men, women, and children. They also sell accessories and a range of articles from a leather goods store.

TURIN

Prenatal Outlet

Piazza Derna 248, Tel. 0112427564
www.prenatal.it
As the name suggests, this outlet has a range of maternity wear, however, it also has plenty of clothing and articles for newborns, babies and toddlers.

TCI HIGHLIGHTS

BORSALINO

Over the years, this brand name has risen to such fame that it is associated with any type of felt hat that appears similar to the original *Borsalino Fedora*, which arose out of Giuseppe Borsalino's namesake business in Alessandria. From 1857, when Giuseppe Borsalino began his work, to the eve of the World War I, production levels reached a high of over 2,000,000 annual pieces. In that period the factory played an important role in the Piedmontese economy. Even though there has been a decline in the number of people who wear this type of hat, production still continues. The fame of the Borsalino hat was spread further by the film *Borsalino* (1970), made with Alain Delon and Jean-Paul Belmondo. In 2006, a museum dedicated to the history of the hat was inaugurated in Alessandria.

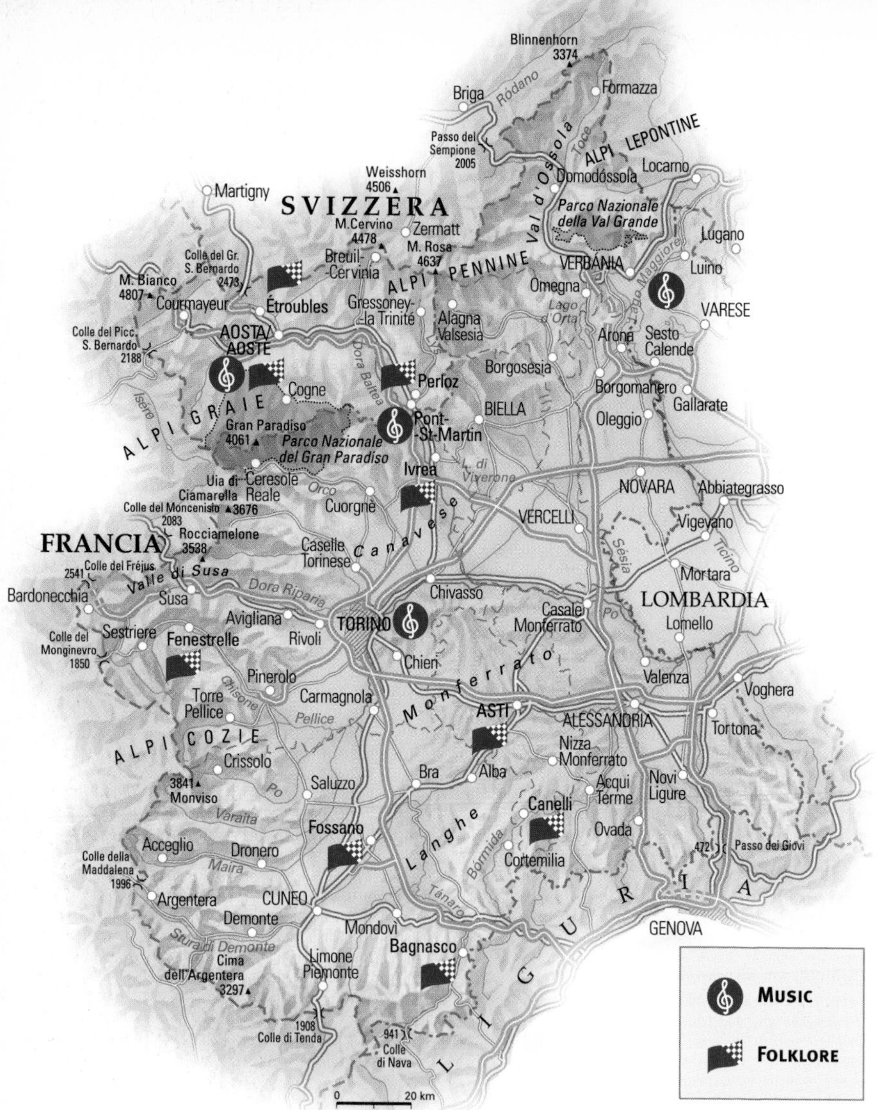

The folk events and popular festivals held in the cities and towns of Piedmont and the Valle d'Aosta are the result of traditions and customs which have been part of the local culture for centuries. Although, in Piedmont, folklore often takes the form of historical re-enactments, such as the *Assedio di Canelli* and the *Battaglia dell'Assietta* at Fenestrelle, which recall a siege and a battle respectively, in the Valle d'Aosta, the valley's rural roots come to the fore in the many *Batailles des Reines* (battles of the cows) and *Batailles des Chèvres* (battles of the goats). For music lovers, as

Events

well as prestigious events organized in Aosta and Turin, music festivals are held in charming, elegant settings, like the concerts which take place on summer evenings by Lake Maggiore.

Highlights

- The exciting Batailles festivals in the Valle d'Aosta.
- Delightful historical re-enactments at Canelli and Fenestrelle.
- Music festivals in Turin.
- Concerts on Lake Maggiore in gorgeous historic settings.

Inside

206 **Music**
208 **Folklore**

MUSIC IN THE VALLE D'AOSTA

The music from Valle d'Aosta performed in public places has religious roots, while in the manors, amateur music was developed to please the nobility. Recently, the region has shown a new interest in music by promoting impromptu events, especially during the summer, and creating new musical institutions, like l'*Orchestre d'Harmonie du Val d'Aoste*.

AOSTA

Aosta Blues Festival

First half of July

Includes nightly concerts with music ranging from blues to opera performed by Italian and international artists and unfolds within the striking framework of the Roman theater in Aosta.
For further information:
Tel. 0165231273,
www.comune.aosta.it

Roman theater in Aosta.

Aosta Classica

July and August

This festival enlivens Aosta's old town center with several types of music, including chamber, contemporary, singer-songwriter, folk, and ethnic music.
For further information:
Tel. 0165361164, www.aostaclassica.it

Assemblée régionale de Chant Choral - Assemblea Regionale di Canto Corale

Last week of May to first week of June

This festival includes performances by choruses and folk groups from the Valle d'Aosta, such as the Giacosa Theater in Aosta, at the church of S. Orso in Aosta. Concludes with a five to six- hour long open-air performance on the first Sunday in June at Tsanté de Bouva in Fénis.
For further information:
Tel. 0165273277, www.regione.vda.it

Concert de Noël - Concerto di Natale

Week before Christmas

The Concerto di Natale takes place at the Cathedral of Aosta in celebration of Christmas. This concert is varied, with a host of performers ranging from gospel groups to accompanied choral choirs and symphonic orchestras, and events.
For further information:
Tel. 0165273277, www.regione.vda.it

GRESSONEY-SAINT-JEAN

Castel Savoia

Summer

This castle was constructed in stone taken from the area between 1900 and 1904, for Queen Margherita. Original decorations have been conserved inside. In the summer, it is the venue for the chamber music concerts of Amici della Musica, a group of musicians from Gressoney.
For further information: Tel. 0125355185,
www.aiatmonterosawalser.it

PONT-SAINT-MARTIN

Concert du Nouvel An - Concerto di Capodanno

Week following the New Year

The Concerto di Capodanno takes place at the Auditorium in celebration of the New Year and presents audiences with the regularly scheduled performance by the Orchestre d'Harmonie du Val d'Aoste, an orchestra founded in 1985 by musician and conductor Lino Blanchod.
For further information:
Tel. 0165273277, www.regione.vda.it

SARRE

Castello Reale

Summer

This castle has medieval origins, but it has been restructured many times. It belonged to many noble families from the area until 1869, when it passed into the hands of the Savoy family after being bought by Vittorio Emanuele II. In the summer, it serves as the venue for the Festival Internazionale di Sarre, which includes performances of different musical genres, from classical music to early music and melodrama.
For further information:
Tel.0165215611, www.comune.sarre.ao.it

MUSIC IN PIEDMONT

Turin plays non-stop host to events, but Piedmont's most important city is not the only one that shares a passion for performance. The region is rich in communities that love to organize musical events. These festivals present the perfect occasion for getting to know the area and for discovering the secrets to its beauty. Turin is the main stage of this cultural vitality.

TURIN

Blues al femminile
October to December
The season features blues music and improvisation from a woman's perspective. For further information: Tel. 011884477, www.centrojazztorino.it

Chicobum Festival
June to July
Music is performed, entertainment provided, and suggestions taken on the summer evenings during this festival. For further information: Tel. 0118194347 www.chicobumfestival.com

Concerti del Lingotto
October to June
These concerts, accompanied by symphonic and classical musical performances, are staged at the Agnelli Auditorium and at the Sala Cinquecento of Lingotto. For further information: Tel. 0116677415, www.lingottomusica.it

Dalle Nuove Musiche al Suono Mondiale
Spring and Fall
A contemporary music festival featuring a new generation of music and sounds. For further information: Tel. 0114343333, www.musica90.net

Linguaggi Jazz
January to March
This concert season offers jazz music and improvisation. For further information: Tel. 011884477, www.centrojazztorino.it

Rai Nuova Musica
January to February
This contemporary music exhibition, staged at the Rai Auditorium, offers an array of new music, free of charge. For further information: Tel. 0118104653-0118104961 www.orchestrasinfonica.rai.it

Stagione Sinfonica
October to June
These symphonic music seasons consist of around 30 concerts performed at the Rai Auditorium. For further information: Tel. 0118104653-0118104961, www.orchestrasinfonica.rai.it

Teatro Regio
From October to June
The Teatro Regio offers a symphonic choral and chamber music season, as well as an opera season presenting at least 10 titles. For further information: Tel. 0118815557-0118815241/242 www.teatroregio.torino.it

Torino Settembre Musica
September
A music festival including performances of national and international importance. For further information: Tel. 0114424777 www.comune.torino.it/settembremusica

Torino World Music Meeting
July
The TWMM is one of the most important Italian music festivals presenting world music. For further information: Tel. 0114343333, www.musica90.net

Traffic - Torino Free Festival
July
A festival combining several disciplines and exploring diverse artistic productions. For further information: Tel. 800015475, www.trafficfestival.com

VERBANO-CUSIO-OSSOLA

Settimane Musicali di Stresa e del Lago Maggiore
August to September
The calendar of events for this music festival presents about thirty concerts with programs including an eclectic blend of music ranging from Baroque to contemporary, as well as the performances of original productions. Performances include symphonic and chamber concerts and instrumental and vocal recitals immersed in an elegant setting, rich in history and art. For further information: Tel. 032331095-032330459 www.settimanemusicali.net

FOLKLORE IN THE VALLE D'AOSTA

The way of life and the traditions that one finds in the Valle d'Aosta are influenced by its particular geographical position. This influence may be noted in the similarities that its rituals present with the rituals characteristic of bordering countries or in the attachment that its people have to the mountains and the farming and pastoral traditions.

AOSTA

La Bataille des Reines

15 August and third Sunday in October

The Bataille des Reines is a fight for predominance among cows from the pasture. This battle is a struggle of bloodless force among the queens of every herd. The victorious animal is considered the Reine and, subsequently, is the one that leads the herd.
After 20 days of preliminary rounds, which are held in different towns throughout the province during the summer, the queens contest in the regional finals before 10,000 spectators at the Arena Croix Noir.
Information: Tel. 0165236627, www.regione.vda.it

ÉTROUBLES

Veillà

Second Saturday in August

This particular event consists of the historic re-creation of the arts and crafts movement in the houses, streets, and squares found in the ancient village of Étroubles. Men and women dressed as craftsmen manufacture butter and cheese, spin wool, and strike iron. Choruses and folk dances can be enjoyed in the evening.
Information: Tel. 016578559, www.gransanbernardo.net

PERLOZ

Bataille des Chèvres

Last Sunday in October

Inspired by the Batailles des Reines, the Bataille des Chèvres includes goats that challenge one another in a harmless battle by throwing blows at each other with their horns. After six preliminary rounds (three in the Spring and three in the Fall) that are held in various locations, a total of 172 goats, a group comprising the best goats from the zone along with the four reigning queens from the previous year, participate in the finals of Tour d'Hereraz (Perloz).
Information: Tel. 0125806269 – 0125807974

TCI HIGHLIGHTS

The Carnival in the Valle del Gran San Bernardo

In the hollow of Gran San Bernardo, however, from Signayes to Étroubles and then up to Saint- Rhemy-en-Bosses, where the Carnival most successfully takes on the main characteristics of the Valley, immerging itself in the most ancient traditions of the Alps and welcoming emotional stories from the past that spark intriguing interest. In Étroubles, participants wear frock coats, decorated in sequins, mirrors, and cockades (see picture). In the valley of Bosses, in a whirlwind of bright colors that appeal to the crowd's fantasy, the masked men march together disguised as symbolic commissioned officers of Napoleon's Grand Armée that passed, descending from San Bernardo, in the Spring of 1800.

Information: www.comune.courmayeur.ao.it, www.carnevalepelline.it, www.gransanbernardo.net

FOLKLORE IN PIEDMONT

Despite the remarkable industrialization that has made the region a leader for the past several decades, the Piedmontese population has been very careful in preserving its own traditions and folkloristic education. In this way, it is able to offer tourists the possibility to attend many events that are as varied as they are interesting and particular.

ASTI

Palio

Third Sunday in September

The flag-wavers demonstration in the morning welcomes crowds to the *Palio* di Asti. The palio is a medieval tradition that consists of a horse race in which jockeys ride saddleless. This event takes place after the historic majestic procession, where participants are dressed in medieval costumes.

Information: Tel. 0141399486, www.comune.ast.it

CANELLI

L'Assedio di Canelli

Third weekend in June

The re-enactment of the assedio di Canelli begins on the Saturday: participants play the roles of farmers and housewives withdrawing themselves behind the wall while forces engage in fighting. Tourists are also able to take part in the event. A fireworks display may also be enjoyed. The Sunday, when the Canelli's forces finally beat back troops, the abundant *pranzo della vittoria* (Victory Lunch), accompanied by a 17th-century menu, is celebrated in the *osterias*.

Information: Tel. 0141820231, www.comune.canelli.at.it

CUNEO

BAGNASCO

Bal do Sabre

Carnival

This fencing ball includes twelve dancers, who daringly hold each other at swords length and move swiftly to the beat of the drum.

The swords glorify their movements and eventually unite the group in a circle or chain.

Information: Tel. 017476047, www.comune.bagnasco.cn.it

FOSSANO

Palio dei Borghi

Second weekend in June

The palio, which consists of a horse race in which knights attempt to hit a model goose target, is one of the many festivities that take place at the Palio dei Borghi. This festival also includes archers who attempt to throw a bow at a moving target, as well as the inhabitants of the seven old *borghi* (villages) of Fossano who parade the streets in costumes and compete in a chivalrous joust. By exploring the village, one may admire the representations of old crafts and taste recipes characteristic of the medieval period. Concludes with fireworks in the castle churchyard.

Information: Tel. 0172699649, www.commune.fossano.cn.it

TURIN

FENESTRELLE

La battaglia dell'Assietta

Third Sunday in July

At the battaglia dell'Assietta, hundreds of participants portray the protagonists of the Battle of 1747, in which the French and Spanish militias joined forces against the army of Carlo Emanuele the III of Savoy. The re-enactment of events takes place in the morning upon the Colle dell'Assietta (literally the hill of Assietta), with every detail being faithfully re-created.

Weitere Informationen: Tel. 012183617, www.comune.fenestrelle.to.it

IVREA

Carnevale

Carnival

Among the different events into which the carnival is divided is the very particular and spectacular *battaglia delle arance* (battle of the oranges) in which teams of orange-throwers join forces against those on board carts drawn by horses.

Information: Tel. 0125618131 www.carnevalediivrea.it

The Valle d'Aosta and Piedmont are two regions with an enviably high quality of life. In this context, its luxurious, elegant, well-manicured spa complexes and wellness centers, often surrounded by beautiful natural landscape, offer visitors the chance to take a rest from the rigors of cultural tourism and allow themselves to be pampered in excellently-equipped, pleasant surroundings. From the viewing terrace of the spa at Saint-Vincent to Piedmont's historic spa complexes, this region offers a wide choice of spa centers where traditional prestige goes hand in hand with state-of-

Wellness

the-art technology, with an offering which, in addition to psychological and physical well-being, has interesting possibilities in terms of sport and leisure.

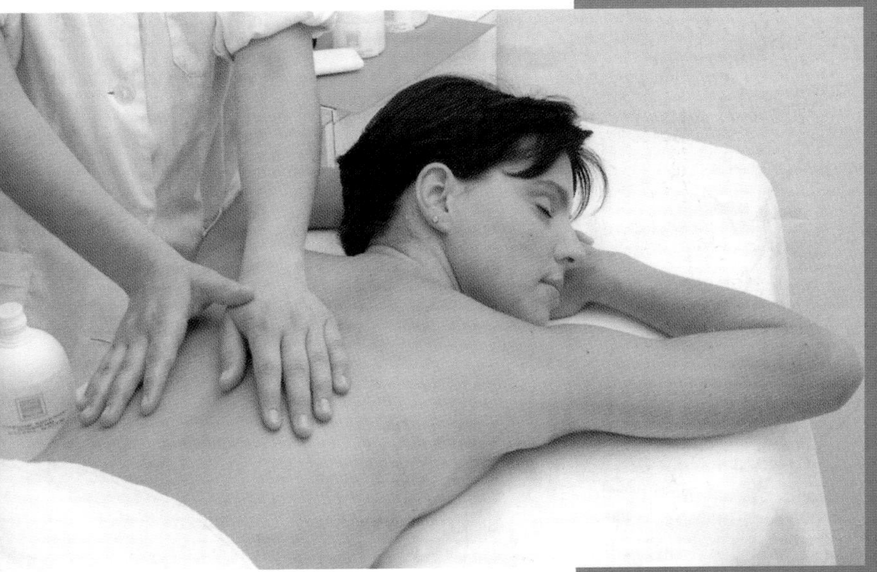

Highlights

- The viewing terrace at the spa of Saint-Vincent.
- Acqui Terme, a spa town for centuries.
- The Istituto Idrotermale di Lurisia, classified by the Italian Ministry of Health as a Super First Class spa.
- The Terme Reali di Valdieri, set in a glorious garden.

Inside

212 **Saint Vincent**
212 **Acqui Terme**
213 **Agliano Terme**
213 **Bagni di Vinadio**
214 **Bognanco**
214 **Garessio**
214 **Terme di Lurisia**
215 **Terme di Valdieri**

SAINT VINCENT

Terme di Saint-Vincent

Viale IV Novembre 100, Tel. 0166512693
Open from April to November
Disabled facilities

The Fons Salutis (Spring of Health) is the only spa in the whole of the Valle d'Aosta and is well-known for the curative effects of its low mineral-content waters, excellent for the digestion and liver problems. The complex is just a few minutes from the town center and can easily be reached by the funicular railway which leaves from the parish church square. The spa itself has a wonderful view over the sweeping Dora Baltea valley from its large, semi-circular covered terrace that dominates the town below. The drive leads to the ground floor entrance, next to the funicular station, where the ticket office, administrative offices and main pump room are all housed. A shady tree-lined avenue runs through the park and gardens, linking the original spa buildings to the new pavilion. Every year the spa organises health week packages in Saint Vincent for visitors that include treatments, various forms of entertainment and concerts.

Elena ***
Via Biavaz 2, Tel. 0166512140
www.hotelelena.be
6 rooms, closed during the second half of December
Just a stone's throw from the spa and the Casino de la Vallée, Elena offers its guests a range of services including sauna, Turkish bath, hydromassage, massage room and a small gym with a relax area. Manipulative and therapeutic treatments are also available on request.

ACQUI TERME

Terme di Acqui

Via XX Settembre 5,
Tel. 0144324390,
www.termediacqui.it
Open all year
Disabled facilities

The Acqui Terme spa complex in the province of Alessandria is divided into two separate parts: the original historical Antiche Terme spa and the Regina spa in the Bagni (or "baths") area on the far side of the Bormida river, and the Nuove Terme, or "New Spa" built at the end of the 19th century in the town center. The characteristic feature of the Bagni area is its huge park with a spa swimming pool and a spa lake, fed by approximately 40 hot springs (55°C/131°F) rich in sodium chloride, bromide and iodide mineral content. The

Grand Hotel Nuove Terme ****
Piazza Italia 1, Tel. 014458555
www.antichedimore.com
145 rooms, open all year round
An extremely smart hotel with its elegant architecture and sumptuously decorated interior, complete with original 19th century frescoes. The hotel's wellness center is equipped with a spa water swimming pool, two saunas and the chance to experience spa baths as the ancient Romans knew them, as well as cubicles for beauty and osteopathic treatments. The mud treatment department can be accessed directly from the hotel bedrooms.

Pineta ***
Via alla Salita 1, Tel. 0144320688,
www.hotelpineta.org
100 rooms, open April-October
The hotel nestles in the middle of a pine wood in the Acqui Terme spa area. A free shuttle service provided for guests links the hotel to the town center and the Regina spa. The wellness center's treatments, baths and swimming pools are fed by waters from the nearby lake with its hot sulfur springs. The center offers a complete range of beauty treatments, as well as therapeutic massages and manipulations that are available following a medical examination. Constant medical supervision is guaranteed.

springs are the source of the muds used for a number of spa treatments. The construction of the Nuove Terme more than a hundred years ago gave the Acqui spa a new lease of life. The 19th-century hotel is fully equipped to provide its customers with a wide range of spa treatments and is near the La Bollente (boiling) spring. The water gushes from its marble aedicola, built in 1870, at the exceptionally high temperature of 75°C/167°F. During the reign of Augustus, to cool it down, Roman engineers built an aqueduct to feed in a constant supply of cold water.

AGLIANO TERME

Fons Salutis Terme di Agliano

Via Fonti 133, Tel. 0141954242,
www.termediagliano.it
Open all year
Disabled facilities

The Agliano spa is situated just under 20 km from Asti. This spa with its Fons Salutis treatment center, has won several prizes for the high quality of its services over the last hundred years. The wellness center is built round a large, airy central hall with direct access to the surgeries, the inhalation treatment department and a section for children.
The spa rehabilitation treatment center comprises a swimming pool, gym and treatment cycle for circul rich in sodium chloride, sulfur and magnesium, excellent for treating circulation, liver, biliary and digestive problems.

BAGNI DI VINADIO

Vinadio Terme Centro Benessere

Tel. 0171959395,
www.termedivinadio.com
Open all year

The therapeutic qualities of the sulfur waters of the Vinadio baths, in Cuneo province, were already appreciated in ancient Roman times. It subsequently became popular as a rest and recreation center to cure the aches and pains of army officers during the reign of the Savoy kings in Turin. Today the original spa buildings have been supplemented by an adjacent modern hotel complex, complete with beauty farm and well-equipped sports center. There is a spa water indoor swimming pool on the lower ground floor and a mud treatment department on the ground floor.

The Vinadio Spa entrance.

Grand Hotel Terme di Vinadio* **

Strada Maestra,
Tel. 0171959395,
www.termedivinadio.com
86 rooms, open all year

The spa and hotel nestle in the Stura valley, in the midst of the stunning scenery and wealth of wild life peculiar to the Argentera nature reserve. The valley also benefits from a particularly mild climate. The hotel itself is still housed in its original 19th century building and the wellness center has a complete range of facilities with a vertical hydromassage tub, an indoor spa water swimming pool and waterfall at a constant temperature of 37°C/99°F and sauna grottoes. The gym is fully equipped with everything necessary for muscle-toning and body-building training programmes. The mineral water spring is near the wellness center and its calcium, sulfur, lithium and chlorine mineral content makes it particularly suitable for treating many types of dermatological problems. Visitors can also enjoy beauty treatments, therapeutic massages and manipulations.

BOGNANCO

Terme di Bognanco

Fonti, Piazzale Rampone 1,
Tel. 0324234137,
www.termebognanco.it
Open from June to September

Tradition has it that the Luigia spring, which has now dried up, was discovered in 1863 by a little shepherdess who was surprised at the strange taste of the water. The local parish priest guessed that the water might be profitable, bought the land it was on, had the required tests carried out and started a business bottling and selling it. Initial difficulties were caused by the bottles breaking due to the pressure of the gas building up as they were transported on foot in panniers. Subsequently a lawyer from Pavia, Emilio Cavallini, bought the spring and its surrounding land and discovered several other mineral water springs in the area, the Ausonia, the Adelaide and the San Lorenzo springs, each with different characteristics and either rich or poor in particular minerals.
He then transformed the little town into a resort and curative spa center. Bognanco waters (Verbano-Cusio-Ossola) are held to be especially good for the treatment of liver and bile tract conditions, and are also excellent for purifying the digestive and urinary tracts.

GARESSIO

Fonti San Bernardo

Via al Santuario 2,
Tel. 017481101
Open from June to mid-September
Disabled facilities

The therapeutic qualities of the S. Bernardo waters became widely known at the beginning of the 20th century, although the local people had long been aware of its healing nature, to the extent that it was considered miraculous. Napoleon basked in its waters on his first Italian campaign, when he passed through Garessio, near Cuneo, and Vittorio Emanuele II of Savoy was a frequent visitor to the upper Tanaro Valley.
In 1926 a permit was granted to bottle and sell S. Bernardo mineral water. It most easily digestible waters in the post-war period and recommended for the preparation of babyfood. Nowadays the mineral water is bottled elsewhere and the S. Bernardo Springs Park has a wellness center with five separate halls, facilities and staff for various treatments including a medical center, a pump room, massage and fitness. There are also tennis courts, dance halls and other amenities in the immediate surrounding area. The Rocciaviva spring water are excellent for the treatment of liver and bile tract conditions, and are also useful for purifying the digestive and urinary tracts.

TERME DI LURISIA

Istituto Idrotermale di Lurisia

Via delle Terme 60, Tel. 0174683421,
www.lurisia.it
Open from April to January

The Lurisia spring, province of Cuneo, only began to be exploited when radioactive traces were discovered in a local stone quarry in 1913. However the wellness center, today known as the Istituto Idrotermale di Lurisia and

The Lurisia Spa, in the quiet of the Mondovì valleys.

classified by the Italian Health Ministry as a superior first class facility, was not built until 1949. Lurisia's mineral water comes from springs in a 360 m-deep tunnel in the mountainside. The main wellness center is built in local style and set in the Spa Park (Parco delle Terme). Visitors can experiment a complete range of spa treatments, including mud packs, inhalations and water therapy, as well as curative therapies for arthritis, rheumatism, varicous veins, circulatory problems, sinusitis and headaches. Beauty and cellulitis treatments are also popular. During the summer Lurisia entertains its guests with a series of concerts, parties, dances, outings and sporting activities.

Reale ***
Via alle Terme 10,
Tel. 0174583005,
www.hotelreale.it
66 rooms, open all year
A pleasant hotel set conveniently in an enormous garden just a stone's throw from the wellness spa complex. Among the facilities provided, guests can make use of a modern, well-equipped fitness area with everything necessary for carrying out a toning programme. The hotel wellness area includes a Turkish bath, an individual hydromassage tub, tanning cubicles with multi-panel Uva lamps and a solarium. Hotel guests benefit from priority booking for therapeutic treatments at the nearby spa. The spa complex itself is an elegant building pleasantly positioned in extensive pine and chestnut woods. Visitors can alternate spa cures and treatments with various sporting activities along the paths of the park that surrounds the institute.

TERME DI VALDIERI

Terme Reali di Valdieri

Regione Terme, Tel. 0171261666,
www.termedivaldieri.it
Open from June to September
Disabled facilities

The Valdieri Spa is set in a large park dotted with pines and and ancient beech trees in the Province of Cuneo. It is generally well-equipped with modern facilities (therapy units, spa water swimming pools, gym and tennis courts) but its outstanding feature is undoubtedly its sulfurous vapor grottoes. Dug out of the side of Mt Matto, these are heated by hot springs to a temperature of 46°C/114°F while the air is saturated with sulfurous vapors. As a result, the curative properties of the humid heat are combined with the benefits of inhaling the gas and the vapors. Another unusual natural feature of the spa is the growth of algae thanks to a series of particular circumstances: the water, its temperature and the effect of the light on the stone steps which convey the water. These algae are used as packs, rather like mud packs, to get the most out of their sulfur content. The spa complex has three halls with hot stoves or vapor grottoes, two halls for aerosol treatments and inhalations, a gynaecological wing and a treatment center for mud and algae packs, beauty treatments and massage, including shiatzu and Ayurvedic techniques.

The large swimming pool at the Valdieri Spa.

Royal Centro Benessere ***
Via Po 20, Tel. 017197106,
www.termedivaldieri.it
110 rooms, open from May to September
The hotel is set in the midst of a huge park dotted with pines and and ancient beech trees. The beautiful surroundings, rich in vegetation and wildlife, blend happily with a particularly mild climate. The wellness complex includes a spa water swimming pool naturally heated to a constant temperature of 34 °C/93°F, sauna, gym and fitness equipment. Guests can book various types of therapeutic massages and manipulations as well as a range of beauty treatments and facials.

THE A-Z OF WHAT YOU NEED TO KNOW

GETTING TO

By plane to the Valle d'Aosta

Saint Christophe – Airport Corrado Gex

Information about flights and services Tel. 0165303350, www.avda-aosta.it

Airvallee, Tel. 0165303303 www.airvallee.com

To and from **Aeroporto Corrado** Gex – Corrado Gex airport is 5 minutes from Aosta town center.

The A5 Torino/Milano/Genova highway, Aosta-Est exit is about 4km away from the airport.

Opposite the airport the Pronto Taxi service can be found. Bookings and information:

Tel. 016531831/800682477

The 14/B coach service connects the airport with the town center.

By plane to Piedmont

Turin – Aeroporto Caselle

Strada San Maurizio 12, Caselle Torinese.

Information about flights:

Tel. 0115676361-0115676362 www.turin-airport.com

Ticket office Tel. 0115676373

Lost luggage Tel. 0115676200

Turin airport is 16km from Turin and can be reached via the highway connecting Caselle to the most important towns of Piedmont, North of Italy and South of France.

The taxi rank can be found outside Arrivals, on the left hand side. Information:

Pronto taxi Tel. 0115737
Radio taxi

Tel. 0115730/0113399

CTA (Consorzio Taxisti Aeroporto) - taxi/van/limousine chaffeur service 24 hours a day. Information:

Tel. 0119963090, www.ctataxi.it

The coach service from Turin town center and the airport stops at Porta Nuova and Porta Susa railway stations.

Sadem Tel. 0113000611 www.sadem.it

A railway service connects Caselle Airport with Dora GTT Station in Turin. Trains depart every 30 minutes.

Infomation:

Tel. 0112165352, www.gtt.to.it

By train to the Valle d'Aosta and Piedmont

For timetables and fares:
Trenitalia, Tel. 892021, every day, from 7 to 21, only from Italy, www.trenitalia.com

By car to the Valle d'Aosta and Piedmont

The Valle d'Aosta can be easily reached from the A5 Torino-Aosta-Monte Bianco highway and from the Mont Blanc tunnel which connects the Valle d'Aosta with France and the small town of Chamonix Mont Blanc.

The efficient Piedmont highway network not only connects all the region's main towns but also the rest of Italy (A4 to Milan, A26 to Genoa), France (A10 to Nice, A32 to Lyon) and Switzerland.

Highway information center: Freephone 800269269 www.autostrade.it

TRANSPORT

By train

All the main towns in Valle d'Aosta and Piedmont can be reached by train.

Trenitalia operates services all over the region.

Information: Tel. 892021, www.trenitalia.com

Coaches in the Valle d'Aosta

Aosta – SAVDA, Tel. 0165361244 www.savda.it

Arnad – VITA

Tel. 0125966546/7/8 www.vitagroup.it

Charvensod – SVAP

Tel. 016541125, www.svap.it

Coaches in Piedmont

Alessandria – ARFEA

Tel. 0131445433

ATM, Tel. 0131323811 www.atm-alessandria.it

Asti – ASP, Tel. 0141434711 www.asp.asti.it

Biella – ATAP, Tel. 0158408117 www.atapspa.it

Cuneo – information:

Tel. 0116910000 www.provincia.cuneo.it/trasporti

Novara – SAF www.safduemila.com

SUN, Tel. 0321626222 www.sun.novara.it

STN, Tel. 0321472647 www.stnnet.it

Turin – GTT, Tel. 800333444 www.5t.torino.it

Verbania – Autoservizi Nerini Tel. 0323552172 www.comune.verbania.it/citta/trasporti

SAF, Tel. 0323552172 www.safduemila.com

VCO, Tel. 0323518711

Vercelli – information: www.comune.vercelli.it

Car rental in the Valle d'Aosta

Europcar – www.europcar.it Corrado Gex Airport, Tel. 016541432

Aosta, Tel. 016541423

Car rental in Piedmont

Avis – www.avisautonoleggio.it

Caselle Airport, Tel. 0115678020-0114701528

Turin, Tel. 011501107-011503263-0112427559-0112053547

Porta Nuova Station, Tel. 0116699800

Europcar – www.europcar.it

Caselle Airport, Tel. 0115678048

Turin, Tel. 0116279429-0112229802-0117730941-0116503603

Hertz – www.hertz.it

Caselle Airport, Tel. 0115678166

Turin, Tel. 011502080-0115096008

Cable cars in the Valle d'Aosta

AVIF - the association for the Valle d'Aosta cable cars service.

Practical info

CLIMATE

Climate in the Valle d'Aosta and Piedmont

The Valle d'Aosta has a typically Alpine climate with very cold winters and cool summers. The abundance of snow in winter is now being affected by global warming. The valley of the Dora Baltea has milder weather than the mountains around it. The unusual morphological characteristics of Piedmont, situated as it is at the top of the Po Valley and surrounded on three sides by mountains, account for its unusual weather. In fact, Piedmont has various micro-climates, however, since the region is cut off from the sea it generally has a fairly typical continental climate, with considerable differences in temperature and high rainfall, especially in spring and autumn. In the area of the Alps, the winters are cold and dry and the summers are cool. In the plain, the winters are humid and the summers are hot and sultry. During the autumn and winter, banks of thick fog form in the plain. On the shores of the lakes, the weather is mild.

INFORMATION

Website of Regione Valle d'Aosta: www.regione.vda.it

Website of Regione Piemonte: www.regione.piemonte.it

Most of the websites of the various municipalities have similar addresses, for example: www.comune.aosta.it

Information: AVIF, Grande Charrière 46, Saint Christophe, Tel. 016533327 - www.avif.it

Boat services on Lake Maggiore (Piedmont)

Taking a boat trip on Lake Maggiore is an excellent way to admire the very beautiful scenery of this area from an unusual point of view. Excellent, regular hydrofoil and ferry services operate various routes around the lake. Some of them enter Switzerland and make scheduled stops at the most interesting towns on the lake shore.

Italian routes:

Arona-Angera (Angera Castle)

Intra-Isole Borromee-Stresa-S.Caterina (Intra-Villa Taranto-Pallanza-Isola Madre-Feriolo-Baveno-Isola Pescatori-Isola Bella-Carciano-Stresa-S.Caterina)

Porto Ronco-Isole di Brissago

International routes:

Arona-Stresa-Isole Borromee-Locarno (Arona-Angera-Meina-Ranco-Ispra-Lesa-Belgirate-Santa Caterina-Stresa-Carciano-Isola Bella-Isola Pescatori-Baveno-Isola Madre-Pallanza-Villa Taranto-Intra-Laveno-Ghiffa-Porto Valtravaglia-Oggebbio-Cannero-Luino-Maccagno-Cannobio-Isole di Brissago-Porto Ronco-Ascona-Locarno). There is also a car ferry service operating between Intra and Laveno on the other side of the lake and viceversa.

Information:

Tel. 800551801-0322233200

www.navigazionelaghi.it-www.lagomaggioreonline.it

Inside

Tourist information

Hotels and restaurants

At night

Museums and Monuments

EMERGENCY NUMBERS

112	Military Police (Carabinieri)
113	State Police (Polizia)
115	Fire Department
117	Financial Police
118	Medical Emergencies
1515	Fire-watch
1518	Road Information
803116	Road Assistance

ANTAGNOD

AIAT Monte Rosa
Via E.Chanoux
Tel. 0125306335

Museums, Monuments and Churches

Museo di Arte Sacra
c/o Parrocchiale
Tel. 0125306629
July-August: Saturdays-Sundays 10.00-12.00, 16.30-18.30

AOSTA

AIAT Aosta
Piazza Chanoux 45
Tel. 016533352
www.aiataosta.com

Hotels

ClassHotel Aosta* * ♿ ★**
Corso Ivrea 146
Tel. 016541845
www.classhotel.com
105 Rooms
Built in the 1960s, this hotel has pleasant communal rooms, comfortable bedrooms, a restaurant that serves local dishes and a sauna.

Europe* ***
Piazza Narbonne 8
Tel. 0165236363
www.ethotels.com
63 Rooms
Restaurant
Credit cards: American Express, Diners Club, Visa, Bancomat
Situated in the town center, the hotel has pleasant rooms with classical furnishing. There is also a restaurant.

Milleluci* * ♿★**
Porossan Roppoz 15
Tel. 0165235278
www.hotelmilleluci.com
31 Rooms
Surrounded by a park with a beautiful view of Aosta, it is constructed in stone and wood combining a traditional environment with all modern comforts. It also offers a health center with sauna, Turkish bath and hydro-massage as well as a playground for young children.

Rayon de Soleil* **
Viale Gran San Bernardo, Km 12
Tel. 0165262247
www.rayondesoleil.it
45 Rooms
Swimming pool.
Situated in a quiet, panoramic position near the cable car for Pila, the hotel has a large garden and swimming pool for the guests.

Restaurants

***Hostaria del Calvino* 🍴**
Via Croce di Città 24
Tel. 0165231650
Closed Sundays except Summer
Credit cards: American Express, Diners Club, Visa, Mastercard, Bancomat
This welcoming hotel on three floors serves classical dishes, hors d'oeuvres of cured meats and local cheeses followed by home-made desserts.

***Le Pélerin Gourmand* 🍴**
Via De Tillier 9/B
Tel. 0165231850
www.peleringourmand.it
Closed Thursdays
Credit cards: American Express, Diners Club
This small restaurant is the ideal venue for a pleasant evening where you can enjoy local cuisine.

***Trattoria degli Artisti* 🍴🍴**
Via Maillet 5/7
Tel. 016540960
Closed Sundays and Mondays
Credit cards: American Express, Diners Club, Visa, Mastercard
A pleasant restaurant that serves dishes typical to the Aosta region.

***Trattoria Praetoria* 🍴**
Via S. Anselmo 9
Tel. 016544356
Closed Wednesday evenings and Thursdays
Credit cards: American Express, Visa, Mastercard
A warm welcome awaits you in these five small dining rooms with arched ceilings in open stonework or wood panelling. The menu includes both classical and local cuisine.

***Vecchia Aosta* 🍴🍴**
Piazza Porte Pretoriane 4
Tel. 0165361186
www.mediavallee.it/vecchiaaosta
Closed Wednesdays (except July and August)
Credit cards: American Express, Diners Club, Visa, Mastercard
Situated in an evocative position in the ancient urban center of Porta Pretoria, this elegant restaurant offers regional dishes, local cheeses and a good selection of wines and spirits.

***Vecchio Ristoro da Alfio e Katia* 🍴🍴**
Via Tourneuve 4, Tel. 016533238
www.ristorantevecchioristoro.it
Closed Sundays and Mondays
Credit cards: American Express, Diners Club, Visa, Mastercard, Bancomat
An evocative atmosphere characterises this restaurant set in an old water mill. It serves local dishes and a large selection of oils and cheeses.

***Xavier 12* 🍴🍴**
Via Xavier de Maistre 12
Tel. 0165261771
www.ristorantexavier.it
Closed Sundays
Credit cards: American Express, Visa, Mastercard, Bancomat
A pleasant venue with arched ceilings, stonework and country-style furnishing that serves both classical and local dishes.

Rural lodgins

La Ferme
Chabloz 18
Tel. 0165551647
This stone and wood chalet is surrounded by vegetable gardens, orchards and vineyards. Accommodation with use of the kitchen where guests are offered breakfast, fruit, vegetables and wine. Excursions and alpine sports can be enjoyed nearby.

***Plan d'Avie* ♿**
Arpuilles
Tel. 016551126
This holiday farm is situated on a plateau surrounded by meadows overlooking the splendid scenery of Aosta. Guests can prepare barbecues and eat in the open air in the shade of a large wooden patio and alpine sports can be enjoyed in the immediate vicinity.

Museums, Monuments and Churches

Complesso Monumentale della Collegiata di Sant'Orso
Via S. Orso
Tel. 0165275965-0165275987
www.regione.vda.it
March-June and September: Mondays-Sundays 9.00-19.00. July-August: Mondays-Sundays 9.00-20.00. October-February: Mondays-Saturday 10.00-12.30, 13.30-17.00; Sundays and holidays 10.00-12.30, 13.30-18.00

***Museo Archeologico Regionale* ★**
Piazza Roncas 12
Tel. 0165275902-0165230545
www.regione.vda.it
Mondays-Sundays 9.00-19.00; last entry 18.00

Museo del Tesoro della Cattedrale di Aosta
Piazza Giovanni XXIII
Tel. 016540251-0165340413-3402808758
April-September: weekdays 9.00-11.30, 15.00-17.30; holidays 8.30-10.00, 10.45-11.30.

October-March: holidays 8.30-10.00, 10.45-11.30, 15.00-17.30. Closed during the religious functions

ARNAD

Municipio
Closè 1
Tel. 0125966121

Museums, Monuments and Churches

Piccolo Museo Parrocchiale
Arnad Le Vieux, Tel. 0125966116
Visits by request.

AYAS

AIAT Monte Rosa
Champoluc, Via Varasc 16
Tel. 0125307113

Hotels

***Monte Rosa* *** ♿**
Periasc, Via Periasc la val 7
Tel. 0125305735
www.monterosahotel.com
20 Rooms
This simple but elegant house built in the 1920s is situated in a sunny, panoramic position near the cross country ski trails.

Rural Lodgins

Goïl
Antagnod, Tel. 0125306370
Open July-August, holidays, weekends
In a lovely position with a view of Mt Rosa,this farm produces milk, butter and fontina cheese. Accommodation is in small stone cottages and the restaurant serves local dishes.

BARD

Museums, Monuments and Churches

Museo delle Alpi - Forte di Bard
Tel. 0125809811
www.fortedibard.it
Tuesdays-Fridays 10.00-18.00; Saturdays and Sundays 10.00-20.00

BREUIL-CERVINIA

AIAT Monte Cervino
Via Guido Rey 17
tel 0166949136
www.montecervino.it

Hotels

Bucaneve* ***
Piazza Jumeaux 10
Tel. 0166949119
www.hotel-bucaneve.it
26 Rooms
Credit cards: American Express, Visa, Mastercard, Bancomat
This hotel and restaurant with a splendid view of Mt Cervino and the Grandes Murailles also offers guests the use of sauna and gym.

Chalet Valdôtain* ***
Via Lac Bleu 2
Tel. 0166949428
www.chaletvaldotain.it
35 Rooms
Credit cards: American Express, Diners Club, Visa, Mastercard, Bancomat
This characteristic Alpine building overlooks the Blue Lake. The restaurant serves local dishes and has a sauna, swimming pool and gym.

***Edelweiss* *** ♿**
Via G. Rey 18
Tel. 0166949078
www.matterhorn.it
29 Rooms
Credit cards: American Express, Diners Club, Visa, Mastercard, Bancomat
With spacious communal rooms and comfortable bedrooms, this hotel has a sauna, a gym and a restaurant that serves local dishes.

Europa* ***
Via C. Pellissier 2
Tel. 0166948660
www.htl-europa.com
61 Rooms
Credit cards: American Express, Visa, Mastercard, Bancomat
This hotel, situated in a quiet, sunny position next to the ski lifts and golf course, has a sauna, swimming pool and gym. The restaurant specializes in local cuisine.

Excelsior-Planet* * ♿**
Piazzale Planet 1
Tel. 0166949426
www.excelsiorplanet.com
46 Rooms
Credit cards: Visa, Mastercard, Bancomat
Situated just a few meters from the ski slopes, this hotel has a restaurant, sauna and swimming pool.

Lyskamm* **
Via Bich 12
Tel. 0166949074
www.hotellyskamm.com
17 Rooms
Credit cards: Visa
This typical alpine style hotel is opposite the ski slopes with a view of Mt Cervino. It has a sauna and a restaurant serving traditional dishes.

Sertorelli Sporthotel* * ♿**
Via Rey 28
Tel. 0166949797
www.sertorelli-cervinia.it
65 Rooms
Credit cards: American Express, Visa, Mastercard, Bancomat
Situated in a panoramic position with a view of Mt Cervino and the Grandes Murailles, this typical alpine hotel is near the center of the town and the ski lifts. It has a restaurant, sauna and gym.

Restaurants

***Hermitage* 🍴🍴🍴**
Via Piolet 1
Tel. 0166948998
www.hotelhermitage.com
Credit cards: American Express, Diners Club, Visa, Mastercard, Bancomat
A delightful restaurant just above the village, it serves typical dishes from the Valle d'Aosta and Piedmont regions.

***Les Neiges d'Antan* 🍴🍴**
Perreres 10
Tel. 0166948775
www.lesneigesdantan.it
Credit cards: Visa, Mastercard, Bancomat
In a little chalet surrounded by woods and meadows, this restaurant serves typical dishes and local cheeses. There is a vast selection of wines and spirits.

CHALLAND-SAINT-VICTOR

Museums, Monuments and Churches

Museo Parrocchiale di Saint-Victor
Sizan Tel. 0125967317
July-August: Mondays-Sundays 9.00-11.30 and 15.00-18.30. September-June: Mondays, Wednesdays, Fridays 9.00-11.30 and 15.00-17.30

CHAMPOLUC

AIAT Monterosa
Via Varasc 16
Tel. 0125307113
www.aiatmonterosa.com

Hotels

Breithorn* * ♿★**
Via Ramey 27
Tel. 0125308734
www.breithornhotel.com
31 Rooms
Credit cards: American Express, Visa, Mastercard, Bancomat
This house, dating from the beginning of the 1900s

and built in the style of the antique Walser houses, is situated in the center of the Champoluc village, the rooms are very comfortable.
The restaurant serves typical alpine dishes. The sauna is available for guests.

Relais des Glaciers* * ♿**
Via G.B. Dondeynaz
Tel. 0125308721
www.hotelrelaisdesglaciers.com
42 Rooms
Just a short distance from the ski lifts, this characteristic stone and wood building has a restaurant and health-center. The rooms are very comfortable.

***Santa San* *** ♿★**
Antagnod,
Strada per Barmasc 1,
Tel. 0125306597
www.hotelsantasan.com
12 Rooms
This lovely traditional-style building is situated near the chair lifts; extra charge for rooms with cooking facilities.

Restaurants

***Le Petit Coq* ★**
Villy,
Tel. 0125307997
Closed Tuesdays
Credit cards: American Express, Diners Club, Visa, Mastercard, Bancomat
An alpine-style wooden chalet where typical dishes made from local products are served.

CHAMPORCHER

Municipio
Lore' 42
Tel. 012537106

Museums, Monuments and Churches

Museo Parrocchiale di San Nicola
Castello, Tel. 012537107
July-August: Mondays-Sundays 9.00-18.30.
September-June: Saturdays, Sundays and holidays 9.00-18.30

CHÂTILLON

Centro Informazioni Turistiche Comunità Montana Monte Cervino
Perolle 20,
Tel. 016662787–016662791
www.montecervino.org

Hotels

***La Rocca* *** ♿**
Perolle 18, Tel. 0166563214
www.hotel-larocca.com
30 Rooms
A well-equipped hotel on four floors with a restaurant.

***Le Verger* *** ♿★**
Via Tour de Grange 53,
Tel. 016662314
www.leverger.it
21 Rooms
Credit cards: Visa, Mastercard
A typical house in the local style surrounded by a flourishing orchard. The furniture is made by local craftsmen.

Relais du Foyer* * ♿**
Panorama 37,
Tel. 0166511251
www.relaisdufoyer.it
32 Rooms
An elegant, well-equipped structure. Breakfast is a sweet or savory buffet. This structure has a restaurant, and for the guest a sauna with gym.

Restaurants

La Terrazza
Panorama 3,
Tel. 0166512548
Closed Wednesdays
Credit cards: American Express, Diners Club, Visa
In this elegant restaurant that serves local dishes and pizzas, guests can dine on the terrace that gives the restaurant its name.

Privé Parisien
Panorama 1,
Tel. 0166537053
Closed Thursdays
Credit cards: American Express, Diners Club, Visa, Mastercard
Set in an imposing farmhouse, this restaurant uses local produce and offers a vast selection of excellent wines and spirits.

Museums, Monuments and Churches

Museo Parrocchiale della Chiesa di San Pietro
Via Gervasone 18,
Tel. 0166563040
Mondays-Sundays 8.00-18.00

COGNE

AIAT Cogne Gran Paradiso
Via Bourgeois 34
Tel. 016574056,
www.cogne.org

Hotels

Bellevue* * ♿**
Via Gran Paradiso 22,
Tel. 016574825
www.hotelbellevue.it
38 Rooms
Credit cards: American Express, Diners Club, Visa, Mastercard
This chalet is situated near the Parco Nazionale del Gran Paradiso. The furniture and lacework is made by local craftsmen and there is a restaurant, swimming pool and health center.

***La Barme* ** ♿**
Valnontey,
Tel. 0165749177
www.hotellabarme.com
15 Rooms
Credit cards: American Express, Visa, Bancomat
An ideal starting point for excursions in the Parco Nazionale del Gran Paradiso, it has a restaurant that serves local dishes and guests can also enjoy a sauna or massage. Storage for bicycles or skis available.

Sant'Orso* * ♿**
Via Bourgeois 2,
Tel. 016574821
www.cognevacanze.com
27 Rooms
Credit cards: American Express, Diners Club, Visa, Mastercard
An Art Noveau-style building on the edge of the Grande Prato di S.Orso. It has a restaurant and fitness area with sauna and gym. This hotel has a parking for the guests.

Restaurants

Brasserie du Bon Bec
Via Bourgeois 72,
Tel. 0165749288
www.hotelbellevue.it
Closed Mondays (in low season)
Credit cards: American Express, Diners Club, Visa, Mastercard, JCB
A charming little bistrot that serves local dishes. It is furnished with antique objects and embroidered tablecloths.

Notre Maison
Crétaz 8,
Tel. 016574104
www.notremaison.it
Credit cards: Diners Club, Visa, Mastercard, Bancomat
A dining room in light wood and stone with a large central fireplace. It serves local dishes and there is a good selection of cheeses, cured meats. It offers excellent wines and distilled drinks.

Museums, Monuments and Churches

Mostra Permanente del Merletto
Via Dr. Grappein 50,
Tel. 0165749282

COURMAYEUR

ℹ **AIAT Monte Bianco**
Piazzale Monte Bianco 13
Tel. 0165842060

Hotels

Auberge de la Maison ******* ♿
Entrèves
Via Passerin,
Tel. 0165869811
www.aubergemaison.it
33 Rooms
Credit cards: American Express, Diners Club, Visa, Mastercard
A chalet situated at the feet of Mont Blanc. The rooms have a large balcony and some have a split-level area, hydro massage baths and fireplace. There is a fitness center and gym and a restaurant that offers local cuisine.

Bouton d'Or ******* ★
S.S. 26 10,
Tel. 0165846729
www.hotelboutondor.com
35 Rooms
Parking, sauna
Credit cards: American Express, Visa, Mastercard
Only a short distance from the ski lifts, this alpine style hotel has a sauna and offers home-made cakes and local cheeses for breakfast.

Chalet Val Ferret ******
Arnouva 1,
Tel. 0165844959
www.chaletvalferret.com
7 Rooms
Parking, restaurant
Credit cards: Visa, Mastercard
Set in a renovated alpine shepherd's hut, this typical alpine hotel has a view of Mont Blanc. In the hall and communal areas guests can admire traditional objects made by local craftsmen.

Courmayeur *******
Via Roma 158,
Tel. 0165846732
www.hotelcourmayeur.it
27 Rooms
Credit cards: American Express, Diners Club, Visa, Mastercard, Bancomat
This house, built in the 1950s, has a restaurant specializing in local dishes. It offers easy access to the ski lifts.

Dei Camosci ******
Via Entreves 7,
Tel. 0165842338
www.hoteldeicamosci.com
25 Rooms
Credit cards: American Express, Diners Club, Visa, Mastercard, Bancomat
An Alpine chalet with a splendid view of Mont Blanc and restaurant with local cuisine.

Del Viale ******* ★
Viale Monte Bianco 74,
Tel. 0165846712
www.hoteldelviale.com
23 Rooms
Surrounded by greenery and with a magnificient view of Mont Blanc,this hotel, built in the 1970s, has alpine-style furnishing and a restaurant that serves local dishes.

Dente del Gigante *******
Strada La Palud 42,
Tel. 016589145
www.dentedelgigante.com
13 Rooms
Credit cards: Diners Club, Visa, Mastercard
This characteristic stone and wood chalet is situated at the feet of Mont Blanc. The restaurant serves local specialties.

Dolonne *******
Dolonne, Via della Vittoria 62,
Tel. 0165846674
www.hoteldolonne.it
32 Rooms
Credit cards: American Express, Diners Club, Visa, Mastercard, Bancomat
A charming venue for mountain lovers. In the winter the ski slopes are close by and in the summer there are numerous walks and excursions. It offers large, alpine style bedrooms and a restaurant.

Gran Baita ******** ♿★
Strada Larzey 2,
Tel. 0165844040
www.sogliahotels.com
53 Rooms
Credit cards: American Express, Diners Club, Visa
A chalet with a panoramic terrace, heated swimming pool, sauna, gym and beauty center. There is a restaurant and transport is provided to and from the village and the ski lifts.

Maison lo Campagnar *******
Dolonne, Rue des Granges 14,
Tel. 0165846840
www.maisonlocampagnar.com
11 Rooms
Credit cards: American Express, Visa, Mastercard, Bancomat
This delightful stone and wood chalet at the feet of Mt Checrouit can be reached "with your skis on your feet". It has charming communal areas, sauna and restaurant.

Mont Blanc ******* ♿★
S.S. 26 18,
Tel. 0165846555
www.altamarea.it
45 Rooms
Credit cards: American Express, Diners Club, Visa, Mastercard
Near the funicular railway leading to Plan Checrouit and just a short distance from the pedestrian town center, this characteristic wooden building has a sauna and restaurant serving local dishes.

Pilier d'Angle ******* ★
Entrèves,Tel. 0165869760
www.pilierdangle.it
19 Rooms
Credit cards: American Express, Diners Club, Visa, Mastercard, Bancomat, JCB
Close to the funicular railways leading to Veny valley and Mont Blanc, this stone and wood chalet also has a restaurant.

Romantik Hotel Villa Novecento ******** ♿
Viale Monte Bianco 64,
Tel. 0165843000
www.villanovecento.it
26 Rooms
Credit cards: American Express, Diners Club, Visa, Bancomat
Early-20th century villa furnished with antiques and precious fabrics, it has a fitness center with sauna, hydro-massage, Turkish bath and gym. The restaurant serves local specialties.

Royal e Golf ******** ♿
Via Roma 87,
Tel. 0165831611
www.royalegolf.com
86 Rooms
Credit cards: American Express, Diners Club, Visa, Mastercard
A comfortable hotel ideal for relaxation and physical well-being. The restaurant serves local dishes.

Vallée Blanche ******* ★
La Palud,
Tel. 0165897002
www.hotelvalleeblanche.com
22 Rooms
Credit cards: Visa, Mastercard, Bancomat
Situated near the funicular railway for Mont Blanc and the entrance to Ferret valley, it combines its convenient position with the advantages of a family run hotel. It offers a sweet and savoury buffet breakfast including home-made cakes and yoghurt.

Restaurants

Dente del Gigante 🍴
Strada La Palud 42,
Tel. 016589145
www.dentedelgigante.com
Closed Mondays
Credit cards: Diners Club, Visa, Mastercard

A refined atmosphere and creative dishes that combine innovative and traditional cuisine.

La Clotze ¶¶
Planpincieux 21,
Tel. 0165869720
www.laclotze.com
Closed Tuesdays and Wednesdays
Credit cards: American Express, Diners Club, Visa, Mastercard, Bancomat
A typical alpine restaurant serving local products and traditional specialties.

La Grolla ¶¶
Peindein Val Veny 104,
Tel. 0165869095
www.lagrolla.it
Credit cards: Visa, Mastercard, Bancomat
Home cooking typical of the Aosta region is the specialty of this restaurant situated in a panoramic position directly on the ski slopes.

La Maison de Filippo ¶¶
Entrèves,
Tel. 0165869797
www.lamaison.com
Closed Tuesdays
Credit cards: Visa, Mastercard
Dining rooms, intimate dining areas and a small cellar in country style with some kitsch items and traditional cuisine.

Pierre Alexis 1877 ¶¶
Via Marconi 50/A,
Tel. 0165843517
Closed Mondays in low season
Credit cards: American Express, Diners Club, Visa, Mastercard, Bancomat
A historial venue with good local cuisine.

Rural Lodgins

Le Rêve
Plan-Gorret, rue du Biolley 3,
Tel. 0165842861
Credit cards: Visa, Mastercard, Bancomat
A pleasant building set in 40 hectares of land with stables, vegetable gardens and orchards that produce raspberries, black-currents and bilberries from which the owner's wife makes fruit juices and jams. It has a splendid view of Mont Blanc and the Rutor group. Guests can enjoy sport, relaxation, walks and excursions.

Museums, Monuments and Churches

Museo Alpino Duca degli Abruzzi
Strada Villair 2,
Tel. 0165842064
Mondays-Sundays 9.00-12.00, 16.00-19.00; Wednesdays only 16.00-19.00. November and June: Tuesdays-Sundays 16.00-19.00. Special opening hours during the exhibitions.

ÉTROUBLES

AIAT Gran San Bernardo
Etroubles, S.S. Gran San Bernardo 13, Tel. 016578559
www.gransanbernardo.net

Hotels

Col Serena* **
Rue des Vergers 5,
Tel. 016578218
www.hotelcolserena.com
16 Rooms
Set in a delightful position, this hotel and restaurant serves both classical and local dishes. Just twenty meters away is a gym and tennis court.

Restaurants

Croix Blanche ¶¶
S.S. Gran S. Bernardo 10,
Tel. 016578238
Closed Tuesdays
Credit cards: Visa, Mastercard
Situated in a 17th-century inn where post carriages used to change horses, this restaurant serves local dishes based on meat and vegetables cooked on stone. Visitors can buy wines and spirits and enjoy live piano music at the weekends.

GIGNOD

Municipio
Castello, Tel. 0165256211

Hotels

La Clusaz* **
La Clusaz,
Tel. 016556075
www.laclusaz.it
14 Rooms
Credit cards: American Express, Diners Club, Visa, Mastercard, Bancomat
Just outside Gignod, this is a small hotel and restaurant where you can re-live the medieval atmosphere of ancient eating places. With its typical alpine furnishing and hand-made ornaments it has an old-fashioned charm.

Rural Lodgins

Le Myosotis
Arliod 7, Tel. 0165256893
Closed mid-January to mid-February
Enjoy a stay in this 19th-century house where the warmth from the open fireplace makes a delightful background to your evenings. Quiet and welcoming, it is the ideal starting point for excursions.

Museums, Monuments and Churches

Museo Parrocchiale di Sant'Ilario
Via Capoluogo 3, Tel. 016556004
www.regione.vda.it
Mondays-Sundays 8.00-19.30

GRAN SAN BERNARDO (COLLE DEL)

AIAT Gran San Bernardo
Etroubles, S.S. Gran San Bernardo 13, Tel. 016578559
www.gransanbernardo.net

Museums, Monuments and Churches

Museo del Colle del Gran San Bernardo
Bourg-Saint-Pierre (Switzerland),
Tel. 0041277871236
Museum and kennels: June and September 9.00-12.00, 13.00-18.00; July-August: 9.00-19.00.
Refuge open all year.

GRESSONEY-LA-TRINITÉ

IAT Gressoney-la-Trinité
Edelboden Inferiore
Tel. 0125366143
www.aiatmonterosawalser.it

Hotels

Jolanda Sport* ***
Edelboden, Tel. 0125366140
www.hoteljolandasport.com
33 Rooms
Credit cards: American Express, Visa, Mastercard
Situated by the chair lift for Punta Jolanda, this alpine style house has a restaurant, health center, swimming pool, gym and games room.

Lo Scoiattolo* **
Tache 6, Tel. 0125366313
www.htlscoiattolo.com
14 Rooms
Credit cards: American Express, Diners Club, Visa
This hotel at the feet of Mt Rosa offers bedrooms with panoramic balconies and alpine-style furnishing. It also has a restaurant specializing in local cuisine, a health center, gym and access to the Internet.

Restaurants

Castore Lounge 🍴🍴
Tache,
Tel. 0125366809
www.castorelounge.com
Closed Tuesdays
Credit cards: Visa, Mastercard
Set in a renovated historical building, the elegant restaurant serves good local wines.

Rifugio Gabiet 🍴🍴
Gabiet,
Tel. 0125366258
www.rifugiogabiet.it
A refuge set amid meadows and woods that can be easily reached by the funicular railway. It specializes in traditional local cuisine.

GRESSONEY-SAINT-JEAN

AIAT Monte Rosa Walser
Villa Deslex
Tel 0125355185
www.aiatmonterosawalser.it

Hotels

Gressoney ******** ♿
Via Lys 3,
Tel. 0125355986
www.hotelsgressoney.com
25 Rooms
Credit cards: American Express, Diners Club, Visa, Mastercard, Bancomat
Built in wood and stone, this hotel has a restaurant that serves local dishes, a sauna, gym and hydromassage pool.

La Gran Baita ******* ♿
Strada Castello Savoia 26,
Tel. 0125356441
www.hotelgranbaita.it
12 Rooms
Credit cards: Visa, Mastercard, Bancomat
Situated in a small, alpine-style chalet, it has communal areas with wooden furnishing, sauna, gym, Turkish bath and Nordic-style external pool.
The restaurant serves regional dishes.

Restaurants

Il Braciere 🍴🍴
Ondrò Verdebio 2,
Tel. 0125355526
Closed Wednesdays
Credit cards: American Express, Visa, Mastercard
Typical alpine hotel with Aosta and Piedmont cuisine. Specialties include local cured meats, home-made cakes and sweets and regional wines.

Nordkapp 🍴
Piazza Umberto I 11,
Tel. 0125355096
www.nordkapprestaurant.com
Credit cards: American Express, Diners Club, Visa, Mastercard, Bancomat
Furnished in alpine style, it offers traditional gastronomic specialties made from fresh, seasonal products, home-made bread and a good selection of national and local wines.

Principe 🍴
Piazza Beck Peccoz 3,
Tel. 0125355117
Closed Mondays
Credit cards: American Express, Diners Club, Visa, Mastercard, Bancomat
Delicious dishes typical of the Aosta region.

Stambecco 🍴
Via Deffeyes 14,
Tel. 0125355201
Closed Tuesdays in low season
A spacious dining room with a large, antique fireplace. The menu includes dishes from Aosta and Piedmont as well as pizza cooked in a wood-fired oven.

Museums, Monuments and Churches

Museo Parrocchiale
chiesa di S. Giovanni Battista,
Tel. 0125355200
www.regione.vda.it
Mondays-Sundays 8.00-19.00

Museo Regionale di Fauna Alpina «Beck Peccoz»
Predeloasch 9,
Tel. 0125355406
www.regione.vda.it
9.00-12.30, 15.00-18.30. Closed Wednesdays and from 1st November to second Sunday in June, except Christmas holidays.

ISSIME

Pro Loco
www.prolocoissime.it

Museums, Monuments and Churches

Museo Parrocchiale di San Giacomo
Piazza Comunale,
Tel. 0125344010
www.regione.vda.it
May-September: Mondays-Sundays 8.00-19.00.
October-April: Mondays-Sundays 8.00-17.00

LA SALLE

IAT (open July and August)
Via Gerbollier
Tel. 0165862562

Hotels

Les Combes ******* ♿
Cheverel, Tel. 0165863982
www.lescombes.it
8 Rooms
Set in a panoramic position with a view of the Mont Blanc chain, it offers rooms furnished in walnut with split-level area or balcony, two panoramic terraces and a restaurant serving local specialties.

Mont Blanc Hotel Village ******** ♿
La Croisette 36,
Tel. 0165864111
www.hotelmontblanc.it
53 Rooms
This hotel in stone and wood has a swimming pool, tennis court, gym, health center and two restaurants for guests.

Restaurants

La Cassolette 🍴🍴🍴
La Croisette 36,
Tel. 0165864111
www.hotelmontblanc.it
Closed Mondays
Credit cards: American Express, Diners Club, Visa, Mastercard, Bancomat
Situated near Mont Blanc, it has antique, local furnishing and large windows overlooking the garden. Regional cuisine.

La Roueige 🍴🍴
Lazey 100, Tel. 0165861091
Situated at a high altitude above the village, it is only open on center request. It serves simple, genuine local dishes.

Rural Lodgins

Le Perce Neige
Château 39, Tel. 0165862422
Closed mid September-mid October and for a period in May
Situated amidst the typical scenery of the upper Dora Baltea valley about half way up from the floor of the valley, it has an enviable view of the surrounding countryside.

Museums, Monuments and Churches

Museo Etnografico «L'Homme et la Pente»
Cheverel,
Tel. 0165862769-0165961908
June-September, Easter and Christmas holidays: Tuesday-Sundays 10.00-12.00, 14.30-17.30.

Museo Parrocchiale di San Cassiano
Piazza S. Cassiano,
Tel. 0165861288
www.regione.vda.it
Mondays-Sundays 6.30-21.00

LA THUILE

AIAT La Thuile Petit Saint Bernard
Via M. Collomb 3
Tel. 0165884179
www.lathuile.it

Hotels

Chalet Alpina ***
Arly 42, Tel. 0165884187
www.chaletalpina.it
14 Rooms
Parking, tennis court, swimming pool
Credit cards: Visa, Mastercard
Near the ski lifts, this typical mountain chalet has a heated, open-air swimming pool, tennis court and storage for skis and boots.

Chateau Blanc ***
Entrèves 39,
Tel. 0165885341
www.chateaublanc.it
13 Rooms
Credit cards: American Express, Diners Club, Visa, Mastercard
A small, alpine-style house near the ski slopes; sauna available.

Restaurants

La Bricole
Entrèves 56, Tel. 0165884149
Closed Monday midday
Credit cards: Visa, Mastercard
A restaurant in harmony with the surrounding area specializing in local and traditional cuisine.

MONGNOD

Ufficio Turistico di Torgnon
Piazza Frutaz 11
Tel. 0166540433
www.torgnon.net

Museums, Monuments and Churches

Museo Etnografico «Petit Monde»
Triatel, Tel. 0166540433
www.torgnon.net
July-August: 10.00-12.00, 15.00-18.00. In other periods visits by request

Museo Parrocchiale di Saint-Roch
Tel. 0166540241
www.regione.vda.it
July-August: Saturdays 14.00-18.30; Sundays 9.00-18.30. September-June: visits by request

PILA

IAT Gressan
Pila
Tel. 0165521008

Hotels

Plan Bois ***
Printemps, Tel. 0165521052
www.planbois.it
31 Rooms
Credit cards: American Express, Diners Club, Visa, Mastercard
Situated in the quiet of the Pila valley, this hotel has a restaurant that serves dishes typical to the Aosta region, communal areas with fireplace, sauna and gym.

Restaurants

Brasserie du Petit Coin
Tel. 0165521108
Closed Thursdays
Credit cards: Visa, Bancomat
A country atmosphere characterises this restaurant with an open air dining area. It serves local dishes prepared with fresh, seasonal products and offers a good selection of local wines.

RHÊMES-NOTRE-DAME

Municipio
Bruil 13
Tel. 0165936114

Hotels

Grande Rousse **
Chanavey 22,
Tel. 0165936105
www.granderousse.it
37 Rooms
Credit cards: American Express, Visa, Mastercard
A country-style building on two floors, it also has a restaurant service.

Rural Lodgins

Lo Sabot
Bruil, Tel. 0165936150
This spacious chalet with balconies is situated in a large, grassy hollow in the Rhêmes valley. The farmyard, vegetable garden and sheds produce the ingredients for the simple home cooking. Lovely walks in the Parco Nazionale del Gran Paradiso.

Museums, Monuments and Churches

Centro Visita del Parco Nazionale del Gran Paradiso
Chanavey,
Tel. 0165936193
www.grand-paradis.it
January, February, June and September: Saturdays and Sundays 9.00-12.00, 14.00-18.00. Easter holidays: 9.00-12.00, 14.00-18.00. April-May: Wednesdays, Fridays, Saturday and Sundays 10.00-16.00. July and August: Mondays-Sundays 9.30-12.30, 15.30-19.30

RHÊMES-SAINT-GEORGES

Municipio
Tel. 0165907634

Rural Lodgins

Edelweiss
Melignon, Tel. 0165936178
www.agriturismoedelweiss.it
Situated in a small hamlet surrounded by larch trees, this old stone building welcomes guests who are looking for the quiet pleasures of farm life and the natural beauty of the Parco Nazionale del Gran Paradiso. The valley also offers the chance to practice alpine sports.

Le Vieux Créton
Créton, Tel. 0165907612
Open April-October
An ideal spot for nature lovers in the Parco Nazionale del Gran Paradiso where the wooded slopes give way to mountain pastures. A group of stone houses that have guarded the road into the valley since 1600s still conserve the old architecture with original stone fireplaces and wooden balconies. A perfect starting point for excursions.

L'Echo
Voix, Tel. 016595218
At the entrance to the Parco Nazionale del Gran Paradiso, this typical alpine chalet offers accommodation in spacious, well-furnished apartments. Ideal for excursions and trekking.

Museums, Monuments and Churches

Museo Parrocchiale di San Giorgio
Coveyrand-Vieux,
Tel. 0165907631
www.regione.vda.it
Summer: Mondays-Saturdays 9.00-17.00.
Winter: visits by request

SAINT-CHRISTOPHE

AIAT Aosta
Aosta, Piazza Chanoux 45
Tel. 016533352
www.aiataosta.com

Hotels

Casale* **
Condemine 1,
Tel. 0165541272
www.hotelristorantecasale.it
25 Rooms
Credit cards: American Express, Diners Club, Visa, Mastercard, JCB
Set in a delightful position, this typical alpine house in stone and wood has a restaurant and swimming pool.

SAINT-PIERRE

Pro Loco
Via Corrado Gex 3
Tel. 0165903159

Hotels

La Meridiana* **
Chateau Feuillet 17,
Tel. 0165903626
www.albergomeridiana.it
18 Rooms
Credit cards: Visa
A small country house furnished in the style of a typical 19th-century Aosta home. Good food and wine cellar where you can taste local wines.

***Notre Maison* *** ★**
Vetan 4,
Tel. 0165908960
www.nih.it/hotelnotremaison
22 Rooms
Credit cards: Diners Club, Visa, Mastercard, Bancomat
Situated in a panoramic position, this chalet offers a buffet breakfast and a restaurant serving regional specialties.

Restaurants

Les Ecureuils
Homené Dessus 8,
Tel. 0165903831
www.lesecureuils.it
Restaurant and holiday farm in an 18th-century building in a panoramic position at an altitude of 1,500 m. Traditional cuisine enriched with products from the farm. Selection of local wines and home-made goats' milk cheeses.

Vetan
Vetan-Dessous 77,
Tel. 0165908830
Closed Tuesdays in low season
An antique building situated at an altitude of 1,700 m with a terrace and a splendid view of the mountains. Menu featuring local cuisine.

Rural Lodgins

L'Abri
Vetan Dessous 83,
Tel. 0165908830
Open February-October and Christmas-6 January
Credit cards: Visa, Mastercard, Bancomat
Situated in a panoramic plateau overlooking the Dora Baltea valley, this stone chalet has rooms in the local style. The farm produces fruit, wines and vegetables and also organizes courses where guests can learn to carve flowers from wood. For sports lovers there is tobogganing and bob-sledding in the winter and mountain bike escursions in the summer.

Les Ecureuils
Homené Dessus 8,
Tel. 0165903831
www.lesecureuils.it
Closed December-January
Peace and quiet amidst meadows and woods. Accommodation in an 18th-century complex with a farm that provides the genuine products for the restaurant. Guests can assist with cheese-making.

Verger Plein Soleil
Jacquemin 5,
Tel. 0165903366
www.vergerpleinsoleil.com
In a panoramic position opposite the Parco Nazionale del Gran Paradiso, accommodation in apartments. The area offers beautiful walks in the summer and just a few kilometers away, guests can enjoy winter sports including skiing by night.

Museums, Monuments and Churches

Museo Regionale di Scienze Naturali
Tache, Castello di Saint Pierre,
Tel. 0165903485
www.mrsn.vda.it
April-September: Mondays-Sundays 9.00-19.00, last entry 18.30

SAINT-VINCENT

AIAT Saint-Vincent
Via Roma 62
Tel. 0166512239
www.saintvincentvda.it

Hotels

Alla Posta* **
Piazza 28 Aprile 1,
Tel. 0166512250
www.hotelpostavda.it
36 Rooms
Near the casino and spa, this hotel has been renovated in its original style. Restaurant with local cuisine.

Atahotel Miramonti* * ★**
Via Ponte Romano 25/27,
Tel. 0166525611
www.atahotels.it
50 Rooms
Credit cards: American Express, Diners Club, Visa, Mastercard, Bancomat
Comfortable rooms and restaurant with local and traditional cuisine.

***Bijou* *** ★**
Piazza Cavalieri di Vittorio Veneto 3, Tel. 0166510067
www.bijouhotel.it
31 Rooms
Well-equipped rooms and restaurant situated in the pedestrian area of the town.

Suisse* **
Via Ponte Romano 80,
Tel. 0166511633
www.suissestvincent.com
37 Rooms
Credit cards: Visa, Mastercard
Near the funicular railway for the health spa, comfortable rooms and restaurant.

Restaurants

***Batezar* ★**
Via G. Marconi 1,
Tel. 0166513164
Closed Wednesdays
Credit cards: American Express, Diners Club, Visa, Mastercard, Bancomat
Situated near the casino, the restaurant has antique furniture and serves dishes typical to the Aosta and Piedmont regions. Good selection of wines and spirits, cheeses, cured meats, cakes and ice-creams, all home produced.

Del Viale
Viale Piemonte 7,
Tel. 0166512569
www.ristorantedelviale.com
Closed Thursdays and Friday midday
Credit cards: Visa, Mastercard, Bancomat
Exquisite cutlery and tablecloths in Flanders fabric in this elegant restaurant with an outdoors dining area.

Le Grenier
Piazza Zerbion 1,
Tel. 0166510138
Closed Wednesdays
Credit cards: Diners Club, Visa, Mastercard, Bancomat
A traditional atmosphere is

created by a lovely fireplace, a good wine cellar and traditional dishes made from local seasonal products.

Museums, Monuments and Churches

Museo Parrocchiale di San Vincenzo
Piazza della Chiesa 7,
Tel. 0166512350
www.regione.vda.it
Mondays-Sundays 7.30-12.00, 14.30-20.30, except during worship.

VALGRISENCHE

Pro Loco
Capoluogo
Tel. 016597193

Hotels

Grande Sassière **
Gerbelle, Tel. 016597113
14 Rooms
Surrounded by meadows and pine woods, this well furnished house offers genuine home cooking.

Perret **
Bonne 1, Tel. 016597107
www.hotelperret.it
18 Rooms
Parking, sauna, restaurant
Credit cards: Visa
In a quiet, panoramic position, this typical chalet made of wood and stone has country-style furnishing and home cooking.

Museums, Monuments and Churches

Museo Parrocchiale di San Grato
Piazza della Chiesa,
Tel. 016597102
www.regione.vda.it
Summer: Mondays-Sundays 8.00-20.00. Winter: visits by request

VALPELLINE

AIAT Valpelline
Capoluogo 1
Tel. 0165713502
www.gransanbernardo.net

Hotels

Le Lièvre Amoureux *** ♿
Chozod 12,
Tel. 0165713966
www.lievre.it
31 Rooms
Set on a gentle slope in a clearing in the woods, this typical alpine building has a restaurant, sauna and gym.

Restaurants

Brasserie du Petit Coin
Tel. 0165521108
Closed Thursdays
Credit cards: Visa, Bancomat
This pleasant, country restaurant with an outdoors dining area offers local dishes prepared exclusively with seasonal, locally produced ingredients. A good selection of regional wines.

Museums, Monuments and Churches

Museo Parrocchiale di San Pantaleone
San Pantaleone,
Tel. 016573205
www.regione.vda.it
Mondays-Sundays 7.30-19.00

VALSAVARENCHE

Ufficio Turistico Valsavarenche
Degioz 52
Tel. 0165905816
www.valsavarenche.org

Hotels

A l'Hostellerie du Paradis *** ♿
Eau-Rousse,
Tel. 0165905972
www.hostellerieduparadis.it
30 Rooms
Credit cards: American Express, Diners Club, Visa, Mastercard, Bancomat
Set in a delightful position, ideal for excursions in the Parco Nazionale del Gran Paradiso, the hotel offers a sweet or savoury buffet breakfast, sauna, swimming pool and restaurant.

Genzianella ***
Pont,
Tel. 016595393
www.genzianella.aosta.it
26 Rooms
A warm welcome awaits you in this hotel and restaurant surrounded by the mountains in the quiet of the nearby Parco Nazionale del Gran Paradiso.

Restaurants

A l'Hostellerie du Paradis
Eau-Rousse,
Tel. 0165905972
www.hostellerieduparadis.it
Credit cards: American Express, Diners Club, Visa, Mastercard, Bancomat
A typical alpine atmosphere and good local cuisine in this restaurant with outdoors dining area and pastry shop.

Rural Lodgins

Lo Mayen ♿
Bien,
Tel. 0165905735
Open by arrangement
Set in the heart of the Parco Nazionale del Gran Paradiso surrounded by pines and larch trees, this farm offers home cooking (evenings only) and is an ideal starting point for walks in the splendid surrounding countryside.

Museums, Monuments and Churches

Museo Parrocchiale della Madonna del Carmelo
Dégioz, Tel. 0165905715
www.regione.vda.it
Mondays-Sundays 9.00-16.00

VALTOURNENCHE

AIAT Monte Cervino
Via Roma 80
Tel. 016692029
www.montecervino.it

Hotels

Grandes Murailles *** ♿
Via Roma 78, Tel. 0166932702
www.hotelgmurailles.com
16 Rooms
A small hotel in a pleasant position with wooden floors, antique furniture, original fireplace and sauna, it specializes in regional cuisine.

Tourist *** ♿
Via Roma 32, Tel. 016692070
www.hotel-tourist.it
34 Rooms
Constructed in the 1950s, this hotel has a bar, a restaurant with local cuisine and transport to and from the ski lifts.

Rural Lodgins

La Péra Doussa ♿
Loz 31, Tel. 016692777
Closed for a period in June
Credit cards: American Express, Diners Club, Bancomat
Set in a clearing in the woods, this spacious chalet has rooms with wood panelling and a restaurant. In the winter guests can reach the ski lifts of Cime Bianche on skis and in the summer they can go up to the Plateau Rosa from the nearby Breuil-Cervinia or go on excursions on horseback.

Museums, Monuments and Churches

Museo Parrocchiale di Sant'Antonio
Tel. 016692005
www.regione.vda.it
Mondays-Sundays 9.00-18.00

ALESSANDRIA

IAT Alessandria
Via Gagliaudo 2
Tel. 0131234794
www.comune.alessandria.it

Hotels

Lux* * ♿★**
Via Piacenza 72,
Tel. 0131251661
www.hotelluxalessandria.it
45 Rooms
Credit cards: American Express, Diners Club, Visa, Bancomat
Soundproofed rooms with all comforts, including multi-media. Sweet and savoury buffet breakfast and restaurant with special prices for hotel guests.

Marengo* * ♿★**
Spinetta Marengo
Via Genova 30,
Tel. 0131213800
www.marengohotel.com
72 Rooms
Credit cards: American Express, Diners Club, Visa, Mastercard, Bancomat
Prestigious hotel with comfortable rooms and communal area equipped with audio-video equipment and Internet points. Restaurant specializing in classical and Piedmont cuisine.

Mercure Alessandria-Alli Due Buoi Rossi* * ♿★**
Via Cavour 32, Tel. 0131517171
www.mercurehotels.com
48 Rooms
Credit cards: American Express, Diners Club, Visa, Mastercard, Bancomat
A carefully restored mid-18th century building with comfortable rooms, access to Internet and restaurants.

Restaurants

Asmara
Corso Romita 35,
Tel. 0131260484
Closed Saturday midday
A small restaurant specializing in cuisine from the Piedmont and Monferrato areas.

Gagliaudo
Via Schiavina 13,
Tel. 0131263095
www.gagliaudo.it
Closed Wednesdays
Credit cards: American Express, Diners Club, Visa, Mastercard
An elegant restaurant with classical and Piedmont cuisine.

***Grappolo* ★**
Via Casale 28,
Tel. 0131253217
www.ristoranteilgrappolo.it
Closed Monday evenings and Tuesdays
Credit cards: American Express, Diners Club, Visa, Mastercard, Bancomat
A restaurant specializing in regional cuisine with home-made bread and pasta. Open-air dining area in the summer.

L'Arcimboldo
Via Legnano 2,
Tel. 013152022
www.ristorantearcimboldo.it
Closed Sundays
A small, elegant restaurant near the railway station. Local cuisine and a vast selection of well-known cheeses and wines from the Piedmont region as well as a choice of spirits.

Osteria al Giardinetto
Viale Milite Ignoto 112,
Tel. 0131223718
Closed Tuesdays and Wednesdays
Credit cards: American Express, Diners Club, Visa, Mastercard, Bancomat
A small restaurant where you can enjoy good, traditional food from Piedmont at a reasonable price. Home-made pasta, confectionery and other traditional specialties.

Trattoria Cappelverde
Via S. Pio V 26,
Tel. 0131251265
Closed Tuesdays
Credit cards: American Express, Visa, Mastercard, Bancomat
A small restaurant in a 19th-century building between the hospital and the Duomo. The menu is a combination of traditional dishes from Piedmont and Liguria and there is also a selection of toma cheese from alpine pastures.

Trattoria da Gina
Valmadonna
Via Pavia 11,
Tel. 0131221024
Closed Mondays
Credit cards: Diners Club, Visa, Mastercard, Bancomat
Near the Tanaro River, a quiet restaurant that serves classical and Piedmont dishes such as potato gnocchi and home-made noodles.

ARONA

Ufficio Turismo
Via S. Carlo 2
Tel. 0322243601
www.comune.arona.no.it

Hotels

Concorde* ***
Via Verbano 1,
Tel. 0322249321
www.concordearona.com
82 Rooms
Credit cards: American Express, Diners Club, Visa, Mastercard, Bancomat
A hotel with comfortable sound-proofed and air conditioned rooms. It has a restaurant, swimming pool and beauty center.

Giardino* **
Corso della Repubblica 1,
Tel. 032245994
www.giardinoarona.com
56 Rooms
Credit cards: American Express, Diners Club, Visa, Mastercard
Situated on the lake shore, this late 19th-century house offers comfortable, modern rooms, some with hydromassage bath.

Restaurants

Del Barcaiolo
Piazza del Popolo 23,
Tel. 0322243388
Closed Wednesdays and Thursday midday
Credit cards: American Express, Diners Club, Visa, Mastercard, Bancomat
Set in a 15th-century building, there are two country style dining rooms and during the summer meals are served outdoors under a porch. The menu is based on fish dishes.

Taverna del Pittore
Piazza del Popolo 39,
Tel. 0322243366
www.ristorantetaverna delpittore.it
Closed Mondays
Credit cards: American Express, Diners Club, Visa, Mastercard, Bancomat
An old, evocative atmosphere for this restaurant with a lovely terrace overlooking the lake. The menu changes with the seasons.

ASTI

IAT Asti
Piazza Alfieri 29
Tel. 014153035
www.comune.asti.it

Hotels

***Antica Dogana* *** ♿★**
Quarto Inferiore,
Tel. 0141293755
www.albergoanticadogana.it
25 Rooms
Credit cards: American Express, Diners Club, Visa, Mastercard

Situated just outside the town of Asti, this late 19th-century country home has retained the original characteristics of the old customs house.

Reale *** ♿
Piazza Alfieri 6,
Tel. 0141530240
www.hotelristorantereale.it
27 Rooms
Credit cards: American Express, Diners Club, Visa, Mastercard
Situated right in the town center, the hotel and restaurant is in a historical building with lovely vaulted ceilings where guests can relax in comfort.

Salera **** ♿
Via Mons. Marello 19,
Tel. 0141410169
www.hotelsalera.it
50 Rooms
Credit cards: American Express, Diners Club, Visa, Mastercard, Bancomat
Surrounded by parks and gardens, this hotel guarantees a quiet, relaxing stay. It has comfortable rooms, a restaurant serving local dishes and access to the Internet.

Restaurants

Angolo del Beato 🍴🍴
Via Guttuari 12,
Tel. 0141531668
www.angolodelbeato.it
Closed Sundays
Credit cards: American Express, Diners Club, Visa, Mastercard
A characteristic restaurant in a 12th-century building. Typical cuisine from the Asti area and a delightful cellar with a good selection of wines.

Barolo & Co 🍴
Via Cesare Battisti 14,
Tel. 0141592059
Closed Mondays
Credit cards: American Express, Diners Club, Visa, Mastercard, Bancomat
In the year 1200 the building was a refuge run by Certosini monks and today it is a restaurant and wine cellar specializing in cuisine from the Asti and Monferrato areas as well as dishes created from mediaeval recipes.

Convivio Vini e Cucina 🍴
Via Giuliani 4/6,
Tel. 0141594188
www.turismodoc.it
Closed Sundays
Credit cards: American Express, Diners Club, Visa, Mastercard, Bancomat
A 19th-century building in the old town center, the menu serves typical dishes based on home-made pasta, a selection of local cheeses and a good choice of wines from the Piedmont region.

Falcon Vecchio 🍴
Via Mameli 11,
Tel. 0141593106
www.hotelpalio.com
Closed Sunday evenings and Monday midday
Traditional local dishes but also dishes based on fish from Liguria. A good selection of local cheeses and cured meats.

La Grotta 🍴
Corso Torino 366,
Tel. 0141214168
Closed Monday evenings and Tuesdays
Credit cards: American Express, Diners Club, Visa, Mastercard
Traditional Asti cuisine featuring a trolley of roast meats and mixed boiled meats. There is also a bar.

Osteria ai Binari 🍴
Mombarone 145,
Tel. 0141294228
Closed Mondays
Credit cards: Visa, Mastercard, Bancomat
19th-century furnishing give this restaurant a romantic atmosphere where you can enjoy dishes from the Piedmont region.

Osteria del Diavolo 🍴
Piazza S. Martino 6,
Tel. 014130221
www.osteriadeldiavolo.it
Closed Mondays and Tuesdays
Credit cards: Visa, Bancomat
Situated among the lovely antique buildings in the town center, this restaurant serves dishes that combine traditional Piedmont cuisine with specialties from neighbouring Liguria.

Museums, Monuments and Churches

Biblioteca Astense
Corso Alfieri 375,
Tel. 0141593002-0141531117
Tuesdays-Thursdays 8.30-20.00, Fridays 8.30-22.00, Saturdays 8.30-13.00

Centro Nazionale di Studi Alfieriani
Via Bonzanigo Giuseppe Maria 34,
Tel. 0141538284
Temporarily closed

Complesso di San Pietro Consavia e Musei Paleontologico e Archeologico
Corso Alfieri 2,
Tel. 0141353072
www.comune.asti.it/cultura/index.shtml
Summer: Tuesdays-Sundays 10.00-13.00, 16.00-19.00. Winter: Tuesdays-Sundays 10.00-13.00, 15.00-18.00

Cripta e Museo Lapidario di Sant'Anastasio
Corso Alfieri 365/a,
Tel. 0141437454
www.comune.asti.it/cultura/index.shtml
Summer: Tuesdays-Sundays 10.00-13.00, 16.00-19.00. Winter: Tuesdays-Sundays 10.00-13.00, 15.00-18.00

Museo degli Arazzi Scassa
Via dell'Arazzeria 60,
Tel. 0141271164-0141271352
www.arazzeriascassa.com
Visits by prior arrangement.

BIELLA

ℹ ***Ufficio Turismo Biella***
c/o Villa Schneider,
Piazza La Marmora 6,
Tel. 0153506613
www.comune.biella.it

Hotels

Agorà Palace **** ♿
Via Lamarmora 13/A,
Tel. 0158407324
www.agorapalace.it
58 Rooms
Credit cards: American Express, Diners Club, Visa, Mastercard, Bancomat
A spacious, elegant reception area, lovely rooms, a large terrace with a roof garden and a restaurant that serves local dishes.

Bugella *** ♿
Via Cottolengo 65,
Tel. 015406607
www.hotelbugella.it
24 Rooms
An antique building at the entrance to the town, it offers lovely rooms and a restaurant.

Restaurants

Al Bucaniere 🍴🍴
Via Pietro Micca 32,
Tel. 01521346
Closed Mondays
Typical cuisine
Credit cards: American Express, Diners Club, Visa, Mastercard, Bancomat
A country-style restaurant with wooden ceilings where you can enjoy fresh fish dishes. The menu changes frequently according to the season and it offers good value for money.

Baracca ★
Via S. Eusebio 12,
Tel. 01521941
www.baraccaristorante.it
Closed Saturdays and Sundays
A restaurant with a long tradition of local home cooking.

Museums, Monuments and Churches

Museo del Territorio Biellese ★
Chiostro di S. Sebastiano,
Via Q. Sella, Tel. 0152529345
www.museodelterritorio.biella.it
Thursdays, Saturdays 10.00-12.00, 15.00-19.00; Fridays 15.00-22.00; Sundays 15.00-19.00. Tuesdays and Wednesdays guided tours and school visits. Closed August

CUNEO

IAT Cuneo
Via Roma 28
Tel. 0171693258
www.comune.cuneo.it

Hotels

ClassHotel Cuneo *** ♿★
Madonna dell'Olmo
Via Cascina Magnina 3/A,
Tel. 0171413188
www.classhotel.com
82 Rooms
Credit cards: American Express, Diners Club, Visa, Mastercard, Bancomat
Soundproofed, air-conditioned rooms with all modern comforts, it has a restaurant and serves a buffet breakfast.

Palazzo Lovera **** ♿★
Via Roma 37, Tel. 0171690420
www.palazzolovera.com
47 Rooms
Credit cards: American Express, Diners Club, Visa, Mastercard, Bancomat
An 18th-century nobleman's residence in the old town center, this hotel has a sauna, gym and restaurant.

Royal Superga *** ♿★
Via Pascal 3, Tel. 0171693223
www.hotelroyalsuperga.com
29 Rooms
Credit cards: American Express, Diners Club, Visa, Mastercard, Bancomat
A late-19th century building in the old town center, it offers comfortable, elegant rooms and a buffet breakfast.

Restaurants

Bistro Trattoria Lovera
Via Roma 37,
Tel. 0171690420
www.palazzolovera.com
Closed Sundays and Saturday midday and Mondays
Situated in the old town center, this cosy little bistro serves typical Piedmont dishes with home-made bread and pasta, a good selection of oils and local cheeses and truffles from Alba when in season.

Delle Antiche Contrade
Via Savigliano 11,
Tel. 0171690429
www.antichecontrade.it
Closed Sundays
Credit cards: American Express, Diners Club, Visa, Mastercard
Situated in what was once an old postal station, it serves local and fish dishes with home-made bread and pasta, a good selection of oils and local cheeses and truffles from Alba when in season.

Locanda da Peju
Madonna dell'Olmo
Via Valle Po 10,
Tel. 0171412174
www.locandadapeju.com
Closed Mondays
Credit cards: American Express, Diners Club, Visa, Mastercard, Bancomat
An informal atmosphere where you can enjoy specialties from Piedmont. Open- air dining area during the summer.

Osteria della Chiocciola
Via Fossano 1, Tel. 017166277
Closed Sundays
Credit cards: American Express, Diners Club, Visa, Mastercard, Bancomat
Right in the town center, a restaurant where local cuisine blends with other specialties. It has a well-stocked wine cellar downstairs.

San Michele
Mondovì 2, Tel. 0171681962
Closed Mondays
Credit cards: American Express, Diners Club, Visa, Mastercard, Bancomat
Set in a 16th-century building, this elegant restaurant serves creative dishes based on traditional recipes.

Trattoria Zuavo
Via Roma 23,
Tel. 0171602020
Closed Wednesdays and Thursday midday
Credit cards: American Express, Visa, Mastercard, Bancomat
Situated in the courtyard of an old building in the town center,this restaurant offers good value for money. It serves local dishes, home-made pasta and a variety of local cheeses.

Museums, Monuments and Churches

Museo Civico
Via S. Maria 10, Tel. 0171634175
www.comune.cuneo.it
Tuesdays, Saturdays 8.30-13.00, 14.30-17.30; Wednesdays-Fridays 8.30-13.00, 14.30-17.00; Sundays and holidays 15.00-19.00. Closed 15 June-30 June

NOVARA

URP Novara
Via Fratelli Rosselli 1
Tel. 03213702218-03213702231
www.comune.novara.it

Hotels

Italia ****
Via P. Solaroli 10,
Tel. 0321399316
www.pancioIihotels.it
63 Rooms
Credit cards: American Express, Diners Club, Visa
An elegant hotel in the old town center, it has well-furnished rooms, pleasant communal areas and a restaurant where it serves sweet and savoury buffet breakfasts.

Museums, Monuments and Churches

Museo Lapidario del Broletto
Via Fratelli Rosselli 20,
Tel. 0321623021-0321627037
www.comune.novara.it
Mondays-Sundays 7.30-19.00

Museo Lapidario del Duomo
Chiostro della Canonica del Duomo, Vicolo Canonica
Tel. 0321661661
Visits by request

ORTA SAN GIULIO

Ufficio Turistico Orta San Giulio
Via Circonvallazione,
Tel. 0322905614-0322905163
www.distrettolaghi.it

Hotels

La Bussola *** ♿
Strada Panoramica 24,
Tel. 0322911913
www.orta.net/bussola
38 Rooms
Credit cards: American Express, Diners Club, Visa, Mastercard, Bancomat
Accommodation in an old residence situated on the upper part of the promontory. It has a large garden, restaurant and swimming pool.

La Contrada dei Monti *** ♿
Via dei Monti 10,
Tel. 0322905114
www.lacontradadeimonti.it

17 Rooms

In a characteristic alley in the old town center, this hotel has vaulted arches, rooms with beamed ceilings and arte povera furnishing for a pleasant, welcoming atmosphere.

Restaurants

Leon d'Oro 🍴🍴 ★
Piazza Motta 43,
Tel. 0322911991
www.albergoleondoro.it

Credit cards: American Express, Diners Club, Visa, Bancomat

Set in an early-19th century residence overlooking the lake, the menu offers traditional, seasonal dishes. Specialties include lake fish, mushrooms, cheeses and local cured meats.

Sacro Monte 🍴🍴
Sacro Monte,
Tel. 032290220
Closed Tuesdays

Credit cards: American Express, Visa, Mastercard

Situated in the center of the Nature Reserve just behind the village, it has a well and granite fireplace. It serves classical and typical Piedmont dishes including mushrooms and snails when in season.

STRESA

*ℹ **Pro Loco Stresa***
Piazza Marconi 16
Tel. 032330150

Hotels

La Palma **** ♿★
Corso Umberto I, 33,
Tel. 032332401,
www.hlapalma.it

124 Rooms

Credit cards: American Express, Diners Club, Visa, Mastercard, Bancomat

A hotel and restaurant with a refined atmosphere, elegant furnishing, sports equipment and panoramic solarium.

Regina Palace **** ♿
Corso Umberto I, 33,
Tel. 0323936936
sales@regina-palace.it
www.regina-palace.it

170 Rooms

Credit cards: American Express, Diners Club, Visa, Mastercard, Bancomat

An early-20th century residence on the lake front facing the Borromee Islands. It is set in a lovely park which gives it a 1920s atmosphere. It has two restaurants, live piano music in the evenings, sauna, swimming pool, tennis court and gym.

Restaurants

Casa Bella 🍴🍴
Isola dei Pescatori
Via del Marinaio,
Tel. 032333471
www.isola-pescatori.it/casabella
Closed Tuesdays

Credit cards: American Express, Diners Club, Visa, Mastercard

In a magical position on a romantic island, this restaurant serves local dishes mainly based on lake fish. It is good value for money.

Vecchio Tram 🍴🍴
Via per Vedasco,
Tel. 032331757
www.vecchiotram.net
Closed Tuesdays

Credit cards: American Express, Diners Club, Visa, Mastercard, Bancomat

Not far from the town center, an elegant atmosphere where you can enjoy both regional and Mediterranean cuisine.

Museums, Monuments and Churches

Museo di Palazzo Borromeo
Isola Bella, Tel. 032330556
www.borromeoturismo.it
March-October: Mondays-Sundays 9.00-17.30. Closed November-February

Museo Storico di Antonio Rosmini
Corso Umberto I, 15,
Tel. 032330091
www.rosmini.it
Mondays-Fridays 9.00-12.00, 15.00-18.00.
Visits by request for groups

STUPINIGI

Restaurants

Le Cascine 🍴
Strada Stupinigi per Orbassano,
Tel. 0119002581
www.ristorantelecascine.com
Closed Tuesday evenings

Credit cards: American Express, Diners Club, Visa, Mastercard, Bancomat

Situated in a delightful park with large windows overlooking a dance floor set among the trees.

Museums, Monuments and Churches

Museo di Storia, Arte ed Ammobiliamento - Palazzina di Caccia di Stupinigi ★
Piazza Principe Amedeo 7,
Tel. 0113581220
www.mauriziano.it
Fridays-Saturdays and Sundays 9.45-12.15, 13.30-15.15

TURIN

*ℹ **URP Torino***
Piazza Palazzo di Città 9/A,
Tel. 0114423010-0114423014
www.comune.torino.it

Atrium Torino
Piazza Solferino,
Tel. 011535181
www.turismotorino.org

Hotels

AC Torino ***** ♿
Via Bisalta 11,
Tel. 0116395031
www.ac-hotels.com

89 Rooms

Facing the Lingotto, it is a fascinating blend of history, luxury, art and technology. It offers comfortable rooms, restaurant and gym.

Alexandra *** ♿
lungodora Napoli 14,
Tel. 011858327
www.hotel-alexandra.it

56 Rooms

Credit cards: American Express, Diners Club, Visa, Mastercard

Situated on the banks of the River Dora, it has sound-proofed rooms with all comforts.

Art Hotel Boston **** ♿
Via Massena 70,
Tel. 011500359
www.hotelbostontorino.it

87 Rooms

Credit cards: American Express, Diners Club, Visa, Mastercard

Original, refined and modern, it is both a hotel and art gallery. The reception and communal areas exhibit paintings and the rooms are all furnished in unique, individual styles. There is also a restaurant.

Artuà & Solferino *** ★
Via Brofferio 1/3, Tel. 0115175301
www.artua.it

10 Rooms

Credit cards: American Express, Diners Club, Visa, Mastercard

This late-19th century residence is situated in the heart of the city just 300 m from the Egyptian Museum. It has comfortable, sound-proofed rooms, Internet point and serves a sweet and savoury buffet breakfast.

Atahotel Concord **** ♿★
Via Lagrange 47,
Tel. 0115176756
www.hotelconcord.com

139 Rooms

Credit cards: American Express, Diners Club, Visa, Mastercard

A mid-19th century residence in the city center, it has a warm, family atmosphere. It offers comfortable rooms and the restaurant serves regional specialties.

***Best Western Hotel Genio* *** ♿**
Corso Vittorio Emanuele II, 47
Tel. 0116505771
www.hotelgenio.it
128 Rooms
Credit cards: American Express, Diners Club, Visa, Mastercard, Bancomat

A 19th-century building with accommodation in comfortable rooms and a sweet and savoury buffet breakfast.

***Best Western Hotel Piemontese* *** ★**
Via Berthollet 21,
Tel. 0116698101
www.bestwestern.it/piemontese_to
37 Rooms
Credit cards: American Express, Diners Club, Visa, Mastercard

In a late 19th-century Art Noveau residence situated in a quiet street in the old town center close to the main museums and the Parco del Valentino, the hotel has welcoming, sound-proofed, air conditioned rooms.

***Cairo* *** ♿★**
Via La Loggia 6,
Tel. 0113171555
www.italyhotels.it
56 Rooms
Credit cards: American Express, Visa, Mastercard, Bancomat

A modern building characterised by classical furnishing. The restaurant serves regional dishes.

***Chelsea* *** ★**
Via XX Settembre 79/E corner Via Cappel Verde
Tel. 0114360100
www.hotelchelsea.it
15 Rooms
Credit cards: American Express, Diners Club, Visa, Mastercard, Bancomat

This hotel and restaurant is situated in the heart of the artistic and museum district, an ideal position for tourists.

G.H. Sitea* * ♿★**
Via Carlo Alberto 35,
Tel. 0115170171, www.sitea.thi.it
120 Rooms
Credit cards: American Express, Diners Club, Visa, Mastercard, Bancomat, JCB

This early-20th-century residence, situated in the town center just behind Piazza S. Carlo, has classically furnished rooms, a gym and restaurant.

Holiday Inn Turin City Centre* * ♿**
Via Assietta 3, Tel. 0115167111
www.holiday-inn.com/turin-cityctr
57 Rooms
Credit cards: American Express, Diners Club, Visa, Mastercard, Bancomat

A 19th-century residence with comfortable rooms equipped with hydro massage bath, shower, sauna or Turkish bath. Restaurant only in the evenings.

Jolly Hotel Ambasciatori* * ♿★**
Corso Vittorio Emanuele II, 104,
Tel. 0115752,
www.jollyhotels.com
199 Rooms
Credit cards: American Express, Diners Club, Visa, Mastercard

In a central position, it has spacious rooms and a restaurant specializing in traditional cuisine.

Jolly Hotel Ligure* * ★**
Piazza Carlo Felice 85,
Tel. 01155641, www.jollyhotels.it
169 Rooms
Credit cards: American Express, Diners Club, Visa, Bancomat, JCB

Dating from the early-20th century, this comfortable hotel has a restaurant specializing in local cuisine and also offers weeks with special theme menus.

***Le Petit Hotel* *** ♿★**
Via S. Francesco d'Assisi 21,
Tel. 0115612626
www.lepetithotel.it
82 Rooms
Credit cards: American Express, Diners Club, Visa, Mastercard, Bancomat

Set in a historic residence in the pedestrian area of the old center, this hotel and restaurant is an ideal base for tourists.

***Roma e Rocca Cavour* *** ♿★**
Piazza Carlo Felice 60,
Tel. 0115612772
www.romarocca.it
86 Rooms
Credit cards: American Express, Diners Club, Visa, Mastercard

In a central position in an elegant early-19th century residence, the hotel has antique furnishing and spacious communal areas.

Turin Palace Hotel* * ♿**
Via Sacchi 8, Tel. 0115625511
www.thi.it
120 Rooms

In a building dating from the second half of the 19th century, it has classically furnished rooms and pleasant communal areas. The restaurant serves local dishes and a sweet and savoury buffet breakfast.

Restaurants

***Al Bue Rosso* 🍴🍴 ★**
Corso Casale 10, Tel. 0118191393
Closed Mondays and Saturday midday
Credit cards: American Express, Diners Club, Visa, Mastercard

Traditional Piedmont cuisine in an early-20th century atmosphere.

***Antica Trattoria ! "Con Calma"* 🍴🍴**
Strada Comunale del Cartman 59, Tel. 0118980229
www.concalma.it
Closed Mondays
Credit cards: American Express, Diners Club, Visa, Mastercard, Bancomat

A pleasant inn where you can enjoy local dishes. Fine selection of cheeses and cured meats.

***Carignano* 🍴🍴🍴🍴 ★**
Via Carlo Alberto 35
Tel. 0115170171
www.sitea.thi.it
Closed Saturday midday
Credit cards: American Express, Diners Club, Visa, Mastercard

Situated in the old town center, it is one of the best-known restaurants in the city.

***Casa Vicina* 🍴🍴🍴**
Via Massena 66,
Tel. 011590949
www.casavicina.it
Closed Sunday evenings and Monday
Credit cards: American Express, Diners Club, Visa, Mastercard, Bancomat

A restaurant specializing in traditional dishes from the Canavese area. A good selection of cheeses and home-made desserts and special theme evenings.

***Cubico* 🍴🍴**
Via Saluzzo 86/Bis,
Tel. 01119714546
www.cubicoristorante.it
Closed Sundays
Credit cards: American Express, Diners Club, Visa, Mastercard, Bancomat

A restaurant that offers both classical and local dishes made from carefully selected products. It is also a laboratory where home-made pasta, bread sticks and ice cream (in summer) are produced. A selection of wines, mainly produced locally, it offers good value for money.

Del Cambio
Piazza Carignano 2,
Tel. 011546690, www.thi.it
Closed Sundays
Credit cards: American Express, Diners Club, Visa, Mastercard
Famous since 1757, this elegant restaurant serves regional specialties. It has a wide choice of wines, particularly those produced locally, spirits and cheeses from Piedmont.

Fortin
Via Damiano Chiesa 8,
Tel. 0112731672
www.fortin.it
Closed Sundays and Saturday midday
Credit cards: American Express, Diners Club, Visa, Mastercard, Bancomat
A fascinating environment characterised by 19th-century furnishing and a collection of paintings divided into periods for each dining room. Traditional cuisine and outdoor dining area in the summer.

Ij Brandè
Via Massena 5,
Tel. 011537279
www.ij-brande.it
Closed Sunday and Monday midday
Credit cards: American Express, Diners Club, Visa, Mastercard, Bancomat
A small, classical restaurant with traditional cuisine. It has a good choice of oils and local cheeses.

'L Birichin
Via Vincenzo Monti 16/A,
Tel. 011657457
www.birichin.it
Closed Sundays
Credit cards: American Express, Diners Club, Visa, Mastercard, Bancomat
An intimate atmosphere with silverware and furnishing in arte povera style for candlelit dinners. Traditional cuisine with innovative touches.

La Cloche
Strada Traforo del Pino 106,
Tel. 0118994213,
www.lacloche.it
Closed Sunday evenings and Mondays
Situated on the slopes of a hill, this restaurant has a terrace where, in the summer, guests can enjoy regional cuisine. It offers a selection of local cheeses, wines and spirits and, in autumn, mushrooms and white truffles. Evenings with special theme menus.

Locanda Mongreno
Strada Comunale Mongreno 50,
Tel. 0118980417
Closed Mondays
Credit cards: American Express, Visa, Mastercard, Bancomat
Old-style atmosphere with large red table lamps and traditional dishes with immaginative touches.

Micamale
Via Corte d'Appello 13,
Tel. 0114362288
www.ristorantemicamale.com
Saturday midday and Sundays
Credit cards: American Express, Diners Club, Visa, Mastercard, Bancomat
Situated in the old town center, it offers a modernized version of the local cuisine. Special theme evenings, a chocolate menu, surprise menu and medieval dishes.

Moreno-La Prima dal 1979 ★
Corso Unione Sovietica 244,
Tel. 0113179657
www.laprimamoreno.it
Credit cards: American Express, Diners Club, Visa, Mastercard, Bancomat
An elegant atmosphere for this restaurant that serves a reasonably priced tourist menu at midday. Menu according to the season.

Solferino ★
Piazza Solferino 3,
Tel. 011535851
www.ristorantesolferino.it
Closed Friday evenings and Saturdays
Credit cards: American Express, Diners Club, Visa, Mastercard
Set in a late 19th-century residence, this restaurant serves traditional food at a reasonable price. Mushrooms and truffles in season and homemade desserts.

Torricelli
Via Torricelli 51,
Tel. 011599814
www.trattoriatorricelli.it
Closed Sundays and Monday midday
Credit cards: American Express, Diners Club, Visa, Mastercard, Bancomat
Built at the beginning of the 20th century, this restaurant serves local dishes utilizing seasonal produce a well as special theme evenings. Chance to taste chocolate with spirits.

Tre Galline
Via Bellezia 37,
Tel. 0114366553
www.3galline.it
Closed Sundays and Monday midday
Credit cards: American Express, Diners Club, Visa, Mastercard, Bancomat
Situated in a 17th-century building in the old town center, the cuisine is based on traditional menus using high quality ingredients.

Villa Somis
Strada Val Pattonera 138,
Tel. 0116312617
www.villasomis.it
Closed Sunday evenings and Mondays
Credit cards: American Express, Diners Club, Visa, Mastercard, Bancomat
Set in an 18th-century residence surrounded by a park with centuries old trees, the elegant furnishing give an aristocratic atmosphere to this restaurant where guests can enjoy traditional cuisine.

At night

Fluido
Viale Umberto Cagni 7,
Tel. 0116694557
www.fluido.to
Set in the evocative atmosphere of Valentino park, this is the ideal place to pass your time. Day or night, summer or winter, you can enjoy interesting musical events.

Kogin's Club
Corso Sicilia 6,
Tel. 0116610546
www.koginsclub.com
Restaurant, cocktail bar and music club, it has spacious terraces and large windows overlooking the colored play of lights on the river. A surrealistic atmosphere where you can enjoy good music.

Il Magazzino di Gilgamesh
Piazza Moncenisio 13/b,
Tel. 0117492801
www.ilmagazzinodigilgamesh.com
A night club where you can also dine, it has a rich programme of blues, jazz and rock concerts as well as Latin American and other music. The upper floor houses exhibitions and events.

Maison Musique
Rivoli, Via Rosta 23,
Tel. 011537636-0119538780
www.maisonmusique.it
Auditorium, restaurant, bar and a lovely park where you can enjoy theatrical performances, exhibitions and concerts.

Museums, Monuments and Churches

Armeria Reale
Piazza Castello 191,
Tel. 011543889-0115184358
www.artito.arti.beniculturali.it

Hotels | Restaurants | Disabled | ★ Special TCI Rates

Tuesdays-Fridays 9.00-14.00; Saturdays-Sundays 13.00-19.00

Fondazione Sandretto Re Rebaudengo convenzionato ★
Via Modane 16,
Tel. 01119831600-01119831616
www.fondsrr.org
Tuesdays-Sundays 12.00-20.00; Thursdays 12.00-23.00

Galleria Civica d'Arte Moderna e Contemporanea - GAM ★
Via Magenta 31,
Tel. 0115629911-0114429518
www.gamtorino.it
Tuesdays-Sundays 9.00-19.00

Galleria Sabauda
Via Accademia delle Scienze 6,
Tel. 0115641755-0115641748-0115641749
www.artito.arti.beniculturali.it
Tuesdays, Fridays, Saturdays and Sundays 8.30-14; Wednesdays 14-19.30; Thurdays 10-19.30. June-August: Tuesdays-Sundays 14-19.30

Museo Civico di Arte Antica e Palazzo Madama ★
Piazza Castello,
Tel. 0115611446-0114429929
www.palazzomadamatorino.it
Scalone and Corte Medievale
Tuesdays-Fridays, Sundays: 9-19; Saturdays: 9-20
Museo Civico d'Arte Antica
Tuesdays-Fridays Sundays: 10-18; Saturdays: 10-20; Closed on Mondays (tickets can be bought up to one hour before)

Museo del Grande Torino - Basilica di Superga
Strada Basilica di Superga 75,
Tel. 0118997456
www.basilicadisuperga.com
April-September: Saturdays and Sundays 14.30-19.00. October-March: Saturdays and Sundays 14.30-18.00

Museo della Sindone ★
Via S. Domenico 28,
Tel. 0114365832
www.sindone.org/it/museo.htm
Mondays-Sundays 9.00-12.00, 15.00-19.00. Bookings on request for groups and schools

Museo di Antichità Archeologica
Via XX Settembre 88 c,
Tel. 0114396140
www.museoantichita.it
Tuesdays-Sundays 8.30-19.30. Free of charge guided tours on Sundays at 16.00

Museo Egizio
Via Accademia delle Scienze 6,
Tel. 0115617776
www.museoegizio.org
Tuesdays-Sundays 8.30-19.30

Museo Nazionale del Cinema ★
Mole Antoneliana,
Via Montebello 20
Tel. 0118138511
www.museocinema.it
Tuesdays-Fridays and Sundays 9.00-20.00; Saturdays 9.00-23.00

Museo Nazionale del Risorgimento Italiano ★
Via Accademia delle Scienze 5,
Tel. 0115621147-0115623719
www.regione.piemonte.it/cultura/risorgimento
Tuesdays-Sundays 9.00-19.00 (last entry 18.00)

Museo Nazionale della Montagna «Duca degli Abruzzi» ★
Via G.E. Giardino 39,
Tel. 0116604104
www.museomontagna.org
Tuesdays-Sundays 9.00-19.00. Modern exibitions only

Museo Nazionale dell'Automobile «Carlo Biscaretti di Ruffia» ★
Corso Unità d'Italia 40,
Tel. 011677666
www.museoauto.it
Tuesdays, Wednesdays, Fridays and Saturdays 10.00-18.30; Thursdays 10.00-22.00; Sundays 10.00-20.30

Palazzo Falletti di Barolo -Appartamenti Storici
Via delle Orfane 7,
Tel. 0114360311
www.palazzobarolo.it
Mondays,Wednesdays 10.00-12.00, 15.00-17.00; Fridays 10.00-12.00. In August open in the mornings only. Closed on mid-August week holiday

Palazzo Reale - Appartamenti Reali
Piazzetta Reale - Piazza Castello,
Tel. 0114361455
www.ambienteto.arti.beniculturali.it
Tuesdays-Sundays 8.30-19.30 (last entry 18.20)

Pinacoteca del Lingotto «Giovanni e Marella Agnelli» ★
Via Nizza 262/103,
Tel. 0110062008-0110062713
www.pinacoteca-agnelli.it
Tuesdays-Sundays 9.00-19.00

Reali Tombe di Casa Savoia - Basilica di Superga ★
Strada Basilica di Superga 75,
Tel. 0118997456
www.basilicadisuperga.com
April-October: Mondays-Fridays 9.30-19.30. November-March: Saturdays, Sundays and holidays 9.30-18.00

VARALLO

Ufficio Turismo Varallo
Corso Roma 38,
Tel. 0163564404
www.comunevarallo.com

Museums, Monuments and Churches

Museo «Calderini»
Via Pio Franzani 2,
Tel. 016351424
www.provincia.vercelli.it/musei/index.htm
June-September: Tuesdays-Sundays 10-12.30/14-18 or on request

Pinacoteca
Via Pio Franzani 2,
Tel. 016351424
www.provincia.vercelli.it/musei/index.htm
Tuesdays-Sundays 10.30-12.30, 14.30-18.00

VERBANIA

IAT Verbania
Corso Zanitello 6,
Tel. 0323556669-0323503249
www.distrettolaghi.it

Hotels

G.H. Majestic * ♿***
Pallanza, Via Vittorio Veneto 32,
Tel. 0323504305
www.grandhotelmajestic.it
95 Rooms
Credit cards: American Express, Diners Club, Visa, Mastercard, Bancomat
Situated on the lake, this hotel has elegant rooms, garden and private beach, restaurant, sauna, swimming pool, tennis court and gym.

Il Chiostro *** ♿
Via F.lli Cervi 14,
Tel. 0323404077
www.chiostrovb.it
100 Rooms
Credit cards: American Express, Visa, Mastercard
Not far from the quays where the boats leave, this hotel is set in part of a 16th-century monastry which still conserves the original cloisters, rooms with cross vaults and spacious halls. Internet point, gym and restaurant serving traditional dishes.

Restaurants

Il Torchio
Pallanza, Via Manzoni 20,
Tel. 0323503352
www.iltorchio.net
Closed Wednesdays and Thursday midday

Credit cards: American Express, Diners Club, Visa, Mastercard, Bancomat

A restaurant with wooden wall panelling and a beamed ceiling. It serves traditional but innovative dishes making use of seasonal products and locally caught fish.

Milano ¥¥¥ ★
Pallanza, Corso Zanitello 2, Tel. 0323556816

Closed Monday evenings and Tuesdays

Credit cards: American Express, Visa, Mastercard

A comfortable, Art Nouveau atmosphere for this restaurant with large windows overlooking the lake. Traditional Piedmont cuisine with both meat and fish.

Piccolo Lago ¥¥¥ ★
Fondotoce, Via Turati 87, Tel. 0323586792
www.piccololago.it

Closed Mondays and Tuesdays (in Winter also Sunday evenings)

Credit cards: American Express, Diners Club, Visa, Mastercard, Bancomat

A bar and restaurant situated in a quiet position with a private lido where boats can moor. Large veranda overlooking the lake and local dishes both from the land and the lake.

Rural Lodgins

Monterosso
Cima Monterosso 30, Tel. 0323556510
www.ilmonterosso.it

Closed mid January-mid February

Bicycle hire

Credit cards: Visa, Mastercard

Set in the countryside of Verbania, it has a wonderful view of Mt Mottarone and Lakes Mergozzo and Maggiore. Accommodation in a farmhouse surrounded by woods with indicated trails, ideal for walking, cycling or horseriding.

Museums, Monuments and Churches

Giardini Botanici di Villa Taranto
Pallanza, Via Vittorio Veneto 111, Tel. 0323556667
www.villataranto.it

April-October: Mondays-Sundays 8.30-18.30. Closed from November to March

Museo Civico
Via S. Maria 10, Tel. 0171634175
www.comune.cuneo.it

Tuesdays, Saturdays 8.30-13.00, 14.30-17.30; Wednesdays-Fridays 8.30-13.00, 14.30-17.00; Sundays and holidays 15.00-19.00. Closed 15 June-30 June

VERCELLI

URP Vercelli
Palazzo Comunale, Piazza Municipio 4
Tel. 0161596333
www.comune.vercelli.it

Hotels

Modo Hotel *** ♿
Piazza Medaglie d'Oro 21, Tel. 0161217300

62 Rooms

Credit cards: American Express, Diners Club, Visa, Bancomat

Conveniently situated, this hotel has well-equipped rooms and a restaurant specializing in both classical and local cuisine.

Restaurants

Giardinetto ¥¥
Via Sereno 3, Tel. 0161257230

Closed Mondays

Situated in a 19th-century residence with large windows overlooking an internal garden, the restaurant serves traditional, seasonal dishes, also based on fish. Comfortable accommodation is available.

Paiolo ¥
Viale Garibaldi 72, Tel. 0161250577

Closed Thursdays

Credit cards: Visa, Mastercard, Bancomat

Situated in a historical house, it serves traditional dishes from the Piedmont region.

Museums, Monuments and Churches

Museo «Camillo Leone»
Via Verdi 30, Tel. 0161253204
www.museoleonevc.it

Tuesdays, Thursdays 15.00-17.30; Saturdays 15.00-18.00; Sundays 10.00-12.00 and 15.00-18.00

Museo «Francesco Borgogna» ★
Via Borgogna 4/6, Tel. 0161252776-0161211338
www.museoborgogna.it

Tuesdays-Fridays 15.00-17.30; Saturdays 10.00-12.30; Sundays 10.00-12.30 (in some periods 14.00-18.00)

Museo del Tesoro del Duomo
Piazza D'Angennes 5, Tel. 016151650
www.provincia.vercelli.it/musei/index.htm

Wednesdays 9.00-12.00; Saturdays 9.00-12.00, 15.00-18.00; Sundays 15.00-18.00

METRIC CONVERTIONS

Distance

Kilometres/Miles		Meters/Feet	
km to mi	mi to km	m to ft	ft to m
1 = 0.62	1 = 1.6	1 = 3.3	1 = 0.30
2 = 1.2	2 = 3.2	2 = 6.6	2 = 0.61
3 = 1.9	3 = 4.8	3 = 9.8	3 = 0.91
4 = 2.5	4 = 6.4	4 = 13.1	4 = 1.2
5 = 3.1	5 = 8.1	5 = 16.4	5 = 1.5
6 = 3.7	6 = 9.7	6 = 19.7	6 = 1.8
7 = 4.3	7 = 11.3	7 = 23.0	7 = 2.1
8 = 5.0	8 = 12.9	8 = 26.2	8 = 2.4

Weight

Kilograms/Pounds		Grams/Ounces	
kg to lb	lb to kg	g to oz	oz to g
1 = 2.2	1 = 0.45	1 = 0.04	1 = 28
2 = 4.4	2 = 0.91	2 = 0.07	2 = 57
3 = 6.6	3 = 1.4	3 = 0.11	3 = 85
4 = 8.8	4 = 1.8	4 = 0.14	4 = 114
5 = 11.0	5 = 2.3	5 = 0.18	5 = 142
6 = 13.2	6 = 2.7	6 = 0.21	6 = 170
7 = 15.4	7 = 3.2	7 = 0.25	7 = 199
8 = 17.6	8 = 3.6	8 = 0.28	8 = 227

Liquid volume

Liters/U.S. Gallons		Liters/U.S. Gallons	
l to gal	gal to l	l to gal	gal to l
1 = 0.26	1 = 3.8	5 = 1.3	5 = 18.9
2 = 0.53	2 = 7.6	6 = 1.6	6 = 22.7
3 = 0.79	3 = 11.4	7 = 1.8	7 = 26.5
4 = 1.1	4 = 15.1	8 = 2.1	8 = 30.3

Temperature

Fahrenheit/Celsius

F	C
0	-17.8
5	-15.0
10	-12.2
15	-9.4
20	-6.7
25	-3.9
30	-1.1
32	0
35	1.7
40	4.4
45	7.2
50	10.0
55	12.8
60	15.5
65	18.3
70	21.1
75	23.9
80	26.7
85	29.4
90	32.2
95	35.0
100	37.8

INDEX OF NAMES

A

Agnelli, a family of Businessmen from Turin – p. 66

Agnelli Gianni (Giovanni, known as), Turin, Businessman, 1921-2003 – p. 66

Agnelli Giovanni, Villar Perosa (Turin), Businessman, 1866-1945 – p. 66

Alexander III (Rolando Bandinelli), Pope, died 1181 – p. 72

Alfieri Benedetto, Rome, Architect, 1700-67 – pp. 57, 59, 89, 91

Alfieri Vittorio, Asti, Poet and Playwright, 1749-1803 – pp. 75, 76

Amedeo VI (Conte Verde, known as), Count of Savoy, Chambéry (France), 1334-83 – p. 59

Antonelli Alessandro, Ghemme (Novara), Architect, 1798-1888 – pp. 62, 84

Antonello da Messina, Messina, Painter, 1430 c. -1479 – p. 54

Augustus (Octavian, known as), Roman Emperor, Rome, 63 BC-14 AD – p. 33

B

Bianchi Francesco, Painter and Stuccoer active in Turin in the first half of the 17C – p. 64

Bianchi Isidoro, Campione d'Italia (Como), Painter and Stuccoer, 1602-62 – p. 64

Bianchi Pompeo, Painter and Stuccoer, active in Turin in the first half of the 17C – p. 64

C

Calvin John (Cauvin Jean), Noyon (France), Religious Reformer, 1509-1564 – p. 21

Canaletto (Giovanni Antonio Cànal, known as), Venice, Painter and Engraver, 1697-1768 – p. 66

Canova Antonio, Possagno (Treviso), Sculptor and Painter, 1757-1822 – p. 66

Carlo Alberto of Savoy, King of Sardinia, Turin, 1798-1849 – pp. 55, 57, 61

Carlo Emanuele II, Duke of Savoy, Turin, 1634-75 – p. 56

Carlo Felice of Savoy, King of Sardinia, Turin, 1756-1831 – p. 60

Charlemagne, Frankish King and Emperor, Aachen (Germany), 742-814 – p. 25

Carlo III Borromeo, Count of Arona, 1586-1652 – p. 88

Casorati Felice, Novara, Painter, Architect, Engraver and Scenographer, 1886-1963 – p. 63

Castellamonte (di) Carlo, Turin, Architect, 1560-1641 – pp. 56, 59, 60, 71

Cesa (della) Pompeo, armorer, documented 1572-99 – p. 55

Challant (family), pp. 20, 43, 48

D

Drovetti Bernardino, Barbania Canavese (Turin), Diplomat and Archeologist, 1776-1852 – p. 60

E

Emanuele Filiberto (Testa di Ferro, known as), Duke of Savoy, Chambéry (France), 1528-80 – pp. 56, 67

F

Ferrari Gaudenzio, Valduggia (Vercelli), Painter, 1475 c. -1546 – pp. 92, 93

Frederick Barbarossa, Weiblingen (Germany), Emperor, c. 1123-90 – pp. 25, 72

G

Galletti Ignazio Amedeo, Turin, Architect, 1726-92 – p. 89

Gandolfino d'Asti (or da Roreto), Roreto (Cuneo), Painter, documented 1493-1510 – p. 77

Guarini Guarino, Modena, Architect, 1642-83 – pp. 56, 67

H

Henry IV, Emperor, 1050-1106 – p. 25

I

Isabella d'Adda, spouse of Carlo III Borromeo, 17C – p. 88

J

Juvarra Filippo, Messina, Architect, Engraver and Scenographer, 1678-1736 – pp. 57, 58, 67, 68, 69, 71, 89

L

Lanzani Andrea, San Colombano al Lambro (Milan), 1650 c. -1712 – p. 73

Leonardo da Vinci (Florence), Painter, Sculptor, Engineer and Architect, 1452-1519 – p. 55

Louis XIV (Re Sole, known as), Saint-Germain-en-Laye (France), King of France, 1638-1715 – p. 62

M

Manet Édouard, Paris, Painter, 1832-83 – p. 66

Martini Arturo, Treviso, Painter and Engraver, 1889-1947 – p. 63

Mastroianni Umberto, Fontana Liri (Frosinone), Sculptor, 1910-1988 – p. 54

Matisse, Henri-Èmile, Le Cateau (France), Painter and Sculptor, 1869-1954 – p. 66

Mellis Gerolamo, Vespolate (Novara), Carver, documented 1546 – p. 79

Miel Jan, Anversa (Belgium), Painter, 1599-1663 – p. 71

Modigliani Amedeo, Livorno, Painter and Sculptor, 1884-1920 – pp. 63, 66

Molineri Giovanni Antonio the Older, Savigliano (Cuneo), Painter and Engraver, 1577 c. - 1645 c. – p. 81

Morello Carlo, Architect and Engineer, died 1665 – p. 56

N

Napoleon Bonaparte, Emperor, Ajaccio (France), 1769-1821 – pp. 25, 72, 88

P

Palagi Pelagio, Bologna, Painter, Sculptor and Architect, 1775-1860 – pp. 57, 59

Pellico Silvio, Saluzzo (Cuneo), Patriot and Writer, 1789-1854 – p. 62

Piano Renzo, Genova, Architect, born 1937 – pp. 65, 66

Picasso Pablo Ruiz, Malaga (Spain), Painter, Sculptor, Engraver and Ceramist, 1881-1973 – p. 66

Ponti Giò, Milan, Architect, 1891-1979 – p. 79

Pozzo Giovanni Pietro, Painter active in Piedmont, 1713-98 – p. 73

Pozzo Pietro Antonio the Younger, Painter, active in Piedmont, 1727-88 – p. 73

R

Rembrandt Harmenszoon van Rijn, Leida (Holland), Painter and Engraver, 1606-69 – p. 61

Renoir Pierre-Auguste, Limoges (France), Painter, 1841-1919 – p. 66

Rosmini Antonio, Rovereto (Trent), Philosopher, 1797-1855 – p. 88

S

St Anselmo, Aosta, Theologian and Philosopher, and later Archbishop of Canterbury, 1033-1109 – p. 32

St Bernard from Mentone (or di Aosta), Archdeacon of Aosta and Preacher, died 1081 – p. 25

St Carlo Borromeo, Arona (Novara), 1538-84 – p. 85

St Orso, Aosta, Priest, 5-8C – p. 18

Savoy, dynasty of Dukes and later of King of Sardinia and King of Italy – pp. 27, 51, 55, 57, 60, 67, 68, 69, 71

Savoy-Carignano Emanuele Filiberto, Prince of Carignano, 1628-1709 – p. 69

Schiaparelli Ernesto, Occhieppo Inferiore (Biella), Egyptologist, 1856-1928 – p. 60

Seyter Daniel, Vienna, Painter, 1649-1705 – p. 57

T

Tibaldi Pellegrino, Puria di Valsolda (Como), Architect, Sculptor and Painter, 1527-96 – p. 85

Tiepolo Giambattista, Venice, Painter, 1696-1770 – p. 66

V

Vaglio Giovanni, Biella, Carver, 1660-97 – p. 78

Van Eyck Hubert, Flemish Painter, died 1426 – p. 54

Van Eyck Jan, Maaseik (Belgium), Painter, 1390 c. -1441 – pp. 54, 61

Vittone Bernardo Antonio, Turin, Architect, 1705-70 – p. 89

Vittorio Amedeo II, Turin, Duke of Savoy, King of Sicily and later King of Sardinia, 1666-1732 – pp. 57, 68

Vittorio Emanuele II, Turin, King of Sardinia and later King of Italy, 1820-78 – p. 71

Vittozzi Ascanio, Orvieto (Terni), Architect, 1539-1615 – p. 56

GENERAL INDEX

A

Acqui Terme pp. 73, 210

Agliano Terme pp. 166, 211

Agliè p. 181

Ayas (valley) pp. 48, 104

Alba pp. 81, 172, 181, 190, 193

Alessandria pp. 72, 166, 180, 189, 201, 203, 227

Allein p. 191

Antagnod p. 48, 218

Antey-Saint-André p. 49

Aosta pp. 18, 160, 164, 169, 176, 186, 197, 200, 203, 206, 208, 218

Arnad pp. 42, 164, 169, 191, 219

Arona pp. 85, 173, 227

Artesina-Prato Nevoso p. 121

Arvier p. 30

Asti pp. 75, 166, 172, 180, 189, 193, 199, 201, 209, 228

Avigliana p. 162

Avise p. 30

Ayas (valley) pp. 48, 104, 219

Aymavilles pp. 32, 176

B

Baceno p. 173

Bagnasco p. 209

Bagni di Vinadio p. 211

Bagnolo Piemonte p. 172

Barbaresco p. 181

Bard pp. 41, 219

Bardonecchia p. 118

Biella pp. 78, 162, 166, 172, 189, 203, 228

Bobbio Pellice p. 173

Bognanco p. 214

Borgomanero p. 193

Borgo San Dalmazzo p. 203

Bossea Cave p. 82

Boves p. 166

Bra pp. 166, 172, 190

Breuil-Cervinia pp. 50, 101, 219

C

Caltignaga p. 203

Cameri p. 173

Canelli p. 209

Cantalupa p. 173

Carmagnola p. 192

Casale Monferrato pp. 189, 201

Castello di Annone p. 166

Castelmagno p. 172

Castiglione d'Asti p. 192

Castiglione Falletto p. 167

Cavour p. 167

Cesana Torinese p. 112

Challand-Saint-Victor p. 48, 219

Chambave pp. 169, 176, 191

Champoluc pp. 48, 219

Champorcher pp. 47, 197, 220

Champorcher (valley) p. 47

Charvensod p. 25

Châtillon pp. 44, 169, 186, 220

Cherasco p. 201

Chivasso p. 190

Claviere p. 114

Cocconato pp. 166, 192

Coggiola p. 166

Cogne pp. 33, 164, 220

Cogne (valley) p. 32

Cortemilia p. 167

Courmayeur pp. 37, 99, 160, 169, 186, 200, 221

Crevaldossola p. 173

Cuneo pp. 80, 162, 166, 172, 181, 190, 201, 203, 209, 229

D

Degioz p. 34

Donnas pp. 41, 169, 200

E

Eau-Rousse p. 34

Étroubles pp. 26, 208, 222

F

Fara Novarese p. 181

Feisoglio p. 172

Fenestrelle pp. 133, 209

Fenis p. 45

Ferret (valley) p. 39

Fossano p. 209

Frabosa Soprana p. 192

G

Gabiano p. 201

Garessio p. 214

Gattinara p. 181

Ghemme p. 181

Gignod pp. 26, 164, 191, 222

Gran Paradiso, National Park p. 128

Great St Bernard p. 25, 222

Gressan p. 26

Gressoney-La-Trinité p. 47, 222

Gressoney Saint-Jean pp. 46, 206, 223

Gressoney (valley) pp. 45, 105

I

Introd p. 34

Isole Borromee p. 88

Issime pp. 45, 223

Issogne p. 42

Ivrea pp. 68, 167, 209

L

La Morra p. 181

La Salle pp. 31, 164, 223

La Thuile pp. 37, 96, 224

Limone Piemonte p. 124

Little St Bernard p. 37

Little St Bernard (valley) p. 37

M

Macugnaga pp. 118, 202

Marene p. 173

Melignon p. 35

Melle p. 173

Monastero Bormida p. 192

Moncalvo pp. 192, 193

Mondovì p. 201
Mont Blanc p. 38
Mont Blanc (valley) p. 39
Montjovet p. 43
Morgex pp. 31, 176

N
Naturpark Côte de Gargantua p. 26
Neive p. 181
Nizza Monferrato p. 180
Novara pp. 84, 173, 181, 190, 199, 203, 229
Nus pp. 169, 186

O
Olivola p. 180
Ollomont (valley) p. 27
Oropa, Sanctuary of p. 79
Orta San Giulio p. 86, 229
Oyace pp. 26, 191
Ozein p. 33

P
Pancalieri p. 202
Perloz pp. 40, 208
Pila p. 107, 224
Piode p. 173
Planaval p. 36
Pontboset p. 47
Pont Canavese p. 202
Ponti p. 192
Pont-Saint-Martin pp. 40, 197, 200, 206
Pont-Suaz, Sanctuary of p. 27
Porossan p. 26
Pre-Saint-Didier pp. 31, 200

Q
Quart pp. 27, 176, 203

R
Rhêmes-Notre-Dame pp. 35, 224
Rhêmes-Saint-Georges pp. 35, 224
Rhêmes (valley) p. 35
Rivoli p. 167
Roccaverano p. 172
Rochefort, Sanctuary of p. 36

S
Sacra di San Michele p. 69
Sacro Monte di Crea p. 73
Sacro Monte di Varallo p. 92
Saint-Christophe pp. 27, 169, 225
Saint-Oyen pp. 27, 191
Saint-Pierre pp. 29, 169, 197, 225
Saint-Rhemy-en-Bosses p. 164
Saint-Vincent pp. 44, 186, 197, 212, 225
Saluzzo pp. 173, 201
San Costanzo sul Monte p. 82
San Giorgio Canavese p. 181
Sansicario p. 110
Santa Maria di Vezzolano p. 77
Santa Maria Maggiore p. 167
Sarre pp. 29, 206
Sauze d'Oulx pp. 116, 173
Savigliano p. 202
Serravalle Scrivia p. 203
Sestriere p. 109
Stresa pp. 88, 230
Stupinigi pp. 69, 230
Superga p. 68
Susa pp. 70, 167

T
Terme di Lurisia p. 214
Terme di Valdieri p. 215
Torgnon p. 49
Turin pp. 51, 134, 144, 162, 167, 173, 181, 190, 199, 202, 203, 207, 209, 230

V
Vaie p. 192
Valdigne p. 29
Val Grande, National Park p. 130
Valgrisenche p. 36, 226
Valnontey (valley) p. 33
Valpelline (valley) pp. 28, 191, 226
Valsavarenche (valley) pp. 34 226
Valtournenche (valley) pp. 49, 50, 101, 169, 197,226
Varallo pp. 92, 202, 233
Venarìa Reale p. 71
Venasca p. 193
Veny (valley) p. 39
Verbania pp. 87, 173, 190, 233
Verbano-Cusio-Ossola pp. 87, 167, 173, 190, 202, 207
Vercelli pp. 89, 173, 181, 190, 199, 202, 234
Verrès pp. 43, 200
Vicoforte, Sanctuary of p. 83
Vignale Monferrato p. 180
Villeneuve pp. 30, 186

GLOSSARY

Apse
a semi-circular or polygonal projection of a building, especially at east end of a church.

Atrium
lobby.

Baita
a typical wooden house in the western Alps.

Basilica
rectangular-shaped.

Building
in Roman times, used for the administration of justice; in early Christian times, used for worship, and generally with a central nave and side aisles, possibly with apse/s.

Calidarium
room for hot or steam baths in a Roman bath.

Capital
part which links a column to the structure above. In classical architecture, capitals were Doric, Ionian, or Corinthian.

Cavea
spectator seating of a theater or amphitheater, usually divided into sections which were assigned to different social classes.

Chemin-de-ronde
internal raised pathway in medieval fortifications.

Codex (pl. codices)
early, hand-written books.

Deambulatory
an aisle encircling the choir or chancel of a church.

Dosseret
supplementary capital set above a column capital to receive the thrust of the arch.

Embrasure
with a splayed (angled) opening.

Forum (pl. fora)
large flat area in an Ancient Roman town, the center of political life.

Frigidarium
room for cold baths in a Roman bath.

Ghibelline
term used in the Middle Ages to refer to supporters of the Holy Roman Emperor.

Guelph (or Guelf)
term used in the Middle Ages to refer to supporters of the Papacy.

Loggia
a colonnaded or arcaded space within the body of a building but open on one side.

Lunette
an area in the plane of a wall framed by an arch or vault containing a painting or sculpture.

Majolica
a type of early Italian earthenware covered with an opaque tin glaze.

Matroneum
overhead gallery in an early church reserved for the worship of women.

Merlon
one of the solid parts between the crenellations of a battlement on a fortified medieval building.

Multifoiled
having several lobes.

Narthex
the portico before the nave of an early Christian or Byzantine church.

Piano nobile
upper floor occupied by the nobility.

Pilaster
shallow rectangular feature protruding from a wall with a capital and a base.

Podium
the raised platform encircling the arena of a Roman amphitheater.

Polyptych
altar-piece consisting of a number of panels. A diptych has two panels; a triptych has three.

Presbytery
the part of a church reserved for the officiating clergy.

Pronaos
a vestibule before the main part of the church.

Quadriporticus
a portico running around four sides of a courtyard, especially in front of early Christian or Romanesque churches.

Rascard
wooden mountain store-room raised on stone pillars.

Rood screen
stone or wooden balustrade separating the main part of the church from the presbytery.

Sacristy
part of church where furnishings and vestments are kept, and where clergy prepare for services.

Tepidarium
the hot room in a Roman bath.

Tiburium
architectural structure enclosing and supporting a dome, used in early and Romanesque Lombard churches.

Transept
the major transverse part of a cruciform church.

Triptych
a painting or panel with a main central part and two lateral parts.

Tympanum
the space between an arch and the horizontal head of the door or window below.

PICTURE CREDITS

Agenzia La Presse, p. 119

Agenzia Sole di Vetro, p. 182 bottom/ L. Beretta p. 150; p. Giussani p. 148; C. Re p. 147 top and bottom, 149

Agenzia StudioNovanta, pp. 171, 172, 190

AIAT Cogne Gran Paradiso, p. 33

Anghi Foto (Marco Anghinoni), p. 8

Archivio AIAT Monte Bianco, p. 100

Archivio Alinari, pp. 54, 60 right and left, 61

Archivio Associazione Turistica Artesina, p. 123

Archivio Buysschaert &Malerba, p. 166

Archivio Comune di Macugnaga, p. 121

Archivio Pila Spa/ Camisasca, p. 108 top and bottom

Archivio Regione Piemonte, p. 167

Archivio Scala, p. 185
Archivio TCI, p. 66

Archivio TCI/Radino, pp. 76, 85

Archivio TCI/ A. Sampietro, p. 32 top, 34, 37

Archivio Vialattea, pp. 109, 111, 112, 117

F. Ardito, pp. 25, 26, 28 top, 28 bottom, 31

Assessorato del Turismo, p. 206

Associazione Produttori Suini del Piemonte, p. 165

M. Bassi, p. 197

L. Boetti, p. 64

G. Carfagna e Associati/G. Carfagna, p. 199

R. Carnovalini, p. 129

P. Cattaneo, p. 91

G. Cervi, p. 62

Cubo Images/C. Beduschi, p. 35
Cubo Images/
F. Meneghetti, p. 21, 23, 24 top and bottom
Cubo Images/G. Roli, p. 39 bottom

Il Decumano, p. 41, 42, 46, 48, 49

Image Bank, p. 201

F. Fiori, p. 202

Foto Camerlenghi, p. 152

Foto Soletti, p. 170

Foto M. Tosello, p. 124

S. Giussani, p. 101, 148

Mairani, p. 140, 143, 159, 174, 177, 178-179

Marka, p. 160, 161, 162 left/D. Donandoni p. 32 bottom/Fuste Raga p. 57

D. Necchi, p. 39 top

Panda Photo/ S. Meyers, p. 128
Panda Photo/B. Midali, p. 131
L. Pasi, p. 45
Photos.com, p. 162 right

F. Rameni, p. 36

Realy Easy Star/T. Spagone, pp. 59, 63, 71, 135, 136, 139, 142, 145, 158 top, 182 top, 196, 213

M. G. Schiapparelli, p. 27, 30, 40

Sime Photo/J. Huber, p. 20

Tahir 'Attar, p. 208

Tips Images/G. A. Rossi, p. 50

Turismo Torino, pp. 51, 55, 67 top and bottom

Webphoto, p. 134

Drawings by Antonello and Chiara Vincenti

Some owners of photographic copyright have been impossible to trace; they are invited to contact the publisher.

Notes

Pinacoteca Giovanni e Marella Agnelli

Via Nizza, 230 - 10126 Torino - Tel. +39 011.0062713 - Fax +39 011.0062712
www.pinacoteca-agnelli.it

In a fascinating space designed by Renzo Piano inside the historic industrial complex of the Lingotto in Turin, the Pinacoteca Giovanni e Marella Agnelli permanently houses 25 masterpieces from Mr. and Mrs. Agnelli's private collection. Opened on September 20th, 2002, the Pinacoteca displays an extraordinary collection of works of art dating from between the 18th and the 20th century and ranging from the Venice of Canaletto and the Dresden of Bellotto to a group, unique in Italy, of seven masterpieces by Matisse.The collection then moves on to the great French masters Manet and Renoir, followed by two pictures by Picasso, works by the Italian Futurists Balla and Severini, and concludes with Modigliani's celebrated painting Nu couché (Reclining Nude).

Giovanni Antonio Canal, detto il Canaletto
Il Bucintoro al molo nel giorno dell'Ascensione 1740 circa
Fondazione Pinacoteca Giovanni e Marella Agnelli

Opening Hours:
from Tuesday to Sunday 10 a.m. - 7 p.m.
Closed on Monday. The Ticket Office closes at 6.15 p.m.

Admission:
Permanent Collection + Temporary Exhibition
Full Price: 6 euros. Reductions for Groups: 5 euros
Reductions for Schools: 4 euros

Only Permanent Collection:
Full price: 4 euros; Reductions: 2,50 euros

Booking:
Groups, Schools and Guided Tours:
Tel. +39.011. 0062713

Bookshop:
Managed by ArtBook, it offers a broad range of Art, Architecture and Design Publications

Copyright Enrico Cano

AN ESSENTIAL TOOL FOR TRAVELLERS.
Italy's clearest mapping !
Touring Club Italiano
Piemonte e Valle d'Aosta
Lombardia
Emilia Romagna
Sicilia
Italia meridionale
Italia Sicilia, Sardegna
Italia centro nord
Italia centro sud
www.touringclub.com
Touring Club Italiano
OLTRE IL VIAGGIO